WITHDRAWN

HARVARD LIBRARY

WITHDRAWN

DANIEL WARNER AND THE PARADOX OF RELIGIOUS DEMOCRACY IN NINETEENTH-CENTURY AMERICA

Daniel Warner

DANIEL WARNER AND THE PARADOX OF RELIGIOUS DEMOCRACY IN NINETEENTH-CENTURY AMERICA

Thomas A. Fudge

Studies in American Religion
Volume 68

The Edwin Mellen Press
Lewiston•Queenston•Lampeter

BX
7027
.Z8
W324
1998

Library of Congress Cataloging-in-Publication Data

Fudge, Thomas A.
   Daniel Warner and the paradox of religious democracy in nineteenth
-century America / Thomas A. Fudge.
      p. cm.-- (Studies in American religion ; v. 68)
   Includes bibliographical references and index.
   ISBN 0-7734-8249-0 (hardcover)
   1. Warner, D. S. (Daniel Sidney), 1842-1895. 2. Church of God
(Anderson, Ind.)--Clergy--Biography. 3. Democracy--Religious
aspects--Christianity--History of doctrines--19th century.
I. Title. II. Series.
BX7027.Z8W324 1998
289.9--dc21   98-44210
[b]   CIP

This is volume 68 in the continuing series
Studies in American Religion
Volume 68 ISBN 0-7734-8249-0
SAR Series ISBN 0-88946-992-X

A CIP catalog record for this book is available from the British Library.

Copyright © 1998 Thomas A. Fudge

All rights reserved. For information contact

      The Edwin Mellen Press   The Edwin Mellen Press
              Box 450   Box 67
        Lewiston, New York   Queenston, Ontario
        USA 14092-0450   CANADA L0S 1L0

The Edwin Mellen Press, Ltd.
Lampeter, Ceredigion, Wales
UNITED KINGDOM SA48 8LT

Printed in the United States of America

**For the Faculty
of
Warner Pacific College**

docendo discimus

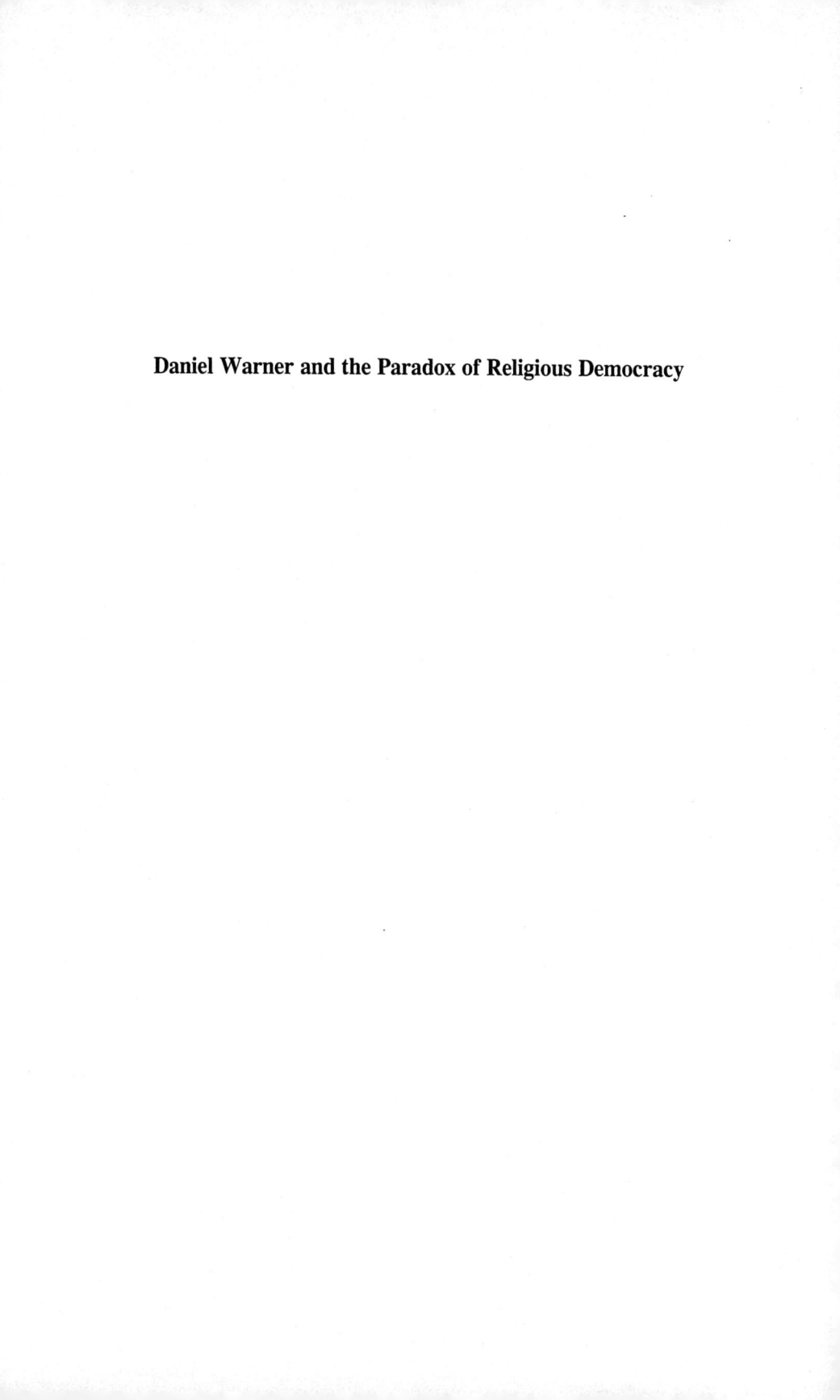

Daniel Warner and the Paradox of Religious Democracy

TABLE OF CONTENTS

List of Illustrations   x
Acknowledgements   xi
Foreword   xiii
Introduction   1

Chapter 1   **The Nineteenth-Century American Religious Experience**   11

    I.   The Fight Between Carnival and Lent   13
    II.   Industrializing the New World   24
    III.   The Paradox of Religious Leaders:
         Responses to American Culture   30

        a.   Prophets, Preachers and Preaching   37
        b.   Popular Religion   59
        c.   The Culture of Religious Print   82

    IV.   The Search for Order   97

Chapter 2   **Holiness as Challenge to Religious Culture**   113

    I.   'Perfection' in the thought of John Wesley   116
    II.   A Second Work of Grace   124
    III.   Holiness or Hell!—Contours of a Radical Cause   140

        a.   War on Worldliness   147
        b.   Divisions of Perfection   156

| Chapter 3 | John Winebrenner and the 'Come-Out' Option | 161 |

| | I. | Origins of the Church of God | 163 |
| | II. | 'A Narrower Way' | 176 |

| Chapter 4 | Daniel Warner and the Battle against 'Babylon' | 181 |

| Chapter 5 | Conflict and Crisis in the Kingdom of God in Ohio | 203 |

	I.	Denouncing 'Come-Out' Christianity	205
	II.	Creating the Warner Myth	216
	III.	Demonizing the Angel Sarah	223
	IV.	God, the Devil and Warner's Books	234
	V.	Shout at the Devil	271
	VI.	Shadows in the Evening Light	276

| Chapter 6 | Democracy and Dictatorship: A Gordian Knot | 287 |

Appendices 305

	a.	Daniel Warner, 'A Fallen Woman'	305
	b.	Daniel Warner, 'Soul Cripple City'	313
	c.	Charles Naylor, 'The Teachings of D.S. Warner and his Associates'	331
	d.	Andrew Byers, 'In Vindication of D.S. Warner and His Work'	342
	e.	The hymns of Daniel Warner	347

Bibliography 351

Index 371

LIST OF ILLUSTRATIONS

1.	Peter Bruegel, 'The Fight between Carnival and Lent' (1559)	15
2.	'The Circuit Riding Preacher' (1867)	52
3.	'Puck's Camp Meeting Sketches, no. 2' (mid-nineteenth century)	79
4.	'A Millerite preparing for the 23rd of April' (1843)	83
5.	'Grand Ascension of the Miller Tabernacle' (1844)	110
6.	Daniel Warner with his son Sidney (*c.* 1887)	182
7.	Sarah Warner (1880s)	225

ACKNOWLEDGEMENTS

Illustrations used in this book have been made possible through the courtesy of several agencies. Figure 1, Peter Bruegel's 'The Fight between Carnival and Lent', Kunsthistorisches Museum, Vienna; figure 2, 'The Circuit Riding Preacher' and figure 3, 'Puck's Camp Meeting Sketches, no. 2', The Billy Graham Center Museum; figure 4, 'A Millerite preparing for the 23rd of April', The Houghton Library, Harvard University; figure 5, 'Grand Ascension of the Miller Tabernacle', Review and Herald Publishing Association; figure 6, Daniel S. Warner and figure 7, Sarah Warner, Warner Press and the Archives of the Church of God, Anderson University. Permission to use these illustrations from these archives, libraries and museums is gratefully acknowledged.

FOREWORD

On the canvas of American Protestantism one will find portraits of colorful and dynamic women and men who rose to prominence especially during the nineteenth century's heady days of religious democracy. A host of social and political forces combined in the new republic to open up the possibility of dissent from the inherited religious traditions of Europe. This democratic combination of dissent and ferment gave birth to the rise of many colorful and often charismatic personalities such as 'Crazy' Lorenzo Dow and Peter Cartwright who were popular preachers. That is to say, they were preachers of the people. Their authority and influence were not grounded in formal education or privileged social position. Rather, they rose from and among the folk who were their primary congregation, preaching religion in common sense in the common tongue. The religious democracy of the nineteenth century permitted, even encouraged, the rise of such men and women to regional and even national prominence.

Although they owed much of their popularity and success to a religious culture of democracy, some of these personalities became leaders of new religious movements where dissent was not only unwelcome; it was not tolerated. Many of those who benefitted from the open religious environment of nineteenth-century America were not prepared to extend that democracy to their own followers. There is more than a little irony in a situation where, as Thomas A. Fudge observes, dissenters themselves do not tolerate dissent. That is the paradox of religious democracy so ably described in this very fine study.

Professor Fudge examines this paradox through the prism of the early ministry of Daniel S. Warner, a holiness 'people's preacher' of the last third of the nineteenth century who was the founder of a new group that called itself the Church of God movement. In Fudge's hands, this particular prism refracts the beam of American religious history in a spectrum that exposes several important insights. In the first place, he situates helpfully the story of Daniel Warner and the Church of God movement in the larger narrative of nineteenth-century American Protestantism. Secondly, in very personal terms, Fudge helps us to see the tension and sometimes human costs involved in the struggle between history and the myths that religious movements often make around their founders. In a larger vein, Fudge also numbers this struggle and others among the issues that contribute to the paradox that is the central theme of his story. And finally, his account requires a reconsideration of the bipolar lens through which much of American religious history has been viewed. Fudge's skilful treatment opens again the question whether the story of American religion is best told simply as a debate between liberal accomodationists and conservative champions of orthodoxy. Perhaps, however, there were men and women who saw themselves and their missions in other terms, whose view of the religious terrain was defined by other landmarks. Through his examination of Warner's rise and the issues in which his early ministry and personal life were embroiled, Fudge brings to light one such individual. In so doing he adds a portrait to the vast mosaic of American Protestantism.

Merle D. Strege
Professor of Historical Theology
Historian of the Church of God
Anderson University
Anderson, Indiana

INTRODUCTION

Martin E. Marty, that astute observer of American religious history, is once reported to have said that religion in America was three thousand miles wide and an inch deep. That remark is at once profoundly true and dangerously misleading. It is true in the sense that American religion historically has embraced nearly every conceivable variety and variation of Christianity. The nineteenth and twentieth centuries constitute a veritable theatre of religious expression and experimentation. Numerous alternative religious movements have risen and fallen. Others have undergone substantive modification while still others maintain persistently the quintessential elements of a religious *ancien régime*. From sea to shining sea, it is difficult to find a non-religious enclave amid the cultural landscape of historic America. In the United States, religion is indeed three thousand miles wide.

That conclusion is uncontested. That such religion lacks depth in quite another matter. It is entirely possible to argue that religious traditions in America have not all been planted on sand or stony ground. The scorching sun of secularism and skepticism dried up only a few of those widely planted seeds. Others found insurmountable difficulties among the thorns of oppression and assimilation which in the end choked their vitality and altered their original objectives. All of these may well have sunk roots only an inch deep into the *terra firma* of the much-heralded promised land. The long harvest of religion in America has demonstrated, however, that the five barley loaves and two small fishes of her humble beginnings have yielded up an abundant crop and the storehouses have overflowed. Five hundred years of American religion leaves little doubt that many forms of Christianity found a place in good ground where their long extending roots sank deep enough to find vast wells of living water in the collective consciousness and identity of the American public. Thus they have flourished. This enduring legacy helped to shape a nation.

It would be an exaggeration to assume that Daniel Warner and the Church of God Reformation Movement either shaped a nation or carved out the direction of religious discourse in American history. That said, it would be equally erroneous to classify Warner and his church as a superficial experiment on the far-flung plains of religion in the new world. Daniel Warner was not, by almost any non-parochial definition, a towering figure. He cannot be numbered among the giants of American Christendom. The religious movement he nurtured into existence cannot be included among the largest or most influential churches in the United States, past or present. Nevertheless, at least in the context of the nineteenth century, Warner and his followers had their feet anchored to a rock of certainty, conviction and vision. Though never a main player, Warner remained perennial. While never a heavy hitter, the Come-Out movement went the distance. In this respect, it is defensible to include Warner among those who helped to inaugurate a new era in American history.

Daniel Warner was the kind of man who made middle ground virtually obsolete. He was either accoladed or vilified. He begat both devoted disciples and vitriolic enemies. As with all shadowy figures of the past, an examination of the historical context has again proven essential and illuminating. The key to understanding Warner lies in the evolving ethos of nineteenth-century America. The clue to unlocking the riddle of this itinerant preacher is inseparable from the context which came to bear upon his life and career. On the face of it, this sounds pedantic and painfully obvious to the historian. But Warner has never been fully contextually examined. This book has attempted to situate Warner in the evolutionary process of American religion and interpret him neither as a 'man of God' nor as a religious fanatic. Instead, Warner has been approached as an historical figure, born in the struggles of competing ideas and contending ideologies. Daniel Warner was a product of his century, a prisoner of his own time. He cannot be detached from his context nor understood apart from it. The mythologizing of the man which occurred in the years following his death were, in the main, products of uncritical history. Ostensibly, such endeavors perceived the nineteenth century naïvely as motionless religious history, a time when nothing happened apart from the rise of the Kingdom of God, directed by the very hand of God. It was an era in which only the final reformation of Christianity transpired, and that in a virtual metahistorical fashion. Warner was an instrument in the hand of God soaring through the evening light of human history. What was important was his message, an urgent divine oracle, and the 'truth' he expounded. The historical context was a mere vehicle, not something intrinsically essential for interpreting the man. In this methodological conviction, history did not produce the man, Warner created history. Such an approach does not recover the past at all. Instead of history, it results in the preservation and perpetuation of myth and devotion to religious predispositions. Heritage is enlarged, history is ignored. The corpus of Warner historiography from C.E. Brown and Andrew Byers to John W.V. Smith and Barry Callen may provide valuable interpretations of Daniel Warner. None of them, however, can be regarded as successful examples of interpreting Warner as a product of nineteenth-century American religious history.

This study is not a religious biography. Indeed, it is not a biography at all. Nor can this book be regarded as a study of Warner's thought and certainly not as a systematic treatment of Warner's religious vision or theological program. In some ways, despite the title, the book is not about Warner at all. It is rather an investigation into the problem of American religious history exemplified in the vicissitudes of the nineteenth century. The upheaval of politics, culture and society in the years following the American Revolution had consequences for religion in the republic from the Atlantic to the Pacific; from the Gulf of Mexico to Canada. This new historical situation became the foundation for all subsequent developments in American Christianity and its enduring and protracted maturation produced an army of church builders and religious architects and among them Daniel Warner.

Several years ago the Notre Dame historian Nathan Hatch published what has become a classic study of religion in the nineteenth century. *The Democratization of American Christianity* has been regarded in some quarters as the most significant book ever written on the subject. Hatch's thesis has proven to be both compelling and influential. The marriage of democracy and religion transformed irrevocably the shape of Christianity in America and yielded an impressive, albeit diverse harvest. Hatch's book has rightly been received in a favorable light. The significance of the Hatch text, however, extends well beyond the bounds of *The Democratization of American Christianity*. Implicit in the argument is another vital concept which neither Hatch nor his disciples have developed or articulated. The theologizing of democracy carries with it a latent paradox which manifested itself consistently in the phenomenon of dictators disguised as democrats. The democratizing of Christianity proved itself unequal to the task of applying democratic principles to the realm of spiritual leadership. Following the decline of Calvinism, religion in America advanced the idea that all people were capable of responding to the gospel independently and could participate with God in the matter of personal salvation. A new soteriological principle emerged. Concomitant with this religious vision arose a qualification of this *laissez-faire* doctrine of salvation. This qualifying factor, rather than negating, encouraged the rise of a firm, spiritual direction in the lives of the converted. If the Bible became open for all to read, dictators disguised as democrats became channels for the voice of God. These individuals interpreted the Bible for the multitudes and functioned as guides along the path to salvation. Surely, there was 'no creed but the Bible' but the matter could not so easily be reduced. That slogan was a declaration of conscience and conviction but it betrayed acceptance of a complicated religious confession.

This paradox of religious democracy is a key for interpreting and understanding Daniel Warner. This book is about that paradox and Warner is the case study for an evaluation of its meaning and influence. Following the American Revolution and the precipitous decline of Calvinism, religious reform swept many sectors of American Christianity. Revivals, popular preaching, the religious press, camp meetings and widespread religious experimentation became hallmarks of the American religious experience. By mid-century Holiness emphases emerged and while they embraced the aforementioned aspects of 'reformed' religion they insisted on a narrowing of the religious experience, to wit, the experience of sanctification. Religious leaders such as Daniel Warner accepted these tenets but insisted on a further narrowing. Religion of necessity had to take another radical step and 'come-out' of the traditional structures of denominationalism. At each turn in this process the democratization of American Christianity was apparent. At the same time the persistent presence of leaders who felt they represented divine truth can also be seen. More often than not the process of religious democracy found its development marked by such dictators who used democratic principles to a certain extent to advance their own vision of God's kingdom. There is a *prima facie* case for numbering Daniel Warner among those religious reformers typifying the paradox of the trends evident in the development of religious history in the nineteenth century. Indeed, Warner could not countenance the raw material of democratized religion. He did not suffer religious diversity gladly and found the idea of multiple 'truths' insufferable.

Coming to terms with Warner necessitated an integrated look at the nineteenth century. The major themes include the protracted struggle between Calvinism and Jacksonian democracy, immigration and industrialization and the formation and development of popular religion. Nineteenth-century popular religion found expression in preaching, camp meetings, revivals and a religiously saturated culture. The rise of religious print and an on-going search for order characterized American history. The Holiness movements and the tradition engendered by John Winebrenner forms the immediate background for a consideration of Daniel Warner. Apart from the delineation of the aforementioned paradox little or no analysis of these themes has been attempted. The research proceeded along the lines of themes to people to context in an attempt to explicate the dilemma of democratized Christianity and the rise of its dictatorial leaders and spokespersons. The essence of the study emerges in chapters one and five. Chapter one attempts to demonstrate the paradoxical phenomenon of Christian dictators and religious democrats. The fifth chapter takes up the unprecedented drama in American religious history wherein Sarah Warner left her husband and attacked his teaching in the public press. Running the risk of anachronism it can be suggested that Daniel Warner was accused by his wife of becoming a religious dictator and thus perpetuating the thorny difficulty of Christianity in its multiple religious worlds in America. This attack forms the basis for a study of Warner as an entrée into a formal consideration of the perplexing paradox of American religious history in the nineteenth century.

This book constitutes the first major study of Daniel Warner outside the tradition of the Church of God (Anderson). It is written, however, from the perspective of an informed outsider. Its early research was conducted while I was a member of the faculty at Warner Pacific College and was intended as an article to mark the centenary of Warner's death in 1995. For reasons never fully explained to the author, the journal which solicited the original article declined to publish it. Since that time it has grown into a monograph. In terms of investigating Warner in the context of the paradox of American religious history, the emphasis has been placed heavily upon those primary sources still extant. Archival research has endeavored to take into consideration the entire typology of available sources: Warner's books, his private, personal journal, pamphlets, *Gospel Trumpet* articles and editorials, other unpublished papers, songs, poems, those volumes in his collected personal library, and extant correspondence. A number of these sources represent genres hitherto unexplored in studies of Daniel Warner. With respect to Sarah Warner, admittedly there is considerably less data and an even greater paucity of primary documentation. Nevertheless, data in archives presumably either unknown or unused in previous discussions of her have been appropriated in an attempt to avoid the pastiche of stereotypes which surround her memory. All of these sources have been synthesized in the hope of coming to terms with a balanced understanding of the war of the Warners and an effective case study of the paradox of American religion. The value of this type of scholarly pursuit has as its aim the hope of an in-depth analysis of Daniel and Sarah Warner which has heretofore not been fully or adequately explored.

There are a variety of individuals and institutions to be acknowledged. My former student Laurie Moore, an honors graduate of Warner Pacific College and now Senior Pastor of the Boston Heights Church of God in Great Falls, Montana, worked in collaboration with me on this project during 1994-95. An earlier version of chapter five constituted the fruits of our labors. I am indebted to Alice Kienberger, Library Director at Warner Pacific College, for providing me a place to work on several occasions and for advice. Alice was generous enough to allow a number of items from the college archives to be transported across the Pacific. Sandra Ajami, former Associate Library Director at Warner Pacific tirelessly assisted me in tracking down a variety of obscure sources. Both librarians made available their considerable skills at a number of important junctures. I am further grateful to Mandi Miller for collecting materials on my behalf and for seeing to it that they arrived safely in New Zealand, sometimes via personal delivery. Her enthusiasm for the project has been both encouraging and gratifying. Charles T. Kendall, Archivist and Theological Studies Librarian at the Anderson University Archives facilitated my research there and has proven helpful over the course of this project in answering numerous queries. I am further indebted to him for making available the unpublished writings of Charles W. Naylor and Andrew L. Byers. During my research in Anderson, Indiana I had the good fortune of discussing some of my findings and conclusions with Merle D. Strege, Professor of Historical Theology and current historian of the Church of God, as well as

Barry L. Callen, University Professor of Christian Studies. Early versions of chapter five were read and commented upon at length by the Warner Pacific College faculty writer's group. Officially known as 'Writer's Cramps', but referred to by its members as 'the inept group', this collection of scholars helped me think through some of the difficulties which cropped up during research. I am especially grateful to Professor Daniel Cole-McCullough now at the University of Alaska-Fairbanks, and the remaining members of that august group, Cole Dawson, Lou Foltz, Steve Arndt and Dennis Plies. I also benefited much from an interview with the late Milo L. Chapman, President Emeritus of Warner Pacific College. It is my keen regret he did not live to see publication.

Merle Strege, Cole Dawson and Jim Wilkins of Lee University read the entire manuscript and commented shrewdly on its improvement. I am particularly in Cole Dawson's debt. His acumen as a scholar of American history and his understanding of the Warner legacy have been exceptional resources he has consistently allowed me to draw upon. As one of my first history teachers, then faculty colleague and now scholarly collaborator and friend, I have found his support and contribution to my work both generous and fulfilling. These words are an inadequate expression of the value I attach to our continuing association. Irv Brendlinger of George Fox University read an earlier version of chapter five and also critiqued my treatment of John Wesley. In both cases the text has been much improved. He may be disappointed to find I have elected to disregard certain aspects of his counsel with respect to Wesley. Though I have not always followed his advice, the exchange consistently has been stimulating and our friendship has not suffered in the heat of debate. Diana Looser proofread the text and rescued me from numerous errors and prevented the occasional literary *faux pas*. Inconsistencies and errors which persist cannot be attributed to any of the aforementioned individuals and must remain solely my responsibility.

Thanks are also due to my colleagues in the History Department at the University of Canterbury, Christchurch, New Zealand, for their response and comments to my presentation on this topic in June 1997 at a Friday 'Kite-Flying' history seminar. Their reaction to a European historian 'flying a kite' in the winds of nineteenth-century American religious history was both enthusiastic and invigorating. I am further grateful to the department for financial assistance which made possible several trips to archives in the northern hemisphere during 1997. My father, Reverend James G. Fudge, hunted down a near impossible text on my behalf, Rosemary Russo prepared the appendices, and Arthur Kelly at Warner Press helped arrange permission for illustrations. Robert H. Reardon and Harold L. Phillips answered a number of questions in a helpful and stimulating manner and their reflection on past events within the history of the Church of God has proven invaluable. I am also grateful to Thomas Miller, Professor of Music at Warner Pacific College, for sharing with me his boyhood recollections of meeting Charles Naylor. Subsequent discussions of early Church of God hymnody and historic issues within the legacy of Daniel Warner also proved both helpful and stimulating.

Thomas Jefferson once wrote, 'it is in our lives and not our words that our religion must be read.' Daniel Warner doubtless would have agreed. The rhetoric of religious democracy and the reality of its inherent paradox encompassed the dialectic of living, speaking and reading. In the fusion of these horizons a new hermeneutic emerged. The subsequent religious discourse underscored a paradigm shift in the nineteenth-century American religious experience. Daniel Warner lived it, Sarah Warner spoke of it and we are left to read of it. There are those who may wish to ignore its import. But the prudent words of King Lear's 'poor fool' when the mad king was about to throw all his clothes away in the midst of a ferocious tempest are instructive:

> Prithee, nuncle, be contented;
> 'Tis a naughty night to swim in.

Mt. Tabor
Portland, Oregon

CHAPTER 1

The Nineteenth-Century American Religious Experience

The following Thursday was designated as the day to build the meeting house. People assembled with their axes, and soon they were lifted up against thick trees. Logs were cut off at the proper length, but they were far too heavy to be brought into the necessary position without a yoke of oxen. Unfortunately the only team of oxen in the entire settlement belonged to a professed infidel, and no one wanted to approach him on the subject. Just as the necessity became pressing, who should appear approaching through the woods but the infidel with his yoke of sturdy oxen, shouting in a merry voice, 'Here comes the devil with his oxen to help you build your meeting-house,' and the work happily went on. The next important event was the appearance of Thomas McLean with a small, flat keg of whiskey under his arm. This was placed in the minister's hands, and starting with the minister and ending with the donor, everyone had a drink. Then there were three cheers for Thomas McLean, and the promise that when the church was organized he would be the first elder. And this promise was fulfilled. 'By sundown, the church was built, covered with clapboards, floored with puncheons, and round logs rolled in for seats. The house was so located that a huge stump answered the purpose of a pulpit, with two puncheons set upright in front, and one across secured to the uprights with pins, on which the Bible might be placed. A puncheon seat for the minister completed the arrangement.'[1]

♠ ♠

The nineteenth-century American religious experience was a lamp and a

---

[1] This was the building of the Presbyterian Church in Cool Spring, Mercer County, Pennsylvania in the spring of 1800 under the direction of the Rev. Samuel Tait. S.J.M. Eaton, *History of the Presbytery of Erie; Embracing in its Ancient Boundaries the whole of Northwestern Pennsylvania and Northeastern Ohio, with Biographical Sketches of all its Ministers, etc.* (New York: Hurd and Houghton, 1868), pp.31-2.

mirror of the wider culture. Religion transformed society, but at the same time was constrained and shaped by that same context. Neither pulpits nor pews could be separated from the historical particularity of their essential *Sitz im leben*. It is not too far afield to agree with sociologists of religion that ordinary life was transformed by political and economic trends and therefore religion was similarly transformed.[2] Even the city set on a hill cannot be hid from the vicissitudes of the world it overlooks.

Post-revolutionary America seethed with discontent, dissent, and discovery. Nowhere was this more evident than in the fiery furnace of religion. In the early 1830s foreign observers concluded that nowhere else on earth did religion exert such a profound influence over the lives of men and women than in America.[3] Alexis de Tocqueville's oft-quoted assessment may be overwrought but the rhetoric and the reality did not have a great gulf between them. Domestic authorities confirmed de Tocqueville's observations.[4] From Cane Ridge to Dwight Moody, New England to California, the identity of religion in America experienced phenomenal growth, modification and a permanent shattering of all semblance of Christian unity. This is not to suggest that religion had lost any of its impact. Rather, there is a *prima facie* case against excluding or minimizing religion from the development of American history. What it inherited from the eighteenth century amounted to a particular American identity. Already in the eighteenth century the colonies had begun forging that new sense of identity, a process which

---

[2] George M. Thomas, *Revivalism and Cultural Change: Christianity, Nation Building, and the Market in the Nineteenth-Century United States* (Chicago and London: University of Chicago Press, 1989), pp. 161-2.

[3] Alexis de Tocqueville, *Democracy in America*, trans, George Lawrence, ed., J.P. Mayer (Garden City: Doubleday & Company, Inc., 1969), p. 291. He was in America from May 1831 until February 1832.

[4] Philip Schaff reflected that ' . . . Christianity is the most powerful factor in our society and the pillar of our institutions . . . .' Quoted in Stephen R. Graham, *Cosmos in the Chaos: Philip Schaff's Interpretation of Nineteenth-Century American Religion* (Grand Rapids and Cambridge: William B. Eerdmans, 1995), p. 141.

produced independence from British rule, the American Revolution, the framing of the Constitution and ultimately the creation of the United States. These historical events and realities played no mean rôle in shaping the American religious experience. The inheritance of history bequeathed to the nineteenth century eager expectation, unbridled enthusiasm and restless ferment.[5] These elements precipitated a veritable religious revolution on a scale not witnessed since the European reformations of the sixteenth century. It contributed to the modern American nation.

I. The Fight Between Carnival and Lent

> Shipmates . . . . all the things that God would have us do are hard for us to do—remember that—and hence, he oftener commands us than endeavors to persuade. And if we obey God, we must disobey ourselves; and it is in this disobeying ourselves, wherein the hardness of obeying God consists.[6]

♠   ♠

Within the stark walls of the Whaleman's Chapel in New Bedford, between marble reliefs remembering those lost at sea, fallen overboard and dragged down by whales, Father Mapple shouted these words to Captain Ahab and his assembled crew. The aged whaler-turned-preacher had ascended to the heights of the pulpit. Once Father Mapple had climbed the vertical ladder he dragged the ladder up behind him, step by step. Now the preacher was cut off from the whalers below. Suspended between heaven and earth, God and humanity, he spoke words which might well have been uttered by an orthodox Calvinist theologian. Father Mapple's

---

[5] Winthrop S. Hudson, *Religion in America*, fourth edition (New York: MacMillan Publishing Company, 1987), p. 172.

[6] Herman Melville, *Moby-Dick or, The Whale* (New York: Penguin Books, 1992), pp. 47-8.

sermon provides a splendid comparison to John Winthrop's discourse, 'A Modell of Christian Charity' and Jonathan Edwards', 'Sinners in the Hands of an Angry God.'[7]

In 1559 the Flemish artist Peter Bruegel painted one of his most famous works depicting popular culture. He called it 'The Fight Between Carnival and Lent'. On one side is a church, on the other a pub called 'At the Sign of the Blue Ship'. Accompanying the church are signs of piety, religious activity, works of mercy and religious persons. Associated with the pub are games and dancing, a dirty bride, a couple kiss in a window and the poor are neglected in the street. The central aspect of Bruegel's art piece is a mock combat between Carnival and Lent. Prince Carnival is shown as a fat man riding on a large wine cask with an enormous pie as a head-dress. His weapons for the battle consist of a long spit upon which appear a pig's head and other delicacies. His opponent, Lent, is a skinny old hag with a beehive for a head-dress. Her principle weapon is a long-handled wooden shovel upon which are two small herring. Her chair rests on a wheeled platform pulled by a monk and a nun. Lent has a bundle of switches in her left hand which are used on the backs of penitents. At her feet are pretzels and other traditional Lenten food. Accompanying Carnival is a rich, hearty fare, while following Lent is a spartan frugal form of nourishment. The church and Lent are marked by austerity, while Carnival is made out in costumes and masks. While people in bright clothes chain-dance with Carnival, those on the other side in dark clothes carry their prayer stools from the church. While the adherents of Lent give alms to the poor, men playing bagpipes lead processions, a ridiculously dressed fool carries a torch and water is poured out of upstairs windows onto the heads of those below in celebration of Carnival's festivals. In the end, the fight resolves

---

[7] The Winthrop text appears in Perry Miller and Thomas H. Johnson, eds., *The Puritans: A Sourcebook of their Writings*, 2 vols (New York: Harper & Row, Publishers, 1963), vol. 1, pp. 195-9. Edwards' sermon is in Clarence H. Faust and Thomas H. Johnson, eds., *Jonathan Edwards: Representative Selections* (New York: Hill and Wang, 1962), pp. 155-72.

The Nineteenth-Century American Religious Experience 15

Figure 1   Peter Bruegel, 'The Fight between Carnival and Lent'
           Courtesy of the Kunsthistorisches Museum, Vienna

itself predictably. Lent always triumphs. Carnival is predestined to perpetual defeat as the seasons of the year ever evolve from Carnival to Lent. Indeed, Carnival was often executed in effigy at the conclusion of the season of carnival.

In the American context, the early nineteenth century featured another fight between Carnival and Lent. Here, the corpulent figure of Carnival appeared as Andrew Jackson while the emaciated, stern figure of Lent was that of John Calvin.[8] War was waged between Jacksonian democracy and Calvinism. Lent was not destined to prevail in the New World as she had with regularity in the Old World. In this context Lent found herself subjected to a long, bitter defeat. Yet, even in this apparent defeat, Lent, or Calvinism, was not vanquished. As in the Bruegel painting, Carnival can exist only in the shadow of Lent, and the haggard old crone only achieves her identity in conflict with Carnival. Both dimensions of popular culture influence and define the other. In nineteenth-century America, the fight between Carnival and Lent was ongoing. There were no clear victors. The struggle defined the contours of the American religious experience.

One of the most powerful and pervasive systems of the Christian religion had been Calvinism. From its monumental roots in *The Institutes of the Christian Religion*, written by John Calvin the French Protestant reformer, to its appropriation and modification by the Synod of Dort and the rise of the Calvinists,

---

[8] The carnivalesque atmosphere surrounding Jackson's inauguration on 4 March 1829 was a sharp contrast to the pessimistic seriousness associated with Calvinism. As many as 30,000 people converged on the Capitol and the streets were filled. Jackson's inaugural speech was nearly drowned out by the cheering multitudes. When Jackson finished taking the oath of office the unruly mob broke through the retraining barriers. People poured into the White House. Barrels of orange punch and pails of liquor were overturned in the rush. Several thousand dollars in smashed china and glassware was lost. Men with mud-covered boots stood on satin-covered chairs, while other clambered on couches in an attempt to catch a glimpse of the president. To the more sedate 'the reign of KING MOB seemed triumphant.' Drinks were hastily transferred outside to relieve the building. The exit from the building took place by way of doors and windows and the mayhem continued on the lawns. 'Never before had there been such an inauguration of a President . . . .' Robert V. Remini, *Andrew Jackson and the Course of American Freedom 1822-1832*, volume 2 (New York: Harper & Row, Publishers, 1981), pp. 173-80.

the religion developed at Geneva proved to be a truly international form of Christianity. Unlike other varieties of sixteenth-century Protestantism, Calvinism was rooted specifically neither in ethnic nor cultural contexts. In some ways it might be said that Calvin transcended culture. Yet it is not so much Calvin who came to dominate as the Calvinists. That Calvin was not a Calvinist is an assumption for another venue. By the time his disciples had concluded their deliberations at Dordrecht in 1619 a system for posterity had been arrived at. The heart of the Calvinist doctrine might well be summarized adequately from the canons of the Synod of Dort: total depravity, unconditional election, limited atonement, irresistible grace and the perseverance of the saints.[9] More than anything else Calvinism came to symbolize the teaching of the doctrines of election and predestination. Calvin did not invent those doctrines but in his appropriation of SS. Paul and Augustine transformed an idea into an ideology. 'It is an awful decree, I confess; but no one can deny that God foreknew the final fate of man before he created him, and that he did foreknow it because it was appointed by his own decree.'[10] According to the will of God some were elected to eternal salvation while others were condemned to hell and both to the glory of God. Augustine had granted the former but remained silent on the latter. Where Augustine chose not to comment, Calvin drew bold conclusions. Whatever was done by humans was accomplished according to the eternal will and purpose of God.[11] Determinism was not a charge Calvinism could refute easily. A doggerel in nineteenth-century America ruefully expressed the popular understanding of Calvinism:

> You can and you can't
> You shall and you shan't

---

[9] Philip Schaff, ed., *The Creeds of Christendom* (Grand Rapids: Baker Book House, 1985), volume 3, pp. 550-97.

[10] John Calvin, *Institutes of the Christian Religion*, 2 volumes, trans. John Allen (Philadelphia: Presbyterian Board of Christian Education, n.d.), volume 2, p. 206.

[11] This is the conclusion Calvin reached in his magisterial exposition of the Protestant faith.

> You will and you won't
> You're damned if you do
> And damned if you don't.[12]

Despite its historical and theological reputation, Calvinism was less a rigid system, at least in America, than an ambiguous attempt at resolving a whole series of knotty religious conundrums. Calvinism seemed to work well for the Puritans who imported it to the new world and bequeathed it to a nation as part of its legacy. By the nineteenth century Calvinism had become increasingly incongruent with the American experience in general. In several ways the forensic system of Calvinism was challenged and in due course successfully overthrown. The kind of God-centered universe imagined by Calvinists gradually faded in a world aglow with human and scientific accomplishments. The equally impressive promise of continued human progress contributed further to the fatal malaise contacted by Calvinism.[13]

The rise and fall of Calvinism has been called one of the major themes in the intellectual history of the western world.[14] Its decline began in Europe under oppressive political policy in some areas and while rebirth seemed somewhat likely

---

[12] The saying has been attributed to Lorenzo Dow but oft-repeated and appropriated. See Nathan O. Hatch, *The Democratization of American Christianity* (New Haven and London: Yale University Press, 1989), p. 130. For example, it was quoted by Charles Finney in *Sermons on Various Subjects* (New York: Taylor & Gould, 1835), p. 71. The idea of determinism carried over into popular culture. Prior to his conversion James Finley was asked by his father if he prayed. Finley replied that he did not. When asked why, he answered: 'Because I do not see any use in it. If I am one of the elect, I will be saved in God's good time; and if I am one of the non-elect, praying will do me no good, as Christ did not die for them.' James B. Finley, *Autobiography of Rev. James B. Finley or, Pioneer Life in the West* (Cincinnati: Cranston and Curts; New York: Hunt and Eaton, 1853), p. 162.

[13] Mark A. Noll, *Princeton and the Republic 1768-1822* (Princeton: Princeton University Press, 1989), p. 209.

[14] Daniel Walker Howe, 'The Decline of Calvinism: An Approach to its Study' *Comparative Studies in Society and History* 14 (No. 3, 1972), p. 306. Howe argues that governmental action in many places in Europe in the course of the later sixteenth and seventeenth centuries contributed to a gradual decline of Calvinism, p. 311.

in seventeenth century America the period between the Second Great Awakening and the Civil War marked a steep decline in Calvinist fortunes in the new world, contributing to a serious erosion of Calvinism. Over the extended period of the Second Great Awakening a reaction to Calvinism evolved into a legacy which constituted a turning point in its eventual dénouement.[15] The protracted offspring of the American Revolution included rebellion against Calvinist hegemony and its authority. Arguably this was foreordained in the political struggle against Federalism. Indeed, Calvinism had provided an intellectual structure for the feeling of absolute religious dependence, an understanding both of salvation and history, *heilsgeschichte*, the dilemma over human will, and the rôle of God's interaction in the world. Fear was an essential ingredient and Calvinism functioned as a manifestation of social mood, alternatively among shifts of contentment and fear.[16] Calvinism made quite clear that God was in total control and that human destiny had already been predetermined, not on the basis of foreknowledge but on the conviction of divine election. For a time, Calvinism was an effective prophylactic against attempts to rebuild the Tower of Babel.

The American Revolution stood as a watershed in the history of theological development, and its defining of American culture and consciousness proved precipitous for Calvinism.[17] Differences in perception and reality caused some to conceive the collapse of Calvinism as altogether sudden.

> Have you heard of the wonderful one-hoss shay,
> That was built in such a logical way,

---

[15] Donald G. Matthews, 'The Second Great Awakening as an Organizing Process, 1780-1830: An Hypothesis' *American Quarterly* 21 (No. 1, 1969), p. 42 makes the observation that the Second Great Awakening cannot be seen as a revolt against Calvinism at least in its original design.

[16] Howe, 'The Decline of Calvinism', p. 322.

[17] See Nathan O. Hatch, *The Sacred Cause of Liberty: Republican Thought and the Millennium in Revolutionary New England* (New Haven and London: Yale University Press, 1977).

It ran a hundred years to a day,
And then, of a sudden, it—ah . . . .

All at once the horse stood still,
Close by the meet'n'—house on the hill.
—First a shiver, and then a thrill,
Then something decidedly like a spill,—
And the parson was sitting upon a rock, ...

The poor old chaise in a heap or mound
As if it had been to the mill and ground
You see, of course, if you're not a dunce
How it went to pieces all at once,—
All at once, and nothing first,—
Just as bubbles do when they burst . . . .[18]

The dramatic shift in Calvinist fortunes did not come to fruition overnight. Post-revolutionary America did witness the emergence of several motifs which ran counter to the ethos and convictions of Calvinism. A free market economy and political independence with all of its implications quite rapidly became translated into religious independence. More importantly political democracy produced a keen sense of soteriological democracy. The dogma of the Calvinists fell victim to patterns of social change. Even erstwhile Calvinist adherents began yielding to the democratic sense of salvation. In the wake of independence sprang political, social and economic freedom. Among the new-found liberties was individual freedom and nineteenth-century religion proved to be a breeding ground for the exercise of individual freedom. In terms of salvation a *laissez-faire* attitude took root. This transformed the faltering Calvinist hegemony into one option among many; an option that as the century progressed proved less and less viable. In the early

---

[18] 'The Deacon's masterpiece: or, the Wonderful "One-Hoss Shay"'. Oliver Wendell Holmes, *Humorous Poems* (London: Ward, Lock Bowden, and Co., 1875), pp. 109-14. The poem humorously announced the collapse of Calvinism, caricaturing the logical and well-built system which instead of wearing out gradually all at once simply fell to pieces. Its historical intention had been to parody Jonathan Edwards and the rigid system of Calvinism he and others espoused.

republic there were at least six clearly discernable value systems competing for allegiance in America: Calvinist orthodoxy, Anglican moralism, civic humanism, classical liberalism, Thomas Paine's radicalism and common sense philosophy.[19] At the outset of the nineteenth century Calvinism was losing the battle against the emerging Republican values of human reliance and determination and her enemies sang lustily, 'blest be the tie which no longer binds.' For perhaps the first time in a long and distinguished career, Calvinism was waging a war it could not win. Volunteerism seemed a viable option. Democracy, as Nathan Hatch has shown, created and transformed a nation and in that creation and transformation recast the meaning of American Christianity.

The strategies for overthrowing Calvinism were both deliberate and consequential. Indeed, religion and culture in America were strange bed-fellows. The force of impact they exerted upon each other had serious implications for 'official' forms of religion. These traditionally 'official' imported forms of Christianity, namely Anglicanism, Roman Catholicism, Lutheranism and Calvinism could no longer presume to operate under the established European social and political rubric *cuius regio, eius religio*. The first half of the nineteenth century produced a plethora of alternative religious experiments which challenged these established churches in a manner unknown in early modern American history. The eventual wearying of Calvinism was not uniform. Indeed, its decline can be observed most sharply in urban centers, within towns and along trade routes. Nonetheless it remained strong throughout much of the nineteenth century in the American hinterlands.[20] The sense of freedom, independence and self-sufficiency which in due course pervaded urban America was not immediately reflected throughout the rural context. 'Where capitalism most flourished,

---

[19] John M. Murrin, 'Religion and Politics in America from the First Settlements to the Civil War', in *Religion & American Politics*, ed., Mark A. Noll (New York and Oxford: Oxford University Press, 1990), p. 27.

[20] Howe, 'The Decline of Calvinism', p. 323.

22   *The Nineteenth-Century American Religious Experience*

Calvinism declined.'[21] Nevertheless, Calvinism retained its ardent defenders and there were continued efforts made from the eighteenth through the twentieth centuries to blend Calvinism, Republicanism and Enlightenment principles. John Witherspoon, Samuel Stanhope Smith, Henry Ward Beecher, Woodrow Wilson, Reinhold Niebuhr and Ralph Bellah may be numbered among those who have sought meaningful synthesis between the traditions of Calvinism and the realities of the New World.[22]

The decline in Calvinist hegemony as a theological assumption did not precipitate a decline in theology. The growth and evolution of theological emphases as a social factor is revealed in an examination of church records, synodal proceedings and ministerial examinations throughout the nineteenth century which leaves no doubt that theology remained vital in many quarters.[23]

The key to understanding American religion in the nineteenth century is connected to the democratic principle. This does not mean that theological developments away from Calvinism may be understood strictly as religious expressions of Jacksonian democracy. But democracy could neither be restrained from entering the spheres of religious inquiry nor yet from becoming ingrained in the consciousness of the American people.[24] This influenced both doctrine and practice. If the focus of soteriology could shift from election to free will doctrinally, then by natural extension spiritual power could no longer be restricted to a gender specific protocol. As the nineteenth-century American religious

---

[21]   *Ibid.*

[22]   Noll, *Princeton and the Republic 1768-1822*, p. 294.

[23]   A collection of such documents may be found in William Warren Sweet, ed., *Religion on the American Frontier 1783-1840: A Collection of Source Materials*, 4 volumes (New York: Cooper Square Publishers, Inc., 1964).

[24]   The principle of democracy upon which Jefferson rode to office merged with evangelical Christianity. Both of these factors should be regarded as products of an unprecedented social disintegration in American history. Gordon S. Wood, 'Evangelical America and Early Mormonism' *New York History* 61 (October 1980), p. 365.

experience revealed, the active involvement of women in leadership capacities constituted no minor rôle.[25] Katherine Ferguson opened New York's first Sabbath school in 1793. In the course of the nineteenth century Sojourner Truth became an abolitionist, reformer and women's rights advocate. Mary Lyon founded Mt. Holyoke Female Seminary in 1836 while Laura Haviland and Harriet Tubman gained fame and notoriety as agents on the underground rail road. Ida B. Wells campaigned for the rights of Blacks and women and organized the first Black Women's Suffrage Organization. Joanna Graham Bethune and Isabella Marshall Graham founded the Society for the Relief of Poor Widows with Small Children in 1797 and the Orphan Asylum Society in 1806. Josephine Shaw Lowell worked for improvements in jails and established the House of Refuge for Women. For her literary efforts Harriet Beecher Stowe assumed a prominent place in American society. At Seneca Falls, New York in 1848, Elizabeth Cady Stanton and her colleagues represented a watershed for women. Susan B. Anthony was a tireless campaigner for the abolition of slavery, as were Sarah and Angelina Grimké, and the heroic efforts of Prudence Crandall, a Connecticut Quaker school-mistress, for integrated schools, are but a few of the many women who assumed the mantle of leadership. Phoebe Palmer, Sarah Lankford, Amanda Berry Smith and a host of other women also assumed prominent places in the realm of religion.[26] Alma White, Ellen G. White and Mary Baker Eddy are among those women who founded churches or new religious movements. Women must be acknowledged as leading lights in a variety of social movements. These were areas wherein women could exercise authority. If political oligarchy could be dispatched *de facto* and *de iure* then the absence of iron-fisted rule allowed religion to find its own way and

---

[25] See Robert H. Abzug, *Cosmos Crumbling: American Reform and the Religious Imagination* (New York and Oxford: Oxford University Press, 1994), pp. 183-203.

[26] See Rosemary Radford Ruether and Rosemary Skinner Keller, eds., *Women and Religion in America*, 3 volumes (San Francisco: Harper & Row, 1981-6), especially volume 1 for the nineteenth century and Nancy A. Hardesty, *Women Called to Witness: Evangelical Feminism in the 19th Century* (Nashville: Abingdon Press, 1984).

the democratizing principle of inherent necessity permitted religious exploration and expression on an unprecedented scale.

II. Industrializing the New World

> All is hurry, bustle and confusion in the street, in the mill, and in the overflowing boarding house. If there chance to be an intelligent mind in that crowd which is striving to lay up treasures of knowledge, how unfavorably it is situated!. . . . Behold what disorder, confusion and disquietude reigns . . . . Incarcerated within the walls of a factory—while as yet mere children—drilled there from five till seven o'clock, year after year—thrown into company with all sorts and descriptions of minds, dispositions and intellects, without counsellor or friends. . . surrounded on all sides with the vain ostentation of fashion, vanity and light frivolity—beset with temptations without, and the carnal propensities of nature within, what *must*, what *will* be the natural, rational result? What but ignorance, misery, and *premature decay* of both *body* and *intellect*? Our country will be but one great hospital filled with worn out operatives and colored slaves! . . . . What but a race weak, sickly, imbecile, both mental and physical? A race fit only for corporation tools and time-serving slaves? . . . . the yoke of tyranny . . . has crushed and is crushing its millions in the old world to earth; yea, to starvation and death . . . .[27]

♣ ♣

The image of grim, gray cities with mills and factories dominating the urban skyline, smoke pouring from stacks blackening everything for miles around is one of the portraits often considered in the process of industrialization. Faceless

---

[27] A young woman by the name of Julianna writing of life and work in the factories at Lowell, Massachusetts in 1845. In John Mack Faragher, Mari Jo Buhle, Daniel Czitrom and Susan H. Armitage, eds., *Out of Many: A History of the American People, Documents Set*, volume 1 (Englewood Cliffs, NJ: Prentice-Hall Inc., 1994), pp. 162-3. See also Philip S. Foner, *The Factory Girls* (Urbana: University of Illinois Press, 1977) for a collection of primary source documents illustrating the lives of industrial employees written by women who worked in the factories of New England in the 1840s.

workers, shuffling to and from their duties, laboring endlessly in constant danger from heat, noise and machines, earning a pitiful wage, living in crowded conditions, barely getting by, rounds out the popular vision. The image of a sudden, dramatic and total transformation is only partially true.[28] Nonetheless, among the major themes of the nineteenth century must be numbered the relatively rapid pace of industrialization. Not only did early America witness significant economic shifts, the process of industrialization and urbanization altered irrevocably the shape of American culture. This impacted dramatically religious culture. The rise of cities with their machines, factories, mass production and strict schedules replaced the pre-industrial economy. This was a century-long process. Not until the 1880s were large factories widely common. In 1800 more than ninety percent of Americans lived on farms. While agrarian society did not disappear, the yeoman existence of farms and families was gradually transformed. Horace Bushnell in an 1851 sermon spoke of the complete revolution of domestic life and manners. The local system of bartering and mutual obligations was replaced by a cash economy. This occurred following the conflict rural people found themselves in, caught on the horns of a dilemma; the ethics of local exchange and the profitability of long distance trade.[29] The production of crops for family use gave way to commercialism. The sale of dairy products, wood and livestock became overshadowed by the rise of the factories. The learning of trades through an apprenticeship program now found itself in serious competition with machines and technology. Where once the family all worked together now family life and work increasingly came to have no relationship. Gender rôles underwent some stereotyping producing revised views of women and domesticity. The order produced from chaos which became the industrializing of America not only recast

---

[28] Walter Licht, *Industrializing America: The Nineteenth Century* (Baltimore and London: The Johns Hopkins University Press, 1995), p. 21.

[29] Christopher Clark, *The Roots of Rural Capitalism: Western Massachusetts, 1780-1860* (Ithaca and London: Cornell University Press, 1990), p. 195.

economic life but likewise altered cultural discourse and invented a 'symbolic repertoire' which would be appropriated by religious reformers in their quest for order.[30] These changes in economic circumstances were among the reasons why some people found themselves pushed from their homes, driven from their places of birth, uprooted from the security of the surroundings which had imparted to them the indelible marks of identity.[31] Some deplored these developments, lamenting the decline of a 'system of labor, which made every farm-house and hamlet a virtuous manufactuory.' Industrialization had virtually swept this away, technology had reduced individual souls to 'mere parts of a vast system of machinery.'[32]

Despite this, industrialization facilitated the growth of religion. Transient urban workers formed congregations of hearers for city evangelists and in the formation of these congregations achieved a new sense of identity and belonging. Such individuals proved themselves more amenable to evangelical preachers than to labor activists. Political and social forms of salvation were enticing but not as compelling as religious salvation. These ready-made urban mission fields did much to provide the early context for revivals in the cities associated with Charles Finney and others. Long standing ecclesiastical hegemony in many towns collapsed as a consequence and in the ensuing disorder revivalism and new religious movements flourished. New, temporary, congregations sprang up comprised of these transient urban workers and this contributed to the formation of a new religious culture forged in the red-hot spontaneous combustion of revivalism.[33]

---

[30] Abzug, *Cosmos Crumbling: American Reform and the Religious Imagination*, p. 5

[31] Licht, *Industrializing America*, p. 64.

[32] George Duffield, a Presbyterian minister. Quoted in Robert Whalen, 'Calvinism and Chiliasm: The Sociology of Nineteenth Century American Millenarianism' *American Presbyterians* 70 (No. 3, 1992), p. 169.

[33] Licht, *Industrializing America*, pp. 71-2. See also Charles Sellers, *The Market Revolution: Jacksonian America, 1815-1846* (New York and Oxford: Oxford University

The industrializing of the new world which began in the eighteenth century persisted well into the twentieth century. Samuel Slater's cotton textile mill on Pawtucket Falls, Rhode Island in 1790 was but the beginning. The cotton gin was invented in 1793 and before the end of the decade Eli Whitney was proposing new advances in technology. The Embargo Act of 1807 excluded British manufactures and allowed big business in America to flourish, but at a cost. In the second decade of the nineteenth century the cotton boom in the south led to significant trade from 1815 onwards. The first factory at Lowell, Massachusetts opened in 1823. Two years later the 364 mile Erie Canal was completed. Ten years later labor disputes and strikes convulsed the economy, but there could be no turning back. Matthias Baldwin in Philadelphia and Cyrus McCormick in Chicago were proposing ideas in manufacturing technology which would have far-reaching consequences. The expansive rail linkages into all parts of the country extended and hastened the inevitable process of industrializing America. In 1830 there were only thirteen miles of rail linkage in the country. By 1850 there were almost 9000 miles of rail in the United States. This precipitated a revolution in transportation. The age of the canals figures prominently as well, together with the development of regular steamboats from 1807. Mining, slaughterhouses and the sprawling stockyards of Chicago were all indicative of these social changes.

Religion was neither immune nor unresponsive to these changes. Methods were adopted, theologies adapted, and religion, through challenge and support, kept pace with society throughout the nineteenth century. Certain elements within Christendom facilitated this more than others. It could be argued that Unitarianism was most responsible for helping to shape American Christianity to the market mentality. Arising in the neighborhood of Boston, this new 'liberal' approach to religion was perhaps the unintended consequence of the Puritan experiment with

---

Press, 1991), pp. 202-36 on religion within the Industrial Revolution and Clark, *The Roots of Rural Capitalism*, pp. 116-7 on the economic power shifts in the context of a revivalist culture.

rationalism. In this experiment, Augustinian-Calvinism became wedded somewhat uneasily to a Pelagian-Arminian ethic of human works and efforts. The revolution in religious order paralleled the revolution in social and political order. Freedom from Calvin went hand in hand with liberation from the British Crown. Unitarianism facilitated the decline of supernaturalism and declared the idea of the Trinity absurd. Rationalism arose in the place of the supernatural and in the stead of a triune God emerged a remote deity who had endowed humankind with self-reliance. God had given to the world the greatest divine gift, not of theological dogma but the human ability to succeed. In the ethos of the early nineteenth century the 'Unitarian God . . . [proved] irresistible.'[34] The connection of religion and economics helped to create a social matrix which altered the shape both of religion and economics in nineteenth-century America.

Out of the countryside and small towns early American culture had reached its primitive definition. Now cities and their immediate environs assumed the lead in the creation of a nation. It bears repeating, however, that while this became increasingly true, at the end of the nineteenth century forty percent of Americans still worked on farms.[35] Significant for the decline of Calvinism, the transformation of American culture and religion were the waves of immigrants which brought new and varied peoples to the shores of the new world. This influx of immigrants to the new world bringing with them diverse Christian and non-Christian expressions both diversified and complicated the growth of religion in America making it quite impossible to speak of western European, Protestant Christianity as the exclusive, even dominant description of religion in America.[36] Moreover, the three million

---

[34] Sellers, *The Market Revolution*, p. 202.

[35] Licht, *Industrializing America*, p. xiv.

[36] See R. Lawrence Moore, *Religious Outsiders and the Making of Americans* (New York and Oxford: Oxford University Press, 1986) and Jay P. Dolan, *The Immigrant Church: New York's Irish and German Catholics, 1815-1865* (Baltimore: The Johns Hopkins University Press, 1975).

immigrants who arrived between 1845 and 1854 posed a real threat to the social cohesion of the republic.[37] Between 1775 and 1850 the population of the nation swelled from less than three million to around twenty million. In addition, many of these newcomers came from environments quite diverse from the predominant Protestant heritage of the Puritans and the Anglicans. Immigration was only one reason for this astonishing increase in population.[38] The rise of cities and the dramatic increase in population posed new and difficult social problems. The concomitant industrialization may be held culpable in part for a new set of ethical, social, labor and political problems which confounded the ability of former solutions and prompted revision.[39] Rapid change was the order of the day. The cities exacerbated this rapid change and the influence of secular universities and the secularizing of religious institutions played an important rôle as well.[40] In the course of the century John D. Rockefeller, Andrew Carnegie, Jay Gould and J.P.

---

[37] Richard J. Carwardine, *Evangelicals and Politics in Antebellum America* (New Haven and London: Yale University Press, 1993), p. 199.

[38] Hatch, *The Democratization of American Christianity*, pp. 3-4.

[39] George M. Marsden, *Fundamentalism and American Culture: The Shaping of Twentieth-Century Evangelicalism 1870-1925* (New York and Oxford: Oxford University Press, 1980), pp. 21-2.

[40] Winton U. Solberg, 'The Conflict Between Religion and Secularism at the University of Illinois, 1867-1894' *American Quarterly* 18 (No. 2, 1966), pp. 183-99 is an excellent illustration and case study of the conflict generated by regulated, required religious observances in American institutions of higher learning. Essential for its insights is George M. Marsden and Bradley J. Longfield, eds., *The Secularization of the Academy* (New York and Oxford: Oxford University Press, 1992). The magisterial study by George M. Marsden, *The Soul of the American University: From Protestant Establishment to Established Nonbelief* (Oxford and New York: Oxford University Press, 1994) is to be noted in this connection. Many institutions suffered the sometime debilitating effects of power struggles between opposing religious forces. Transylvania University founded in 1799 at Lexington was the scene of a protracted battle for control between Presbyterians and liberals. Marsden, *Ibid.*, p. 72. Of the 516 colleges and universities founded before the Civil War in America only a few were without religious affiliation. Hudson, *Religion in America*, p. 147.

Morgan, among others emerged.[41] In the end, population growth, inequalities in wealth distribution and propertylessness reshaped American society.[42] Not all these changes were for the better. On an individual level the woes expressed by Julianna from the Lowell factories indicated one type of social plight. On a larger scale, the ravaged land, displaced masses of humanity and democratic contradictions served to illuminate social conundrums which continued to defy explanation and solution and which remained hallmarks of the industrial legacy.[43]

III. The Paradox of Religious Leaders:
Responses to American Culture

Your prayers are so very cold they do not rise more than six feet high; you must strive hard and struggle—you must groan, you must agonize, why you must pray till your nose bleeds, or it will not avail. If you do not do better I must soon shake my garments against you and clear out and be gone. I would not have you think that I will *stay here* and go *to hell* along with the rest of you.[44]

♠ ♠

From medieval times religion functioned in western society in a central capacity. Frequently religion regulated social order providing boundaries and

---

[41] On the use of big business see Licht, *Industrializing America*, pp. 133-65.

[42] Clark, *The Roots of Rural Capitalism*, p. 261.

[43] Sellers, *The Market Revolution*, p. 427.

[44] Charles Finney preaching in the town of Western, New York. Finney also referred to the town as Westernville. Cited in William G. McLoughlin, Jr., *Modern Revivalism: Charles Grandison Finney to Billy Graham* (New York: The Ronald Press Company, 1959), p. 27.

establishing control. Yet not all religion operated on the cutting edge of society. There were religious expressions which tended to retreat from visibility. The rise of new religious emphases in nineteenth-century America were all in one way or another responses to the unique evolving culture and social identity. There were religious responses and ideas formed on social issues such as the Fugitive Slave Law, the Dred Scott decision, John Brown's raid at Harper's Ferry, the Kansas-Nebraska Act and so on. By culture it is reasonable to accept the definition encompassing common beliefs, values, and assumptions identifying a group of people in oral, literary, artistic, political and educational forms.[45]

American religion might be said in some instances to have become subsumed within culture. This cardboard sign in a saloon window in Gillette, Wyoming at the end of the nineteenth century suggests such a relation:

> Preaching at 7:30 P.M.
> Dance at 9:00 P.M.
> After Dance, Big Poker Game[46]

Other forms of religious expression were entirely world-negating and indicative of a serious ambivalence toward social structures. Francis Asbury upon visiting Washington in 1806 remarked in his journal: ' . . . Congress does not interest me: I am a man of another world, in mind and calling . . . . '[47] Worldliness collided with other-worldliness in the religious experience and ethos of nineteenth-century America. The prophets and priests of religion proclaimed their visions to the people and in each and every instance those visions and the actions predicated upon them constituted a response to the way in which the new world was evolving. While the Amish and Hutterites withdrew from society, the Salvation Army

---

[45] Marsden, *Fundamentalism and American Culture*, p. v.

[46] Cited in Ferenc Morton Szasz, *The Protestant Clergy in the Great Plains and Mountain West, 1865-1915* (Albuquerque: University of New Mexico Press, 1988), p. 101.

[47] *The Journal and Letters of Francis Asbury*, eds., Elmer T. Clark, J. Manning Potts and Jacob S. Payton, 3 volumes (London and Nashville: Epworth Press and Abingdon Press, 1958). Entry for 5 March, volume 2, p. 497.

attempted to address social ills in a variety of philanthropic ways. William Miller and the Adventists declared the world at an end, Transcendentalists embraced the meaning and mystery of the human experience. Washington Gladden and Walter Rauschenbusch critiqued the established social order, while some advocates of the extreme manifest destiny persuasion exulted in the godliness of the American system. If John Humphrey Noyes and his Oneida community celebrated the goodness of love and sexuality, Ann Lee and the Shakers eschewed all forms of sexual expression. While disease ravaged the nation, Charles and Myrtle Fillmore, Mary Baker Eddy and the Christian Scientists preached a unique idea of deliverance from sickness. While Quakers persisted in their pacifist ways, mainline Christian denominations blessed troops who fought on both sides of the Civil War. Fundamentalists attempted to narrow certain forms of inquiry while Unitarians and Universalists pushed for relaxed standards of Christianity. The Holiness movements sought to transform the world and reform society, while the Mormons under Joseph Smith and Brigham Young were among those groups to abandon efforts at reforming society and simply went off into the great frontier wilderness to built their own alternative version of the kingdom of God. Others practised communist principles of common living, shared possessions and simple lifestyles.[48] The emancipation of Blacks from slavery in the wake of the Civil War resulted in a mass exodus from white churches and the establishment of a variety of Black churches. The age of the great revivals constituted a completely different aspect of American religion. Out of this vortex, the diversity among those bearing the same name is altogether astounding. The Baptists were representative. They included Anti-Mission Baptists, Free Will Baptists, General Baptists, Particular Baptists, Primitive Baptists, Regular Baptists, Old School Baptists, Hard Shell Baptists,

---

[48] See Lawrence Foster, *Religion and Sexuality: Three American Communal Experiments of the Nineteenth Century* (New York and Oxford: Oxford University Press, 1981) for discussions of the Shakers, Mormons and the Oneida Community. See also Dolores Hayden, *Seven American Utopias: The Architecture of Communitarian Socialism, 1790-1915* (Cambridge, MA and London: The MIT Press, 1976). Hayden lists 130 communities and alludes to hundreds more, pp. 362-6.

Landmark Baptists, Northern Baptists, Southern Baptists, Separate Baptists, Dutch River Baptists, Permanent Baptists, Two-Seed-in-the-Spirit Baptists and a smattering of other types. The democratic principle seemed to know no bounds in the realm of religion. Volunteerism had become an essential ingredient in the American religious experience in many quarters.

If the principle *e pluribus unum* could be applied to American culture and the formation of a nation it could in no wise be made a rule for the nineteenth-century American religious experience. Out of the many came an even greater variety and diversity. The idea of oneness in American religion has never been a reality. From the very beginning any search for a single religious *successio* must end in failure.[49] The Puritans may have predominated for a time in the early Massachusetts Bay Colony but diversity soon emerged. This could only be but a natural consequence of immigration and those fleeing religious oppression in the old world in search of liberty in the new.[50] When that liberty seemed to be in hand, the conviction arose that a strict conformity must be imposed in order to preserve freedom. This resulted in life and death; a simultaneous broadening and constricting of democracy, socially and religiously. Philip Schaff remarked at mid-century that '. . . America is *the grave of all European nationalities*; but a *Phenix* [sic] *grave*, from which they shall rise to new life . . . in a new . . . form.'[51] These new forms assumed religious clothing in more than isolated instances.

---

[49] A good and sound caution is issued with respect to the futility of searching for a single origin in light of the radical diversity and complexity of American religion in Jerald C. Brauer, 'Regionalism and Religion in America' *Church History* 54 (No. 3, 1985), p. 368.

[50] On this see W.R. Ward, *The Protestant Evangelical Awakening* (Cambridge: Cambridge University Press, 1992), pp. 241-65.

[51] *America: A Sketch of its Political, Social, and Religious Character*, ed., Perry Miller (Cambridge, MA: The Belknap Press of Harvard University Press, 1961), p. 51. The work originally appeared in 1855.

'Immigration, which was America's historic *raison d'être* has been the most persistent and the most pervasive influence in her development.'[52] What appears as hyperbole should be looked at closely. America was the immigration destination in the nineteenth century. The fear of an attractive and unknown situation was not sufficient to keep these people in their unattractive, well-known contexts. But there was a price to pay beyond the trans-Atlantic voyage. These immigrants were uprooted from their familiar environments in the old world and received the inheritance of alienation in the new world. They had rejected old world traditions and embraced freedom as citizens of a new world. Even this exuberance bore bitter fruit. The growth of freedom mirrored the decline of order but in the chaos, a new order emerged. In the end, immigration was not a problem to be solved but a reality to be integrated into the evolution of a nation.[53]

As the offspring of immigration, ethnic diversity represented and perpetuated religious diversity. Religious America matched social America as a complex mosaic. One of the implications of the American Revolution was the recognition of religious tolerance as a social norm.[54] That said, men like Thomas Jefferson were convinced that no liberty, including religious liberty, 'should be left hanging on the whimsy of public opinion.'[55] Indeed, scholars have demonstrated the spiritual free-for-all which seemed to characterize the early nineteenth century was a veneer for a growing crisis which appeared to be evolving out of control. As de Tocqueville noted, 'where there is no authority in religion or politics, men are soon frightened by the limitless independence with which they are faced . . . they

---

[52] Maldwyn Allen Jones, *American Immigration*, second edition (Chicago and London: The University of Chicago Press, 1992), p. 1.

[53] I am indebted to Oscar Handlin, *The Uprooted* (Boston: Little, Brown, 1951) for the foregoing. The paragraph is essentially the thesis of Handlin's book.

[54] Abzug, *Cosmos Crumbling: American Reform and the Religious Imagination*, p. 5.

[55] Edwin Gaustad, *Sworn on the Altar of God: A Religious Biography of Thomas Jefferson* (Grand Rapids: William B. Eerdmans, 1996), pp. 51-2.

cannot accept their ancient beliefs again, they hand themselves over to a master.'[56] In religious matters that master would turn out to be various and sundry dictators disguised as democrats. There would be, after all, order in the community, order within religion. But that order would exist in many cases as a thinly disguised autocracy. Yet the success of these movements was clearly evident and undeniable and their appeal nothing short of extraordinary.

By mid century the American frontier had been pushed westward to the Pacific. The American world no longer could be regarded as centered in New England and its boundaries no longer restricted to the Atlantic fringe. Hundreds of wagon trains annually pulled out of Independence, Missouri, the jumping off point for the Oregon Trail and the fabled fortunes of California. In 1846 the tragic, almost mythic Donner Party began their legendary trek into the wild, largely uncharted wilderness. The mood of the nation was westward. Expansion seemed to be on the minds of many, not least among them the religious entrepreneurs and innovators. Missionaries Jason Lee, the Whitmans and Spaldings made their mark in the Oregon Territory by the 1840s. It was 1846 when the Mormons set out for the Great Salt Lake Basin. That same year the Mexican War began which effectively added Texas, New Mexico and California to the burgeoning United States. Between 1845 and 1848 the territory of America increased by a full fifty percent and by 1848 encompassed the land from sea to shining sea. The territorial expansion of the United States is of course fundamental for understanding the meaning and complexity of nineteenth-century American history.

In the 1830s, reports of religious life across the Mississippi River could be briefly summarized: 'No Sunday west of St. Louis, no God west of Fort Smith.'[57] Religious fervor in the east aimed to change all that. The American religious experience followed parallel lines with the expansion of the nation. The recognized

---

[56] Alexis de Tocqueville, *Democracy in America*, p. 444.

[57] An old cowboy saying noted in Frederick A. Norwood, *The Story of American Methodism* (New York and Nashville: Abingdon Press, 1974), p. 264.

social norm of religious toleration following the turn of the nineteenth century persistently widened, though in a curious fashion. Pluralism and denominationalism spread out with national expansion aided by missions enthusiasm. As in earliest America no form of official or standard religious practice may be evidenced along the overland trails west nor yet in those western territories. Settlers pushing west brought their own brand of Christianity with them. All along the Oregon, Santa Fe, Gila River, California and Old Spanish Trails were the traces of Roman Catholicism, Baptists, Methodism, the Presbyterians, Hutterites, Mormons, Congregationalists, Quakers, Unitarians, Lutherans, Disciples of Christ, non Christians and many others. Along these same trails rode itinerant evangelists, revivalists and popular preachers. Each brought their own peculiar brand of religion, each seeking to missionize the frontier. They brought with them a social and religious culture which shaped their converts and transformed the identity of the wilderness. An old adage asserted that 'the Baptists came on foot; the Methodists came in a Conestoga wagon; the Presbyterians rode the train; and the Episcopalians arrived in the Pullman car.' While expressing the diversity of religious and social culture this adage reflects accurately social status more than it does historical reality.[58] The question of social status quite certainly had a key rôle to play in the emerging structures of denominationalism.[59] Thus, in due course, theology and religious institutions crossed the frontier into the uncharted vastness of the American west. The churches and theologies adapted to their new surroundings and made efforts to increase their numbers and evangelize those already there. The Kickapoos, Choctaws, Chickasaws, Flatheads and other

---

[58] Cited in Szasz, *The Protestant Clergy in the Great Plains and Mountain West, 1865-1915*, p. 11.

[59] Anne C. Rose, 'Social Sources of Denominationalism Reconsidered: Post-Revolutionary Boston as a Case Study' *American Quarterly* 38 (No. 2, 1986), pp. 243-64 offers evidence to support this assumption.

indigenous peoples were natural mission fields.[60] Their savagery of life and religion generally found little toleration among the Christian settlers and missionaries. Roger Williams upon purchasing Rhode Island from natives in the seventeenth century is reported to have advised them, 'why do you paint yourselves? Wipe it off! The God who made you will be unable to recognize you.' The same paternal attitude marked the nineteenth century. Despite these sentiments and much conflict, religious diversity in the new world must be numbered among the components of the American religious experience in the nineteenth century. The archdeacon of Surrey, Samuel Wilberforce, visiting America in the mid-1840s put it thus: 'Nowhere have the restless waters of the multitude of sects tossed themselves in wilder madness than in the new world.'[61] The seeds of religious democracy had been irrevocably sown. The harvest of the early nineteenth century was yet to come.

A. Prophets, Preachers and Preaching

Breethring, I see yonder a man that's a sinner! I know he's a sinner! Thar he stands, a missuble old crittur, with his head a-blossomin' for the grave! A few more short years, and d-o-w-n he'll go to perdition, lessen the Lord have mer-cy on him! Come up here, you old hoary-headed sinner, a-n-d git down upon your knees, a-n-d put up your cry for the Lord to snatch you from the bottomless pit! You're ripe for the devil; you're b-o-u-n-d for hell, and the Lord knows what'll become on you.[62]

---

[60] For documents relating to missionary efforts among the native American peoples see Sweet, ed., *Religion on the American Frontier*, volume 2, pp. 605-48 for the Presbyterians, volume 3, pp. 340-67 for the Congregationalists, and volume 4, pp. 499-551 for the Methodists.

[61] Cited in Christopher Adamson, 'God's Continent Divided: Politics and Religion in Upper Canada and the Northern and Western United States, 1775 to 1841' *Comparative Studies in Society and History* 36 (1994), p. 418 n. 39.

[62] An Alabama camp meeting preacher in mid-sermon exhorting Captain Simon Suggs of the Old Southwest. The incident is noted in Charles A. Johnson, *The Frontier Camp Meeting: Religion's Harvest Time* (Dallas: Southern Methodist University Press,

♠ ♠

Religion provided a context for so much of what happened in the course of the nineteenth century. In the morass of politics, social change and cultural developments the emerging new religious identities in America created the parameters for continued revival, reform and reformation. This process of narrowing continued to define the American religious experience.

The failure of Calvinism, the expansion of the nation and the democratizing of religion produced a culture of reformers not unlike those soldiers of the faith in sixteenth-century Europe who sought single-handedly to slay the Goliath of organized, official religion. In America it seemed the context for such religious innovation was even more inviting than the crisis-ridden societies of early modern Europe. General themes which emerged from these reforming attempts centered on revivalism, the preaching of sin, access by all to the benefits of Christ with respect to salvation and the ability of all persons to respond. Of course none of these emphases differ substantially from those of the seventeenth or eighteenth centuries. In the nineteenth century, however, these traditional motifs became tinged with a sense of urgency. This urgency was shaped by its social and historical context. Familiar ideas were transformed. This new wine in old wineskins burst forth in unexpected ways. Social distinctions, for the most part tended to evaporate. Emphases upon spontaneity and a rejection of formality were widely evident. In the wake of the loss of traditional authority these reformers initially found identity and security in religious democracy. On the foundations of social and political democratic principles, religious reformers began rebuilding Christianity. Nathan Hatch has identified three areas of reform common to several movements. In the first instance, a social levelling whereby ecclesiastical revolution placed laity and clergy on a similar standing. A wholesale rejection of academic or intellectual theology followed, only to be replaced by a new

---

1985), p. 267 n.6.

hermeneutic and system of theology. Finally, and perhaps most significant, lip-service was paid to the principle that each believer had the inalienable right to read and interpret the Bible for him or herself.[63] In other words, everyone ought to be 'wholly free to examine for [them]selves, what is truth, without being bound to any catechism, creed, confession of faith, discipline or any rule excepting the scriptures.'[64] This was religious democracy in principle, a *laissez-faire* theology.

Between the rhetoric and the reality emerged dictators disguised as democrats. Between the pulpit and the pew persisted a great gulf of separation. The democratizing of Christianity and the de-Calvinizing of theology certainly transformed religious discourse but some of the old traditional categories remained and resisted steadfastly all attempts at their elimination. Nowhere could this be more evident than in the distinction between the pulpit and the pew. Father Mapple's pulpit in *Moby-Dick* only physically exaggerated a spiritual reality. The word dictatorship is perhaps too strong but the spiritual oligarchy found in the higher echelons of many of the religious movements in nineteenth-century America is undeniable. Thomas Jefferson may have loudly proclaimed: '. . . I have sworn upon the altar of god eternal hostility against every form of tyranny over the mind of man' but that libertarian sentiment did not find productive soil in nineteenth-century religion.[65] The Methodists preached holiness, personal responsiveness and individual conversion while maintaining leadership, direction and discipline by means of a firm episcopal authority. Wesley may have decried this approach in England but, despite his correspondence with Francis Asbury the latter persisted

---

[63]   Hatch, *The Democratization of American Christianity*, pp. 71-3.

[64]   Elias Smith in 1809. Quoted in Wood, 'Evangelical America and Early Mormonism', p. 374.

[65]   This frequently quoted comment appears in a letter addressed to Benjamin Rush, dated 23 September 1800. The letter has been published in Dickinson W. Adams, ed., *Jefferson's Extracts from the Gospels*, in *The Papers of Thomas Jefferson*, second series (Princeton: Princeton University Press, 1983), pp. 319-21 at p. 320. The idea of tyranny of course meant different things to different people.

in maintaining American Methodism in this manner.[66] The rigid authoritarian hierarchy of movements like the Mormons cannot be considered exceptional. The emergence of the *Book of Mormon* under the auspices of Joseph Smith naturally endowed Smith with power and authority well beyond that of Mormon underlings in the early days of the movement.[67] Not all Mormon converts were necessarily amenable to this type of leadership but options for reform within the Mormon kingdom proved both few and fruitless. Dissenters like Oliver Cowdery wanted a more open society, one existing closer to the values and traditions of evangelical Protestantism and New England 'town' democracy. Smith and his cadre of supporters insisted on an essentially closed community founded on an ethic and doctrine beyond the traditional boundaries of historic Protestantism. The result was crisis in Kirtland, Ohio in 1836-7, a confrontation which only Joseph Smith ultimately could win.[68] In his own words, 'Truth is "Mormonism". God is the author of it.'[69] To dismiss and denounce Smith as the originator of a cult is patently absurd. Smith's posture cannot be seen as something other than a reflection of the prevailing ethos of many religious movements within the culture of the nineteenth century. Alexis de Tocqueville was not far off the mark in his suggestion that

---

[66] 'How can you, how dare you, suffer yourself to be called Bishop? I shudder, I start at the very thought! Men may call me a knave or a fool, a rascal, a scoundrel, and I am content: But they shall never, by my consent, call me Bishop! For my sake, for God's sake, for Christ's sake, put a full end to this! Let the Presbyterians do what they please, but let the Methodists know their calling better.
Thus, my dear Franky, I have told you all that is in my heart.' Wesley to Asbury, 20 September 1788 in *The Works of John Wesley*, volume 13 (Grand Rapids: Baker Book House, 1979), pp. 74-5.

[67] See for example, Richard L. Bushman, 'The Book of Mormon and the American Revolution' *Brigham Young University Studies* 17 (1976), pp. 3-20.

[68] On this see especially Marvin S. Hill, 'Cultural Crisis in the Mormon Kingdom: A Reconsideration of the causes of the Kirtland Dissent' *Church History* 49 (No. 3, 1980), pp. 286-97.

[69] Smith, *History of the Church of Jesus Christ of Latter-Day Saints*, ed., Brigham H. Roberts (Salt Lake City: Deseret News Press, 1948), volume 3, p. 297.

freedom proved to be a harder taskmaster than bondage and for this reason men and women were not unhappy to release themselves to the guidance and wisdom of spiritual prophets, holy men and women of God. Was de Tocqueville in error when he affirmed that 'religion in America is a world apart in which the clergyman is supreme . . . .'?[70]

Prophets and charismatic leaders wielded power and authority in the new world religious experience on a scale not unlike that administered by popes, bishops and patriarchs in the old world. Powerful individuals such as Alexander Campbell emerged as a leader of exceptional presence, a man who knew divine truth and as such had little time or patience for religious dissent and did not gladly abide challenge. John Humphrey Noyes made all final decisions and oversaw an autocratic administration at Putney, Vermont and Oneida, New York. In 1837 he set forth his political philosophy in this manner. 'I would never connect myself with any individual or association in religion unless I was acknowledged leader.'[71] Noyes remained adamant on this point. 'Never will I be compelled by ministers or anyone else to accept any doctrine that does not commend itself to my mind and conscience.'[72] There was little separation between the rhetoric and the reality. Noyes' son summarized it this way: 'My father was the center of life at Oneida.'[73] The self-acclaimed prophet Robert Matthews left no doubt as to the nature of his authority: 'God speaks through me.'[74] Charles Finney did not consider his

---

[70] *Democracy in America*, p. 448.

[71] Cited in Spencer C. Olin, 'The Oneida Community and the Instability of Charismatic Authority' *The Journal of American History* 67 (No. 2, 1980), p. 289.

[72] Cited in Nathan O. Hatch, 'Sola Scriptura and Novus Ordo Seclorum', in *The Bible in America: Essays in Cultural History*, eds., Nathan Hatch and Mark Noll (New York and Oxford: Oxford University Press, 1982), p. 70.

[73] Pierrepont Noyes, *My Father's House: An Oneida Boyhood* (Gloucester, MA: Peter Smith, 1966), p. 125.

[74] Paul E. Johnson and Sean Wilentz, *The Kingdom of Matthias* (New York and Oxford: Oxford University Press, 1994), p. 112. According to John Nevin, contempt for

authority any less binding on his hearers. Finney was reported once to have declared publicly that he was one of the brigadier generals of Jesus Christ. As such he possessed a special commission from the heavenly court to preach. All who refused to believe him would suffer eternal damnation.[75] Francis Asbury 'wielded supreme authority.'[76]

Following the assassination of Joseph Smith in the Carthage, Illinois jail a short but intense power struggle convulsed the Mormon movement. A charismatic movement cannot flourish for long in the absence of a prophet. Sidney Rigdon, John C. Bennett, Benjamin Winchester, Lyman Wright and James J. Strang stood ready to fill the void. But these Latter-Day Saints and aspiring prophets one by one failed. The reasons are complex and ultimately negated on account of the prophet who did succeed and who led the Latter-Day Saints out of the chaos of Carthage and into the light of the kingdom of God on the desolate desert shores of Salt Lake.[77] Brigham Young ultimately prevailed on the strength of democratic principles but even his persuasion proved itself in the sun-baked sands of Utah to be autocracy in the gown of democracy. The charismatic basis for the legitimacy of leadership was both appealing and problematic. Despite the clear theologizing of democracy on one hand, there remained an autocratic element in the leadership of new, burgeoning religious movements. The voice of God, *vox dei*, and the voice of the people, *vox populi*, might now be intimately related. The Bible was declared

---

history and authority and reliance upon one's own sense of divine commission was a mark both of the sects and of antichrist. John W. Nevin, *Anti-christ; or the Spirit of Sect and Schism* (New York: John S. Taylor, 1848), p. 54.

[75]   The report appeared in Buffalo, New York in the *Gospel Advocate* (13 January 1826), pp. 3,5. Cited in McLoughlin, *Modern Revivalism: Charles Grandison Finney to Billy Graham*, p. 27.

[76]   Charles H. Goodwin, 'The Greatest Itinerant Francis Asbury 1745-1816' *Proceedings of the Wesley Historical Society* 50 (May 1995), p. 52.

[77]   Thomas F. O'Dea, *The Mormons* (Chicago: University of Chicago Press, 1957), pp. 70-1 sets forth the context of the power struggle precipitated by Smith's untimely demise.

open for all to read and accept, the masses were encouraged, even implored to seek God, surrender to that God and be converted on the basis of free, unhindered will. But dictators disguised as democrats channelled the voice of God, interpreted the Bible for the multitudes and declared the true narrow path to salvation while pointing out in unequivocal terms the many and varied broad roads leading downward to destruction.

It is worth noting the pattern dissent followed in early American religion. Intolerance in white churches in Philadelphia caused Richard Allen (1760-1831) and Absalom Jones (1746-1818) to leave Methodism and found a separate congregation which in time would produce the African Methodist Episcopal Church. Intolerance when it has conceived brings forth further intolerance and Allen became a dictator, presiding over segregated Sabbaths.[78]

The slogan 'no creed but the Bible' was a declaration of conscience but at the same time an admission of an even more complex confession than of those who subscribed to the Augsburg Confession or the 'Thirty-Nine Articles'. The reality of religious democratic leadership is often one filled with paradox. In 1842 McKendree College conferred on Peter Cartwright the degree 'Doctor of Divinity'. From that time on he seemed to regard it as an insult, or a personal affront, if he were not addressed as 'doctor'.[79] Position, pride and personality were the quintessential factors in the rise of the American preacher. There was a fine line between 'authentic servanthood and exploitive demagoguery.'[80] This collision of

---

[78] See Carol V.R. George, *Segregated Sabbaths: Richard Allen and the Rise of the Independent Black Churches, 1760-1840* (New York: Oxford University Press, 1973), Clarence E. Walker, *A Rock in a Weary Land: The African Methodist Episcopal Church During the Civil War and Reconstruction* (Baton Rouge and London: Louisiana State University Press, 1982), pp. 4-29 and Harry V. Richardson, *Dark Salvation: The Story of Methodism as it Developed among Blacks in America* (Garden City, N.Y.: Doubleday, 1976), pp. 76-116.

[79] See the note in Richard A. Chrisman, 'Peter Cartwright as a Presiding Elder' *Methodist History* 27 (No. 3, 1989), p. 159.

[80] Hatch, *The Democratization of American Christianity*, p. 208.

realities has thus far proven nearly unavoidable in the history of popular religious leaders, whether European or American.

The monumental shifts in religion brought about by the reformations of the sixteenth century and reopened in the drama of post-revolutionary America underscored the crisis of authority which the abandonment of tradition invariably creates. The nineteenth-century American religious experience had to come to terms with the devastating loss of confidence in the existing social and theological order. Ostensibly an ideology of reformation had been inaugurated in politics, jurisprudence, economy and society in general. There was no compelling reason not to extend those lines of inquiry into a thorough *renovatio* and *reformatio* of religious structures. The defeat of religious hierarchy did help to create its own unique sense of confidence, both evidenced in the widespread rise of charismatic leadership and in the perfectionism of the Holiness movements. Debates on authority stemming from the American Revolution, the framing of the Constitution and the political upheavals of the 1790s left no doubt that on the eve of the nineteenth century profound social and cultural changes signalled a crisis for the emerging American nation. This crisis had implications not only for government and institutional structures, but also for members of the republic in general. The consequences of revolution could not be brushed aside and even in the intoxication of liberty and independence there remained nagging fears about the future. Trends prompted by close association with Britain and Europe throughout the early colonial period were now suspended. The transformation of society and culture, with its implications for religion, had only just begun. The struggle against the crisis of authority had violent consequences. The uprooting of generations of tradition, thought, wisdom, custom and social order were among the offspring of proclaiming liberty and freedom for all. What did this mean, other than that the American revolution was both a securing of independence from British rule and an attempt to forge meaning and order out of the chaos and flux of the primeval forests?[81] The popular ferment which percolated down through the social order sought answers, direction and, from a religious perspective, divine presence in the midst of democratic ambiguity. The popular preacher and charismatic religious leader encountered plenty of fertile soil to till in the early nineteenth century. The intermingling of politics and religion found common ground and congruent expression in the continued decline of Calvinism and the persistent theologizing of democracy. Joseph Smith, Lorenzo Dow, William Miller, Ellen G. White and a host of others were able without the benefit of training or formal education to create powerful and pervasive religious movements seemingly *ex nihilo*. The blending of democratic persuasion and proclamations of divine wisdom attracted mass followings. The function of the church and state in de-Calvinized America utilized similar tools. Wherever popular preachers were present, politicians appeared. Politicians were preachers and preachers were politicians.[82] This close association might appear curious in light of the First Amendment but politics and religion have always been closely aligned and during the nineteenth century the line of demarcation was blurred to such a degree that separation frequently proved virtually impossible. 'Politics are a part of religion in such a country as this . . . .'[83] The Methodists were particularly active in politics. By 1870 Methodists had governed twenty-four of the thirty-seven states and by the end of the century

---

[81] For the foregoing I am especially indebted to Edmund S. Morgan, *The Challenge of the American Revolution* (New York: W.W. Norton & Company, Inc.,1976), James H. Kettner, *The Development of American Citizenship, 1608-1870* (Chapel Hill: University of North Carolina Press, 1978), pp. 173-209, John H. Murrin, 'Political Development', in *Colonial British America: Essays in the New History of the early Modern Era*, eds., Jack P. Greene and J.R. Pole (Baltimore: The Johns Hopkins University Press, 1984), pp. 414-56, Gordon S. Wood, ed., *The Rising Glory of America, 1760-1820* (New York: George Braziller, 1971), pp. 1-22, Wood, *The Creation of the American Republic 1776-1787* (New York: Norton, 1972) and Hatch, *The Democratization of American Christianity*, pp. 22-4.

[82] Alexis de Tocqueville, *Democracy in America*, p. 293.

[83] Charles G. Finney, *Lectures on Revivals of Religion* (Oberlin: E.J. Goodrich, 1868), p. 282.

had seen four of their adherents in the White House.[84] There were those who accepted this relation and others who vehemently decried it. James Gordon Bennett visiting upstate New York in 1831, declared that religion and politics had become so closely aligned as to produce 'a religion like the Jesuits.'[85]

The political uses of religion constitute an entirely different inquiry which in this context cannot be explored in any detail. The revering of men like George Washington in religious terms is of course fundamentally misguided. Abraham Lincoln's use of the Bible and religion to political ends is well known. Religion also provided a structure for political parody. 'Whigs in 1844 sang lustily of an apostate now returned to the fold "like a prodigal son." Political "conversions" might be accompanied by mock baptisms (high-spirited Democrats allegedly baptized a new member "in the name of Andrew JACKSON, the Father! James K. POLK, the Son! and TEXAS, the Holy Ghost!!!") and by mock communion services, involving the distribution of whiskey or cider and corn bread as "sacraments."'[86]

The greatest slave insurrection in nineteenth-century American history was a religiously motivated event. Nat Turner used the medium of preaching to garner a following. As in medieval history he preached a crusade. With those sermons, appeals to the Bible, and repeated references to his revelations, Turner marched by the cross to liberate his people from the hand of their oppressors. As it turned out, he would march by the cross to die. Turner's men executed whites and those slaves loyal to them in the dramatic events of 'Old Nat's War'. After being

---

[84] Roger Robins, 'Vernacular American Landscape: Methodists, Camp Meetings, and Social Respectability' *Religion and American Culture* 4 (No. 2, 1994), p. 168. In 1845 the closet Methodist James Polk, in 1869 the irregular Ulysses S. Grant, in 1877 the indifferent Rutherford B. Hayes and in 1897 the devout William McKinley were those elected to the presidency of the United States. The adjectives describing the Methodism of these men belongs to Robins.

[85] Cited in Paul Johnson, *A Shopkeeper's Millennium: Society and Revivals in Rochester, New York, 1815-1837* (New York: Hill and Wang, 1978), pp. 134-5.

[86] Cited in Carwardine, *Evangelicals and Politics in Antebellum America*, p. 53.

captured Turner confessed that five years earlier he had received power from God to control weather, heal and lead his movement. Turner had been, before the events of 1831, regarded as a preacher and a prophet.[87] When asked prior to his execution by hanging if it were not now clear that his revelations had been wrong, Turner replied, 'was not Christ crucified?'[88] Social revolution was cast as a religious crusade and the political uses of religion pressed to their limits, but even at the extremes there were those prepared to heed the word of the preacher.

Authoritarian religious leaders masquerading as proponents of religious democracy had no intention, for the most part, of deceiving anyone. They believed in the principles of democracy in a social, economic and political sense and to a certain extent could ratify the use of democratic ideals in theology. In the common search for order, however, many of these individuals regarded history as corrupted and perceived themselves as the true restorer by divine mandate. Studying the remains of their legacies through their works and in the traditions they engendered leads one to believe that very few indeed, if any, did not wholeheartedly adopt a Messiah complex. Their dictatorship, then, was born out of an intense desire to turn the world from wickedness and this drive was matched by an unshakable belief in their own destiny as men and women of God. That this conviction produced fanaticism, self-righteousness and manipulation can scarcely be denied.

The lamp and the mirror provided by the nineteenth-century American religious experience illuminated and reflected these convictions and realities. The battle between Carnival and Lent, Jacksonian democracy and Calvinism, served to

---

[87] 'Verbatim Record of the Trials in the Court of Oyer & Terminer of Southampton County, Held Between 31 August and 21 November 1831 . . . .' in Henry I. Tragle, *The Southampton Slave Revolt of 1834: A Compilation of Source Material* (Amherst: The University of Massachusetts Press, 1971), pp. 222, 372 and 407. See also Albert J. Raboteau, *Slave Religion: The 'Invisible Institution' in the Antebellum South* (New York: Oxford University Press, 1978), pp. 163-4.

[88] Gayrand S. Wilmore, *Black Religion and Black Radicalism* (Garden City, N.Y.: Doubleday, 1972), pp. 87-102.

exacerbate both the chasm and the symbiosis which simultaneously widened and closed within the religious experience of nineteenth-century America. That chasm between faith and culture, and the symbiotic relationship of religion and society must be numbered among the plethora of causes producing the paradox of religious democracy. The city of God challenges the city of humankind, but once again the city set on the hill remains vulnerable to the world it overlooks.

Religious responses to American culture were profoundly stimulated by visions of the end of history. According to some, God had kept America hidden for centuries until the last days.[89] Now that the last days had seized upon human history America became the theater of war for the cosmic battle between God and the Devil.[90] If the American Revolution had pitted God against Antichrist, then nineteenth-century America perceived that struggle as yet unfolding.[91] The precipitous and monumental struggle enacted between Fort Sumter and Appomattox has gone down in certain religious historiography as the Armageddon of the Republic.[92] Indeed, the Civil War was widely seen as an apocalyptic contest,

---

[89]   Hudson, *Religion in America*, p. 33. The term 'manifest destiny' was coined in the 1840s but the idea is considerably older. Anders Stephanson, *Manifest Destiny: American Expansionism and the Empire of the Right* (New York: Hill and Wang, 1995), p. 5.

[90]   'Thro all the West, revivals of any power are almost unknown . . . . here is to be the battle field of the world. Here Satans [sic] seat is. A mighty effort must be made to dislodge him *soon*, or the West is undone.' A letter of Theodore Weld to Charles Finney from Cincinnati on 28 February 1832. Gilbert H. Barnes and Dwight L. Drumond, eds., *Letters of Theodore Dwight Weld, Angelina Grimké Weld and Sarah Grimké, 1822-1844* (New York and London: D. Appleton-Century Company, Inc., 1934), volume 1, pp. 66-8.

[91]   See for example Nathan O. Hatch, 'The Origins of Civil Millennialism in America: New England Clergymen, War with France and the Revolution' *The William and Mary Quarterly* third series, 31 (No. 3, 1974), pp. 407-30.

[92]   James H. Moorhead, 'Between Progress and Apocalypse: A Reassessment of Millennialism in American Religious Thought, 1800-1880' *The Journal of American History* 71 (No. 3, 1984), p. 524.

the supreme test of evangelical civilization.[93] The influence and presence of Christianity in the events leading up to this conflict occupied a prevalent place. For many, including popular preachers, judgment hung in deep, dark gloom over the earth, the Day of Wrath loomed on the horizon, and to certain discerning minds, apocalyptic imagery, signs of the end, were all around. This eschatological expectation, coupled with bizarre apocalyptic portents and a keen sense of millennial fervor had long existed in America. From the beginnings of colonization, millennialism had been part of the religious and cultural tradition imported into the new world by the Puritans.[94] These emphases did not remain long the sole provenance of Puritans. By the nineteenth century Shakers, the Oneida Community, Mormons, Adventists, Jehovah's Witnesses, Holiness movements and many other traditions subscribed in one form or another to the ideas that the second coming of Christ was at hand. The whole gamut of millenarian expectation proved to be an important ingredient in the rise and proliferation of revivalism.[95] The 'day of great disappointment' may have derailed the Millerites and influenced the eschatological doctrines of other Adventist groups, but it did little to disrupt general religious preoccupation with the impending parousia. New theories were advanced to suggest revised strategies for reading the end of the world. The Miller failure of 1844 contributed to the severity of a gradual religious recession which climaxed in the Civil War. The Methodists lost 56,847 converts to the Millerites but this recession did not prove strong enough to seriously disrupt either the

---

[93] Marsden, *Fundamentalism and American Culture*, p. 11.

[94] Ira V. Brown, 'Watchers for the Second Coming: The Millenarian Tradition in America' *The Mississippi Valley Historical Review* 39 (No. 3, 1952), p. 444.

[95] Millenarianism must be seen as separate from Millerism and it is worth noting that the former belief was not a marginalized aspect of American Christianity. The chiliasts frequently were individuals of notable education and standing within the evangelical communities. Whalen, 'Calvinism and Chiliasm', p. 164.

progress of American Christianity in general or that of the Methodists specifically.[96]

Not everyone lived in the shadow of impending gloom. There were prophets of progress and human advancement within the religious community.

> Religion is steadily becoming more spiritual and more ethical, less formal, less dogmatic, less crudely emotional; theology is more moral and less materialistic in its conceptions than once it was; liberty and toleration are taking the place of bigotry and tyranny; character and conduct are exalted above opinion and theory; and love as compassion, and love as good-will is slowly but steadily gaining upon cruelty and strife.[97]

Despite the this-worldliness of Washington Gladden and others, apocalyptic angst and eschatological anticipation carried popular religion along well beyond the end of the century. By that time John Nelson Darby had invented yet another strategy for reading the script of the end of time which proved altogether compelling in many conservative sectors of American Christianity.[98] An entire genre of literature grew up around these prophetic utterances that human history was at an end.[99]

---

[96] Richard Carwardine, *Trans-Atlantic Revivalism: Popular Evangelicalism in Britain and America, 1790-1865* (London and Westport: Greenwood Press, 1978), p. 53. On the Methodist figures see John Leland Peters, *Christian Perfection and American Methodism* (New York and Nashville: Abingdon Press, 1956), p. 118.

[97] Washington Gladden, *Burning Questions of the life that now is, and of that which is to come* (New York: The Century Co., 1891), p. 242.

[98] Marsden, *Fundamentalism and American Culture*, p. 51. See also Timothy P. Weber, *Living in the Shadow of the Second Coming: American Premillennialism, 1875-1982* (Chicago and London: University of Chicago Press, 1987), pp. 13-42 for the last quarter of the nineteenth century and comments on dispensationalism and Paul Boyer, *When Time Shall Be No More: Prophecy and Belief in Modern American Culture* (Cambridge: The Belknap Press of Harvard University Press, 1992), pp. 80-100.

[99] See Ruth L. Bloch, 'The Social and Political Base of Millennial Literature in Late Eighteenth-Century America' *American Quarterly* 40 (No. 3, 1988), pp. 378-96. Bloch attempts to postulate who was responsible for the creation and publication of this literature and perhaps more importantly who might have read it. See also David D. Hall, *Worlds of Wonder, Days of Judgment: Popular Religious Belief in Early New England* (New York: Alfred A. Knopf, 1989) for background.

The Nineteenth-Century American Religious Experience

If apocalyptic anxiety gripped many Christian minds in nineteenth-century America the place of preaching and the rôle of the pulpit stood central in the American religious experience. '. . . for the pulpit is ever this earth's foremost part; all the rest comes in its rear; the pulpit leads the world. From thence it is the storm of God's quick wrath is first descried, and the bow must bear the earliest brunt. From thence it is the God of breezes fair or foul is first invoked for favorable winds. Yes, the world's a ship on its passage out, and not a voyage complete; and the pulpit is its prow.'[100] Popular preaching in the first half of the nineteenth century frequently constituted the preaching of reformation in the search for a revived church. Only a church unspotted by the world could offer an appropriate response to a culture tottering on the brink of apocalypse. The essence of reform was to radically join together heaven and earth within the social structure. But while this ideal struggled for realization the joining together of heaven and earth more often than not resulted in a withdrawal from the world.[101]

Among the enduring images of nineteenth-century American religion were the circuit-riding preachers and the charismatic revival orators. Francis Asbury's own spartan career exemplifies the former. Asbury's visit to America lasted forty-five years. For thirty-one of those years he served as Methodist bishop and for more than three decades rode a circuit ranging over some five thousand miles every one of those years, travelling more than 275,000 miles. Sixty-two times he crossed the Allegheny Mountains on horseback. Preaching daily, visiting the faithful in the most remote hamlets, sleeping wherever he could find shelter, Asbury pursued the vanishing kingdom of God through forest, canyon, valley and town. He organized a veritable army of itinerant preachers which by the time of his death numbered

---

[100] Melville, *Moby-Dick*, p. 45.

[101] Abzug, *Cosmos Crumbling: American Reform and the Religious Imagination*, p. 8.

52   *The Nineteenth-Century American Religious Experience*

Figure 2   'The Circuit Riding Preacher', hand-colored wood engraving by A.R. Waud, from *Harper's Weekley*, 12 October 1867. Courtesy of the Billy Graham Center Museum

more than seven hundred.[102] The lifestyle of the Methodist itinerant did not differ much from many of the popular preachers who roamed the backwoods of America seeking for lost souls to preach to. They did not forever remain in rural areas but often appeared, abruptly out of the hills, in centers of civilization, wild, uncouth figures preaching a message of judgment and repentance. Such was 'Crazy' Lorenzo Dow who bewildered, amused and spellbound audiences across eastern America.

> Lorenzo [Dow] was not only uncouth in his person and appearance, but his voice was harsh, his action hard and rectangular. It is scarcely possible to conceive of a person more entirely destitute of all natural eloquence. But he understood common life, and especially vulgar life—its tastes, prejudices, and weaknesses; and he possessed a cunning knack of adapting his discourses to such audiences. He told stories with considerable art, and his memory being stored with them, he could always point a moral or clinch a proposition by an anecdote. He knew that with simple people an illustration is better than logic, and when he ran short of Scripture, or argument failed, he usually resorted to some pertinent story or adapted allegory . . . .[103]

Lorenzo Dow was a master of popular preaching and mass appeal. His sermons fanned the flames of popular ferment and discontent. He was a performer and an impressive stage presence. At one moment he could have the crowd howling with laughter, the next on the verge of tears. He shrank neither from calling attention

---

[102] All of this is set forth in some detail in *The Journal and Letters of Francis Asbury*. In all, Asbury likely preached more than 16,000 sermons. The distances he covered exceeds even that amassed by Wesley. In 1771 there were twelve preachers and about 1,200 Methodists in America. By the time of Asbury's death there were almost 700 preachers and 214,000 Methodist adherents. Goodwin, 'The Greatest Itinerant Francis Asbury 1745-1816', pp. 47-50.

[103] Boston publisher Samuel Goodrich in 1856 describing Dow. Cited in Hatch, *The Democratization of American Christianity*, p. 125. The epithet 'crazy' was attached to Dow by those unsympathetic either with his message or approach. He left a literary legacy. See for example, *The Dealings of God, Man, and the Devil; as exemplified in the Life, Experiences, and Travels of Lorenzo Dow, in a period of over half a century: Together with his Polemic and Miscellaneous Writings, Complete. To which is added The Vicissitudes of Life by Peggy Dow*, 2 vols. (New York: Sheldon, Lamport & Blakeman, 1856).

to sinners in the audience nor from employing emotional props to support his sermon. Trumpets might blow at a pre-arranged moment in the homily or Dow might smash some object to smithereens.[104] The description of Lorenzo Dow quite clearly is a stereotype, but nonetheless an accurate one of the frontier preacher. Other eccentrics like 'Jumping Jesus' in New York might be regarded as the lunatic fringe of nineteenth-century American religion.[105] The 'holy whine' of frontier preaching was both appealing and repulsive. It helped create a religious experience.

The frequency of popular preaching and the length of these sermons is worth noting. Daily sermons became a feature of American culture. Sermons preached in churches and meeting houses, at camp meetings and in houses functioned as a dominant element of popular culture. It was not uncommon for preachers to carry on a discourse for several hours. Daniel Warner is reported to have preached without stopping for up to four hours at a time.[106] In this he was certainly not anomalous. Peter Cartwright preached a three hour sermon at the Goose Creek camp meeting in Kentucky in 1822,[107] Richard Whatcoat preached three sermons in a day, James Gilruth preached thrice on 9 August 1834 and went 'to bed about 9. pretty tired.' He arose the following day 'preached at 11 . . .

---

[104] Dow's preaching is described by Hatch, *The Democratization of American Christianity*, pp. 130-3. It begs comparison to the early twentieth-century revivalist Billy Sunday. Sunday would jump up on the pulpit, wave flags, shout, and smash chairs. As an ex-baseball player he would use his erstwhile athletic skills to his advantage and crowds would enjoy the point immensely when he ran full-tilt across the stage and slid 'into home' to Jesus. Lyle W. Dorsett, *Billy Sunday and the Redemption of Urban America* (Grand Rapids: William B. Eerdmans, 1991).

[105] Johnson and Wilentz, *The Kingdom of Matthias*, p. 59. Matthews, who took the name Matthias, was so nicknamed by workers in New York. On 20 June 1830 'Jumping Jesus' commissioned Elijah Pierson to go about as Elijah the Tisbite. *Ibid.*, p. 92.

[106] Andrew L. Byers, *Birth of a Reformation or the Life and Labors of Daniel S. Warner* (Anderson: Gospel Trumpet Company, 1921), p. 437.

[107] *The Autobiography of Peter Cartwright*, ed., Charles L. Wallis (Nashville: Abingdon Press, 1984), p. 155. Numerous examples could be listed to illustrate the point.

preached at 3 p.m. . . . I preached again at night . . . . to bed about 11. all in a foam of sweat & quite weried. [sic] having laboured excessively hard during the meeting.'[108] In 1830 Charles Finney preached almost daily for six months during the week and three times on Sundays.[109] Traditional forms of Christianity were puzzled and confounded by this approach. 'There are Swarms of false teachers all through the Country—at every Crossroad, in every School house, in every private house—you hear nothing but night meetings, Class meetings, love feasts &c &c.'[110] This complaint from a Catholic priest in 1820s Maryland cannot be considered exaggerated when the habits of popular preachers and circuit riders are closely examined. Occasionally preachers confessed to having preached too much, though such admissions were rare indeed.[111] Even more scarce are admissions of poor preaching on the part of the sermonizers.[112] That aside, preaching and the hearing of sermons formed an integral aspect of the American religious past time.

---

[108] The Journal of Bishop James Whatcoat appears in Sweet, ed., *Religion on the American Frontier*, volume 4, pp. 73-122, reference on p. 119. The Journal of James Gilruth appears in *Ibid.*, pp. 367-468, references on pp. 375-6. Both men were Methodists.

[109] Johnson, *A Shopkeeper's Millennium: Society and Revivals in Rochester, New York, 1815-1837*, p. 95.

[110] Cited in Hatch, *The Democratization of American Christianity*, p. 141.

[111] Among the very few comments see Benjamin Lakin, one of the pioneer Methodist circuit-riders who wrote in his journal for 4 August 1795, 'At night I examined myself and I fear I preach myself too much.' His journal appears in Sweet, ed., *Religion on the American Frontier*, volume 4, pp. 202-60, reference at p. 209.

[112] The Presbyterian William Hill confided to his journal on 22 August 1790: 'Preached today at Tommahock Meeting house [Virginia], but was never so entirely forsaken since I professed religion. I was shut up in every sense of the word. It was a poor jumbled performance indeed,—felt heartily sorry for the people that they should turn out to so little purpose, that I had only hurt their feelings through sympathy for me.—I was afraid I had disgraced the cause of God, & subjected it to ridicule—I was really ashamed to look the people in the face, could have wished to have hid myself & been seen by none of them.' Sweet, ed., *Religion on the American Frontier*, volume 2, pp. 759-60. The Methodist Benjamin Lakin recounted an unfortunate experience in the pulpit on 14 December 1809 that 'when I attempted to preach . . . several times I so lost my subject that I expect I sometimes spoke nonsense.' Sweet, ed., *Ibid.*, volume 4, p. 236.

Part of the success of this kind of preaching may be linked to two innovations. In the first instance the rise of a newly formulated vernacular preaching proved most attractive to the eager masses who flocked to the pulpits of these preachers. In later medieval Europe preaching shifted from Latin to the vernacular and reforming trends both within and beyond the official church utilized this method to communicate ideas to the common people. In America the language remained the same from a technical point of view, but with the advent of preachers like Lorenzo Dow the words changed. Leaving off the technicalities of learned, academic theological discourse popular preachers began to speak specifically to the common situation of ordinary folk. This emphasis on vernacular preaching also paved the way for a shift in the actual preaching of sermons. During the course of the nineteenth century a change in homiletics developed. This adjustment might best be described as a change of emphasis from doctrine or theology to narrative. Storytelling came to dominate the pulpits and between 1870 and 1900 the anecdotal style was widely observed.[113] This encouraged active interaction between preacher and congregation, an element which dominated Black churches. The frontier Baptist preacher and missionary Jacob Bower related this interaction in his autobiography with reference to an incident at a church in St. Louis in 1841.

> ... while I was preaching, with a most powerful feeling [sic] in my whole soul, and a state of deep feeling [sic] in the congregation. The old collerd pastor was siting [sic] in the pulpit behind me; frequently saying, hai-hai-hai. At length he sprung to his feet and exclaimed with a thundering voice. 'I will not hold my peace when truth comes with such *power*. hai.' And soon nearly all the professing part of the congregation were on their feet too, hollowing [sic], Glory to God. Hallelujah. Hallelujah. Glory Hallelujah. Bless the Lord. [P]raise the Lord. Hallelujah. AMEN. AMEN. &c. I think I may safely say, that I never saw a congregation of professing people enjoy themselves so well no where.[114]

---

[113]   See on this shift David S. Reynolds, 'From Doctrine to Narrative: The Rise of Pulpit Storytelling in America' *American Quarterly* 32 (No. 5, 1980), pp. 479-98.

[114]   Bower's autobiography has been edited in Sweet, ed., *Religion on the American Frontier*, volume 1, pp. 185-230. The reference is on p. 221.

It has been suggested that changes in preaching technique might be numbered among the factors explaining the rise and phenomenal success of the Second Great Awakening. It seems unlikely that such a thesis can stand.[115] Indeed, the changes in preaching style were yet to emerge in maturity and certainly not until the later stages of the Second Great Awakening can the homiletical revolution be considered widely influential.

Certainly, preaching did function as a powerful means of social control. This is perhaps best illustrated with reference to the rise of slave religion. 'Were the slave preachers a force for accommodation to the *status quo* or a force for the exercise of slave autonomy?'[116] Nat Turner may have been an anomaly. While slave religion did foster the seeds of liberation and 'exodus', it can be argued that its primary function was as a mechanism for control by white masters. The ethic of the Sermon on the Mount and the promises of the 'sweet by and by' undergirded *status quo* social order.

The rise of popular preaching must be related to the development of the public lecture series which arose in the nineteenth century and served to create a public forum which proved most influential in the communication and spread of ideas. These organized, advertised lectures were not occasional events. For example, in New York City between 1840 and 1860 there were more than 3,000 advertised public lectures. In Boston in 1846 alone, the citizens of that city had the option of no fewer than twenty-six 'courses' of lectures they could attend. These public events were not restricted to the cities nor to centers of higher learning. By the 1840s between 3,500 and 4,000 communities nationwide had an active lecture-sponsoring society. By mid-century conservative estimates indicated that weekly attendance at lectures in the north and west were in the vicinity of 400,000. This

---

[115] Richard D. Shiels, 'The Second Great Awakening in Connecticut: Critique of the Traditional Interpretation' *Church History* 49 (No. 4, 1980), p. 403 for a comment setting aside the idea that changes in preaching technique might explain the revival.

[116] Raboteau, *Slave Religion*, p. 238.

suggests a dimension of culture which might help to explain the appeal of popular preaching. The creation of a common public may be traced to the fact that many of the lecturers traversed the country in crisscross fashion delivering the same lectures to different audiences. This created a common experience, transcended the barriers of illiteracy and forged an American public.[117] The increased attendance at these lectures may well reflect a preoccupation with ideas related to religious liberalism, the application of faith to social issues, the rise of Black and frontier preaching, evangelical sermonizing and the appeal of literary Unitarianism.[118] Preachers like Dow, Henry Ward Beecher, D.L. Moody, Philip S. Brooks, and to a lesser extent Horace Bushnell actively promoted the shift in homiletics.[119]

'[Father Mapple] . . . said no more, but slowly waving a benediction, covered his face with his hands, and so remained, kneeling, till all the people had departed, and he was left alone in the place.'[120] Covering their faces from worldly wickedness they listened intently for the still small voice of God. The preacher and preaching were prophetic aspects among responses to American culture.

---

[117] Donald M. Scott, 'The Popular Lecture and the Creation of a Public in Mid-Nineteenth Century America' *The Journal of American History* 66 (No. 4, 1980), pp. 791-809. Scott suggests plausible reasons for the widespread appeal of the public lecture. Among popular 'name' lecturers were Henry Ward Beecher, Oliver Wendell Holmes, Ralph Waldo Emerson, Starr King and Horace Greeley.

[118] Reynolds, 'From Doctrine to Narrative: The Rise of Pulpit Storytelling in America', p. 485.

[119] Suggestive in a variety of other ways is Lawrence Buell, 'The Unitarian Movement and the Art of Preaching in 19th Century America' *American Quarterly* 24 (No. 2, 1972), pp. 166-90.

[120] Melville, *Moby-Dick*, p. 54.

B. Popular Religion

> ... above a hundred persons, nearly all females, came forward, uttering howlings and groans, so terrible that I shall never cease to shudder when I recall them. They appeared to drag each other forward, and on the word being given, 'let us pray,' they all fell on their knees; but this posture was soon changed for others that permitted greater scope for the convulsive movements of their limbs; and they were soon all lying on the ground in an indescribable confusion of heads and legs. They threw about their limbs with such incessant and violent motion, that I was every instant expecting some serious accident to occur.
>
> But how am I to describe the sounds that proceeded from this strange mass of human beings? I know no words which can convey an idea of it. Hysterical sobbings, convulsive groans, shrieks and screams the most appalling, burst forth on all sides. I felt sick with horror. As if their hoarse and overstrained voices failed to make noise enough, they soon began to clap their hands violently . . . .
>
> One woman near us continued to 'call on the Lord,' as it is termed, in the loudest possible tone, and without a moment's interval, for the two hours that we kept our dreadful station. She became frightfully hoarse, and her face so red as to make me expect she would burst a blood-vessel. Among the rest of her rant, she said, 'I will hold fast to Jesus, I never will let him go; if they take me to hell, I will hold him fast, fast, fast!'
>
> The stunning noise was sometimes varied by the preachers beginning to sing; but the convulsive movements of the poor maniacs only became more violent. At length the atrocious wickedness of this horrible scene increased to a degree of grossness, that drove us from our station; we returned to the carriage at about three o'clock in the morning, and passed the remainder of the night in listening to the ever increasing tumult at the pen. To sleep was impossible. . . .[121]

♠ ♠

Among the dominant images of the nineteenth-century American religious experience were the Bible, the camp meeting, the circuit riding preacher and the

---

[121] This is part of the account written by Frances Trollope of a camp meeting in Indiana on 14 August 1829. The account appeared in her book, *Domestic Manners of the Americans*, ed., Donald Smalley (New York: Vintage Books, 1949), pp. 167-75.

charismatic religious leader. Popular religion and popular culture received and shaped these images in profoundly important ways. It is essential not to overemphasize the peculiarity of popular religion. In a true sense there was no separation of folk and élite religion in America.[122] There were of course different uses and appropriations of a common religion. The similarities outweigh dissimilarities. The rise of vernacular preaching, innovations in homiletics, together with the ever-present preoccupation with apocalyptic themes produced the age of revivals. Beginning with the Great Awakening and continuing through the nineteenth century were a series of unrelated revivals. This age of revivals was marked by much diversity, a continued splintering of denominations, the rise of even further sects and religious movements, and an unrelenting fundamental grassroots appeal. It is none too wide of the mark to see these later revivals as byproducts of the tremendous zeal brought about by the enthusiasm generated by the gaining of emancipation from British domination in the wake of the American Revolutionary war. George Whitefield, Jonathan Edwards, Francis Asbury and Charles Finney are among the names associated with American revivalism. On one level, revivals might be seen as religious responses to encroaching rationalism, liberalism and secularism which were also finding receptive homes in the expanding, democratized new world. The limits of freedom and liberty had yet to be defined. The American religious experience in the context of revivalism involved intense spiritual questing. The Second Great Awakening during the first quarter of the nineteenth century set the pace for revivalism well into the twentieth century.[123] This momentous event has been called the most influential religious

---

[122] Hall, *Worlds of Wonder, Days of Judgment: Popular Religious Belief in Early New England*, p. 6.

[123] Among good studies of the Second Great Awakening should be numbered William G. McLoughlin's survey in *Revivals, Awakenings, and Reform: An Essay on Religion and Social Change in America, 1607-1977* (Chicago and London: The University of Chicago Press, 1978), pp. 98-140.

revival in American religious history.[124] This was a time when people 'preferred their whiskey straight and their religion red-hot.'[125] Revival campaigns set out with the lofty goal of saving America. The infidels and heretics were already making serious inroads and Oregon had become already a Masonic state.[126] The Methodists took a leading rôle in the outgrowth of revivalism and may be said to have been among the vanguard of influence in the Second Great Awakening. Many of the Methodist preachers, especially those in the pattern of Peter Cartwright, saw themselves as confronting scoffers, infidels and deists. Cartwright understood his task as outshouting and outfighting any riffraff who challenged him and furthermore to outwit the Baptists, Shakers, Universalists and other kinds of unregenerates.[127] The strains of anticlericalism and anti-intellectualism which pervaded certain sectors of the revivals brought derision from more learned observers. Suggestions were advanced that since America had thrown aside the yoke of allegiance to England it might as well throw off the yoke of superstition which continued to encumber it.[128] But this was going altogether too far for those imbued with the spirit of revivalism. A popular song sympathetic to the ethos of popular religious reform proclaimed the veracity of revival and boasted that the cause of the Methodists retained divine favor.

---

[124] Mark A. Noll, *A History of Christianity in the United States and Canada* (Grand Rapids: William B. Eerdmans, 1992), p. 166.

[125] Hudson, *Religion in America*, p. 131.

[126] The Methodist preacher Orceneth Fisher described Oregon in this manner around 1878. Sweet, ed., *Religion on the American Frontier*, volume 4, pp. 487-94. The reference is on p. 490.

[127] Peter Cartwright, *Autobiography of Peter Cartwright* and McLoughlin, *Revivals, Awakenings, and Reform: An Essay on Religion and Social Change in America, 1607-1977*, pp. 134-5.

[128] For example, Thomas Paine, *The Age of Reason* (London: Watts & Co., 1915), pp. 2, 22 and throughout. Paine's book originally appeared in 1795.

'The Methodist'

> The world, the Devil and Tom Paine
> Have try'd their force, but all in vain,
> They can't prevail, the reason is,
> The Lord defends the Methodist.
>
> They pray, they sing, they preach the best,
> And do the Devil most molest,
> If Satan had his vicious way,
> He'd kill and damn them all today.
>
> They are despised by Satan's train,
> Because they shout and preach so plain
>
> I'm bound to march in endless bliss
> And die a shouting Methodist.[129]

James Erwin had his congregation sing a variation of this tune:

> The world, John Calvin, and Tom Paine
> May hate the Methodists in vain,
> I know the Lord will then increase,
> And fill the world with Methodists.[130]

Indeed, the phenomenal increase in Methodist fortunes throughout the eighteenth and nineteenth centuries in the face of Calvinist decline is witness to the success of the age of revivals. Between 1820 and 1830 the Methodist movement doubled the number of its adherents and could now boast half a million members.[131]

---

[129] Cited in Charles A. Johnson, 'Camp Meeting Hymnody' *American Quarterly* 4 (No. 2, 1952), pp. 123-4.

[130] cited in Marty E. Marty, *Pilgrims in their own Land: 500 Years of Religion in America* (Boston and Toronto: Little, Brown and Company, 1984), p. 174. Another version went like this:
> The devil, Calvin and Voltaire
> May hate the Methodist in vain;
> Their doctrine shall be downward hurl'd:
> The Methodist will take the world.

Cited in Frederick A. Norwood, *The Story of American Methodism*, p. 232. From 1805 onward many versions of this song circulated.

[131] Hatch, *The Democratization of American Christianity*, p. 3.

Not all were so enthusiastic. The Presbyterian Lyman Beecher claimed that if Charles Finney ever came to New England he would fight him all the way to Boston.[132] Finney came. Beecher did not fight. Instead Finney came because Beecher eventually invited him and by that time Finney had emerged as the leading spokesman for the cause of religious revival. Finney preached to people and at people. Finney would holler, 'Oh God, smite that wicked man . . .', pointing his finger at some cowering unfortunate. To another Finney would accost, 'God Almighty, shake him over hell.'[133] Referring to Theodore Dwight Weld and his apparent unrepentant sinfulness, Finney roared, 'puke it up, Mr. W.' Jonathan Edwards may have never taken his eyes off the bell rope in the rear of the church when he preached notable sermons such as 'sinners in the hands of an angry God', but nineteenth-century revivalists did everything in their power to make their listeners part of the actual sermon. James Axley, a Methodist preacher in eastern Tennessee and friend of Peter Cartwright, gained notoriety for preaching against numerous transgressions and identifying guilty parties attending the sermon. 'That dirty, nasty, filthy tobacco-chewer, sitting on the end of that front row.'[134] Results often were dramatic. Among the most significant and enduring religious phenomena to emerge from the age of revivals was the camp meeting. There were 150 days of camp meetings in 1810. By 1811 Francis Asbury reported between

---

[132] 'Finney, I know your plan, and you know I do; you mean to come into Connecticut and carry a streak of fire to Boston. But if you attempt it, as the Lord liveth, I'll meet you at the State line, and call out all the artillerymen, and fight every inch of the way to Boston, and then I'll fight you there.' *The Autobiography of Lyman Beecher*, ed., Barbara Cross (Cambridge: Belknap Press, 1961), volume 2, p.75. The conflict between Finney and Beecher is told by Keith J. Hardman, *Charles Grandison Finney 1792-1875: Revivalist and Reformer* (Syracuse: Syracuse University Press, 1987), pp. 121-32.

[133] McLoughlin, *Revivals, Awakenings, and Reform*, p. 125.

[134] Sweet, ed., *Religion on the American Frontier*, volume 4, pp. 728-30. In the course of a single sermon Axley pointed out an individual causing noise at the rear of the church while cleaning mud from his boots, a young girl who was 'giggling and chattering', a man who fell asleep as well as the individual who chewed tobacco.

400 and 500 such gatherings in that year alone,[135] while John Sale confidently announced that the Lord had attended them all.[136] By 1816 the number of camp meetings had risen to 600 and by 1820 more than 1000.[137]

Revivalist camp meetings became commonplace in America following the outburst of enthusiasm at Cane Ridge, Kentucky in the late summer of 1801. These gatherings in the hinterlands of America lay beyond the boundaries of ecclesiastical traditions and originated outside the circle of religious and social élites. Camp meetings were expressions of folk religion and popular piety. Cane Ridge was in the vanguard of these mass gatherings. From 6-12 August 1801 somewhere between ten and twenty thousand people gathered in this small Bourbon County settlement. Kentucky had been admitted to the union in 1792 and by 1800 had a population of around 220,000.[138] Over the course of the six day event as many as 20,000, including the governor of Kentucky, thronged over Cane Ridge though it is to be doubted that more than 10,000 were ever there at any one time.[139] Still, even those more conservative figures are significant. The largest town in the state was Lexington which boasted a population of less than 2,000. For six days a

---

[135] 'Our campmeetings, I think, amount to between four and five hundred annually, some of which continue for the space of six or eight days. It is supposed that it is not uncommon for ten thousand persons, including all who come at different periods, to be present at one of those meetings.' Letter to Thomas Coke, 2 September 1811. In *The Journal and Letters of Francis Asbury*, volume 3, pp. 455-6.

[136] Sale was one of the founders of Methodism in Cincinnati and served as a presiding elder in the Ohio and Miami districts. See his letter of 20 February 1807 in Sweet, ed., *Religion on the American Frontier*, volume 4, pp. 159-60.

[137] Robins, 'Vernacular American Landscape: Methodists, Camp Meetings, and Social Respectability', p. 169.

[138] Paul K. Conkin, *Cane Ridge: America's Pentecost* (Madison: University of Wisconsin Press, 1990), p. 64. By comparison, Wesleyan Grove, a Methodist camp founded in 1835 comprised thirty-four acres and approximately 500 buildings. Ellen Weiss, *City in the Woods: The Life and Design of an American Camp Meeting on Martha's Vineyard* (New York and Oxford: Oxford University Press, 1987), p. xi.

[139] Kenneth O. Brown, *Holy Ground: A Study of the American Camp Meeting* (New York and London: Garland Publishing, Inc., 1992), p. 21.

religious theater played on Cane Ridge.[140] Preaching, shrieking, groaning, crying, praying, fainting, singing, shouting and being slain in the spirit regularly occurred, sometimes throughout the night. The masses clapped their hands, hugged each other, kissed, laughed, jerked and yet again cried out and were slain in the spirit. To assert ' . . . that hundreds fell to the ground was beyond dispute; falling was the central phenomenon of Cane Ridge.'[141] What had been planned as a traditional Presbyterian celebration of Holy Communion escalated into a major event in the religious history of America. The background for understanding Cane Ridge lies principally in the context of Scottish-Presbyterianism with its regular three or four day communions, preceded by fasting and prayer and an all-day preparation. What transpired at Cane Ridge was indicative of the expanding religious experience in late eighteenth-century Kentucky and the emergence of new theological-religious emphases stemming from the theologizing of democracy. Cane Ridge was to have been the last in a series of summertime communions in Kentucky. Instead, it became the first in a long line of religious revivals centering in the camp meeting phenomenon. Cane Ridge was the proverbial mountaintop religious experience. It transformed the message of the preachers from propositional theory to existential reality. For once, the rhetoric and the reality matched. This became an enduring feature of the camp meeting. August 1801 in Bourbon County provided six days of other-worldliness for the masses who made the trip to Cane Ridge. For six days ordinary life was set aside and forgotten. For six days the problems and worries of life did not exist. Many people during those historic six days forgot to prepare meals or eat for two or three days. For those six days many neglected to engage in the normal tasks of life. For six days the Holy Spirit descended and Cane Ridge was transformed from an unimportant community into the kingdom of God. It was

---

[140] The term is R. Lawrence Moore's, 'Religion, Secularization, and the Shaping of the Culture Industry in Antebellum America' *American Quarterly* 41 (No. 2, 1989), pp. 228-32.

[141] Conkin, *Cane Ridge: America's Pentecost*, p. 107. Conkin's account is based on contemporary witnesses.

an indelible religious experience for those who came from far and wide.[142] As many as seven preachers preached simultaneously.[143] Some of the adherents of revivalism travelled up to fifty miles to hear the preaching and readily joined in with those slain in the spirit. Contemporary witnesses described the scene of fallen saints like a battlefield where the dead and dying had succumbed in the heat of war. Others reported that the sounds of revival and camp meeting could be heard for miles and the roar resembled that of Niagara Falls.[144]

In the tradition of the Great Awakening emotion played a central part in the camp meeting revivals. Cane Ridge was no exception when it came to physical demonstrations. Jerking, barking, dancing, shouting and falling down slain in the spirit were regular features of camp meetings throughout nineteenth-century America. The religious expressions and experiences had come a long way from the prim and proper Puritan meeting houses of early New England. John Calvin may not have approved but it was all part of religious democracy. Certainly there were abuses and in some cases dire consequences. One rowdy, beginning to experience the jerks himself, made an effort to escape to the nearby woods and fortify himself with some whiskey, but in the excitement his bottle was knocked from his hands and smashed. He became so enraged that he began to curse and rage. 'At length he fetched a very violent jerk, snapped his neck, fell, and soon expired, with his

---

[142] *Ibid.*, p. 177.

[143] *Autobiography of Peter Cartwright*, p. 34. See also Finley, *Autobiography of Rev. James B. Finley*, p. 166 wherein Finley reports 'I counted seven ministers, all preaching at one time . . . .' standing on stumps, in wagons and on fallen trees.

[144] James B. Finley, *Autobiography of Rev. James B. Finley or, Pioneer Life in the West*, pp. 166-7. See also Ellen T. Eslinger, 'The Great Revival in Bourbon County, Kentucky', unpublished Ph.D. dissertation, University of Chicago, 1988 for a discussion of the setting in terms of its political, social and economic context.

mouth full of cursing and bitterness.' This fatality is the only one on record attributed to the jerks.[145]

Fear tactics prevailed. At an 1806 camp meeting Benjamin Lakin affirmed: 'I feel an impression that there is some man or young woman here . . . who will be tramping in hell before this time next year.'[146] The rush to pray was entirely predictable. Many of the revivalist preachers used such tactics with great success. 'Look, look, see the millions of wretches biting and gnawing their tongues as they lift their scalding heads from the burning lake [of fire] . . . . Hear them groan amidst the fiery billows as they lash and lash their burning shores.'[147] The aforementioned Benjamin Lakin related that a 'wicked man' intended to send his daughter to the 'Danceing [sic] School' but the sudden death of the child before the deed could be carried out indicated divine judgment.[148] Elsewhere Lakin drew the same conclusions. A man who cracked nuts outside the church, disturbing Lakin in his preaching, was cursed by the preacher that it might be God's will to cut down the young man and throw him into hell. Lakin reported that later he received word that the man had indeed been called to divine judgment. In the same area a half dozen hooligans were judged by God for their persecution of religion: one lost a leg in an accident, another had died and a third lay at death's door.[149] Elsewhere,

---

[145] The story is told in the *Autobiography of Peter Cartwright*, p. 46. Cartwright asserts that he personally witnessed more than 500 people jerking at the same time during his larger meetings. *Ibid.*, p. 45.

[146] Cited in Johnson, *The Frontier Camp Meeting*, p. 172.

[147] Charles Finney as quoted in McLoughlin, *Modern Revivalism*, p. 89.

[148] On a number of occasions Lakin equated tragedy with divine intervention. 'I feel awfull [sic] apprehensions of some Judgment falling on this peopel [sic].' 'I feel very awfull [sic] at the continual allarms [sic] of Dearth [sic], to Day a man had his head broken to pieces by the fall of a tree, in about 7 months I've heard of 10 or 12 Sudden Deaths. Shurely [sic] the Lord is pouring out his fury on Newriver.' Sweet, ed., *Religion on the American Frontier*, volume 4, pp. 208, 213, 216.

[149] Sweet, ed., *Religion on the American Frontier*, volume 4, p. 225. Similar accounts can be readily found in the sources. See also *The Autobiography of Peter*

a 'boasting disciple' of Thomas Paine who spurned Christ went insane and died.[150] The impact of these stories on the devotees of religion cannot be overestimated. Much of this was brought on by the conviction that hearing sermons and swooning in the spirit was not enough. Each individual had to accept Jesus Christ and make a decision to be converted to the truth of the gospel. The prevailing apocalyptic angst and millennial expectations cannot be ruled out of the fabric of fear tactics. Charles Finney admitted he used the tactics of politicians to garner support in an effort to coax lost souls into the kingdom of God. 'The results justify my methods.'[151] This constituted his response to his critics. It was a case of situation ethics. The end justified the means. According to Dwight Moody, 'it makes no difference how you get a man to God, provided you get him there.'[152] 'Mourners' benches', a camp meeting phenomenon, symbolized the plight of the sinner and the need for salvation. These crude creations also underscored the openness of the altar, free access to divine grace now released from the hegemonic strictures of Calvinist predestination. If the First Great Awakening stressed the sovereignty of God and Calvinist themes, the Second Great Awakening and the ensuing age of revivals and camp meetings emphasized something quite different. If not free will, certainly the choice or ability to come to Christ dominated the revivals of the

---

Cartwright, p. 292.

[150] Finley, *Autobiography of Rev. James B. Finley*, p. 198. Finley also tells of a blasphemer who was knocked from his horse by the power of God and lay unconscious on the ground for thirty hours before arising and becoming saved. *Ibid.*, p. 364.

[151] McLoughlin, *Revivals, Awakenings, and Reform*, p. 126.

[152] cited in James E. Johnson, 'Charles G. Finney and a Theology of Revivalism' *Church History* 38 (No. 3, 1969), p. 357.

nineteenth century.[153] While this is entirely true it would be inaccurate to suggest that revivalism was essentially a religious expression of Jacksonian democracy.[154]

The first half of the nineteenth century witnessed an exponential growth of revivals carried along by the fires of utopian and millenarian enthusiasm. From New England to Ohio there was one revival after another.[155] Millennialism, in its many forms, was one expression of the revivalist ethos.[156] Between 1825 and 1835 more than 1,300 such events occurred in the state of New York.[157] All along the Erie Canal from Albany to Buffalo religious revivals occurred over and over again. Charles Finney preached there and from the seedbed of religious discontent sprang new movements headed by William Miller and Joseph Smith.[158] Millerites and Mormons together with utopian communities like John Humphrey Noyes' Oneida Community and Shaker settlements added different features to the evolving landscape of American religion and presented their own challenges and responses to American culture. This 'burned-over district' was also the headwaters for much antislavery sentiment and the women's rights movement gained impetus here at Seneca Falls. The 'burned-over district' was unique but reflected a microcosm of events happening throughout the nation. Reference to a single year illustrates the

---

[153] Noll, *A History of Christianity in the United States and Canada*, p. 170.

[154] John L. Hammond, 'Revivals, Consensus, and the American Political Culture' *Journal of the American Academy of Religion* 46 (No. 3, 1978), pp. 299-303. Hammond makes this point quite well avoiding extremes on both sides.

[155] Carwardine, *Trans-Atlantic Revivalism: Popular Evangelicalism in Britain and America, 1790-1865*, pp. 45-56 for the topography of revivals between 1790 and 1865. See also Edwin S. Gaustad, *Historical Atlas of Religion in America* (New York: Harper & Row, Publishers, 1976).

[156] James H. Moorhead, 'Between Progress and Apocalypse: A Reassessment of Millennialism in American Religious Thought, 1800-1880', p. 527.

[157] Michael Barkun, *Crucible of the Millennium: The Burned-Over District of New York in the 1840s* (Syracuse: Syracuse University Press, 1986), pp. 2, 23.

[158] On Finney's work there see Johnson, *A Shopkeeper's Millennium: Society and Revivals in Rochester, New York, 1815-1837*.

point. The year 1830 witnessed several significant events: Finney arrived in Rochester, New York and preached a revival which reverberated across the nation. The Shakers had more members in that year than at any other time in their history. Robert Matthews experienced his revelations which precipitated his eccentric career. Alexander Campbell broke from the Baptists and began a path which ultimately led to union with Barton Stone and the creation of the Disciples of Christ. Joseph Smith produced the *Book of Mormon*. At the same time, Americans were drinking more alcohol than ever. It has been suggested that the fervent quest for spirituality and the imbibing of spirits were different reactions to the chaos of democracy.[159]

These revivals, camp meetings and religious awakenings were responses to American culture.[160] At the same time they functioned in the formation of creating new religious communities, strengthening bonds between older communities and reinforcing crucial identities. Camp meetings were symbolically and socially important. Their physical structure set forth and reinforced the prevailing social understanding of human relations and authority. The focus was the preaching stage raised well above the benches. Men and women were divided into pre-assigned seating arrangements. Salvation may have taken on democratic features but the crucial distinction between clergy and laity, men and women, free and slave, was maintained by the camp meeting.[161] Different faiths, facing common problems, found solidarity in the mountaintop experience and in these ways gave birth to

---

[159] Wood, 'Evangelical America and Early Mormonism', p. 360.

[160] Cathy Luchetti, *Under God's Spell: Frontier Evangelists 1772-1915* (New York: Harcourt Brace Jovanovich, Publishers, 1989) contains more than one hundred photographs of frontier religion.

[161] Dickson D. Bruce Jr., *And They All Sang Hallelujah: Plain-Folk Camp Meeting Religion, 1800-1845* (Knoxville: The University of Tennessee Press, 1974), p. 10. Weiss, *City in the Woods: The Life and Design of an American Camp Meeting on Martha's Vineyard*, p. 10 notes that Negro tents were segregated from the others.

vibrant religious communities.[162] Lorenzo Dow at the beginning of the century and Dwight L. Moody at the end preached common concerns but approached the task of revival from opposite ends of the spectrum. If Dow resembled John Baptist from the deserts of the Dead Sea region, Moody was more like St. Paul debating philosophers in the midst of the Areopagus in Athens. Lorenzo Dow the rural enthusiast and Dwight Moody the urban businessman were part of an evolving tradition. Both of these images belong to the history of nineteenth-century revivals and both reflect the American religious experience, even though it must be borne in mind that there were as many discontinuities as continuities across the great divide of the Civil War.

Concomitant with popular preaching, revivalism and popular expressions of piety in camp meeting contexts was the rise and profusion of gospel music. Music, like theology, was effected significantly by the wide reach of democracy.

> I'm pitchin' my tent on the old campground
> Gonna give Satan one more round
> No hidin' place down here.[163]

The camp meeting and its hymnody provide valuable clues into the social meaning of revivalism.[164] These same songs encapsulate the themes of revivalist preaching and summarize the theology of popular religion. Among these themes should be noted the call for sinners to turn from their wicked ways and avoid their fate in hell.

> Stop poor sinners, stop and think,
> Before you further go;
> Will you sport upon the brink of everlasting wo!
> On the verge of ruin stop,

---

[162] Timothy L. Smith, 'Congregation, State, and Denomination: The Forming of the American Religious Structure' *The William and Mary Quarterly* third series, 35 (No. 2, 1968), p. 175.

[163] Cited in Johnson, 'Camp Meeting Hymnody', p. 110.

[164] George M. Thomas in his book *Revivalism and Cultural Change: Christianity, Nation Building, and the Market in the Nineteenth-Century United States* attempts to flesh out the social meaning of the age of revivals.

> Now the friendly warning take;
> Stay your footsteps, ere you drop
> Into the burning lake.[165]

The intersecting of sacred and secular, holy and profane, natural and supernatural was constantly encountered in the camp meeting context. The fight of faith and the clambering up into salvation could only be accomplished once the kingdom of the enemy had been overthrown.

> Shout Old Satan's Kingdom Down
>
> This day my soul has caught new fire
> Halle, hallelujah!
> I feel that heav'n is coming nigh'r
> O glory hallelujah!
>
> Shout, shout, we're gaining ground,
> Halle, hallelujah!
> We'll shout old Satan's kingdom down,
> O glory hallelujah![166]

The goal of all religious revival was salvation and the gaining of eternal life. One of the enduring tunes of the camp meetings, summarizes this hope and theology:

> On Jordan's stormy banks I stand
> And cast a wishful eye,
> To Canaan's fair and happy land
> Where my possession lie.
>
> I'm bound for the promised land,
> I'm bound for the promised land,
> Oh, who will come and go with me?
> I'm bound for the promised land.[167]

---

[165] Cited in Johnson, *The Frontier Camp Meeting*, p. 198. Part of this song is also recorded in the *Autobiography of Rev. James B. Finley*, p. 398.

[166] A number of versions exist containing between fourteen and sixteen verses. This part cited in Johnson, *The Frontier Camp Meeting*, p. 202.

[167] Cited in *Ibid.*, pp. 201-2.

This reflects the message on a cottage sign: 'we'll camp a while in the wilderness and then we're going home.'[168] According to evangelical camp meeting theology, everyone and anyone could come, accept Christ and be saved from sin, hell fire and damnation.

> Come hungry, come thirsty, come ragged, come bare,
> Come filthy, come lousy, come just as you are.[169]

Sacred singing cannot be construed either as unimportant or an indifferent aspect of American religion either in the eighteenth or nineteenth centuries. Rather it can be argued that hymnody, especially in its popular forms, in its universality and publicity made it an important religious media. More than that hymnologists have concluded that gospel songs were perhaps the most sensitive means of appropriating the complex changes brought about by the various religious awakenings and revivals in America.[170] The popular music of the camp meetings encompassed Wesleyan hymns, black spirituals, gospel words sung to bar-room jingles and inventive creations of a various and sundry nature. In time music evolved into a most important accompaniment to revivalist preaching. The names Isaac Watts, Ira D. Sankey, Thomas Hastings and Fanny J. Crosby, among others were one aspect of this remarkable tradition. The Baptists, Methodists, Winebrennerians, Mormons, Millerites, Holiness and Pentecostal movements all successfully utilized popular music and gospel hymnody to advance their cause. These songs became part of the American religious experience.[171]

---

[168] Weiss, *City in the Woods*, p. 57.

[169] These were lines from a popular camp meeting ditty. Johnson, *The Frontier Camp Meeting*, p. 211.

[170] Stephen A. Marini, 'Rehearsal for Revival: Sacred Singing and the Great Awakening in America', in *Sacred Sound: Music in Religious Thought and Practice*, ed., Joyce Irwin (Chico, CA: Scholars Press, 1983), p. 87.

[171] See Charles A. Johnson, 'The Frontier Camp Meeting: Contemporary and Historical Appraisals, 1805-1840' *The Mississippi Valley Historical Review* 37 (No. 1, 1950), pp. 91-110, Johnson, 'Camp Meeting Hymnody', pp. 110-26, Hatch, *The Democratization of American Christianity*, pp. 146-61 and Sandra Sizer, *Gospel Hymns*

The moral and spiritual dilemmas facing American Christianity threatened to disrupt the progress of establishing God's kingdom. Urbanization, industrialization, the persistent problem of slavery and the plethora of difficulties encountered as the nation pressed westward seemed to weigh in on every side. The evangelical sentiment, expressed by none other than Finney, suggested that the political and social behavior of men and women in matters pertaining to morality might be altered if their hearts could be changed.[172] Finney suggested that revivals were hindered when churches supported wrong notions on questions involving human rights.[173] Thus the expediency and zeal of revivalist preaching and the concentrated camp meeting saw as a primary aim the conversion of hearts in order to achieve social order and eliminate pressing social concerns. Slavery remained a paramount source of uneasiness.[174] It represented the limit of political and social revolution. It also seemed to suggest the limits of religious democracy. Was

---

and Social Religion: The Rhetoric of Nineteenth-Century Revivalism (Philadelphia: Temple University Press, 1978).

[172] Sandra Sizer, 'Politics and Apolitical Religion: The Great Urban Revivals of the Late Nineteenth Century' *Church History* 48 (No. 1, 1979), p. 90.

[173] See Roger Joseph Green, 'Charles Grandison Finney: The Social Implications of his Ministry' *The Asbury Theological Journal* 48 (No. 2, 1993), p. 18. The sentiment was not isolated. 'Next to a sound theology . . . the thing we most need in this country is correct political thinking.' Benjamin Crary, *Central Advocate* (24 October 1866). Quoted in Morrow, *Northern Methodism and Reconstruction*, p. 203.

[174] Charles Finney barred slaveholders from holy communion at the Chatham Street Chapel in New York City during his tenure there and condemned slavery as sin. Hardman, *Charles Grandison Finney*, pp. 274, 370. Hardman points out, however, that during Finney's pastorates at the Chatham Street Chapel and the Broadway Tabernacle in New York, blacks remained segregated on one side of the sanctuary. *Ibid.*, p. 262. Elsewhere the Congregational Churches of Illinois passed a resolution in 1836 'That Slaveholders ought not to be admitted to our Pulpits and communion tables.' The document appears in Sweet, ed., *Religion on the American Frontier 1783-1850*, volume 3, p. 178.

Christianity a religion of promise, and if so, to whom did the promise belong, and what did the promise mean in concrete, social terms?[175]

One of the key elements in continued widespread revivalism may be apprehended in an ongoing concern for radical religious and thereby social innovation. As more separatist groups emerged the larger denominations began to institutionalize and secure their fortunes. Groups such as the Holiness movements and their offspring in the later nineteenth century persisted in the fight against antichrist and continued to contend for the faith once delivered to the saints, unprepared to admit that the structures of post-Calvinist Protestantism were indeed the final reformation of the church. 'Much of the evidence, then, seems to indicate that the dry rot of mainstream conservatism, seen on one side as morbidness and on the other as powerlessness, helped to precipitate the religious ferment of the late nineteenth century.'[176] Rather than fading away, revivalism simply took different shape as the century progressed and the second half of the nineteenth century is to be noted for its diversity in religious matters every bit as much as the earlier stages of the century for those recurring religious responses to American culture. The social attraction of the camp meeting persisted and flourished from Martha's Vineyard to the valleys of Oregon and California well into the second half of the nineteenth century. It is entirely accurate to affirm that these events marked a high point in the social routine of common people and their families.[177] Some, like 'Camp Meeting John Allen', found these regular events irresistible. Before he died at the age of ninety-two, John Allen had attended 374 camp meetings.[178]

---

[175] See David Brion Davis, *The Problem of Slavery in the Age of Revolution 1770-1823* (Ithaca and London: Cornell University Press, 1975), pp. 255-84 and pp. 523-56. See also *Ibid.*, *Slavery and Human Progress* (New York and Oxford: Oxford University Press, 1984).

[176] Grant Wacker, 'The Holy Spirit and the Spirit of the Age in American Protestantism, 1880-1910' *The Journal of American History* 72 (No. 1, 1985), p. 62.

[177] Johnson, *The Frontier Camp Meeting*, pp. 209 and 244.

[178] Weiss, *City in the Woods*, p. 21.

Francis Asbury proclaimed confidently that camp meetings constituted the battle axe of Christian warriors and would destroy the godlessness and wickedness of false doctrine, superstition and the power of hell.[179] He had both supporters and detractors. The irony of Asbury's position is that while the camp meetings arguably did dispatch hell and damnation from the lives of many who accepted the persuasive message of the religious prophets they became magnets for that same godlessness and wickedness. Lurking on the periphery of many camp grounds were a regular cadre of distillers armed with an ample supply of whiskey. Various types of undesirables invariably turned up at the camp meetings: merchants peddling wares, horse thieves, whores, book agents, dentists, doctors, barbers and of course the perennial free-loader. These individuals were present for other than spiritual reasons. Some went to camp meeting to pray heaven down, others went to raise hell. James Finley reported that while the services went on within the camp ground, outside 'all manner of wickedness was going on.'[180] 'While the devotees were rolling around on the ground in agonizing fervor to behold, the others were enjoying themselves comfortably with smoking, chewing tobacco, drinking, chatting with the women or talking politics with the men.'[181] Numerous extant reports indicate card playing, various forms of debauchery, and drunks carousing through the woods all night only to pass out, to wake, repent and drink again. Recalcitrant scoffers who became too disorderly were sometimes tied to trees and forced to listen to the sermon.[182] Some contemporary observers remarked that the swooning of bodies being slain in the spirit by day was matched only by the

---

[179] 'Camp-Meetings! The battle ax and weapon of war, it will break down walls of wickedness, part of hell, superstition, false doctrine . . . .' This in a letter to Jacob Gruber, 1 September 1811. *The Journal and Letters of Francis Asbury*, volume 3, pp. 452-3.

[180] *Autobiography of Rev. James B. Finley*, p. 364.

[181] Johnson, *The Frontier Camp Meeting*, p. 222.

[182] Johnson, *Ibid.*, p. 227.

prostrate bodies of illicit lovers by night and nine months or so later many women ostensibly brought into the world bastards as a result of the blessings of the camp meetings.[183] 'Becca Bell,—who often fell [i.e. slain in the spirit], is now big with child to a wicked trifling school master of the name of Brown who says he'll be damned to hell if he ever marries her.' Or, by contrast, 'Polly Moffitt was with child to Petty and died miserably in child bed.' 'Raglin's daughter seems careless . . . Kitty Cummings got careless . . . .'[184] At Cane Ridge on Sunday night an adulterous escapade was interrupted while the previous night, following the worship and preaching, six men, 'lewd fellows of the baser sort', were discovered under the preaching stand alternately taking sexual liberties with a loose woman.[185] John Humphrey Noyes asserted in an 1867 letter that the mixture of social,

---

[183] Cedric B. Cowing, 'Sex and Preaching in the Great Awakening' *American Quarterly* 20 (No. 3, 1968), p. 624.

[184] Robert Davidson, *History of the Presbyterian Church in the State of Kentucky; with a preliminary Sketch of the churches in the Valley of Virginia* (New York: Robert Carter, 1847), pp. 163-4 and Johnson, *The Frontier Camp Meeting*, p. 54.

[185] So noted by the Reverend John Lyle in the first years of the nineteenth century. See Johnson, *The Frontier Camp Meeting*, pp. 54, 65-6. The phrase 'lewd fellows of the baser sort' comes from the biblical *Acts of the Apostles* and was used to describe some individuals at the Three Springs, Illinois campmeeting in 1807. See the account of the event in Johnson, *The Frontier Camp Meeting*, appendix II-C, pp. 259-60. Problems regarding immoral behavior remained a perennial problem throughout the nineteenth century and were not unique to any denomination. The Presbyterians were obliged to proceed against James R. Little in Cape Girardeau County, Missouri in 1839. According to formal charges, Little fondled Louisa Clodfelter, attempted to remove the bed-clothing from Sarah and Catherine Matthews, inappropriately touched Jane Smith on more than one occasion, attempted to fondle Leah Smith while she slept, got into bed with Mrs. Catherine Stevenson who awoke to discover Little's 'hand on my privates.' In a separate incident Little accosted Stevenson 'and turned around his hand and put it on, or as near my privy parts as he could get it, and I could not get it off my lap until he saw fit to take it off . . . .' Little declined to offer any defense and was subsequently suspended from the church. Sweet, ed., *Religion on the America Frontier*, volume 2, pp. 558-62. The Methodists suspended Robert Graham in 1834 for hugging and kissing two women and then denying it. Sweet, ed., *Ibid.*, volume 4, p. 387.

religious and sexual excitement in the camp meeting context ought to be viewed more positively than negatively.[186] His opinion was a distinct minority.

Detractors often caricatured camp meetings with visual lampoons. One representative effort proclaimed such functions as little more than emotional outbursts and money-making scams. In the center of the picture a tent has these words on the front, 'the cause of Christ.' A parson straddles a large beer keg, hand raised, preaching to those gathered. On the left side of the keg the words 'spirits of just men made perfect' can be seen, while on the front 'exalted devotion' has been inscribed. Behind the parson a sign reads, 'come to religion, 10 cents a glass.' Several have gathered around this fount and are guzzling. On the top of the tent a cross and a dollar sign have been amalgamated with the words above reading, 'making the thing go.' Bibles, tracts and money (both coin and paper) fly about the cross-dollar sign symbol. Behind the preacher a man attempts to kiss a woman beneath a side which reads 'love making feast.' He leans against a large box labelled 'case of Bibles tracts.' To the left of the main tent another tent has flying from its top a banner with the word 'pleasure.' A man and woman pause for a kiss. Several others in a circle toss around a large ball which bears several words and phrases: 'sacred names and truths', 'Christ', and 'anything to make it popular.' A sign in the bushes to the far left reads, 'city wolf and camp meeting lamb' as a man leads a woman away into the undergrowth. A sign over their heads affixed to a tree reads, 'road to ruin.' In the background to the left a man leans out of his tent to kiss a woman leaning out of her tent beneath a full moon. A sign on the woman's tent reads, 'ladies tent, no admittance.' Between them and the main tent, clothes have been hung up on a make-shift clothes-line above a sign reading, 'total immersion suits' for baptism.

---

[186] Noted in Weiss, *City in the Woods*, p. 75 and Johnson, *The Frontier Camp Meeting*, p. 94.

The Nineteenth-Century American Religious Experience 79

Figure 3 'Puck's Camp Meeting Sketches, no. 2' from *Puck's Magazine*, chromolithograph. Courtesy of the Billy Graham Center Museum

To the right of the main tent well-dressed people can be seen arriving for the camp meeting events beneath a sign, 'beware of pickpockets.' A wagon follows two well-dressed women, laden with boxes and trunks labelled 'dresses' and 'rich satins.' Beneath the feet of the ladies the words, 'come to be converted' can be seen. In the right foreground of the lampoon are two large barrels; one identified as 'Hymn Brandy' and the other, 'Church Rule Whiskey'. Several men have congregated around these barrels. Beneath their feet the words, 'chorus of exhorters - he's worth $100,000' can be seen. An insert on the bottom center of the lampoon features a large poster labelled 'revivalist tent'. The revivalist tent is actually a 'steam boat ticket agency.' A clerk shuffles money while over his shoulder one can read his advertisement: 'Devil, Sharp & Co. special rates to camp meetings.' Opposite the clerk, sitting on a barrel labelled 'Satan's game' sits the Devil wearing a top hat and clutching in his hand three tickets with the word 'souls' on them. At the bottom of the poster it reads, 'one makes the money' and 'the other takes the souls.' Partially visible from behind the poster is a Bible with a greenback sticking out of it indicating the 'outpouring of the spirit.'[187]

Beyond the evidence and propaganda of immoral activity at camp meetings there were further suggestions that inappropriate behavior between preachers and women occurred during the prayer sessions.[188] Much of these allegations were probably malicious and without foundation. However, extant records do reveal cases of clear immorality among ministers.[189] An Alabama girl attending a camp

---

[187] This representative lampoon has been published in color in *Christian History* 14 (No. 1, 1995), p. 10.

[188] Frances Trollope, *Domestic Manners of the Americans*, p. 173. Her comments have to do with a camp meeting in Indiana in 1829.

[189] The notorious case advanced against the Presbyterian minister Rev. Jeremiah Abell in 1824 will suffice to make the point. Charges alleged that Abell approached Mrs. Annas Buchanan while she was in bed, tried ' . . . to excite her passions by thrusting his hand into her bosom & by approaching parts peculiarly feminine . . . .' Later, the same woman was awakened to find Abell's hands on her breasts. Abell was also charged with compelling Mrs. Jane Rayburn to sit on his knee for prolonged periods against her will

meeting wrote to a friend and confided that she had acquired many boyfriends during the event and further that the girls on the whole were enjoying themselves as never before.[190] Alexander Campbell noted in 1830 that there were probably more fights during the day and debauchery at night on the edges of the camp meeting than practically anywhere else.[191] Peter Cartwright once stopped his Sunday morning sermon at Marietta, Ohio in 1806 long enough to personally thrash, singlehandedly, three drunks. A riot ensued but Cartwright's campers prevailed over the 'sons of Belial.'[192] In a celebrated case, a known bandit John A. Murrel, successfully masqueraded as an itinerant preacher in Georgia. He later confessed to having robbed eleven men and even commented on his preaching. 'I preached some d____d fine sermons and scattered some counterfeit United States' paper among my brethren.'[193] Opponents of camp meeting Christianity and religious enthusiasm throughout the nineteenth century cultivated the stories of immorality in all their less than edifying detail and used it as propaganda in an attempt to discredit popular religion and call into question the integrity of its promoters.

---

during which time the defendant 'hugged & kissed her'. Mrs. Sally Johnston testified that Abell had entered her bed chamber and fondled her against her will. Abell was suspended from his ecclesiastical duties. The proceedings of the inquest appear in Sweet, ed., *Religion on the American Frontier*, volume 4, pp. 250-7. The Methodist lay preacher A.G. Meacham was charged in 1839 with twice attempting to seduce Malinda Nichols and 'for making two attempts with wicked intention at illicit intercourse, first with Elisabeth Sawyer . . . and with Malinda Williams . . . .' Meacham confessed and was deposed. Sweet, ed., *Ibid.*, pp. 648-59.

[190] Bruce, *And They All Sang Hallelujah: Plain-Folk Camp Meeting Religion, 1800-1845*, p. 54.

[191] Johnson, 'The Frontier Camp Meeting: Contemporary and Historical Appraisals, 1805-1840', p. 91.

[192] Johnson, *The Frontier Camp Meeting*, p. 226.

[193] Bruce, *And They All Sang Hallelujah: Plain-Folk Camp Meeting Religion, 1800-1845*, p. 46.

C. The Culture of Religious Print

In 1843 an anti-Millerite engraving appeared with this title caption:

> The Salamander Safe
> 'A Millerite preparing for the 23rd of April
> You let it come! I'm ready'!!

The engraving featured a grinning man inside a safe, thumbing his nose at the viewers. His hat hung on the rear wall, while on the inside opened door there is a palm-leaf fan. A barrel of ice in the judgment day larder was just in case the Millerite found himself hell bound. On the well-stocked shelves were neatly stacked contingency provisions, including a block of cheese, flask of brandy, crackers and a carton of Havanna cigars. On the right side of the safe, indicating yet another precaution were the words 'patent fireproof chest.'

♠ ♠

After the Gutenberg revolution, culture in all western societies became cultures of the printed word. Unlike China and Korea movable type and the printing press were not restricted to political administration. Rather, the press penetrated the depth of social relations and lodged itself in the human psyche and beyond that secured for itself a permanent place in public life.[194] If the nineteenth-century American religious experience was extravagant in its revivalism, camp meetings, circuit riders, popular music and vernacular preaching it was a natural course of action to find the publishing industry, under the influence of democratized evangelicalism, creating a culture of religious print. Even in Europe a long tradition of the supremacy of religion in the publishing industry could be

---

[194] Roger Chartier, ed., *The Culture of Print: Power and the Uses of Print in Early Modern Europe*, trans., Lydia C. Cochrane (Princeton: Princeton University Press, 1989), p. 1.

Figure 4 'A Millerite preparing for the 23rd of April', 1843.
Courtesy of the Houghton Library, Harvard University

detected.[195] Working from the assumption that popular culture and religious culture in America shared a system with at least some common values and attitudes, the

---

[195] Roger Chartier, *The Cultural Uses of Print in Early Modern France*, trans., Lydia C. Cochrane (Princeton: Princeton University Press, 1987), pp. 149-51.

marketability of religious print and propaganda in mass dissemination into a total unified culture (artificial as it clearly was) made it possible for the promoters of religious texts to influence an entire nation, one which was expanding too rapidly for circuit riders and itinerant preachers to keep up with. The sheer distances from New England to California, from Georgia to the Oregon Territory proved too great for any aspiring nineteenth-century Asbury to patrol.

At the outset it is essential to define what might be called common or shared values.[196] These common values, widespread beliefs or grassroots mentalities cannot be regarded in any context as homogeneous or clearly defined sets of ideas. Rather, it may be more fruitful to regard the texture of common communities as a mosaic comprised of dynamic conceptions, always changing and being modified and holding within its essential unity a clear element of diversity, even outright contradiction. The fabric holding together such communities, however, is the clue to understanding the processes of culture formation.[197] Nevertheless, it must be borne in mind that popular culture itself is a category of the learned which indicates already its limited scope of usefulness.[198] In general it is possible to move toward a definition of common or shared religious values by suggesting that the ethos of religious democracy is not the provenance of any group or groups. Rather, the principles of popular, democratized American religion were shared by divergent religious movements. After accepting common dominant symbols and values, however, they departed from each other in matters of interpretation and practice. Nonetheless, many of these groups continued to adhere

---

[196]   On the problems and complexities of the study of popular culture one may benefit from the astute essay by Bob Scribner, 'Is a history of popular culture possible?' *History of European Ideas* 10 (1989), pp. 175-91.

[197]   A summary of the dilemmas facing the scholar of popular culture in Scribner, 'Is a history of popular culture possible?' is useful together with Tessa Watt, *Cheap Print and Popular Piety, 1550-1640* (Cambridge: Cambridge University Press, 1991), pp. 1-8.

[198]   Roger Chartier, *Forms and Meanings: Texts, Performances and Audiences from Codex to Computer* (Philadelphia: University of Pennsylvania Press, 1995), p. 83.

to general defining characteristics. Among those values and attitudes might be numbered evangelism, revivalist emphases, apocalyptic expectations, millennial hopes, separatist tendencies, the necessity of the Bible, an observing of the separation between sacred and profane, incipient religious intolerance, charismatic leadership, adherence to the supernatural and amenable to popular expressions of piety. The culture of religious print can neither be limited to nor attributed to groups holding shared values and attitudes. But the nineteenth-century American religious experience witnessed both the proliferation of such movements as well as the creation of an altogether novel culture of print which added a further dimension to the diversity and complexity of the native religious experience.

Central to the ethos of nineteenth-century religion was the image of the Bible. Indeed, it is not inappropriate to refer to the holy scriptures as 'America's Icon.'[199] From the Puritan experiments in New England to twentieth-century revivals, dependence on the Bible was foundational.[200] As Mark Noll has pointed out, fascination and preoccupation with the Bible has its roots in the European reformations of the sixteenth century. Throughout the turbulent years in post-revolutionary America, and following the steep, clearly perceptible decline of Calvinism as a theological assumption, the Bible came to the fore as 'the most pervasive symbol of "Christian America"'.[201] The use of the Bible in the new world following the triumph of democracy took on entirely and uniquely American characteristics. In antebellum Protestant America the Bible was the highest court of appeal.[202] Its social utilization in the Civil War conflict, even to the actual

---

[199] Noll, *A History of Christianity in the United States and Canada*, p. 400.

[200] Harry S. Stout, 'Word and Order in Colonial New England', in Hatch and Noll, eds., *The Bible in America*, p. 19.

[201] Noll, *A History of Christianity in the United States and Canada*, p. 400.

[202] George M. Marsden, 'Everyone One's Own Interpreter? The Bible, Science, and Authority in Mid-Nineteenth-Century America', in *The Bible in America*, eds. Hatch and Noll, p. 79.

86   *The Nineteenth-Century American Religious Experience*

theater of war, was indicative of the significance attached to it. Mark Noll has argued that the ways in which the Bible has been used in public and private spheres amounted to a strategic focus revealing how Americans historically wrote, thought, talked and perceived.[203] In other words the Bible was, in nineteenth-century America, a social force to be reckoned with. This can be ascertained with a brief consideration of two organizations which together facilitated a popular evangelical press. Those two institutions were of course the American Bible Society, founded in 1816 and the American Tract Society, founded in 1825. They were preceded by more than a hundred Bible societies and dozens of tract societies.[204] Driven by missionary zeal to Christianize America these organizations subscribed to the idea of America's manifest destiny, the imminent advent of a millennial reality, and were fully imbued with the spirit of democracy which by the 1820s was for all intents and purposes absolutely prevalent. The creation and facilitation of religious print in the hands of these institutions was greatly advanced. Combining energy and prodigious industry the two organizations managed in the years between 1829 and 1831 to produce and distribute more than one million copies of the Bible and print an average of five pages for every person in the United States. At that time the population of the American nation was less than thirteen million.[205] This kind of mass communication centered on the icon of the Bible was but the tip of the proverbial iceberg. The religious culture of the nation produced in time a veritable sea of print.

From the earliest days of the nineteenth century the pulpit and the press were linked. Indeed, it is neither possible nor desirable to separate them. There were powerful exchanges between preachers and religious leaders on one hand, and popular audiences on the other whether through preaching or religious texts. The

---

[203]   Noll, *A History of Christianity in the United States and Canada*, p. 404.

[204]   David Paul Nord, 'The Evangelical Origins of Mass Media in America, 1815-1835' *Journalism Monographs* 88 (May 1984), p. 4.

[205]   Noll, *A History of Christianity in the United States and Canada*, p. 227.

spoken word acted as an intermediary for the illiterate.[206] Verbal texts which became printed texts were read to those unable to read and again the spoken word remained paramount.[207] The pulpit promoted the press and the press reflected the ethos of the pulpit. There was a strong and prevalent conviction that should the press fail to find adequate support, the pulpit likewise would fall.[208] Elias Smith, a New England enthusiast, popular preacher and general disturber of the peace of a complacent Christendom, launched the first religious newspaper in the United States in 1808. The *Herald of Gospel Liberty* eventually gained more than 1,500 subscribers and numerous distribution agents around the country. Smith's paper was only the beginning of a cultural revolution of religious print. By 1830 religious periodicals were commonplace. Universalists produced no fewer than 138 different journals between 1820 and 1850. Anti-Masons invaded practically every village in New York state between 1826 and 1834 by means of their more than one hundred different newspapers. The circuit riding Methodist preacher was assigned additional duties and became a peddler of religious books and literature. By 1840 the Methodists could boast upwards of 15,000 subscribers to their weekly periodical the *Western Christian Advocate*. Dozens of printers and binders were employed to keep up with demands. Nathan Hatch points out that these impressive statistics are somewhat meager when compared with the herculean efforts of William Miller and the Adventists. Within four years the Millerites churned out more than four million pieces of literature as a result of their strategies for reading the signs of the times. Alexander Campbell, John Humphrey Noyes and Daniel Warner must be numbered among those whose movements benefitted from the culture of religious print. Warner insisted his paper, the *Gospel Trumpet*, was

---

[206] Chartier, *The Cultural Uses of Print in Early Modern France*, p. 225.

[207] Brian Stock, *Listening for the Text: On the Uses of the Past* (Baltimore and London: The Johns Hopkins University Press, 1990), p. 2.

[208] Hatch relates the connection between the press and the pulpit with references to the sources. Hatch, *The Democratization of American Christianity*, p. 142.

God's paper[209] while Noyes declared he would sooner jettison his communal experiments than suffer the demise of his newspaper.[210] Millions of pieces of religious literature, including tracts, propaganda, newspapers, magazines and devotional booklets circulated throughout America. By 1830, as noted earlier, the American Bible Society and the American Tract Society were annually printing more than a million Bibles and six million tracts. Methodist publications, both weekly and monthly, claimed thousands of subscribers allowing that religious movement to be counted as the largest circulator of a journalistic work anywhere in the world. In 1835 the Antislavery Society in America circulated more than one million free pieces of antislavery literature.[211] In that same year the Baptists declared they had used '2500 reams of paper' and turned out '7,000,000 pages' in missionary efforts. Scholars of early modern America and religious journalism have estimated that between 1790 and 1830 nearly six hundred new distinct religious periodicals were created and the number of subscribers increased exponentially from 5,000 to as many as 400,000.[212] The postmaster charge account

---

[209] Warner, 'To our Contemporaries', *Gospel Trumpet* (16 January 1882).

[210] Noyes was involved in several publishing ventures. At last he established the *Witness*. This was replaced by the *Perfectionist* which was succeeded by the *Spiritual Magazine*. Robert David Thomas, *The Man Who Would Be Perfect: John Humphrey Noyes and the Utopian Impulse* (Philadelphia: University of Pennsylvania Press, 1977), p. 96.

[211] This kind of enterprise was later repeated by Evangelicals turned Fundamentalist. Between 1910 and 1915 a series of twelve small books bearing the title *The Fundamentals: A Testimony to the Truth* appeared. Three million copies of the books were distributed free of charge across the nation. Marsden, *Fundamentalism and American Culture*, pp. 118-23.

[212] I have relied heavily on Hatch's survey for these figures and information on the proliferation of religion print in the first half of the nineteenth century. Hatch, *The Democratization of American Christianity*, pp. 73, 125-6 and 142.

books for 1831 and 1832 in Jacksonville, Illinois shows that more than half of the 271 subscriptions were to religious publications.[213]

The rise of a religious culture of print solidified the pulpit drama and translated the spoken word into the written word. Oral texts were captured and preserved in some cases for posterity. These written texts became tools of instruction, direction and propaganda. The power of preaching now was augmented by the reality, 'it is written.' The profusion of print and the culture it engendered also produced texts of singular importance. Not least among them was the *Book of Mormon*. Based on gold plates ostensibly uncovered by Joseph Smith on Cumorah Hill in New York, the 'gold bible' was published in 1830 to much acclaim and derision.[214] The document quickly evolved into a formative influence on the Mormon movement and despite its neglect by historians became unarguably the impetus for Smith's rise to prophetic status and a major attraction for those joining the Latter-Day Saints.[215] The *Book of Mormon* would remain despite numerous trials and tribulations the *chef d'oeuvre* of Smith's movement. The search for order and authority in nineteenth-century America found clear answers and directions within the pages of the *Book of Mormon*. Smith's revelation of an up-to-date Bible, complete with emphasis upon an active supernatural presence of the divine and a voice of authority, provided the ingredients for many seeking order in chaos and

---

[213] Nathan O. Hatch, 'Elias Smith and the rise of Religious Journalism in the early Republic', in *Printing and Society in Early America*, eds., William L. Joyce, David D. Hall, Richard D. Brown and John B. Hench (Worcester: American Antiquarian Society, 1983), p. 270.

[214] Pre-publication rhetoric referred to the *Book of Mormon* as Smith's 'gold Bible.' Philip L. Barlow, *Mormons and the Bible: The Place of the Latter-day Saints in American Religion* (New York and Oxford: Oxford University Press, 1991), p. 26.

[215] Jan Shipps, *Mormonism: The Story of a New Religious Tradition* (Chicago and Urbana: University of Illinois Press, 1985), Richard L. Bushman, 'The Book of Mormon and the American Revolution' *Brigham Young University Studies* 17 (1976), pp. 3-20, Gordon S. Wood, 'Evangelical America and Early Mormonism' *New York History* 61 (October 1980), pp. 359-86 and Hatch, *The Democratization of American Christianity*, pp. 113-21.

secure moorings in an unstable world.[216] His preoccupation with the Bible was extraordinary and in some ways Smith 'out-Bibled' his contemporary biblicists.[217] Yet the *Book of Mormon* rivalled the authority of the Bible itself. According to Joseph Smith '[w]e believe the Bible to be the word of God as far as it is translated correctly; we also believe the Book of Mormon to be the word of God.'[218]

The rise of religious print paralleled to large extent the rise of the secular press. In two decades from 1790 to 1810 newspapers in the United States increased dramatically from ninety to 370.[219] America was awash in a paper sea. The relation between preaching and printing alluded to earlier is of course linked to the religious dimensions of democracy. All of this denoted a transfer of power and authority. The word of God could be handled by all, read by all and seemingly appropriated by all. 'Nothing but the principles of the Bible can save our happy nation or the world . . . .'[220] If the culture of religious print began with the Bible, the ensuing mountain of literature dotting the landscape of the American religious experience may be regarded in large measure as the collection of commentary on

---

[216] Mario S. De Pillis, 'The Quest for Religious Authority and the Rise of Mormonism' *Dialogue: A Journal of Mormon Thought* 1 (March 1966), pp. 68-88.

[217] Barlow, *Mormons and the Bible: The Place of the Latter-day Saints in American Religion*, p. 220.

[218] Smith, 'History of the Latter Day Saints', in John Winebrenner, *History of all the Religious Denominations in the United States: containing authentic accounts of the rise and progress, faith and practice, localities and statistics, of the different persuasions: written expressly for the work, by fifty-three eminent authors, belonging to the respective denominations* (Harrisburg, PA: John Winebrenner, 1854), pp. 344-9 at p. 348.

[219] Hatch, *The Democratization of American Christianity*, p. 25.

[220] *Autobiography of Peter Cartwright*, p. 125. Philip Schaff echoed a similar sentiment. 'Destroy our churches, close our Sunday-schools, abolish the Lord's Day, and our republic would become an empty shell, and our people would tend to heathenism and barbarism. Christianity is the most powerful factor in our society and the pillar of our institutions . . . . Christianity is the only possible religion for the American people, and with Christianity are bound up all our hopes for the future.' Quoted in Graham, *Cosmos in the Chaos: Philip Schaff's Interpretation of Nineteenth-Century American Religion*, p. 141.

that holy book. Of course it did not begin that way. 'No creed but the Bible' was a slogan which reverberated throughout the American religious experience. But given the sometime complexity of biblical nuance and in light of traditional dogmas, preachers and religious leaders soon found the need to carve out their own niche of biblical interpretation. Often this was accomplished without benefit of formal training or consultation. William Miller's intensive, personal study of the Bible yielded up a strategy for reading the end of the world.[221] Adventist publications trumpeted the conviction that everything ought to be proven 'by the Bible and nothing but the Bible.'[222] Charles Finney was adamant that theology could not be accepted on the basis of human authority, ecclesiastical decree or confession of faith. The only plausible method for arriving at a correct interpretation of biblical texts was to pore over the written words in an attitude of prayer. In that way God would reveal the mysteries of the holy book.[223] Once those mysteries had been disclosed it seemed proper to commit them to print lest they be lost from memory. The towering heaps of religious print and biblical commentary notwithstanding, religious leaders like Daniel Warner could claim to be *homo unius libri*, a man of one book.[224] This would present a whole new set of problems and facilitate the further growth of the culture of religious print. Scripture clearly had a wax nose as Luther long ago had observed.[225] That wax nose could be pulled or

---

[221] See Wayne Judd, 'William Miller Disappointed Prophet', in Numbers and Butler, eds., *The Disappointed: Millerism and Millenarianism in the Nineteenth Century*, pp. 20-1.

[222] Hatch, 'Elias Smith and the rise of Religious Journalism in the early Republic', p. 275.

[223] Garth M. Rosell and Richard A.G. Dupuis, eds., *The Memoirs of Charles G. Finney* (Grand Rapids: Academie Books, 1989), pp. 55-7.

[224] This was John Wesley's term for himself in his *A Plain Account of Christian Perfection*, in *The Works of John Wesley*, volume 11 (Grand Rapids: Baker Book House, 1979), p. 373.

[225] '... he who wants to prove ... is able to fashion from Scripture, as from wax, any shape he pleases.' Martin Luther, 'Lectures on Genesis', trans., George V. Schick

turned in any direction and moulded into an infinity of shapes depending upon the perception of divine revelation apparent to the preacher or religious leader. John W. Nevin warned the Christian world that in an age of theological democracy the Bible became a text for all people to use in whatever manner they desired.[226] Nevin was right and the flexible authority of the holy book underscored the varieties of American Christianity.[227]

> Witness the sect of the 'Christians', as they call themselves, in the West, the 'Campbellites' or 'Disciples of Christ', the 'Church of God', as founded a few years since by John Winebreuner [sic], &c. All these agree, in casting off creeds and tradition, and going back to the Bible. That is, they are absolutely unhistorical; and for this very reason their pretended catholicity has no contents or substance whatever.[228]

This produced its own peculiar problems. Popular reading, both in Europe and America, may be described as a discontinuous process which actually dismembered the text, lifted words and sentences from their literary context and assigned a literal meaning to them.[229] 'The Bible is good enough for me: just the old book under

---

in *Luther's Works*, ed., Jaroslav Pelikan (Saint Louis: Concordia Publishing House, 1961), volume 3, p. 191. Luther frequently applied the idea of the 'wax nose' to scripture.

[226] Cited in Hatch, *The Democratization of American Christianity*, p. 182.

[227] '. . . the Bible has proved to be the most flexible of authorities. . . .' Herbert Butterfield, *The Whig Interpretation of History* (London: G. Bell and Sons, 1931), p. 79.

[228] Nevin, *Anti-christ; or the Spirit of Sect and Schism*, p. 82.

[229] This seems very evident in a variety of heresy inquiries in early modern Europe. An example of this was the career and trial of an Italian miller named Menocchio who having gained literacy capabilities formed his own cosmological conclusions based on his reading habits. The story is told with verve in Carlo Ginzburg, *The Cheese and the Worms: The Cosmos of a Sixteenth-Century Miller*, trans. John and Anne Tedeschi (New York: Dorset Press, 1989). Roger Chartier, *Forms and Meanings*, p. 94 uses Menocchio as an example of early modern reading. David Hall notes that reading in early New England was much different from that characteristic in nineteenth-century America. In the former, it was a slow, intense process as compared to the faster pace and marked casualness of the later century. See his 'The Uses of Literacy in New England, 1600-1850' in *Printing and Society in Early America*, eds., William L. Joyce, *et al.*, p. 23.

which I was brought up. I do not want notes or criticism, or explanations about authorship or origin, or even cross-references. I do not need them, and they confuse me.'[230] Grover Cleveland's overheard remark may be extreme but it identified a trend within the American religious experience. More relevant perhaps was the proud boast made by Charles Hodge that in his nearly fifty years at Princeton (1820-78) not a single new idea had been introduced or propounded.[231] Where the word of God was, there was no need for theories and hypotheses. The wax-nosed Bible clearly suffered this fate over and over. The book was equivalent to God.[232]

The diverse uses of the Bible persisted in a variety of forms throughout the early years of Fundamentalism and in similar fashion well into the twentieth century. Religious thinkers on both sides of the Atlantic pointed out the inherent dangers latent in the Roman proverb, 'beware the man of one book.' Søren Kierkegaard wrote in 1848 that the religion of the book had all but strangled the life out of Christianity. Luther's reformation which dispatched the papacy ought

---

[230] Cited in Hatch, 'Sola Scriptura and Novus Ordo Seclorum', in *The Bible in America*, Hatch and Noll, eds., p. 76.

[231] Cited in Martin E. Marty, *Pilgrims in Their Own Land: 500 Years of Religion in America*, p. 303. Espousing the same view was John H. Rice, professor of theology at Union Seminary, Prince Edward, Virginia. In a letter to Rev. Absalom Peters of 31 October 1828 Rice outlined his conception of the Bible. ' . . . in this southern region, we do not want any body, who thinks that he has made new discoveries in religion; or that he can account for things, which none before him ever could account for. We hold here that the religion of the Bible is a religion of facts; and that it is the part of the Christian to receive the facts which God has revealed, because He has told us of them, and He knows. *How* things are, we do not pretend to explain; and we do not want any body to perplex the people by attempts to do what we are assured cannot be done. In a word, the people here know nothing of the *Isms*, which have plagued you all to the North; and we do not wish them to know.' Sweet, ed., *Religion on the American Frontier*, volume 2, pp. 664-5.

[232] For example, the 'Resolution on the Bible Cause' ratified by the 'Constitution of the General Eldership of the Church of God in North America', 'Resolved, That we regard the Bible cause as being emphatically the cause of God . . . .' John Winebrenner, *History of all the Religious Denominations . . .* , p. 184.

now to be repeated and this time dispatch the Bible.[233] In the early 1940s, between the collapse of Fundamentalism and its eventual revival, Reinhold Niebuhr remarked that paradigm shifts in religion with respect to authority had indeed created one culture after another in ecclesiastical history. The authority of the charismatic church in primitive Christianity fell victim to the authority of a bureaucratic institutional administration guided by Constantinian principles. The incident at the Milvium Bridge in 311 causing Emperor Constantine to convert to the Christian faith had enormous political implications for Christianity. Constantinian Christendom lasted until the upheavals of the European reformations when the authority of the church was replaced by the authority of the Bible which proved to be every bit as rigid and unyielding as the medieval church.[234] In the same vein the progressive and influential theologian Karl Barth concluded that a 'paper pope' had replaced the living pope in Rome and exerted a tyranny over the minds of Christians. Indeed this 'paper pope' was wholly given up into the hands of its interpreters and wielded an arbitrary authority of unassailable power.[235]

The impact of religious print upon the spiritual and social life of the nation might suggest that popular culture was being created on one hand and appropriated

---

[233] 'Fundamentally a reformation which did away with the Bible would now be just as valid as Luther's doing away with the Pope. All that about the Bible has developed a religion of learning and law, a mere distraction. . . . The Bible societies have done immeasurable harm. Christendom has long been in need of a hero who, in fear and trembling before God, had the courage to forbid people to read the Bible.' The most recent translation of this passage appears in *Søren Kierkegaard Papers and Journals: A Selection*, trans., Alastair Hannay (London: Penguin Books, 1996), pp. 343-4.

[234] 'The authority of the Bible was used to break the proud authority of the Church; whereupon the Bible became another instrument of human pride.' *The Nature and Destiny of Man*, 2 volumes (New York: Charles Scribner's Sons, 1941-3), volume 2, p. 239.

[235] 'The Bible was now grounded upon itself apart from the mystery of Christ and the Holy Ghost. It became a "paper Pope", and unlike the living Pope in Rome it was wholly given up into the hands of its interpreters. It was no longer a free and spiritual force, but an instrument of human power.' *Church Dogmatics*, volume 1, part 2, trans., G.T. Thomson and Harold Knight, eds., G.W. Bromiley and T.F. Torrance (Edinburgh: T&T Clark, 1956), p. 525.

on the other. The Bible played no mean rôle in the program of popular religion and revivalism.

> Ten thousand reformers like so many moles
> Have plowed all the Bible and cut it [in] holes
> And each has his church at the end of his trace
> Built up as he thinks of the subjects of grace.[236]

Many groups would claim the reformation adage *sola scriptura* but the varieties of American Christianity which were developed under that rubric must surely indicate *scriptura numquam sola*. That Scripture is never alone is well attested by the gargantuan proportions of the culture of religious print. There may well have been 'no creed but the Bible' in many corners of the American religious experience, but the central icon of nineteenth-century religious culture was well supported by commentaries, treatises, written opinion, interpretations and applications. As the devotional life of several groups would indicate, Bible reading effectively became efficacious. In the hands of its many interpreters the Bible fulfilled the Latin dictum *habent sua fata libelli* [books have their own destiny]. The same could be said with respect to all literature. Books can be used in a multitude of ways. Established cultural and social practices, to say nothing of religious influence, provide meaning to printed texts.[237] The tyranny of Calvinism was at an end; a new social force had begun.

As noted earlier the religious element was not the sole component in the culture of print which swept the nation in the early years of the nineteenth century and persisted beyond its close. Indeed, the rapidly developing secular newspapers vied for the lion's share of readers among the American public. Alongside daily and weekly newsprint were almanacs, novels, broadside ballads, chapbooks,

---

[236] So ran the observation of Richard McNemar, a typical Christian pilgrim who successively belonged to the Methodists, Presbyterians, the Christian Church and the Shakers. 'The Mole's Little Pathways' (1807?), MS. copy, Shaker Papers, Library of Congress. Cited in Hatch, 'The Christian Movement and the Demand for a Theology of the People' *The Journal of American History* 67 (No. 3, 1980), p. 566.

[237] Chartier, *The Cultural Uses of Print in Early Modern France*, p. 183.

magazines and political pamphlets.[238] The rise and proliferation of these aspects of culture may help to explain some of the changes in homiletics and preaching techniques already described which by mid century became regular and permanent features of revivalist pulpiteering. All of this together must be considered, as Paul Ricoeur has insisted, in the tensions between the world of the text and the world of the reader.[239] Alongside this culture of print must be noted the rise in institutions of higher learning. For example the Methodists founded thirty-five institutions of higher learning between 1840 and 1860. From the Civil War through the end of the century they established at least one every year.[240] In many ways it is possible to regard colleges and universities as the offspring of religion.[241] The drama of the nineteenth century not only confirmed this reality but likewise endured the influence of secular institutions which by the century's end posed a serious intellectual threat.[242]

---

[238] See R. Lawrence Moore, 'Religion, Secularization, and the Shaping of the Culture Industry in Antebellum America', p. 217.

[239] Paul Ricoeur, *From Text to Action: Essays in Hermeneutics, 11*, trans., Kathleen Blamey and John B. Thompson (Evanston: Northwestern University Press, 1991), pp. 84-6. The point has been reiterated in important ways by Roger Chartier, *The Order of Books: Readers, Authors, and Libraries in Europe between the Fourteenth and Eighteenth Centuries*, trans., Lydia G. Cochrane (Stanford: Stanford University Press, 1994), p. 3.

[240] Nathan O. Hatch, 'The Puzzle of American Methodism' *Church History* 63 (No. 2, 1994), pp. 180-1.

[241] Winton U. Solberg, 'The Conflict Between Religion and Secularism at the University of Illinois, 1867-1894', p. 183. As noted earlier, of the more than 500 institutions of higher learning established prior to the Civil War most were affiliated with some form of religious community.

[242] See George M. Marsden and Bradley J. Longfield, eds., *The Secularization of the Academy* (New York and Oxford: Oxford University Press, 1992) and Marsden, *The Soul of the American University*.

IV. The Search for Order

Sectarians fierce for systems fight,
Each can demonstrate that he's right;
And prove by scripture, blocks and knocks,
That every other is heterodox.
Each claims a right to judge his brother,
And by that right to damn each other,—
Pray God to vindicate their sentence
And smite all others with repentance.[243]

♠ ♠

The absence of a clear magisterium and any means of enforcing one led to a crisis of authority in religious circles. Not even newly formed churches and movements could always successfully assemble an unambiguous authority which could prevent the numerous compelling centrifugal forces from deviating away from the inchoate churches. The search for order took time and in the chaos and uncertainty which invariably followed the displacement of tradition, religious entrepreneurialism flourished. The splintering of religion had reached extreme proportions. Jefferson may have been jesting when he remarked, 'I am of a sect by myself, as far as I know', but there was indication of religious expressions that narrow.[244] There is evidence to suggest that the revolt against Calvinism specifically was in some instances also a revolt against theology generally. In the case of Barton Stone's colleagues Robert Marshall and John Thompson this was

---

[243] An unsigned poem which appeared in the *Farmer's Journal*, 26 September 1791 in Danbury, Connecticut. Cited in William G. McLoughlin, *New England Dissent, 1630-1833: The Baptists and the Separation of Church and State*, volume 2 (Cambridge: Harvard University Press, 1971), p. 916.

[244] This comment to Ezra Stiles Ely, 25 June 1819. In *Jefferson's Extracts from the Gospels* in *The Papers of Thomas Jefferson* second series, p. 386.

almost certainly true.[245] The jettisoning of tradition, theology and learning created opportunities for new and alternative ideas and structures to emerge. In this respect a long tradition preceded the nineteenth century. Bewildered by the competing claims of dogma in the various churches Joseph Smith elected to follow none of them and instead resolved to abandon them all. His regular visits to the solitude of the hills produced Mormonism. Caleb Rich suffered the same kind of confusion in the previous century and in the hinterlands of Massachusetts and New Hampshire, ostensibly guided by angels, preached his own doctrine of universal salvation.[246] The prophet Matthias stalked around New York City clad in an extravagant costume, wearing a two-edged sword and carrying an iron rod with which he eventually expected to rule the world. He was seldom without a great iron chain and key in the expectation of locking Satan up. He paraded around town, clanking and shouting his gospel. Traditional religion had no place in the ministry of 'Jumping Jesus.'[247] Elhanan Winchester, Elias Smith, Abner Jones, William Smythe Babcock and Lucy Mack Smith should be numbered among those casting off the yoke of traditional theology and embracing a personal version of religion.[248] It would be facile to ignore the success of such movements. Many of these revival-preaching itinerants gained wide hearing and some like Charles Finney precipitated not only religious fervor but social change. In late 1825 Finney arrived in Rome, New York on the Erie Canal in the heart of the 'burned-over district'. Reports indicated that Finney's presence and preaching brought to a virtual standstill secular business, and religion became the standard topic of conversation in the

---

[245] Nathan O. Hatch, 'The Christian Movement and the Demand for a Theology of the People', p. 557.

[246] Stephen A. Marini, *Radical Sects of Revolutionary New England* (Cambridge, MA: Harvard University Press, 1982), pp. 72-5. I have been unable to consult Rich's own narrative, 'A Narrative of Elder Caleb Rich' *Candid Examiner* 2 (1827), pp. 179-80.

[247] Johnson and Wilentz, *The Kingdom of Matthias*, p. 98.

[248] There are sketches of these individuals with references to the sources in Nathan O. Hatch, *The Democratization of American Christianity*, pp. 41-3.

streets and even within taverns. The imbibing of alcohol apparently trailed off significantly, public quarrels came to an end and the Sabbath was strictly observed.[249] The social moralism brought about temporarily or otherwise by religion can also be witnessed in the textile manufacturing town of Lowell, Massachusetts. Around 1840 the town had a population of 20,000 and featured numerous cotton and wool factories. Employment in the factories was refused to 'anyone who is habitually absent from public worship on the Sabbath, or known to be guilty of immorality.'[250] The nineteenth-century American religious experience demonstrated time and again that social life and religiosity were almost synonymous.[251]

The powerful images of American religion, the Bible, camp meetings, revivalist preaching, popular music and the work of the Holy Spirit were not external aspects of a propositional religious ideology. Symbols participate in the reality they signify. Religious symbols, filled as they always are with intense emotion and commitment do not remain isolated entities. Instead, such symbols become incorporated into the lives of those who recognize them. Those participating in the theologizing of democracy not only believed in the veracity of such symbols, they thought about them, felt them and acted them out. The symbol

---

[249] An overview of these events with references to the sources may be found in Abzug, *Cosmos Crumbling: American Reform and the Religious Imagination*, p. 68. See also Hardman, *Charles Grandison Finney*, pp. 72-4. An excellent regional study on religion and the transformation of communities is Curtis D. Johnson, *Islands of Holiness: Rural Religion in Upstate New York, 1790-1860* (Ithaca and London: Cornell University Press, 1989. The study investigates Cortland County.

[250] Carwardine, *Trans-Atlantic Revivalism: Popular Evangelicalism in Britain and America, 1790-1865*, p. 27. The reality did not always match the rhetoric. The PBS series 'The American Experience' feature 'The Sins of our Mothers' (1989) tells the story of Emeline Gurney, born to impoverished parents in Maine and sent to work in the mills of Lowell. The story of sexual liaison within the mill structure and the ensuing tragedy could not have been isolated.

[251] Szasz, *The Protestant Clergy in the Great Plains and Mountain West, 1865-1915*, p. 8.

created a dimension of popular imagination and a religious *mentalité*.[252] These symbols and mentalities only fuelled the already present intellectual ferment now reaching boiling stage within popular culture.[253] The continuing search for religious order and an acceptable central authority actively promoted the exploration of the boundaries of Christian democracy. The search for order in democratic institutions may in the end be wholly illusory. In post-bellum America significant social flux exacerbated difficulties hindering the quest for order. Religious fundamentalism which characterized many strands comprising the paradox of theologized democracy underscores this assumption. The phenomenon of fundamentalism may be regarded as a manufactured order which allowed the faithful to manage a stable faith in an unstable culture.

Still, religion was indispensable in the creation of both individual and communal identities. This was apparent on both sides of the racial frontier. The First African Baptist Church of Savannah was founded in the late eighteenth century. By 1830 under the leadership of Andrew Marshall the congregation numbered 2,417 members.[254] The greatest achievement, however, of churches such as this one, was not in their phenomenal growth. It could not even be assigned to the fact that they had been capable of assimilating the Christian religion into their cultural outlook. Instead, what was truly amazing was that in a slave state they could control their own institution, take in members and expel others. Moreover, they could hear preaching from one of their own ministers. In other words, a culture existed within a culture, tenuously perhaps but successful nonetheless.[255]

---

[252] Catherine L. Albanese, 'Savage, Sinner, and Saved: Davy Crockett, Camp Meetings, and the Wild Frontier' *American Quarterly* 33 (No. 5, 1981), p. 483.

[253] A good overview of this is Gordon S. Wood, 'Evangelical America and Early Mormonism', pp. 359-86.

[254] Raboteau, *Slave Religion*, p. 189.

[255] Raboteau, *Ibid.*, p. 199. On religious life in slave communities see *Ibid.*, pp. 212-88 and Milton C. Sernett, *Black Religion and American Evangelicalism: White Protestants, Plantation Missions, and the Flowering of Negro Christianity, 1787-1865*

The Nineteenth-Century American Religious Experience 101

With the religious entrepreneur and the generation of prophets arose the faith healer. The 'faith cure', as it was called, perhaps developed as a response to the challenge of biblical criticism and natural science which by mid-century were making serious inroads into American culture. The idea of supernatural intervention in the area of physical healing constituted a definitive religious response to the Tübingen School and Charles Darwin.[256] The power of God was vigorously proclaimed while Ferdinand Christian Baur and David Friedrich Strauss were demonized as prophets of skepticism and rationalism.[257] The conservative trends tugging at the boundaries of the American religious experience could not abide the threat of higher criticism, the doctrine of evolution or the probing queries into the historicity of the gospel narratives. The quest for the historical Jesus aside, evangelists, popular preachers and many Christian colleges were more interested in the power of the Holy Spirit and in defending God and the Holy Scriptures.[258]

(Metuchen, N.J.: The Scarecrow Press, Inc., 1975).

[256] Raymond J. Cunningham, 'From Holiness to Healing: The Faith Cure in America 1872-1892' *Church History* 43 (No. 4, 1974), p. 512.

[257] Baur was a leading representative of the Tübingen School whose work directly challenged the notion of the verbal inspiration of scripture. See for example his *Vorlesungen über neutestamentliche Theologie*, second edition (Darmstadt: Wissenschaftlichen Buchgesellschaft, 1973 reprint). His most important work had to do with ecclesiastical history wherein he worked from the assumption that neither history nor Christianity possessed supernatural elements in terms of origins. *Ferdinand Christian Baur on the Writing of Church History*, ed. and trans., Peter C. Hodgson (New York: Oxford University Press, 1968). The theologian Strauss was a student of Baur's at Tübingen but his early publications were so notorious he forfeited any possibility of an academic career in theology. The most important of his works remained *The Christ of Faith and the Jesus of History*, trans. Leander E. Keck (Philadelphia: Fortress Press, 1977) and *The Life of Jesus Critically Examined*, trans., George Eliot (London: SCM Press, 1973). For the relation of Baur and Strauss to nineteenth-century higher criticism see Roy A. Harrisville and Walter Sundberg, *The Bible in Modern Culture: Theology and Historical-Critical Method from Spinoza to Käsemann* (Grand Rapids: William B. Eerdmans, 1995), pp. 89-130.

[258] One of the essential components of nineteenth-century scholarship in Europe was a general inquiry into the possibilities of recovering the Jesus of history. There were two predominant assumptions of the nineteenth century quest at the outset. First, the objective

This led on to the development of Fundamentalism as a direct response to the recoverability of the past via historical criticism and second, that the Gospels were adequate as sources for an historical reconstruction of the life of Jesus insofar as the details of his ministry was concerned. This quest produced a number of 'Lives of Jesus'. All of these essentially attempted to limit the life of Jesus to natural, psychological causes and motivations and tended in the main to reject or ignore all eschatological dimensions. Among the notable scholars involved in the 'quest' were Hermann Samuel Reimarus (1694-1768), Friedrich Schleiermacher (1768-1834), David Friedrich Strauss (1808-74), Ernest Renan (1823-92), Wilhelm Hermann (1846-1922), Alfred Loisy (1857-1940), Wilhelm Wrede (1859-1906), Shailer Matthews (1863-1941), Johannes Weiss (1863-1914) and Shirley Jackson Case (1872-1947). The quest was abandoned as futile on the grounds of historical skepticism and source criticism which called into serious question the authenticity and reliability of the gospels. Further, theological disinterest in the historical Jesus for dogmatic reasons (Barth) and for eschatological reasons (Bultmann) contributed to its eventual failure. It is somewhat of a puzzle that the Tübingen School so adamant on the centrality of history as a tool for investigation, thus championing historical criticism, should undermine its own foundation by declaring that history was unreliable and that nothing of value could be extracted from the past. Historical criticism was thereby crippled and rendered practically useless. At the turn of the twentieth century Albert Schweitzer summed up the history in his epic *The Quest of the Historical Jesus: A Critical Study of its Progress from Reimarus to Wrede*, trans. W. Montgomery, third edition (London: Adam & Charles Black, 1956). Schweitzer's book, originally appeared in German in 1904, reviewed and summarized the history of the movement. His conclusion was that the eschatological outlook of Jesus determined his actions and his teachings. 'In the knowledge that he is the coming son of man, Jesus lays hold of the wheel of the world to set it moving on that last revolution which is to bring all ordinary history to a close. It refuses to turn, and he throws himself upon it. Then it does turn and crushes him. Instead of bringing in the eschatological conditions, he has destroyed them. The wheel rolls onward, and the mangled body of the one immeasurably great man who was strong enough to think of himself as the spiritual ruler of mankind and to bend history to his purpose, is hanging upon it still. That is his victory and his reign.' Schweitzer, *The Psychiatric Study of Jesus*, trans. Charles R. Joy (Boston: Beacon Press, 1948), frontispiece. In the end Schweitzer concluded it was possible to know Christ but only in one's own experience. 'He comes to us as One unknown, without a name, as of old, by the lakeside, He came to those men who knew Him not. He speaks to us the same word: "Follow thou me!" and sets us to the tasks which He has to fulfill for our time. He commands. And to those who obey Him, whether they be wise or simple, He will reveal Himself in the toils, the conflicts, the sufferings which they shall pass through in His fellowship, and, as an ineffable mystery, they shall learn in their own experience Who He is.' *The Quest of the Historical Jesus*, p. 401. Alfred Loisy concluded somewhat differently by insisting 'we know Christ only by the tradition, across the tradition, and in the tradition of the primitive Christians.' In any event Loisy was cynical about Christian history. Jesus had come preaching the kingdom of God, but the world wound up with the church. ['Jésus annocait le royaume, et c'est l'Église qui est venue.'] *L'Évangile et l'Église*, fifth edition (Paris: Émile Nourry, 1929), p. 153. There is an English edition. *The Gospel and the Church*, trans., Christopher Home (Philadelphia: Fortress Press, 1976), p. 166.

encroaching evils of godless science and theology. The central components of the Fundamentalist movement—evangelicalism, biblical inerrancy, premillennialism and separatism—were hewn from the quarry of the conservative American religious experience.[259] The other side of the emphasis must include the neophyte liberal theology movement associated with individuals such as Henry Ward Beecher.[260]

The struggle for religious security and the flux of competing and conflicting paradigms could not avoid yielding up the specter of intolerance. The autocratic emphases of Calvinism had, except perhaps in the remotest hinterlands of the country, been excised from the popular American religious experience. The democratizing of Christianity, however, proved itself unequal to the task of applying democratic principles to the realm of spiritual leadership. Finney and his associates may have preached that people were capable of responding to the gospel independently and were therefore obliged to act responsibly in their response, but this co-participation with God in matters of salvation did not extend beyond that.[261] A *laissez-faire* doctrine of salvation did not negate the necessity for firm, spiritual direction in the lives of the converted. Destroying the fabric of the institutional churches of course eliminated the authority and moral guidance of history and tradition. This development in certain respects brought forth an unintended consequence in the form of an unrestrained subjective piety. This hitherto unforeseen danger, evident in some of the radical fringes of American Christianity, fostered intolerance and destroyed any notion of ideals regarding Christian unity.

---

[259] Marsden has shown this in his excellent study, *Fundamentalism and American Culture*. See also Martin E. Marty and R. Scott Appleby, eds., *Fundamentalisms Observed* [The Fundamentalism Project, volume 1] (Chicago and London: University of Chicago Press, 1991), pp. 4-8.

[260] On Beecher see William G. McLoughlin, *The Meaning of Henry Ward Beecher: An Essay on the Shifting Values of Mid-Victorian America, 1840-1870* (New York: Knopf, 1970) and Clifford E. Clarke, *Henry Ward Beecher: Spokesman for a Middle Class America* (Urbana: University of Illinois Press, 1978).

[261] Timothy L. Smith, 'Righteousness and Hope: Christian Holiness and the Millennial Vision in America, 1800-1900' *American Quarterly* 31 (No. 1, 1979), p. 26.

Opportunities for divergent expressions of faith and religious practice, while certainly tolerated by the law, fell into disrepute at the hands of those who adjudicated themselves spiritual barometers chosen by God. That there were not a few of this persuasion may be evidenced from the numerous bloodless religious wars which were waged across the nation in an unrelenting serious of conflicts. To remove religious authority from the control of bishops and hierarchical churches and place it instead in a personal moral context did indeed do away with the supervisory function of the episcopacy and the church hierarchy. But in its stead it yielded a highly unmanageable feeling of personal autonomy which may indeed have bypassed a variety of religious leaders but which certainly spread in almost epidemic fashion among many of those who claimed the inheritance of political independence and democratic freedom. This was one of the implications of a state with no official religion, but which officially sanctioned religious liberty.[262] It constituted furthermore a conundrum, an unsolvable Gordian knot. The democratization of America in the wake of 1776 legitimated the rhetoric of religious toleration as a social norm. The reality of a profoundly religious culture revealed the hollowness of the ideal. Between the rhetoric and the reality an unbridgeable gulf was formed.

The bane of religious intolerance which remained a permanent aspect of the religious experience in nineteenth-century America was part of the historic succession of Christianity and indeed part of the legacy of Christendom itself stretching all the way back to the early church in New Testament times. If institutions replaced charismatic direction and Bibles subverted those same institutions, the American experience taught the lesson that Bibles in the hands of religious zealots could hardly avoid a collision of monumental proportions with implications and aftershocks beyond human calibration. Joseph Smith, John

---

[262] Abzug, *Cosmos Crumbling: American Reform and the Religious Imagination*, pp. 5-6 suggests that this conundrum may yield clues to understanding the complex configuration of nineteenth-century American religion.

Humphrey Noyes, Daniel Warner and Mary Baker Eddy were not unique in this regard. Each believed without wavering that God had spoken to them personally with a message not for the few, but for the many. Benjamin Lakin was typical in a reliance upon dreams, visions and messages from God.[263] Smith was more direct and to the point. 'The Church of Jesus Christ of Latter Day Saints, was founded upon direct revelation, as the true church of God has ever been, according to the scriptures . . . .'[264] There was little room for negotiation and concession when one represented God and the divine will. Tolerance in such a context became not a virtue but a vice. Philip Schaff may well have declared, 'HERESY IS AN ERROR; INTOLERANCE IS A SIN; PERSECUTION IS A CRIME', but his was a voice crying almost alone in the bellicose wilderness of American religion in the nineteenth century.[265] Religious intolerance led to militancy and a resolute commitment to resist all form and semblance of compromise. The results were at times wholly unedifying. The rhetoric and style of the preachers lent itself to dogmatism, inflexibility and intolerance. Charges and countercharges continued to fan the flames of Christian disunity. Protestants viewed Catholics as religious miscreants and in due course Protestants set themselves against other Protestants. Congregationalists dismissed the Mormons, Universalists and Campbellites as hostile to evangelical doctrine.[266] Methodists attacked Baptists and Presbyterians

---

[263] Lakin's journal is replete with reference to dreams, visions, and proleptic awareness of future events. Sweet, ed., *Religion on the American Frontier*, volume 4, pp. 202-60. Sweet has edited only extracts of Lakin's journal. His complete journal and other papers are in the library of the Divinity School at the University of Chicago.

[264] Smith, 'History of the Latter Day Saints', in Winebrenner, *History of all the Religious Denominations* . . . , p. 344.

[265] This was the subject of Schaff's address at the opening ceremonies for the 1892 academic year at Union Theological Seminary in New York City. Quoted in Graham, *Cosmos in the Chaos*, p. 233.

[266] From the minutes of the Congregational Churches of Illinois, 26 October 1834 with specific reference to Griggsville. Sweet, ed., *Religion on the American Frontier*, vol. 3, p. 164 n. 9.

denounced Unitarians. Cumberland Presbyterians were denounced by other Presbyterians as 'antinomian'. The Presbyterians regarded Methodists as 'deplorably ignorant, bitterly sectarian, & wildly fanatical,' reduced Campbellite doctrine to 'the cold assent of the head' and labelled Baptists as illiterate 'Hard Shells'.[267] Baptists and Presbyterians recognized each other long enough to declare 'the Methodist system is ANTI-CHRIST.'[268] Baptists turned against Baptists, Mormons forsook Mormons and the kingdom of God experienced a further shattering. If the rock of Peter had been split in 1054 and western Christendom broken into pieces in the wake of Luther, Calvin and their colleagues, then the pieces of the rock upon which the church had been built were now ground to powder in the aftermath of a democratic reform of the Christian religion. The barbs were sharp and the wounds often fatal. 'Old, grey headed sinners' were informed that they 'deserved to have been in hell long ago' while 'hypocrites', and 'apostates' were condemned for having led many to hell in the service of Satan. 'You are a reprobate, you are going straight to hell.' Others were accosted with the charge, 'if you don't repent today, you will be in hell tomorrow.'[269] Entire groups fell under the vitriolic rhetoric and the denunciation of the Unitarians as 'the seat

---

[267] These conclusions may be found among the correspondence of the American Home Missionary Society of the Presbyterian Church, 1846. Sweet, ed., *Religion on the American Frontier*, volume 2, pp. 696-8.

[268] Carwardine, *Evangelicals and Politics in Antebellum America*, p. 228. Elsewhere, the Congregationalist Luther Shaw wrote to the secretary of the Home Missions Society from Macomb County, Michigan on 22 August 1835 with this report. 'The current of Infidelity is strong in the Terr'y. Unwearied pains are taken to disseminate error. Infidel Publications are extensively circulated. About 20 or 25 copies come to the P.O. of our Villages every week; these are not all however taken in the Village. Several copies go into the surrounding settlements. Universalism & Deism are the most common and popular errors.' Sweet, ed., *Religion on the American Frontier*, volume 3, p. 315.

[269] These were among the strong words used in polemical confrontations in New York. See Abzug, *Cosmos Crumbling: American Reform and the Religious Imagination*, p. 70 with references. Hardman, *Charles Grandison Finney*, pp. 97-8 likewise covers these incidents. In fairness to Finney it should be noted that later in life he confessed to having 'erred' in his approach and in language. Hardman, *Ibid.*, p. 381.

The Nineteenth-Century American Religious Experience 107

of the devil, the Synagogue of Satan, a nest of vipers, a nest of serpents . . . and rattlesnakes' cannot be considered unusual or uncommon.[270] Peter Cartwright denounced 'Uncle Joe' Smith as an 'imposter' and said that all Mormons ought to be considered and thus treated as outlaws everywhere.[271] On 27 October 1838 Missouri Governor Lilburn W. Boggs issued an order stating that all Mormons must either be expelled from the state or be 'exterminated.'[272] Elsewhere, not everyone was amenable to the 'fatherhood of God, the brotherhood of man and the neighborhood of Boston'. Soon, theological 'truth' was juxtaposed to 'human' errors. *The* faith confidently identified heresies and a declaration of true religion was proclaimed in the face of false doctrine. This religious warfare often affected political and social identities as well. Pamphlet warfare broke out on a number of fronts. Jedidiah Morse put it thus: 'Are you of the Christian or Boston religion?'[273] John Lowell wondered, 'are you a Christian or a Calvinist?' Those of a different persuasion were routinely subjected to bitter attacks by the vitriolic propagandists. Not infrequently during the age of revivals and throughout the Holiness era, revival converts accosted men and women in the streets or in places of business with the shout, 'are you going to hell', or 'are you interested in truth?' That interest in truth could only be measured by one's willingness to accept the gospel message and interpretation of the one preaching, whether that one was in the pulpit or on the street. To decline to be converted brought down the wrath of God and the

---

[270] Abzug, *Cosmos Crumbling: American Reform and the Religious Imagination*, p. 73.

[271] *Autobiography of Peter Cartwright*, pp. 224, 228.

[272] 'The Mormons must be treated as enemies and *must be exterminated* or driven from the state, if necessary for the public good.' cited in Smith, *History of the Church of Jesus Christ of Latter-Day Saints*, volume 3, p. 175. Smith later referred to this exterminating decree in his 'History of the Latter Day Saints', in Winebrenner, *History of all the Religious Denominations* . . . , p. 346.

[273] See James King Morse, *Jedidiah Morse: A Champion of New England Orthodoxy* (New York: AMS Press, 1967).

one who dared withstand truth became 'a damned son of a Bitch.'[274] Efforts at conciliation rarely succeeded. When Alexander Campbell's paper attacked the Baptists, one of the Kentucky Campbellites tried to walk the *via media*. He greeted one of those from the other side, 'Good morning, my brother.' The response was blunt. 'Don't call me brother, sir. I would rather claim kinship with the devil himself.'[275] Xenophobia prevailed. Religious conflict along the great divide of denominationalism could rarely find agreement and solidarity. An exception was the widely contained fear of Roman Catholicism which seemed to occupy not a few of America's religious groups.[276] The Milwaukee *Daily American* on 4 October 1855 proclaimed, 'the man who is a Roman Catholic cannot be an American.'[277] Here, religion and nationalism merged into a unique form of bigotry. Elsewhere, Catholics were identified as 'the infidel' and 'fanatics,'[278] and a desire was expressed that Catholics would go quickly to perdition so that their 'fine Cathedrals [may] be cleansed of their idols and be converted into evangelical sanctuaries.'[279]

---

[274] In 1857 the Methodist preacher Peter Cartwright was accused before the Illinois Annual Conference of having denounced another minister in those terms. Cartwright denied the allegation and the conference declined to sustain the charge. Sweet, ed., *Religion on the American Frontier*, volume 4, p. 672.

[275] Noted in Marty, *Pilgrims in Their Own Land: 500 Years of Religion in America*, p. 197.

[276] On anti-Catholicism in the nineteenth century see Ray Allen Billington, *The Protestant Crusade 1800-1860: A Study of the Origins of American Nativism* (Chicago: Quadrangle, 1964). More than two and a half million Catholics immigrated to America in the 1850s. Graham, *Cosmos in the Chaos*, pp. 58-9.

[277] Cited in Carwardine, *Evangelicals and Politics in Antebellum America*, p. 220.

[278] The first example appears in a letter of 20 August 1830 from the American Home Missionary Society of the Presbyterian Church and signed by Knowles Taylor, treasurer. Sweet, ed., *Religion on the American Frontier*, volume 2, p. 669. The second example comes from a document of 23 March 1843 relating to the Congregational Church in Wisconsin. Sweet, ed., *Religion on the American Frontier*, volume 3, p. 381.

[279] The Presbyterian churchman Joshua L. Wilson in a letter of 12 September 1828. Sweet, ed., *Religion on the American Frontier*, volume 2, p. 734.

The prominent Methodist Episcopal leader William Fisk stated in 1837 that the religion of Rome tended toward idolatry, was incompatible with political and religious freedom, encouraged vice and contributed to the impoverishment of nations and was in fact completely opposed to the principles of political economy.[280] Men such as Lyman Beecher, Daniel Warner and many others never shook off their distrust of the Catholic form of Christianity.[281] Popular culture also reflected these popular beliefs. In New England 'break the pope's neck' was a widely observed game.[282] Pope Day was observed from New England to South Carolina; a carnivalesque event which featured a parade culminating in the execution of the pope in effigy by burning.[283] Democratic dictators played no mean rôle in the perpetuation of such sentiment. Anti-catholicism remained a preoccupation over the *longue durée*. Intolerance persisted until it became one of the boundaries identifying the American religious experience throughout the nineteenth century. Even so intolerance yielded up a measure of toleration. Men like Philip Schaff, who initially opposed sectarianism, came to accept virtually all comers to the Kingdom of God.[284]

Caricature, faithfulness, promise and failure marked the borders of the American religious experience in the nineteenth century. Nowhere was this more

---

[280] See Charles Yrigoyen, Jr., 'Methodists and Roman Catholics in 19th Century America' *Methodist History* 28 (No. 3, 1990), pp. 177-8.

[281] On this theme see also John Wolffe, 'Anti-Catholicism and Evangelical Identity in Britain and the United States, 1830-1860', in Mark A. Noll, David W. Bebbington and George A. Rawlyk, eds., *Evangelicalism: Comparative Studies of Popular Protestantism in North America, the British Isles, and Beyond, 1700-1990* (New York and Oxford: Oxford University Press, 1994), pp. 179-97.

[282] See the comments in the 'Journal of Philip Fithian' in *American Historical Journal* 5 (January 1900), p. 297. Fithian (1747-76) was a tutor in the family of Councillor Robert Carter at Nomini Hall, Westmoreland County, Virginia. He was later a minister and military chaplain.

[283] Billington, *The Protestant Crusade 1800-1860*, pp. 18-19.

[284] Graham, *Cosmos in the Chaos*, pp. 218-19.

110   *The Nineteenth-Century American Religious Experience*

pointed than in 1844 when the prophesies of William Miller collapsed. An anti-Millerite broadsheet published in October of that year put it all succinctly in visual form. The broadsheet titled, 'Grand Ascension of the Miller Tabernacle! Miller in his Glory, Saints and Sinners in one great CONGLOMERATION!', shows the Boston Tabernacle rising into heaven. On the roof, gazing serenely ahead and seated on a prophecy chart is William Miller, seemingly oblivious to the scene. With both hands upraised as if in a fright, Joshua V. Himes, a Miller cohort and chief publicist, stands on the ground surrounded by bags of money, held back by

Figure 5 'Grand Ascension of the Miller Tabernacle', 1844.
Courtesy of the Review and Herald Publishing Association

The Nineteenth-Century American Religious Experience

a devil with a forked-tail who says, 'Joshua V, you must stay with me.' Signs below Joshua's feet read, 'signs of the times', 'midnight cry', and 'advent herald.' On the roof of the ascending tabernacle stands a man blowing a trumpet. Several people are clinging to the flying structure in desperate attempts to hold on, many have slipped and are falling through the air. Clearly the true saints of the Millerite Church are well-positioned while the sinners and unbelievers are left behind. A great throng of people with uplifted hands behold the spectacle. The tragedy of Miller became the triumph of others. His failure contributed to their success, though in the end perhaps the greatest difference between Miller and his detractors may be reduced to mathematics.

In the end, ecumenism failed and intolerance prevailed. The search for order went on and in the midst of chaos, confusion, conflict and competing claims, the nineteenth-century American religious experience produced order, or rather a series of different forms of order, which permitted diversity to not only persist but flourish. In many ways there could be no other acceptable solution. The freedom of religion signalled freedom for denominations and liberty to establish means whereby the work of the churches could be supplemented.[285] But it also meant liberty to challenge religious tradition, overthrow those same churches, or separate from them. Thomas Jefferson had proclaimed that in religious matters, 'united we fall, divided we stand.'[286] The legacy of the American Revolution and the triumph of democracy legitimately could permit no other reality. Theology and democracy, religion and society, liberty and intolerance were the images of an enduring American paradox nurtured to maturity in the search for order and identity.

---

[285] Graham, *Cosmos in the Chaos*, p. 150.

[286] Gaustad, *Sworn on the Altar of God*, p. 214.

CHAPTER 2

Holiness as Challenge to Religious Culture

Oh, now I see the crimson wave, The Fountain deep and wide;
Jesus, my Lord, mighty to save, Points to His wounded side.

I see the new creation rise, I hear the speaking blood;
It speaks! polluted nature dies—Sinks 'neath the cleansing flood.

I rise to walk in heav'n's own light, Above the world and sin,
With hearts made pure and garments white, and Christ enthroned within.

Amazing grace! 'tis heav'n below, To feel the blood applied;
And Jesus, only Jesus know, my Jesus crucified.

> The cleansing stream I see, I see!
> I plunge, and oh it cleanseth me;
> Oh, praise the Lord, it cleanseth me!
> It cleanseth me, yes, cleanseth me.[1]

♠ ♠

'I do not love God. I never did.'[2] These are strange words from the pen of

---

[1] Phoebe Palmer, 'The Cleansing Wave' in *Inspiring Hymns* (Grand Rapids: Singspiration, 1951), no. 189.

[2] 'Dear Brother,—I think you and I have abundantly too little intercourse with each other. Are we not *old acquaintances*? Have we not known each other for half a century? and are we not jointly engaged in such a work as probably no two other men upon earth are? Why, then, do we keep at such a distance? It is a mere device of Satan. But surely

the man commonly referred to as the father of Methodism. They are stranger still as a confession belonging to the individual long regarded by history as the chief progenitor of the teaching of holiness and Christian Perfection.[3] If John Wesley did not love God, how then did his name become attached to the history of the

---

we ought not at this time of day to be ignorant of his devices. Let us therefore make the full use of the little time that remains. We at least should *think aloud* and use to the uttermost the light and grace on each bestowed. We should help each other,
    Of little life the best to make,
    And manage wisely the last stake.
    In one of my last I was saying I do not feel the wrath of God abiding on me; nor can I believe it does. And yet (this is the mystery) [I do not love God. I never did]. Therefore [I never] believed in the Christian sense of the word. Therefore [I am only an] honest heathen, a proselyte of the Temple, one of the φοβούμενοι τὸν Θεόν. And yet to be so employed of God! and so hedged in that I can neither get forward nor backward! Surely there never was such an instance before, from the beginning of the world! If I [ever have had] *that faith*, it would not be so strange. But [I never had any] other ἔλεγχος of the eternal or invisible world than [I have] now; and that is [none at all], unless such as fairly shines from reason's glimmering ray. [I have no] direct witness, I do not say that [I am a child of God], but of anything invisible or eternal.
    And yet I dare not preach otherwise than I do, either concerning faith, or love, or justification, or perfection. And yet I find rather an increase than a decrease of zeal for the whole work of God and every part of it. I am φερόμενος, I know not how, that I can't stand still. I want all the world to come to ὃν οὐκ οἶδα. Neither am I impelled to this by fear of any kind. I have no more fear than love. Or if I have [any fear, it is not that of falling] into hell but of falling into nothing.
    I hope you are with Billy Evans. If there is an Israelite indeed, I think he is one. O insist everywhere on *full* redemption, receivable by *faith alone!* Consequently to be looked for *now*. You are *made*, as it were, for this very thing. Just here you are in your element. In connexion I beat you; but in strong, pointed *sentences* you beat me. Go on, in your *own way*, what God has peculiarly called you to. Press the *instantaneous* blessing: then I shall have more time for my peculiar calling, enforcing the *gradual* work.
    We must have a thorough *reform of the preachers*. I wish you would *come to Leeds* with John James in the machine. It comes in two days; and after staying two days, you might return. I would willingly bear your expenses up and down. I believe it will help, not hurt, your health. My love to Sally.' Letter of John Wesley 27 June 1766 to Charles Wesley in *The Letters of the Rev. John Wesley, A.M.*, ed., John Telford, volume 5 (London: The Epworth Press, 1931), pp. 15-17. The words in brackets were written in shorthand.

[3]   A concise, but helpful, overview of Wesley and perfection can be found in Irv A. Brendlinger, 'A study of the views of major eighteenth century Evangelicals on Slavery and Race, with special attention to John Wesley', unpublished Ph.D. dissertation, University of Edinburgh, 1982, pp. 286-310.

Holiness movements and the teaching of Christian perfection and entire sanctification?

Nineteenth-century American religion witnessed wave after wave of revivalism, renewal and reform. The teaching of holiness and the history of the Holiness movements provide historical evidence that at least sectors of American Christianity did not regard the democratizing of religion as nearly enough. Holiness, as a theological principle and moral practice, must be numbered among the plethora of responses which both challenged religious culture specifically and American society in general. The several great awakenings had, in the end, not been 'great' or radical enough. After the mighty purges of Calvinism from theology and spirituality there had been altogether too much accommodationist baptizing of the status quo. Camp meetings, revivals and the expansion of Christianity into the western frontier had been good but had not gone far enough. The reformation of theology was regarded as a positive advance. The development of democratic soteriology was welcomed as a necessary step. Pervasive evangelical fervor had been embraced as a key to the successful establishment of the primitive church in the new world. Still, none of these measures was altogether satisfactory. There were those in American religion who pushed for a reformation of ethics and morals and a stricter theology of behavior. As these emphases deepened a narrowing of the definition of Christianity occurred. There was a closing of the ranks within the American religious experience. The pregnant possibility of a purely ethical form of Christianity in due season gave birth to the Holiness movements.

By emphasizing applied Christianity, Holiness proponents implied that much of American Christianity had stopped short of a full realization of the kingdom of God. By calling for a manifestation of transformed lives, the varieties of Holiness emphases suggested a radical separation between sound and substance. According to the Holiness program, faith was not just something confessed, but something which actually changed the heart of the confessor which enabled the believer to confess.[4] In other words, this inner experience produced a practised faith.

I. 'Perfection' in the Thought of John Wesley

To retain the grace of God, is much more than to gain it: Hardly one in three does this. And this should be strongly and explicitly urged on all who have tasted of perfect love. If we can prove that any of our Local Preachers or Leaders either directly or indirectly, speak against it, let him be a Local Preacher or Leader no longer. I doubt whether he should continue in the society. Because he that could speak thus in our congregations cannot be an honest man.[5]

♣ ♣

In 1735 John Wesley sailed from England to the New World to convert the Indians. His attempt as a foreign missionary was a debacle. 'I went to America, to convert the Indians; but O! who shall convert me?'[6] Wesley's association with the Moravians and his famous Aldersgate experience after his return from America, wherein he felt his 'heart strangely warmed', are among the stages on his road to

---

[4] The necessity of faith in sanctification is rooted in Wesley. 'Q. 2. Is faith the condition, or the instrument, of sanctification? A. It is both the condition and the instrument of it. When we begin to believe, then sanctification begins. And as faith increases, holiness increases, till we are created anew.' 'Minutes of some late conversations between the Rev. Mr. Wesleys and others', 26 June 1744, in *The Works of John Wesley*, volume 8 (Grand Rapids: Baker Book House, 1979), p. 279.

[5] John Wesley to Adam Clarke, 26 November 1790 in *The Works of John Wesley*, volume 13, pp. 104-5.

[6] *Journal*, 24 January 1738, in *The Works of John Wesley*, volume 1, p. 74.

establishing a religious legacy.[7] With the exception of his ill-fated sojourn in Georgia which lasted less than two years, Wesley had no direct, personal influence in America. Nonetheless, his later ideas on holiness were promulgated far and wide, reinterpreted and appropriated and must be considered among the salient ideas in nineteenth-century American religion.

In some respects, Wesley remained an enigma, a paradoxical figure laboring in the theological cleavage between Calvinism and Arminianism. Claimed by both sides Wesley belonged wholly to neither but from their conflicting theologies he fashioned the 'Wesleyan' conception of holiness; a motif defying conventional systematic theology. At the outset, Wesley affirmed the Protestant Reformation principle of salvation by faith.[8] Wesley left no doubt that salvation was contingent upon the Augustinian conception of grace and not on the free will notion advanced by the Pelagians. The natural ability of humankind was neither the basis nor the impetus for salvation; it was rather divine grace.[9] However, Wesley set forth his opposition to the extreme Calvinist principle of predestination. In a public sermon he stated: Calvinism causes preaching to be entirely superfluous; it removes all incentive for the pursuit of holiness; it breeds contempt for the non-elect; it destroys the motivation for doing good works; it renders Christian revelation useless; it makes the proclamation of the gospel a contradiction; and it

---

[7] 'In the evening I went very unwillingly to a society in Aldersgate-Street, where one was reading Luther's preface to the Epistle to the Romans. About a quarter before nine, while he was describing the change which God works in the heart through faith in Christ, I felt my heart strangely warmed. I felt I did trust in Christ, Christ alone for salvation: And as assurance was given me, that he had taken away *my* sins, even *mine*, and saved *me* from the law of sin and death.' *Journal*, 14 May 1738, in *The Works of John Wesley*, volume 1, p. 103. The emphases are Wesley's. See also the collection of essays in Randy Maddox, ed., *Aldersgate Reconsidered* (Nashville: Kingswood Books, 1990).

[8] Set forth clearly in an Oxford sermon of 18 June 1738 in *The Works of John Wesley*, volume 5, pp. 7-16.

[9] Edward W.H. Vick, 'John Wesley's Teaching Concerning Perfection' *Andrews University Seminary Studies* 4 (1966), p. 203.

causes God to appear to be more unjust than the Devil.[10] It can also be demonstrated that while Wesley withstood the extremes of Calvinism, he did not acquiesce in the tendencies of eighteenth-century humanism. In seeking to avoid the error of what he called 'antinomianism'; Wesley affirmed his willingness to come to 'the very edge of Calvinism' and deny free will and human power above that of divine free grace. Furthermore, Wesley was adamant that all merit must be excluded from humankind even to the extent of that which is done by humans on the basis of God's grace.[11] In other words, Wesley tried to protect both the ideas of justification and sanctification from the encroaching conviction of the supremacy of human achievement.[12] In protecting these doctrines, Wesley also underscored their essential relationship. He conceived justification as what God does for humankind and sanctification as what God accomplishes within men and women. If justification restored humanity to divine favor, then sanctification restored the image of God in humankind.[13]

Over a long and varied career, Wesley consistently perceived his divine mission as the proclamation of holiness.[14] He set forth his understanding of this in

---

[10] Sermon on Free Grace on 26 April 1739 in *The Works of John Wesley*, volume 3, ed., Albert C. Outler (Nashville: Abingdon Press, 1986), pp. 544-63. Elsewhere, 'We think it our duty to oppose Predestination with our whole strength—not as an opinion, but as a dangerous mistake, which appears to be subversive of the very foundations of Christian experience, and which has, in fact, given occasion to the most grievous offences.' Letter to John Newton, 14 May 1765, in *The Letters of the Rev. John Wesley, A.M.*, volume 4, p 298.

[11] The relevant section of the minutes from a conference Wesley held with his associates in 1745, discussing this topic, has been included in Vick, p. 204.

[12] See the insightful comment in William R. Cannon, 'John Wesley's Doctrine of Sanctification and Perfection' *Mennonite Quarterly Review* 35 (No. 2, 1961), p. 95.

[13] Brendlinger, 'A study of the views of major eighteenth century Evangelicals . . . ', p. 295.

[14] 'This doctrine [full sanctification] is the grand depositum which God has lodged with the people called Methodists; and for the sake of propagating this chiefly he appeared to have raised us up.' Letter to Robert Carr Brackenbury, 15 September 1790, in *The Works of John Wesley*, volume 13, p. 9. As the years progressed so did Wesley's resolve

his *Plain Account of Christian Perfection*.[15] In that text Wesley defined perfection under the rubric of love; love for God and for humankind. Such love was wholly consumed with God and God's pleasure and not the fulfilment or advancement of one's self.[16] According to Wesley, an appropriate definition of Christian perfection must come to this conclusion: 'A Christian is so far perfect, as not to commit sin.' Perfection is love for God and neighbor which implies deliverance from all sin in thought, word and deed.[17] Love remains the governing factor and constitutes in essence the reality of Christian Perfection.[18] But love requires substance and definition. St. Augustine once wrote 'love, and do as you please.'[19] There must certainly be some correlation between the love espoused by Augustine and that held up by Wesley as the fountain of sanctification. The essential elements in Wesley's view encompassed 'purity of intention, the renewed image of God in [humankind], and loving God and neighbour.'[20] According to Wesley, '[n]othing is sin, strictly speaking, but a voluntary transgression of a known law of God.'[21] This was

---

to persist in proclaiming the teaching. Brendlinger, 'A study of the views of major eighteenth century Evangelicals . . ., p. 287 n.160.

[15]   The text of 1777 appears in *The Works of John Wesley*, volume 11, pp. 366-446.

[16]   *Ibid.*, pp. 368-9.

[17]   *Ibid.*, pp. 376, 393-4. Wesley claimed to base his teaching on Biblical texts. At mid-career he remarked that he had made the Bible essentially his sole source of doctrine. 'In 1730 I began to be *homo unius libri*, to study (comparatively) no book but the Bible.' Letter to John Newton, 14 May 1765, in *The Letters of the Rev. John Wesley, A.M.*, volume 4, p. 299.

[18]   Wesley, *Plain Account of Christian Perfection*, p. 401.

[19]   'Dilige, et quod vis fac.' St. Augustine, 'Homily VII' on I. John 4:4-12, trans., H. Browne in *The Nicene and Post-Nicene Fathers*, ed., Philip Schaff, volume 7 (Grand Rapids: William B. Eerdmans, 1983), p. 504.

[20]   Brendlinger, 'A study of the views of major eighteenth century Evangelicals . . . .', p. 293.

[21]   Letter to Mrs. Elizabeth Bennis, 16 June 1772 in *The Works of John Wesley*, volume 12, p. 394.

explicated in terms of freedom from evil or sinful thoughts, and 'in one sense freed from temptations.'[22] Wesley clearly meant that this implied the removal of all inward sin.[23] Ostensibly, Wesley did not mean that Christians were incapable of any shortcoming. Mistakes and errors were not necessarily sinful. Even an individual fully imbued with love for God and neighbour could fail in a variety of ways. The context of the *Plain Account of Christian Perfection* bears this out. Notwithstanding, Wesley created a theological dilemma in the suggestion that even though such acts or omissions were not in themselves sin, they yet required the application of the blood of atonement.[24]

Eschewing all suggestion of antinomianism, John Wesley made clear that Christian perfection did not nullify obedience to a moral, ethical standard.[25] Wesley suggested that the experience of sanctification did not necessarily imply entire and permanent deliverance from all things non-essential to salvation. Perfection, in the Wesleyan perspective, was indeed a present but dynamic evolving state. 'Neither dare we affirm, as some have done, that all this salvation is given at once. There is indeed an instantaneous, as well as a gradual, work of God . . . .'[26] When viewed as a whole, Wesley concluded that sanctification was God's greatest work on earth.[27]

John Wesley, in a variety of ways and in several places, made it absolutely clear that he believed in the possibility of the experience and relationality of sanctification. For a man to be so certain of something and yet not claim the

---

[22] Wesley, *Plain Account of Christian Perfection*, pp. 376, 379.

[23] 'Minutes of some late conversations between the Rev. Mr. Wesleys and Others', 26 June, 1744, in *The Works of John Wesley*, volume 8, p. 279.

[24] Wesley, *Plain Account of Christian Perfection*, pp. 394-6.

[25] *Ibid.*, pp. 415-6.

[26] *Ibid.*, pp. 380, 383.

[27] *Ibid.*, p. 427.

reality for himself seems odd. Wesley never gave witness to having achieved Christian perfection. Could this be the reason why he would claim never to have loved God? Perfection, like justification, could never be known for certain, yet Wesley did not hesitate to advance several 'proofs' which might suggest the presence of perfection in the life of an individual: 'clear evidence of exemplary behaviour', the ability to witness as to the time when the act of perfection was experienced, and 'if it appeared that all . . . subsequent words and actions were holy and unblamable.'[28] Nowhere does Wesley commit himself to the position that perfection was a once for all time event effecting a condition which could not be altered. Here, Wesley went against the grain of the Calvinist doctrine of unconditional eternal security wherein the elect are destined for glory irrespective of any act or action. Indeed, 'God does not love men that are inconstant, nor good works that are intermitted. Nothing is pleasing to him, but what has a resemblance of his own immutability.'[29] Wesley's *Plain Account of Christian Perfection* is, in the end, not plain at all. There is no reliable way to navigate the tedious strait between involuntary and willful sins. Moreover, any consistent articulation of the distinction is bedevilled with a thousand difficulties. Even considering the context of the eighteenth century and Wesley's non-systematic approach to the formulation of doctrine, his theology of perfection is incongruent with his teaching on sin. When it came to theological constructs *vis-à-vis* the human propensity toward sinfulness, Wesley wholeheartedly appropriated Augustine in a consistent conviction of total human depravity. But if one could be made perfect why then did mistakes and transgressions persist? And if these 'mistakes' were not really sins, why did Wesley feel compelled to state that the cleansing stream of blood was necessary to cover such wrongs? Clearly, Wesley put great stress on the issue of unconscious and culpable ignorance. A reading of Wesley's works makes manifest that he did in fact define sin in different and conflicting ways. That he consistently

---

[28] *Ibid.*, p. 398.

[29] *Ibid.*, p. 440.

disparaged the term 'perfection' can easily be demonstrated and it is manifestly evident that John Wesley was aware of the plethora of problems associated with absolutizing the idea. He warned of the dangers which lurked when the ideal was set too high or the reality pressed too far and with prescriptive rigidity.

> One word more, concerning setting perfection too high. That *perfection* which I believe, I can boldly preach because I think I see five hundred witnesses of it. Of *that perfection* which you preach, you do not even think you see any witness at all. Why, then you must have far more courage than me, or you could not persist in preaching it. I wonder you do not in this article fall in plumb with Mr. Whitefield. For do not you as well as he ask, 'Where are the perfect ones?' I verily believe there are none upon earth, none dwelling in the body. I cordially assent to his opinion that there is *no such perfection* here as *you* describe—at least, I never met with an instance of it; and I doubt I never shall. Therefore I still think to set perfection so *high* is effectively to renounce it.[30]

There is some substance to the suspicion that Wesley failed to delineate clearly the symbiotic nature of original sin and the experience of perfection. If holiness occurs when one is unaware of sin then why does Wesley place such importance on the moment of realization that perfection has been given? Ostensibly, there is in Wesley the irrefutable conclusion that the ultimate proof for perfection is a subjective one. When theology has failed to explicate the relation between justification and sanctification, perfection and sin, Wesley calmly submitted that the evidence for perfection lies with the individual being conscious of no sinfulness, but mindful only of love. '"But is there no sin in those who are perfect in love?" I believe not: But be that as it may, they feel none . . . . whether sin is suspended, or extinguished, I will not dispute: It is enough that they feel nothing but love.'[31] The verve with which Wesley drew this conclusion may not have prompted feelings of pride in himself, but it did so in those later to promote

---

[30] Letter to Charles Wesley, 9 July 1766 in *The Letters of the Rev. John Wesley, A.M.*, volume 5, p. 19.

[31] Letter of 12 May 1763 to 'Mrs. Maitland', in *The Works of John Wesley*, volume 12, pp. 257-8. The reference is on p. 257.

his teachings. It has been suggested that the very claim to sanctification might entail sin—conscious or otherwise—unless some acknowledgement of one's own potential sinfulness was likewise expressed.[32] But this would destroy the whole idea of perfection, for one, according to Wesley, is perfect when sin is consciously absent and love prevails and triumphs over all. A definite and literal reading of Wesley precludes the possibility of Christian perfection, literally understood, and the Lutheran principle that believers are *simul iustus et peccator* and makes their coexistence mutually exclusive.[33] Despite attempting to substantiate his doctrine on the basis of Scripture, Wesley's 'exegesis is not always convincing.'[34]

John Wesley lived eighty-eight years and not once, as far as extant records indicate, did he claim to have experienced perfection. Indeed, the silence is resounding but curiously punctured by that disturbing sentence, 'I do not love God. I never did.' Perhaps a clue to understanding Wesley's strange confession lies with his very definition of love and Christian perfection. Maybe Wesley was, after all, a closet Lutheran, who, while holding to the doctrine of divine grace could never extricate himself from the consciousness of his own sinfulness. His love for God did not expel totally awareness of his own depravity and thus he could never in good conscience claim to have experienced perfection. If love for God meant the suspension or eradication of sin in one's life, Wesley could honestly, and

---

[32] Vick, *Ibid.*, p. 217.

[33] Luther used terms such as 'simul iustus et peccator', 'semper peccator, semper penitens, semper iustus', and 'ignoranter iusti et scienter iniusti, peccatores in re, iusti autem in spe' to express his understanding of the paradoxical nature of the Christian life. Thus, Christians are 'at one and the same time righteous and a sinner'. 'Always a sinner, always penitent, always justified.' 'In a way we do not understand, we are justified; though at the same time, in a way we do understand, we know that we are unrighteous: sinners indeed, yet righteous in hope.' See for example 'The Disputation Concerning Justification' in *Luther's Works*, volume 34, ed., Lewis W. Spitz (Philadelphia: Muhlenberg Press, 1960), p. 167; 'Exposition of Psalm 51' volume 12, p. 328; 'Lectures on Galatians, 1519', volume 27, pp. 230-1; 'Against Latomus', volume 32, pp. 173 and 213; 'Lectures on Romans' volume 25, p. 260.

[34] Randy L. Maddox, *Responsible Grace: John Wesley's Practical Theology* (Nashville: Kingswood Books, Abingdon Press, 1994), p. 182.

understandably, admit in 1766 that he had never loved God. He had twenty-five years left to live. In that time John Wesley neither said nor wrote anything which has survived to indicate that in his own mind he ever experienced perfection and thereby came to love God.[35]

II. A Second Work of Grace

> . . . Are you ready? Have you on the white robe? No longer think of holiness as a doctrine peculiar to a *sect*, but rather as a doctrine peculiar to the *Bible*, as the only fitness for admission to the society of the bloodwashed in Heaven. . . . If you are not a *holy* Christian, you are not a *Bible* Christian.[36]

♠ ♠

Methodism was in the vanguard of holiness emphases in American Christianity. By 1830 the Methodists could number half a million adherents in the

---

[35] There is plenty of evidence in the wider Wesley corpus of literature to suggest that the key to understanding Wesley's doctrine of sanctification lies more in the idea of relationship than actual state. 'Wesley's understanding of perfection is most accurately seen in terms of a relationship, rather than a state.' Brendlinger, 'A Study of the views of major eighteenth century Evangelicals. . .', p. 301. Brendlinger goes on to insist that the idea of sinless perfection is thus made irrelevant. If sanctification were simply a state then the notion of sinless perfection would be absolutely critical. On the other hand, if sanctification is correctly understood as relationship, then if perfection did exist also, it would of necessity have to be regarded as a by-product rather than as the condition. Brendlinger, *Ibid.*, p. 305. This leads on to the social implications of sanctification, a topic which lies beyond the parameters of this study. If Brendlinger is correct in his interpretation of Wesley's doctrine of sanctification, then it seems evident that the nineteenth-century Holiness movements appropriated Wesley out of context and in certain cases made him an authority for ideas he never espoused.

[36] Phoebe Palmer in the introduction to her *Present to My Christian Friend on Entire Devotion to God* (1845) in Thomas C. Oden, ed., *Phoebe Palmer: Selected Writings* (New York and Mahwah: Paulist Press, 1988), p. 186.

new world.[37] Circuit riding preachers across the American continent preached holiness and encouraged 'heart religion' as opposed to a 'head religion'. Francis Asbury remarked that 1805 was the greatest year in world history and prayed that preachers of the evangelical gospel would be holy. Commenting on a Maryland meeting Asbury noted: 'Five hundred and eighty were said to be converted; and one hundred and twenty confirmed and sanctified. Lord, let this work be general.'[38] Asbury rode more than 275,000 miles on horseback through the American frontier preaching holiness. Peter Cartwright rode Methodist circuits for fifty-three years. In the far west William Roberts toiled for forty-one years on the Pacific coast. By the time he died in 1888 at Dayton, Oregon he had travelled more than 200,000 miles on behalf of the Holiness message, a distance exceeded by no other than Asbury.[39] The Methodist circuit riders may well have done much to bring order from chaos but not all in the new world were receptive to the teaching of holiness. One man successively moved his family from Virginia to Georgia to the Mississippi Territory in efforts to avoid the Methodists. He was unsuccessful. The spread of Methodism was a virtually unchecked phenomenon. Circuit rider Richard Nolley finally caught up with the religious fugitive and gave him this piece of advice: 'My friend, if you go to heaven you'll find Methodist preachers there; and if you go to hell, I am afraid you will find some there; and you see how it is in this world so you had better make terms with us, and be at peace.'[40] Hyperbole notwithstanding, by mid century the preaching of holiness in the United States was

---

[37] Nathan O. Hatch, *The Democratization of American Christianity* (New Haven and London: Yale University Press, 1989), p. 3.

[38] *The Journal and Letters of Francis Asbury*, volume 3, p. 210.

[39] Elizabeth M. Smith, 'William Roberts: Circuit Rider of the Far West' *Methodist History* 20 (No. 2, 1982), pp. 60-74.

[40] Cited in Robert T. Handy, 'American Methodism and its Historic Frontier: Interpreting Methodism on the Western Frontier: Between Romanticism and Realism' *Methodist History* 23 (No. 1, 1984), p. 48.

widespread,[41] and by no means confined to Methodist circles. For example, between 1844 and 1860 a holiness revival swept through the entire Church of the United Brethren.[42] As noted in the last chapter the structure of Calvinism with its pessimism and determinism proved itself unequal to the task of supporting the visions of American idealism in the nineteenth century. There was therefore no meaningful relevance between a theology of the old world and the ideals of the new. On the other hand, the teaching of holiness presented a theology concerned with the advancement and ultimate perfecting of humans and, by natural extension, social institutions. Such theology was indeed fashionable and for a time the nineteenth century proved enthusiastically receptive.

The rise of holiness as a theological option and religious force begins of course with Wesley and Methodism. Beyond that, one may turn specifically to three primary sources in the 1830s and 1840s: Timothy Merritt's *Guide to Christian Perfection*, the 'Tuesday Meeting' of Phoebe Palmer, and the editorial pen of Nathan Bangs.[43] Merritt's new religious magazine first published in Boston in July 1839 was the harbinger of holiness publications. But Merritt did not initiate a movement. Instead, his publication was but a clear indication of the growing strength of the early Holiness movements. Merritt claimed in the first edition of the *Guide to Christian Perfection* that the perfection in love advanced by John Wesley, the basis of sanctification, could result in the number of sanctifications equalling that of conversions. Indeed, this was the goal of Holiness revivalism. Merritt perceived his effort as hastening the spread of sanctification among Christians.

---

[41] Timothy L. Smith, *Called unto Holiness: The Story of the Nazarenes: The Formative Years* (Kansas City, MO: Nazarene Publishing House, 1962), p. 11.

[42] Daryl M. Elliott, 'Entire Sanctification and the Church of the United Brethren in Christ to 1860' *Methodist History* 24 (No. 4, 1987), pp. 203-21.

[43] Allan Coppedge, 'Entire Sanctification in Early American Methodism: 1812-1835' *Wesleyan Theological Journal* 13 (Spring 1978), p. 35.

Merritt's religious magazine was a bench mark on the road to a holiness revival.[44] Occurring simultaneously with the emergence of a culture of holiness print was a venue for the actual practice and appropriation of Christian perfection.

Phoebe Palmer (1807-1874) promoted holiness in a rather different way primarily through 'Tuesday Meetings' in New York City. These meetings commenced in 1837 with the active support of her sister Sarah Lankford (1806-1896) and continued beyond Palmer's death in 1874. Through Bible reading, studies of the scriptures, singing and personal testimonies the 'Tuesday Meeting' evolved into a catalyst for continued holiness teaching, expansion and revival. Palmer's zealous promotion of the notion of sanctification and her innovative adoption of Wesley's thought later figured into the shattering of the Holiness movements. The 'Tuesday Meeting' was in some ways a microcosm of the larger Holiness movement. Palmer's meetings featured regular, personal witnessing to the work of the Holy Spirit in one's life. These testimonies became a rite of passage and a hallmark of Holiness revivalism throughout the nineteenth century. The 'Tuesday Meetings' also featured an ecumenical flavor involving those of various Christian traditions who found union in their common interest in, and pursuit of, holiness. The place of the Bible in the 'Tuesday Meeting' was also indicative of the esteem Holy Scripture was held in the Holiness movements. While the charge of biblicism cannot justifiably be attached to certain sectors of the Holiness revivals, it is doubtful that it may be seen as inappropriate when applied to Phoebe Palmer. The 'Tuesday Meetings' likewise underscored increasing involvement by the laity, a feature which can be seen across the spectrum of American revivalism. The rôle of women in the 'Tuesday Meeting' cannot be overlooked. The main protagonists in its long history were women, principally Palmer and Lankford. Throughout the first century of the American holiness tradition, women played important functions

---

[44] There is a short, useful, overview of Merritt's periodical in Melvin Easterday Dieter, *The Holiness Revival of the Nineteenth Century* (Metuchen, N.J. and London: The Scarecrow Press, Inc., 1980), pp. 1-3.

in the shaping of the American religious experience. While there are historiographical problems associated with the presumed relation between the feminism of antebellum abolitionist perfectionists and the enhanced rôle for women in ecclesiastical circles encouraged by post-bellum holiness leaders,[45] the function and activity of women in nineteenth-century American religion did increase.[46] One might argue that a network of associations and contexts coalesced in the nineteenth century which facilitated the growing place of women in religious endeavors. The personal connections of evangelists, institutions, camp meetings, revivals, the religious press, world mission societies and holiness groups could be numbered among the foundations.[47] Personal testimonies, interdenominationalism, lay involvement, the rôle of women, and the place of the Bible in the 'Tuesday Meetings' reflect accurately trends in American Holiness.[48] The existential experience provided and facilitated by the 'Tuesday Meetings' was not without a reasoned and intellectual framework. Palmer became an authority of some note and a Holiness theologian. Beyond that, there were powerful and persuasive intellectual defenders of the Holiness ethos.

---

[45] Douglas M. Strong, 'The Crusade for Women's Rights and the Formative Antecedents of the Holiness Movement' *Wesleyan Theological Journal* 27 (Nos. 1-2, 1992). p. 133.

[46] The advancement of women in the religious arena was not without controversy. The presence of women studying with men at Oberlin College scandalized some. In January 1836 Amelia Norton wrote to Lydia Finney expressing her disdain for the innovation. 'I must tell you frankly my friend . . . there is something so revolting to the feelings of delicacy and propriety of conduct . . . in connecting a male and female seminary together, that I can never approve of it, and must join with those . . . condemning it in toto.' Cited in Charles E. Hambrick-Stowe, *Charles G. Finney and the Spirit of American Evangelicalism* (Grand Rapids and Cambridge: William B. Eerdmans, 1996), p. 178.

[47] See for example Margaret McFadden, 'The Ironies of Pentecost: Phoebe Palmer, World Evangelism, and Female Networks' *Methodist History* 31 (No. 2, 1993), pp. 63-75, especially p. 74.

[48] On the foregoing I am indebted to the excellent outline in Dieter, *The Holiness Revival of the Nineteenth Century*, pp. 35-45.

Holiness as Challenge to Religious Culture 129

Arguably, Nathan Bangs (1778-1862) became the most influential Methodist leader after Asbury. He stridently opposed what he considered the excesses of the camp meetings and with increasing emphasis, Bangs attempted to wield the whip of the *Methodist Discipline* in an effort to maintain order and decorum in the burgeoning Methodist Church.[49] Through the medium of the *Methodist Monthly* and the weekly *Christian Advocate and Journal*, Bangs supported the cause of holiness, advanced educational concerns, and became the chief architect in the building of Methodism into a middle-class religion.[50] If the circuit riding preachers represented one era in American religious history, Bangs represented another. His relentless pen chronicled the progression of the Methodists, but there was a price. The cost for growth and prestige was the gradual abandonment of the circuits, the camp meetings and the enthusiastic revivalism. But for the cause of holiness, Nathan Bangs stands among the important early proponents. With Palmer and Bangs, the names of Francis Asbury, Charles G. Finney, Asa Mahan, Dwight Moody, Oberlin College and the Keswick influences must be numbered among the lasting luminaries of American Holiness.

The spirit of the times found deep resistance in its encounter with the Holiness movements. The age of American secularism and the age of the Holy Spirit, as defined by holiness proponents specifically and revivalism generally, were essentially incompatible. Christian communities were defined by a variety of features: ritual, the separation of profane and sacred elements, and a series of rites of passage.[51] The Holiness communities were characterized by the doctrine of sanctification and the practice of Christian perfection. Indeed, perfection was the

---

[49] See the note in Hatch, *The Democratization of American Christianity*, p. 202.

[50] By 1875 Methodism quite clearly had evolved into a middle-class Christian denomination. See the discussion in Dieter, *The Holiness Revival of the Nineteenth Century*, pp. 204-5.

[51] Robert H. Abzug, *Cosmos Crumbling: American Reform and the Religious Imagination* (New York and Oxford: Oxford University Press, 1994), pp. 30-1.

single reliable antidote against encroaching apostasy. Out of the Wesleyan-Methodist context of doctrinal holiness emerged the teaching of entire sanctification, or a second work of grace. This motif became a clear line of demarcation between the Holiness movements and the rest of American Christianity. It is essential to maintain the crucial distinction between the idea of a second work of grace, in the Holiness context, and the teaching of Christian morality, regeneration and good works issuing from the state of justification. That said, the doctrine of entire sanctification was different in degree rather than in kind from the mainstream of Methodism. However, the implications for separate movements and organizations became considerably higher than that recognized heretofore by some scholars of religion.[52]

Three key concepts came to define the holiness emphasis: present, total, and necessary. One of the enduring songs from this period was that written by Phoebe Palmer entitled *The Cleansing Wave*. The focus of the song was on the experience of sanctification and that experience was perceived in the here and now. The song purposefully was written in the present tense. Everything happens in the eternal now: seeing, hearing, walking, feeling, and the cleansing. Perfection was neither a future state nor condition and certainly not solely the provenance of those who had passed from death to eternal life. 'Let me assure you, dear friend, that as surely as you need holiness *now*, so surely it is for you *now*.'[53] Palmer's hymn was not an anomaly among the hymnody of the Holiness movements. 'Conspicuous verbs include "cleanse, consume, fill, perfect, restore, sanctify, wash." Adjectives and adverbs encompass "all, every, full, inbred, no more, perfect, spotless." Nouns often focus upon "blood, fire, fountain, glory, love, peace, rest, sin,

---

[52]   T. Rennie Warburton, 'Holiness Religion: An Anomaly of Sectarian Typologies' *Journal for the Scientific Study of Religion* 8 (No. 1, 1969), pp. 130-9 concludes differently stating that there were few implications for separatist organizations. Warburton does make the crucial distinction between Holiness and Pentecostal traditions.

[53]   Phoebe Palmer, *Present to My Christian Friend on Entire Devotion to God* (1845), in Oden, ed., *Phoebe Palmer: Selected Writings*, p. 187.

salvation, victory, waves."'[54]

By the 1850s many within the Holiness circles came to believe that the gospel of Christian perfection was the key to spiritual progress.[55] Sanctification was total, encompassing the whole believer, working perfection through and through in an experience which was paradoxically instantaneous and progressive. Phoebe Palmer taught that any notion that holiness was merely the doctrine of a sect was to be rebuffed. 'It is the crowning doctrine of the crowning dispensation.'[56] The work of holiness was 'unsectarian'.

After declaring that the experience of perfection, as a distinct second work of grace, could be obtained in the present and that it was total help for total need, it was a short step for the leaders of the Holiness movements to conclude in emphatic terms that the experience was both fundamental and an essential component to salvation. Here emerged the embryonic form of a new soteriological principle. Wesley may have avoided drawing such a conclusion but some of his contemporaries did not. Preaching in 1766, the year Wesley declared to his brother Charles that he did not love God, Thomas Webb put a fine point on the necessity of sanctification. 'The words of the text were written by the Apostles after the act of justification had passed on them. But you see, my friends, this was not enough for them. They must receive the Holy Ghost after this. So must you. You must be sanctified. But you are not. You are only Christians in part. You have not received the Holy Ghost. I know it. I can feel your spirits hanging about me like so much dead flesh.'[57] Webb's homily was the first recorded Methodist sermon in the new

---

[54] Mel R. Wilhoit, 'American Holiness Hymnody Some Questions: A Methodology' *Wesleyan Theological Journal* 25 (No. 2, 1990), pp. 40-1.

[55] Smith, *Called Unto Holiness*, p. 12.

[56] See Palmer, ed., *Pioneer Experiences* (New York, 1867), p. vi.

[57] Cited in Vinson Synan, *The Holiness-Pentecostal Movement in the United States*, pp. 19-20.

world. Phoebe Palmer insisted that entire sanctification was essential to salvation.[58] The Methodists Nathan Bangs and George Peck averred the same thing insisting that sanctification which was necessary to full salvation could not be obtained without a second work of grace.[59] Palmer's methodology became controversial and not all of her theology on the matter of perfection and the second work of grace was accepted without question. She placed tremendous emphasis on the altar as the symbol of salvation and her so-called 'altar phraseology' brought objections from several quarters.[60] Nonetheless, Palmer and many other adherents of the Holiness cause believed steadfastly that the second work of grace would bring about a final reformation of the church and unite all God's children in one family. 'Names and sects and parties fall, and Christ alone is all in all.'[61] Whether or not Palmer's teaching was contrary to Wesley is beside the point.[62] This utilization of Wesley was sufficient to make her point and Palmer became the 'international evangelist par excellence' and the 'Mother of the Holiness Movement'.[63] This emphasis on

---

[58] For example, Palmer, *The Way of Holiness* (New York: Palmer & Hughes, 1868), p. 135. The book originally was published in 1843.

[59] See Theodore Hovet, 'Phoebe Palmer's "altar phraseology" and the Spiritual Dimension of Women's Sphere' *The Journal of Religion* 63 (No. 3, 1983), pp. 266-7.

[60] For recent treatments see Hovet, 'Phoebe Palmer's "altar phraseology" and the Spiritual Dimension of Women's Sphere', pp. 264-80 and Charles E. Jones, 'The Inverted Shadow of Phoebe Palmer' *Wesleyan Theological Journal* 31 (No. 2, 1996), pp. 120-31.

[61] Palmer frequently used this verse to express her hope and conviction in Christian unity. Cited in Dieter, *The Holiness Revival of the Nineteenth Century*, p. 81 n. 97.

[62] There are good grounds for assuming that Palmer's teaching was in some ways in direct disagreement with that of John Wesley. The context of this chapter is, however, not concerned with a comparative analysis of Palmer and Wesley on the matter of sanctification. For a short overview of the perceived conflict with the conclusion that Palmer and Wesley were at odds see, Ivan Howard, 'Wesley versus Phoebe Palmer: An Extended Controversy' *Wesleyan Theological Journal* 6 (No. 1, 1971), pp. 31-40.

[63] For the former conclusion see McFadden, 'The Ironies of Pentecost: Phoebe Palmer, World Evangelism, and Female Networks', p. 68. 'Palmer might well be called the "Mother of the Holiness Movement", which eventually gave birth to such denominations as the Church of the Nazarene, the Church of God (Anderson, Indiana),

the second work of grace elevated the teaching of sanctification into a place of central preoccupation in the religious thought of the nineteenth century. It would remain there until nearly the end of the century.[64] While garnering the lion's share of attention of those observing Methodism it may be stated that while the idea of entire sanctification was an important aspect of American Methodism it did not become the dominant feature.[65] It is also instructive to note the subtle shifts of emphases within the various Holiness movements.[66]

The theology of sanctification in the American context combined three principles to create a novel second work of grace. Those elements included the immediacy advocated by Jonathan Edwards, the directness of Charles Finney and the full release from sin proposed by John Wesley. This ideological triumvirate undergirded the fledgling Holiness movements.[67] In other words, salvation sprang from the beginning of the religious experience and could not be understood as the product of a progressive reality. Nevertheless, the notoriety the doctrine of perfection lent to the Holiness movements was sufficient to attract much attention. The leading revivalist of the second quarter of the nineteenth century, Charles Finney, understood entire sanctification as a complete and continual obedience to

---

the Salvation Army, and also Pentecostal groups like the Assemblies of God, the Pentecostal-Holiness Church, and the Church of God (Cleveland, Tennessee).' Nancy Hardesty, *Great Women of Faith: The Strength and Influence of Christian Women* (Grand Rapids: Baker Book House, 1980), p. 88.

[64] Timothy L. Smith, 'Righteousness and Hope: Christian Holiness and the Millennial Vision in America, 1800-1900' *American Quarterly* 31 (No. 1, 1979), p. 27.

[65] E. Dale Dunlap, 'Tuesday Meetings, Camp Meetings, and Cabinet Meetings: A Perspective on the Holiness Movement in the Methodist Church in the United States in the Nineteenth Century' *Methodist History* 13 (April 1975), p. 85.

[66] It has been suggested, however, that the distinction between Wesleyan and Oberlin doctrines of perfection have been overdrawn. See Donald W. Dayton, 'Asa Mahan and the Development of American Holiness Theology' *Wesleyan Theological Journal* 9 (Spring 1974), pp. 60-9, especially p. 60.

[67] I owe this connection to Melvin Dieter, *The Holiness Revival of the Nineteenth Century*, p. 31.

the law of God. Shifting from an Augustinian-Calvinist posture Finney went on to claim that 'entire obedience to God's law is possible on the grounds of natural ability.'[68] However, 'sin . . . is never overcome by any man in his own strength.'[69] That is the work of the Holy Spirit which is contingent upon obedience to God. Such obedience, however was entirely possible through human effort and will. Against both Wesley and Palmer, Finney affirmed that entire sanctification was not a matter of feeling. It was likewise not contingent upon works or human effort.[70] Sanctification came through faith alone.[71] Sinlessness was not humanly possible for Finney, but the state of perfection was possible through faith, obedience and the work of the Holy Spirit.[72] Like Phoebe Palmer, Finney did not hesitate to conclude that entire sanctification was absolutely essential to salvation.[73] As far as Finney was concerned, holiness was the essential condition for salvation. Indeed, God could not save unless one was being sanctified and becoming holy.[74] Finney comes close to, if not actually, committing Pelagianism by making a life of holiness

---

[68] Charles G. Finney, *Lectures on Systematic Theology*, ed., J.H. Fairchild (South Gate, CA: Colporter Kemp, 1944), pp. 406-7.

[69] *Ibid.*, p. 422.

[70] *Ibid.*, pp. 434-5.

[71] *Ibid.*, p. 439.

[72] This did not restrain Finney from declaring that those who were truly regenerate could and did live lives essentially blameless. 'Regeneration, or conversion, is a change in the choice. It is a change in the supreme controlling choice of the mind. The regenerated or converted person prefers God's glory to every thing else . . . . When a person is truly born again, his choice is habitually right, and of course his conduct is in the main, right.' *Lectures to Professing Christians* (New York: Fleming H. Revell, 1878), p. 322.

[73] Keith J. Hardman, *Charles Grandison Finney 1792-1875: Revivalist and Reformer* (Syracuse: Syracuse University Press, 1987), p. 344.

[74] See for example Finney, *Sermons on Gospel Themes* (Oberlin: E.J. Goodrich, 1876), p. 328 and his *Sermons on the Way of Salvation* (Oberlin: E.J. Goodrich, 1891), p. 60.

contingent on persistent obedience to the moral law.

> The sinner should consider that the change of heart is a voluntary thing. You must do it for yourself or it is never done. True, there is a sense in which God changes the heart, but it is only this: God influences the sinner to change, and then the sinner does it. The change is in the sinner's own voluntary act.[75]

The implication of this, as Keith Hardman makes clear, is that if persons strayed inadvertently from complete obedience to God and thus disobeyed in some manner, their salvation was forfeit until such time as thorough repentance was undertaken.[76] There were those both within and beyond the pale of the Holiness movements who attacked this position, soon to be known as the 'Oberlin heresy'. This notion of perfectionism was condemned in scathing terms relentlessly. Finney remained undeterred. Along with his colleague and close associate Asa Mahan, the teaching was consistently propagated at Oberlin College well into the 1870s.

Observers and participants alike in American religious history were shocked by the extreme comments of the Oberlin heretics. Lewis Tappan might have said that the 'devil is at Oberlin sure enough'[77] but to mainstream Christianity Finney never seemed quite so dangerous as 'crazy John Noyes, the Perfectionist.'[78] Noyes

---

[75] Finney, *Sermons on Gospel Themes*, p. 93. The affinity with Phoebe Palmer on this point is instructive. '. . . nothing *but the blood of Jesus* could *sanctify* and *cleanse* from sin . . . . [nevertheless] corresponding *action* is also necessary; the offering must be *brought* and believingly *laid upon the altar* . . . the Spirit helpeth our infirmities . . . but *man must act.*' *The Way of Holiness*, in Oden, ed., *Phoebe Palmer: Selected Writings*, p. 179.

[76] Hardman, *Ibid.*, p. 332.

[77] Cited in Hambrick-Stowe, *Charles G. Finney and the Spirit of American Evangelicalism*, p. 223.

[78] This was the epithet attached to Noyes. Referred to in *Religious Experience of John Humphrey Noyes Founder of the Oneida Community*, ed., George Wallingford Noyes (New York: The MacMillan Company, 1923), p. 257. Noyes was denounced by the main stream Holiness movements. '[T]he great and fundamental errors of the Perfectionists, a sect which rose some years ago in the state of New York . . . .' Asa Mahan, *Scripture Doctrine of Christian Perfection* (Boston: D.S. King, 1839), pp. 174-6 is representative.

professed that as early as November 1833 he had advocated the doctrine of perfection. On 20 February 1834 when queried, he went well beyond the position taken by either John Wesley or Charles Finney. 'Question: 'Don't you commit sin?' Answer: 'No.'[79] In a letter dated 24 February 1834 Noyes took the momentous step of declaring himself free from all present sin.[80] Religious sensibilities were shocked profoundly and the authorities at Yale invited Noyes to depart from their hallowed halls. Finney, who earlier had met Noyes personally, now hastened to disassociate himself from the latter's position. Even Noyes' explanation of his sinlessness did not sit well with the wider religious community. 'I do not pretend to perfection in externals. I only claim purity of heart and the answer of a good conscience toward God. A book may be true and perfect in sentiment and yet be deficient in graces of style and typographical accuracy.'[81] But Noyes' book would not sell even though it is hard to distinguish at this point very much difference between his position and that of other perfectionists. Phoebe Palmer had definitively declared, 'Holiness implies salvation from sin, a redemption from *all* iniquity.'[82] Had not even Wesley declared that sanctification allowed Christians to live above sin? In his *Plain Account of Christian Perfection* he qualified that statement by declaring that mistakes and errors could still creep into the lives of the perfect, but such shortcomings were not sins and perfection was thereby not impaired. The gulf between Wesley's sinless mistakes and the grammatical errors in Noyes' book was barely perceptible. Yet Wesley went down in history as a holy man and Noyes as an incorrigible rascal and, after the communal attempts at Putney and Oneida, a sexual pervert. When pressed, Noyes had this rejoinder. 'Some person asked me whether I should continue to preach

---

[79] Noyes, *Ibid.*, pp. 101 and 110.

[80] The text of the letter appears in *Ibid.*, pp. 178-9.

[81] *Ibid.*, p. 120.

[82] *Present to My Christian Friend on Entire Devotion to God*, in Oden, ed., *Ibid.*, p. 188.

now that the clergy had taken away my license. I replied: "I have taken away their license to sin, and they keep on sinning. So, though they have taken away my license to preach, I shall keep on preaching."'[83] For his ideas, Noyes, like perfectionists before and after him, claimed divine inspiration. His son later explained it this way. 'The Community believed that his inspirations came down what he called the "link and chain": from God to Christ; from Christ to Paul; from Paul to John Humphrey Noyes, and by him made available for the Community.'[84]

Radical extremes within the perfectionist movement, such as the followers of John Humphrey Noyes, did cause much concern within the ranks of the Holiness movements and did effect modification of Holiness theology. The Oberlin heretics, Finney and Mahan, were once approached by a student with this question: 'What degree of sanctification do the Scriptures authorize us to trust Christ for? May we, or may we not, trust Him to save us from all sin, and to sanctify us wholly, and to do it in this present life? I would very earnestly appeal to our beloved instructors, President Mahan and Professor Finney, for a specific answer to this question.'[85] Finney and Mahan were taken aback at the query and for a time were unsure of what answer they should give. Their hesitation stemmed from their abiding worry about Noyes. In due course their answer came in 1839 in the form

---

[83] Noyes, ed., *Ibid.*, p. 125.

[84] Pierrepont Noyes, *My Father's House: An Oneida Boyhood* (Gloucester, MA: Peter Smith, 1966), pp. 132-3. 'Noyes, Bible Communism was more than a compromise since it promised "security from sin" in the Perfectionist mode, and community of property, labor, and love in the Owenite and Fourierist tradition. Noyes went beyond Wesleyan Perfectionism and Millerite insecurity into an antinomian Calvinism which guaranteed inner peace and surety. He went beyond the leadership failures of the phalanxes and extracted the passional and organizational genius of the scheme, but avoided the factional and leadership disputes by offering a theology that was beyond dispute for the leadership.' Robert S. Fogarty, 'Oneida: A Utopian Search for Religious Security' *Labor History* 14 (No. 2, 1973), p. 227.

[85] The story is told in Edward H. Madden and James E. Hamilton, *Freedom and Grace: The Life of Asa Mahan* (Metuchen, N.J. and London: The Scarecrow Press, Inc., 1982), p. 61.

of Mahan's book, *Scripture Doctrine of Christian Perfection*.[86] It was a classic Oberlin answer, couched in the context of Wesleyan doctrine, carefully avoiding the extreme interpretations of perfectionism embraced by the Oneida Community and John Humphrey Noyes. Mahan made clear that while ' . . . holiness may be perfect in *kind* . . . [it was] *finite* in *degree*, and in this sense [was] imperfect . . . .'[87] Still, Mahan could codify the Oberlin teaching by declaring that the promise of the teaching of sanctification was '[e]ntire freedom from all sin, and the transformation of our entire character into a likeness to his own.' The conclusion was inescapable. Those sanctified were ' . . . entirely emancipated from the power of sin.'[88]

As the nineteenth century wore on, the message of the Holiness gospel, despite conflict, crisis and controversy, persisted. Its aim had all along been the eradication of the old sinful nature. For proponents of the Holiness doctrine, Martin Luther had been wrong. A Christian cannot be righteous and a sinner at the same time. Sin excludes all possibility of righteousness. Righteousness, present in the lives of believers, eradicates all trace of human depravity. In 1866 the Methodist preacher H.G. Wells wrote a letter from Horry, South Carolina deploring the state of the church. 'Here as most everywhere the church has suffered terribly. Morals have become lax, backsliding frequent, and in some localities the church is in a condition to dishearten its ministers.'[89] All along the doctrine of entire sanctification, a second work of grace, causing perfection, had been the remedy for such conditions. Holiness destroyed the sinful nature and those

---

[86] Asa Mahan, *Scripture Doctrine of Christian Perfection* (Boston: D.S. King, 1839).

[87] Mahan, *Ibid.*, p. 8.

[88] Mahan, *Ibid.*, pp. 149 and 152.

[89] Published in the *Southern Christian Advocate* (28 September 1866). Quoted in Francis Butler Simkins and Robert Hilliard Woody, *South Carolina During Reconstruction* (Gloucester, MA: Peter Smith, 1966), p. 398.

seeking to be sanctified were also seeking death to self. Occasionally, the enthusiasm for this dying to sin produced humorous situations.

> Two Free Methodist preachers with whom I am well acquainted were holding meetings in Greenburg, PA. In a special service a man was seeking holiness. Their method emphasizes dying-out to sin. The seeker at the altar became desperate and cried out at the top of his voice, 'Let me die; let me die'. The preachers kept saying, 'Kill him, kill him, Lord'. A man on the street heard this and supposed that a murder was being committed. He ran and rang the police alarm, and soon the place of meeting was full of officers in blue coats ready to arrest the murderers, who proved to be harmless holiness preachers.[90]

Speaking for the Methodist Episcopal Church in 1884, J.E. Evans defined holiness thus: '. . . sanctification is distinct from and a higher state of grace than regeneration and the new birth. Whosoever, therefore, teaches contrary to this is not a Methodist in doctrine. . . .'[91] The proponents of the Holiness gospel were convinced that such a position formed the sole effective solution to the decline of religion. The only question regarding its efficacy had to do with whether or not the church in general would support its propagation. At the Christmas conference of the Methodist Episcopal Church in 1784, the church fathers, borrowing from Wesley, identified their mission statement. 'Question: What may we reasonably believe to be God's design in raising up the . . . Methodists? Answer: To reform the Continent and to spread scriptural Holiness over these lands.'[92] This was the place of departure for the Holiness campaign. As late as May 1885 the first General Holiness Assembly in Chicago adopted this doctrinal resolution: 'Entire Sanctification is a second definite work of grace wrought by the Baptism with the Holy Spirit in the heart of the believer subsequent to regeneration, received

---

[90] The story is told in Herbert M. Riggle, *Pioneer Evangelism* (Anderson: Gospel Trumpet Company, 1924), p. 92.

[91] Cited in John Leland Peters, *Christian Perfection and American Methodism* (Nashville and New York: Abingdon Press, 1956), pp. 153-4.

[92] Quoted in Ralph E. Morrow, *Northern Methodism and Reconstruction* (East Lansing: Michigan State University Press, 1956), p. 3.

instantaneously by faith, by which the heart is cleansed from all corruption and filled with the perfect love of God.' The same assembly declared that entire sanctification totally eradicated the carnal mind and obliterated completely the 'birth principle of sin.'[93] Once the Holiness movements had articulated their theological position, an active program of propagation and the implementation of a holiness of the heart began. It challenged religious culture and threatened to inaugurate another reformation of the church.

III. Holiness or Hell!— Contours of a Radical Cause

If you cannot make up your mind to discard sin and obey God
you may as well make up your mind to go to hell! There is no alternative.

♠ ♠

The narrowing of the definition of Christianity and a closing of the ranks within the context of the Holiness movements by natural consequence eliminated all middle ground. One either was saved through the experience of sanctification wrought by a second work of grace effecting perfection, or one belonged to the Devil. Charles Finney did not exaggerate when he called on his hearers to decide either for heaven or hell; God or the Devil. There was no third option. Luther's *simul iustus et peccator* principle had become in American revivalism wholly untenable. The Holiness movements marked out the hour of decision.

Phoebe Palmer maintained that total consecration to God and entire sanctification by God were two sides of the foundation of authentic Christianity. Human action and divine response constituted the heart of what it meant to be a

---

[93] Cited in Peters, *Christian Perfection and American Methodism*, pp. 137 and 162.

'Bible Christian'.[94] The Holiness emphases had been born out of the great age of revivals in American history. The chief protagonists in the 1840s were Finney and Mahan. By the 1850s Phoebe Palmer had emerged as a dominant voice. The charge of Holiness was a challenge to the church and to the world. The question, 'are you going on to perfection?' could realistically only be answered in the affirmative. To answer negatively or agnostically immediately brought the rejoinder, 'where are you going?' Without sanctification no one could escape damnation. 'Every Christian also admits that no one can be saved who does not aim at perfection.'[95] That experience was all-important. Hard-core Holiness preachers like Peter Cartwright were not above making that point painfully clear.

> Monday evening came; the Church was filled to overflowing; every seat was crowded, and many had to stand. After singing and prayer, Brother Mac took his seat in the pulpit. I then read my text: 'What shall it profit a man if he gain the whole world and lose his own soul?' After reading my text I paused. At that moment I saw General [Stonewall] Jackson walking up the aisle; he came to the middle post, and very gracefully leaned against it, and stood, as there were no vacant seats. Just then I felt someone pull my coat in the stand, and turning my head, my fastidious preacher, whispering a little loud, said, 'General Jackson has come in; General Jackson has come in.' I felt a flash of indignation run all over me like an electric shock, and facing about to my congregation, and purposely speaking out audibly, I said, 'Who is General Jackson? If he don't get his soul converted, God will damn him as quick as he would a Guinea negro!'[96]

Cartwright's inference was that God regarded all people as sinners needing a second work of grace. Worldly status had nothing to do with human depravity.

---

[94] Melvin E. Dieter, 'Primitivism in the American Holiness Tradition' *Wesleyan Theological Journal* 30 (No. 1, 1995), p. 83. In the preface to the second edition of her book *The Way of Holiness* in 1844 Palmer revealed that she had debated over calling the work *Bible Christianity*. See the remarks in Oden, ed., *Phoebe Palmer: Selected Writings*, pp. 165-6.

[95] Mahan, *Scripture Doctrine of Christian Perfection*, p. 45.

[96] This in the course of a sermon at the Tennessee Conference in Nashville in October 1818. In Peter Cartwright, *Autobiography of Peter Cartwright* (Nashville: Abingdon Press, 1984), p. 133. See also Katherine L. Dvorak, 'Peter Cartwright and Charisma' *Methodist History* 26 (No. 2, 1988), pp. 113-26.

The doctrine of holiness was propagated in a variety of ways: theological formulation, the passing of resolutions, preaching, publications, camp meetings, the enforcing of rules and regulations, fear, and the utilization of pure logic. Charles Finney's background in the legal profession served him well on numerous occasions when he argued the nature of his theological convictions. To his detractors who claimed that complete obedience was impossible Finney had this to say: 'To say that God requires me, on pain of death to do that which he knows I cannot do, is charging God with infinite tyranny. It is blasphemous.'[97]

Preaching undoubtedly spread the holiness emphases more effectively than any other medium. The American religious experience of the nineteenth century included the age of the preacher. Charles Finney, as previously noted, was among those pulpit giants whose pervasive preaching left an indelible mark upon American religious history. '. . . while heaven calls, and hell groans; while the spirit strives, and Christians pray, will you have the moral courage, the decision of character, the honesty, and manhood, to resolve on immediate submission to Jesus Christ?'[98] Here was the emphasis on the 'now' and the place of human response and decision. Some responded, others refused. Still others indignantly denounced the Holiness preachers as this unregenerate did in the 1860s: All Methodists ought to be hanged and then sent to hell. There was no point of having a hell if damned rascal Methodist preachers were not sent there.[99] To those who did not respond Finney castigated in biting terms. 'Go but a little further, cleave to your enmity but a little longer; and the knell of eternal death shall toll over your damned soul, and all the corners of despair will echo with your groans.'[100] The

---

[97] Finney, *Sermons on Gospel Themes*, pp. 335-6. See also the useful study by James E. Johnson, 'Charles G. Finney and a Theology of Revivalism' *Church History* 38 (No. 3, 1969), pp. 338-58.

[98] Charles G. Finney, *Sermons on Various Subjects*, p. 180.

[99] Cited in Morrow, *Northern Methodism and Reconstruction*, p. 237.

[100] Finney, *Sermons on Various Subjects*, p. 140.

options were clear: holiness or hell. Some remained undeterred and as the last chapter pointed out ruffians frequently sought to disrupt the meetings of the revivalists. Francis Asbury once quieted a gang of such individuals bent on disturbing a camp meeting by telling them that they ought to be duly cautious. While the Methodists were all seeking salvation, they were not yet entirely sanctified and might retaliate.[101]

Holiness preachers perceived that the general decline in religion which they supposed to have set into American Christianity following the age of the great awakenings could be attributed to a failure to fully promote and enforce the doctrine and implications of sanctification. One preacher suggested that his inquiries into this matter revealed that much had been made of sin, redemption through Christ, repentance and justification by faith, but little on the matter of sanctification. Since the doctrine was not being promoted from the pulpit, ordinary Christians had left off their pursuit of heart religion. Once this was perceived, '[I] immediately set about a reform in myself and began to preach and enforce the doctrine of holiness by shewing [sic] the state I found the people to be in and the need of perfecting holiness in the fear of God.'[102]

The Holiness movements took advantage of the culture of religious print and began to spread their message of entire sanctification and perfectionism via the forms of media from the 1830s onward. Timothy Merritt's *Guide to Christian Perfection* was but the beginning of a legion of Holiness periodicals. All of the influential Holiness leaders from the Palmers to Finney to the independent movements in the last quarter of the century employed effectively the medium of

---

[101] Cited in Frederick A. Norwood, *The Story of American Methodism* (New York and Nashville: Abingdon Press, 1974), p. 159.

[102] 'The Journal of Benjamin Lakin', 15 March 1814, in William Warren Sweet, ed., *Religion on the American Frontier, 1783-1840*, volume 4 (New York: Cooper Square Publishers, Inc., 1964), p. 249.

print.[103] John Humphrey Noyes declared in 1837 that his paper *The Witness* was 'one of the most efficient means of commending to the world that heavenly teacher . . . .'[104]

If the Methodist circuit riders turned out to be an integral link in the expanding chain of the holiness doctrine so too another enduring symbol of nineteenth-century American religion became transformed by the waves of holiness which began sweeping the nation by mid-century. The Holiness camp meeting originated with John A. Wood, a Methodist pastor.[105] The impetus for Holiness camp meetings can reasonably be attributed to the conviction that God had so ordained it. In April 1867 William B. Osborn, a Methodist elder in New Jersey, said to John S. Inskip, a leading New York Methodist pastor: 'I feel that God would have us hold a holiness camp-meeting!' The two prayed and together became convinced that it was indeed God's will.[106] In that same year a decision was made to continue the holiness camp meeting tradition and a call went out to found the 'National Camp Meeting Association for the Promotion of Holiness'. This foundation published its two objectives: 'to glorify God in building up the church in holiness and saving sinners.' Yet again, it was announced that the idea had come by divine inspiration. Its usefulness for the Holiness movements would last more than three decades.[107] These Holiness camp meetings were a reflection of the ethos

---

[103] For an overview of the beginning of Holiness printing see Charles E. Jones, *Perfectionist Persuasion: The Holiness Movement and American Methodism, 1867-1936* (Metuchen N.J.: The Scarecrow Press, Inc., 1974), pp. 2-3.

[104] Noyes, ed., *Religious Experience of John Humphrey Noyes*, pp. 376-8.

[105] Kenneth O. Brown, *Holy Ground: A Study of the American Camp Meeting* (New York and London: Garland Publishing Inc., 1992), p. 33.

[106] William McDonald and John E. Searles, *The Life of Rev. John S. Inskip, President of the National Association for the Promotion of Holiness* (Boston: McDonald & Gill, 1885), p. 187.

[107] On this development see Dieter, *The Holiness Revival of the Nineteenth Century*, pp. 104-7 with references to the primary sources.

of the perfectionist movement in general. They were world-negating conclaves designed to provide an escape from the wider world, a retreat into the presence of God, an opportunity for a second work of grace, a context for experiencing entire sanctification, a possibility for perfection. Invitations were often couched in such terminology. '[Come] away to the tented grove! Away from the busy scenes, from the din and conflict of earthly strife! Away to the place of holy convocation . . . .'[108]

Holiness camp meetings ranged the full spectrum from high emotionalism, loud singing, the waving of handkerchiefs, victory marches, to celebrations of holy communion in the middle of the night. Eccentrics, such as those mentioned in the previous chapter also frequented these Holiness convocations. It could be a time of 'glorious confusion'.[109] Some of the larger meetings were events of note. Such was the convocation near Manheim, Pennsylvania in the summer of 1868. More than 300 ministers and 25,000 people crowded onto the camp grounds for the services on Sunday. It was an ecumenical affair. There were Presbyterians, Baptists, Dutch Reformed, Methodists, Quakers and Congregationalists in attendance. On Monday evening following the sermon by John Thompson of Philadelphia over 2000 people were led in prayer by G.W. Woodruff.

> . . . all at once, as sudden as if a flash of lightning from the heavens had fallen upon the people, one simultaneous burst of agony, and then of glory, was heard in all parts of the congregation; and for nearly an hour, the scene beggared all description . . . . Those seated far back in the audience declared that the sensation was as if a strong wind had moved from the stand over the congregation. Several intelligent people, in different parts of the congregation, spoke of the same phenomenon . . . . Sinners stood awe-stricken, and others fled affrighted from the congregation . . . . [many believed they were] face to face with God.'[110]

---

[108] Cited in Dieter, *Ibid.*, p. 112.

[109] The preceding paragraph is based upon the data in Dieter, *Ibid.*, pp. 114-15.

[110] McDonald and Searles, *The Life of Rev. John S. Inskip, President of the National Association for the Promotion of Holiness*, pp. 201-2.

Such events harkened back to the early revivals at Cane Ridge and elsewhere. In other gatherings, it was reported that 'multitudes were sanctified wholly . . . ' all at once.[111] Other events at camp meetings were perceived as the reason why entire denominations went over to the Holiness cause. Reports poured in from around the country declaring that salvation and sanctification prevailed. Holiness seemed to be the main theme. Some reports claimed that ministers attending camp meetings went back to their respective congregations filled with the new power of sanctification. Entire church bodies were reputed to be tarrying at altars around the country seeking the blessing of perfection in a second work of grace.[112] There is some justification for the conclusion that camp meetings in postbellum America passed nearly entirely into the Holiness tradition and became given up to perfectionist emphases.[113]

Despite undeniable, even startling, success, the question about the necessity of a second work of grace continued to dog the Holiness movements. Why was there a need for this second work of grace? What was wrong or deficient with the first work? Samuel Franklin of the Illinois Annual Conference wrote 'A Critical Review of Wesleyan Perfection' in 1866 and charged that sanctification achieved nothing more than what had already been accomplished in the process of regeneration. Predictably the book was denounced by Phoebe Palmer and others as dangerous and unprofitable.[114] But the query, 'why did the first work of grace require a second work of grace?' remained even in the minds of the faithful. 'My mind is much conf[u]sed, and under sore temptation to disbelieve the Doctrine of

---

[111] Such were the reports from the Ocean Grove camp meetings of 1872 and 1878. See Peters, *Christian Perfection and American Methodism*, p. 178.

[112] See as representative a report to the *Philadelphia Home Journal*. Quoted in McDonald and Searles, *The Life of Rev. John S. Inskip*, pp. 210-11.

[113] Dieter, *The Holiness Revival of the Nineteenth Century*, p. 145 n. 60.

[114] Cited in Peters, *Christian Perfection and American Methodism*, p. 150.

Christian perfection.'[115] Benjamin Lakin was not alone with his doubts. If a second work was essential, could there not also be a third necessary work? Still, the majority of the Holiness adherents believed steadfastly in the doctrine of holiness or hell. Their radical cause lacked only a visible sign for the world to see. They had been justified and sanctified. They had experienced redemption and perfection. But could the world see that they were in fact those notable people referred to by the Apostle Peter: a chosen generation, a royal priesthood, a holy nation, a peculiar people?[116] With no *via media* between glory and perdition, the Holiness movements began to demonstrate their perfection in ways which the children of darkness could not mistake.

A. War on Worldliness

> The Dunkard preacher, with his long hair parted in the middle, full beard except the shaved upper lip, peculiarly cut coat, flap trousers, and broad-brimmed hat, all as a part of his religion, and his love for tobacco, was told to clean up and get rid of the 'mark of the beast.'[117]

♠ ♠

---

[115] 'The Journal of Benjamin Lakin', 1 October 1794, in Sweet, ed., *Religion on the American Frontier*, volume 4, p. 211. Doubts such as these persisted and may be found among the sources of the Holiness movements throughout the nineteenth century.

[116] I Peter 2:9.

[117] Daniel Warner and his colleagues when confronting a sectarian at Bucyrus, Ohio around 1881. Enoch E. Byrum, 'Customs and Traditions' *Gospel Trumpet* (1 July 1915), p. 3. During the summer heat of 1908, President James M. Gray of Moody Bible Institute in Chicago sent a letter to the faculty on 29 July expressing his dissatisfaction at such 'unusual' conduct as sitting in offices without wearing coats and vests. According to Gray, such behavior might have detrimental effects upon students who needed the example of conventionality. Gray file, Moody Bible Institute archives. Cited in George M. Marsden, *Fundamentalism and American Culture* (New York and Oxford: Oxford University Press, 1980), p. 131.

Charles Finney may have been speaking in general about revivalism when he said, '[t]he object of our measures is to gain attention.'[118] It cannot be denied that the measures taken by the Holiness movements to enforce a sanctified life gained much attention, generated conflict within the ranks and figured prominently in the 'holiness or hell' attitude. Historically, a clear separation between holy and profane was negotiated within the Holiness ranks. Members of many Holiness groups were forbidden to drink, dance, gamble, play cards, smoke, chew tobacco, or attend places of worldly entertainment. Such places of amusement were identified as plays, movies, fairs, ball games and pool halls. Men and women frequenting beaches and swimming together was likewise actively discouraged. Women were enjoined to cease using makeup, wearing either short skirts or short sleeves and cutting their hair. The wearing of ornamental jewelry was likewise frowned upon. The use of profanity was forbidden and a strict observance of the Lord's day emphasised.[119] Throughout the course of the nineteenth century practically all preachers of the holiness cause condemned worldliness in many of the aforementioned forms, stressing proper dress and behavior for their adherents.[120] Again, Wesley may be seen as a precursory proponent of such emphases and measures.[121]

Such standards of holiness were not advanced in the sense of being

---

[118] Finney, *Lectures on Revivals of Religion*, p. 173.

[119] Benton Johnson, 'Do Holiness Sects Socialize in Dominant Values?' *Social Forces* 39 (No. 4, 1961), p. 313.

[120] Smith, *Called Unto Holiness*, pp. 37-8.

[121] See for example his sermon 'On Dress', in *The Works of John Wesley*, volume 7, pp. 15-26. 'Let your dress be *cheap* as well as plain; otherwise you do but trifle with God, and me, and your own souls. I pray, let there be no costly silks among you . . . . [l]et there be no Quaker-linen . . . no Brussels lace, no elephantine hats or bonnets,–those scandals of female modesty. Be all of a piece, dressed from head to foot as persons *professing godliness* . . . .' *Ibid.*, p. 24. Elsewhere, in his *A Plain Account of Christian Perfection*, Wesley enjoined his followers to '[b]e exemplary in all things; particularly in outward things, (as in dress,) . . . .' *Ibid.*, volume 11, p. 435.

Holiness as Challenge to Religious Culture 149

optional. Indeed, they were promoted as obligatory if one were to seriously pursue the path of holiness. Dressing and behaving in a certain, prescribed manner was attached to the doctrine of entire sanctification and the idea of perfection outside the boundaries of holiness standards was considered virtually impossible. For those who had fled from old world religious persecution seeking freedom in the new world, or those leaving main stream Christianity in search of something different, the need for boundaries was paramount. Dissent is rarely permitted amongst dissenters. Hence, the strict standards of conformity within the Holiness traditions. Such conformity constituted a broadening and a constricting of religious democracy. 'The only way to *retain* the grace of sanctification is by *keeping* all upon the altar.'[122] The advocates of the doctrine of holiness drew very fine lines around the idea of 'keeping all upon the altar.' Thus, Methodist churches attempted to legislate against dancing, theatres, playing cards and horse-racing.[123] According to a southern Methodist, '[l]et the sexes promiscuously indulge in this fascinating art [dancing] and see at once the tendency to dissipation and lasciviousness.'[124] The Baptist Church in Kentucky in October 1807 heard a complaint against 'Bro. Daniel Brown for frolicking and dancing' and referred it to their November meeting whereupon Brown was excluded from the communion because of his said 'frolicking and dancing.'[125] As for the theatre, it was regarded as 'one of the antechambers of hell.'[126] Phoebe Palmer's speculation included the conclusion that

---

[122] Phoebe Palmer, *Present to My Christian Friend on Entire Devotion to God*, in Oden, ed., *Phoebe Palmer: Selected Writings*, p. 200.

[123] Hunter Dickenson Farish, *The Circuit Rider Dismounts: A Social History of Southern Methodism 1865-1900* (New York: Da Carpo Press, 1969), p. 342.

[124] Henry M. Mood in the *Southern Christian Advocate* (18 November 1874). Quoted in Simkins and Woody, *South Carolina During Reconstruction*, p. 405.

[125] See the minutes of these meetings in Sweet, ed., *Religion on the American Frontier*, volume 1, pp. 338-9.

[126] *New Orleans Christian Advocate* (1 February 1868).

Abraham Lincoln was shot because he went to the theatre,[127] thus removing himself temporarily from the protection of divine grace which could on no account abide the sinfulness of the playhouse. On 25 August 1866 the New Orleans *Christian Advocate* reported this plea from a dying man: 'Keep your sons from cards; over them I've murdered time and lost heaven.'[128] Confessions such as this provided ammunition for the continuously smoking cannons of the holiness assault upon worldliness. Lest it be doubted that such prohibitions and attitudes were not linked to matters of salvation and sanctification it is instructive to note that frequently preachers clearly associated their invectives against worldliness with the holiness or hell motif. At the Randolph Grove, Illinois camp meeting in 1831, the preacher James Lotta put it this way in his condemnation of horse-racing: 'There is a class of people who can't go to hell fast enough on foot, so they set on their poor, mean ponies and go to the horse race.'[129] Preaching at the Methodist Conference in Nashville in 1818 James Axley pulled no punches in his declaration that those failing to be conformed to the Holiness patterns of life could in no wise enter heaven.

> Brother Axley rose, sung, prayed, took his text: 'Be not conformed to this world, but be ye transformed by the renewing of your minds;' and if the Lord ever helped mortal man to preach, he surely helped Brother Axley. First he poured the thunders of Sinai against the Egyptians, or slave oppressors; next he showed that no moderate dram-drinker could enter heaven; and then the grape-shot of truth rolled from his mouth against

---

[127] See the comment in McFadden, 'The Ironies of Pentecost: Phoebe Palmer, World Evangelism, and Female Networks', p. 68.

[128] *New Orleans Christian Advocate* (25 August 1866).

[129] Quoted in Johnson, *The Frontier Camp Meeting*, p. 130. 'My greatest concern for my children is that they may be *saved*. Oh how I feel for those in Houston! Do they attend the M.E. Church at all? Have they entirely forgotten their gray headed father's last admonition? Have they turned away from the Lord's house to go to Balls, and parties of pleasure, the feasts of Satan? Will they wade through the prayers and admonitions and tears of their father and mother down to hell? Oh God! have mercy upon them, and undeceive them . . . .' Letter of Orceneth Fisher to his son Asbury, 3 October 1856. In Sweet, ed., *Religion on the American Frontier*, volume 4, pp. 480-2.

rings, ruffles, and all kind of ornamental dress. Dr. Bascom was sitting right before him. He had a gold watch-chain and key, and two very large gold seals. The Rev. H.B. was so excited that unconsciously he took up one of the seals, and he began to play with the other seal with his right hand. Axley saw it, stopped suddenly, and very sternly said to him, 'Put up that chain, and quit playing with those seals, and hear the word of the Lord.'[130]

Worldly attachments were clear indications that one was not properly connected spiritually. The spiritually intuitive could determine from observation whether or not a person was 'right with God.' Francis Asbury often remonstrated with preachers by saying, 'you read books, but I read men.'[131] While in England Phoebe Palmer wrote to Queen Victoria whose soul obviously was in danger. 'Last week I wrote to Queen Victoria . . . . As a Queen, she doubtless merits their admiration. But as an experimental Christian, she cannot be regarded, so long as she patronizes the theatre, and the horse race, etc.'[132] There were standards carefully maintained and patrolled with ever-increasingly vigilance. Failure to observe these many and varied conventions provided inviolable proof that entire sanctification had not yet occurred in the war against worldliness.

The *Augusta News* in Georgia hyperbolically reported in 1883 that the entire city was discussing the question advanced in a sermon by Warren Candler, 'is it possible for one to live without sin?' Candler's holiness sermons were filled with vitriolic denunciations of the sins of drinking, dancing, theatres, cards and even wine on family tables.[133] The enforcement of holiness standards was not isolated. In many cases systematic examinations of adherents were carried out. For

---

[130] Recorded by Peter Cartwright who was present in his *Autobiography of Peter Cartwright*, p. 132.

[131] This according to the report of Peter Cartwright. *Autobiography of Peter Cartwright*, p. 110.

[132] This in a letter to Bishop and Mrs. Hamline, dated 20 August 1860 in Oden, ed., *Phoebe Palmer: Selected Writings*, p. 268.

[133] On this see Vinson Synan, *The Holiness-Pentecostal Movement in the United States*, pp. 43-4.

example, in Madison County, New York, an annual Methodist conference was held at Smithfield on 25 May 1811. Among the minutes preserved in the manuscript 'Journal of Pompey Circuit', are these details. 'The Members of this Conference were particularly examined one by one in each of the following Christian ordinances and Practice . . . baptism . . . Lord's supper. . . Family devotion and Instruction . . . drinking . . . Wearing of Gold and orniminatal [sic] apparal [sic] . . . .'[134] The Presbyterian Synod of Kentucky convening in October 1808 at Lexington made this recommendation: ' . . . that every friend of Zion Should Confess with Sorrow the sins of the age in Neglecting the ordinace [sic] of God's House and the religious education of Youth, in increasing fondness for intemperance, balls, horse-Races and theatrical Amusements and therefore we recommend that Christians implore God for Christs Sake to arrest the calamities with which we are threatened . . . .'[135]

This concern with the disparity between the words of the faith and the actions of the faithful remained a perennial issue for Holiness advocates. Even non-Holiness churchmen expressed their concern. 'The American Sabbath is in danger of being crucified between two thieves,—Irish whiskey and German beer.'[136] At times the gulf separating the two was more than exaggeration on the part of those seeking to negate worldliness. The records of the Old Wateree Conference in South Carolina provide evidence to support claims of a serious decline in morals and church polity.

> Church people 'running for the bottle, getting drunk and turning up jack. A free fight at Carter's Meeting House on the expulsion of a member and the drunkard cursing in the religious assembly at Lancaster Village' . . . .

---

[134] The conference records have been edited and published in Sweet, *Religion on the American Frontier*, volume 4, p. 565.

[135] Minutes of the Synod edited and published in Sweet, *Religion on the American Frontier*, volume 2, p. 373.

[136] Philip Schaff, quoted in Graham, *Cosmos in the Chaos: Philip Schaff's Interpretation of Nineteenth-Century American Religion*, p. 155.

Whisky and peach brandy so abounding that preaching was postponed until the drunkards had gone home.[137]

According to Charles E. Jones, while perfectionist theology did not change, new methods aimed at determining holiness emerged in the preoccupation with combating worldliness. Ultimately certain social requirements became not only standards of holiness but functioned as admission requirements to Holiness groups. In their identification of inner purity with certain types of dress and behavior, Holiness preachers confused the two. Convinced that extravagant dress on the outside indicated pride on the inside, many condemned ruffles, feathers, jewelry (including wedding rings), and corsets.'[138] This confusion helps to explain the emphasis upon externals. If John Wesley was perceived as the originator of the doctrine of Christian perfection, there were those among the Holiness movements who likewise appealed to Wesley for the validity of their standards of holiness. Benjamin Roberts, founder of the Free Methodists, pointed out that Wesley had established rules for admission to meetings. No person was to be granted entrance '. . . till they have left off superfluous ornaments. . . . Allow no exempt case, not even of a married woman. . . Give no ticket to any that wear calashes, high-heads, or enormous bonnets.' Roberts went on to ask whether the Methodists then were simply fanatics or were now backslidden? 'Times may change but God does not change.'[139] The rise of higher criticism and Darwinian science was seen as a threat to the biblical assumptions of Holiness advocates and the perceived worldliness within popular Christianity were regarded as the double-edged sword of the enemy.

---

[137] See the report in the *Southern Christian Advocate* (25 July 1876). Quoted in Simkins and Woody, *South Carolina During Reconstruction*, pp. 402-3.

[138] Jones, *Perfectionist Persuasion*. p. 85. There were instances wherein individuals were expelled from churches after refusing to set aside their wedding rings. See for example a case in Warren County, North Carolina in 1810 in Sweet, ed., *Religion on the American Frontier*, volume 4, pp. 189-91.

[139] Cited in Dieter, *The Holiness Revival of the Nineteenth Century*, p. 151. Wesley's instructions may be found in *The Works of John Wesley*, volume 8, p. 307.

A firm discipline against both attacks seemed crucial for the survival of authentic Christianity. Conviction and fear led to extreme measures and in some cases total fanaticism. There were some who held that they should not sleep on beds, but rather on the ground and should eat crackers out of the dirt or go without food entirely. Others ostensibly refused to eat with, or have any association with, anyone not professing sanctification.[140]

Much was made of the New Testament text, '[s]trive for . . . holiness without which no one will see the Lord.'[141] That holiness encompassed the doctrine of a second work of grace which resulted in entire sanctification and yielded up perfection in the lives of Christians. As we have seen, however, there were certain identifying characteristics of those who were holy, or of those striving for perfection. Consistent violation of the prescribed standards of holiness resulted in exclusion from the church which then impaired or ended one's chances for perfection. The Baptist Church in Kentucky expelled members for 'telling lies', adultery, drinking, horse racing, stealing, swearing, failure to regularly attend church, gambling, disobedience and a variety of other offenses and infractions.[142] When it came to holiness little distinction was made between the 'crime of fornication' committed by Lucy Phillips and the 'complaint' against James Robertson for horse racing.[143] The practical and social consequences were different to be sure, but both were serious hindrances to Christian perfection and the

---

[140] This type of fanaticism was reported in the *Good Way*, one of the leading venues of the Holiness movement in Missouri in 1881. Summarized in Dieter, *The Holiness Revival of the Nineteenth Century*, p. 214.

[141] Hebrews 12:14 Revised Standard Version

[142] Records of the Forks of Elkhorn Baptist Church, Kentucky, 1804-6 in Sweet, ed., *Religion on the American Frontier*, volume 1, pp. 311-24.

[143] Phillips, see the extracts from the session-book of the First Presbyterian Church in Phelps, New York, 7 October 1821 in Sweet, ed., *Religion on the American Frontier*, volume 2, p. 522; Robertson, see the Records of the Forks of Elkhorn Baptist Church, Kentucky, August 1805 in *Ibid.*, volume 1, p. 316.

offenders were summarily excommunicated. The evidence yielded up by various church records from several strands of the Holiness movements reveal that ecclesiastical discipline was applied equally and regularly to both clergy and laity.

The doctrine of justification by faith alone and the idea of a second work of grace were strange and uncomfortable bed fellows in nineteenth-century America. The Protestant principle *sola fide* and the radical conviction 'holiness or hell' produced several serious theological confrontations. The concept of regeneration proposed by Charles Finney and the doctrine of sanctification advanced by Phoebe Palmer in the end seem based more on human work than divine grace.[144] Holiness could not avoid the necessity of good works if Christian perfection was to prevail. Good and bad depended to large measure on the acts and actions of humans. When a Methodist preacher's horse died, the man wondered what he had done which caused God to allow the beast to die.[145] Achievement or failure in the matter of perfection became linked to behavior. Entire sanctification may have issued forth from divine grace, but perfection was neither achieved nor retained without human responses, obedience and work. Finney was adamant that '. . . entire humility is implied in entire sanctification.'[146] This did not bridge the gulf between the rhetoric and the reality in some circles. Wesley had cautioned against the harsh promotion of perfection but in their zeal to reform the church, oppose worldliness and witness the perfecting of the saints, Holiness preachers frequently ignored Wesley's injunction and the gentle, still small voice he

---

[144] See Victor D. Reasoner, 'The American Holiness Movement's Paradigm Shift Concerning Pentecost' *Wesleyan Theological Journal* 31 (No. 2, 1996), pp. 132-46, especially pp. 136-7.

[145] '. . . this Morning I was informed that My horse was Drowned When I heared [sic] it I felt unmoved; But was soon led to Reflect thus why Lord has this hapened [sic] what have I Don[e]. . . .' The Journal of Bishop Richard Whatcoat in Sweet, ed., *Religion on the American Frontier*, volume 4, p. 116.

[146] *Lectures on Systematic Theology*, p. 458.

suggested was drowned out in the storm of holiness or hell.[147] This situation reflects both political and popular uses of tradition and theology.

The gospel message of the Holiness movements became in due course a negative social gospel. Rather than attempting to reform society, perfectionists increasingly began to reject the world. Their ultimate concerns became less and less focussed on the problems of poverty, inequality and inequity and more centered on a new collection of standards of holiness. These standards of holiness constituted a hierarchy of values and the greatest social sins were violations of these values and standards: lipstick and liquor, cigarettes and cards, dancing, ball games and the theatre.[148] The Holiness movements had their own 'rhythms of piety' to ensure they would be entirely sanctified.[149] These rhythms not only challenged religious culture but precipitated dissent, conflict and change.

B. Divisions of Perfection

> But many holiness people—so-called—are fallen, and are impregnated with divers forms of fanaticism, crankism, 'damnable heresies', come-out-ism, and strong hydra-headed doctrines of devils. They are split up into little sects, factions and fads, each claiming to be the only true body of Christ; and while they excommunicate all others from the kingdom of God, they themselves manifest the most intolerant bigotry.[150]

---

[147] On Wesley's injunction see Dieter, *The Holiness Revival of the Nineteenth Century*, p. 32.

[148] See the excellent delineation in Synan, *The Holiness-Pentecostal Movement in the United States*, p. 58.

[149] The term is from Leigh Eric Schmidt, *Holy Fairs: Scottish Communities and American Revivals in the Early Modern Period* (Princeton: Princeton University Press, 1989), pp. 153-8.

[150] Rev. W. W. Hooper in a letter to the *Pentecostal Herald*, cited in Farish, *The Circuit Rider Dismounts*, p. 73 n. 3.

While it may be true that the doctrine of holiness played little or no rôle in Methodist divisions up until the 1860s, the same cannot be maintained for the remainder of the nineteenth century.[151] The Holiness movements soon became increasingly prone to divisiveness, disorganization and division. Growing strife within the varieties of the Holiness revivals gave the upper hand of development to a polarizing, rather than a unifying tendency. This can be explained in part by reference to the leadership of the movements for perfection. Typically, Holiness leaders were self-appointed individuals possessing independent minds, personal ideas and convictions which they then made normative for their particular group of followers.[152] Here again this reality underscores the paradox of religious democracy within the nineteenth-century American religious experience. The collision of varying emphases and the divergence of paths to holiness led to recriminations, animosity, charges of heresy, backsliding or worse. Often such divisiveness came as a result of the conviction that certain sectors of the movement had become weak on the message and were sacrificing the integrity of the Holiness gospel. Wars of holiness religion broke out as one group sought to outstrip the other in a demonstration of perfection. The unity of revival and the oneness of sanctification gave way to conflict and division. The last quarter of the nineteenth century was marked by a fracturing of the Holiness cause into a multiplicity of groups. The period between 1885 and 1905 was peculiarly typical of this shattering.[153]

There were at least two schools of thought within the Holiness movements

---

[151] Jones, *Perfectionist Persuasion*, p. 8.

[152] Hatch, *The Democratization of American Christianity*, p. 214.

[153] Dunlap, 'Tuesday Meetings, Camp Meetings, and Cabinet Meetings: A Perspective on the Holiness Movement in the Methodist Church in the United States in the Nineteenth Century', p. 100.

which led to confrontation and irreconcilable conflict. The first, was that the traditions of the Wesleyan-Methodist heritage ought to be retained in their revivalist context. Peter Cartwright actively contended for this. He steadfastly believed that camp meetings, prayer meetings and love feasts should remain as essential characteristics of sanctified religion. He deplored any and all deviation from them.[154] The circuit riding preachers were simultaneously agents and victims of the institutionalizing of Methodism. By gaining greater control over congregations they became further removed from the earlier religious practices and ethos Cartwright advocated.[155] The other school of thought was reactionary in its stance to promote holiness through ever-increasing strict standards. Admittedly, there had been decline in certain aspects of the Holiness movements. Camp meetings as a religious institution began to vanish. Revivalism took on new and different forms. There persisted the danger of assimilation; holiness being integrated into mainstream Christianity, losing its distinctives and shedding its radical character. In other words, urges to make Holiness respectable, even palatable to traditional Christianity, persisted. Encroaching worldliness terrified the proponents of radical holiness. This report in the New York *Christian Advocate* in the summer of 1872 was symptomatic both of the decline of Holiness and representative of how some proponents of perfection saw their fellow Christians. The report suggested that people were coming to camp meetings partly for health and partly for religious reasons. They '. . . mix Christianity and sea-bathing a little too confusedly.'[156] This was a conundrum. For the perfectionist, swimming and sanctification had no relation. Camp meetings were for the perfecting of holiness

---

[154] See the *Autobiography of Peter Cartwright, passim* and Richard A. Chrisman, 'Peter Cartwright as a Presiding Elder' *Methodist History* 27 (No. 3, 1989), p. 157.

[155] Frank E. Johnson, '"Inspired by Grace": Methodist Itinerants in the early Midwest' *Methodist History* 35 (No. 2, 1997), p. 94.

[156] The report is quoted in Charles H. Lippy, 'The Camp Meeting in Transition: The Character and Legacy of the late Nineteenth Century' *Methodist History* 34 (No. 1, 1995), p. 3.

in the fear of God. While swimming in itself was an entirely neutral activity, it clearly had no place in the context of a Holiness meeting. The decline of holiness standards in certain quarters caused much dismay. '... [A]mong early Methodists .... [p]arents did not allow their children to go to balls or plays; they did not send them to dancing-schools .... If the Methodists had dressed in the same "superfluity of naughtiness" then as they do now, there were very few even out of the Church that would have any confidence in their religion. But O, how have things changed for the worse in this educational age of the world!'[157]

'Holiness or hell' all but disappeared in some streams of Holiness thought. In some sectors of Methodism the doctrine of sanctification was no longer considered among the essential teachings of the church.[158] In others, it became a perpetual reminder that without holiness no one would see God. The Holiness movements had reached their zenith in their present form. If revivalism had transformed the evolving definition of American Christianity in the first half of the century, then the doctrine of entire sanctification had defined another generation of American religious history. From Asbury to Finney there had been a narrowing of the definition of Christianity. From Palmer to the Fundamentalists and Pentecostals there was a further closing of the ranks. Christian perfection was essential before anyone could possibly live a victorious Christian life. The principles of religious democracy had allowed for the rise and proliferation of revivalism and its religious culture. An extension of those same principles had produced the Holiness movements. But there remained those unsatisfied.

---

[157] *Autobiography of Peter Cartwright*, p. 61.

[158] In his 'History of the Methodist Episcopal Church', Nathan Bangs listed twenty-four 'cardinal doctrines' but did not mention sanctification in his survey. In John Winebrenner, *History of all the Religious Denominations in the United States: containing authentic accounts of the rise and progress, faith and practice, localities and statistics, of the different persuasions: written expressly for the work, by fifty-three eminent authors, belonging to the respective denominations* (Harrisburg, PA: John Winebrenner, 1854), pp. 369-71. This contrasts sharply with the aforementioned note that Bangs did consider sanctification essential to salvation.

Ecclesiastical reformation now came to be viewed as somehow hindered by the very structures it sought to renew and reform. In the face of this conviction there was no other alternative but to come out from tradition, abandon the organization of Constantinian Christendom altogether, and return to the perceived simplicity of primitive Christianity. The time had come for 'heart religion' to separate from 'head religion'.

CHAPTER 3

John Winebrenner and the 'Come-Out' Option

The leaders in the holiness movement are all, or nearly so, zealous advocates of come-outism. For the last ten years in some of these states [Illinois, Iowa, Missouri, Nebraska, Kansas, California] the Holiness Associations have been a standing menace to the spirit of the Gospel of Jesus Christ. As associations they have been, and are to-day, religious anarchists.[1]

♠ ♠

Convinced of the unscriptural nature of denominationalism, numerous leaders in the Holiness movements tradition elected to separate from the churches they were in, in order to practice true and complete holiness. They became known as the 'come-outers.' Among the early prominent come-out leaders were Solomon B. Shaw, John P. Brooks, Hardin Wallace and Daniel S. Warner. There is a measure of validity in the observation that after some consideration with the teaching and practice, radical holiness and its expressions were relinquished quietly by several denominations. The come-outers found this objectionable and unconscionable. If a weariness of controversy and a striving after perfection eventually pervaded the ranks of Methodism by the 1880s, the cause was adopted and championed by the come-out movement. Rather than contending for the

---

[1] T.J. Wheat, presiding Methodist elder cited in Peters, *Christian Perfection and American Methodism*, p. 140.

holiness faith and practice within organized religion the more radical Holiness spokesmen withdrew. To loyal churchmen this was a most disturbing development.[2] Philip Schaff identified sectarianism among the most dangerous pitfalls in American religion.[3] This tendency constituted the most serious dimension of the shattering of the unity of Holiness. Notwithstanding the eagerness to withdraw from organized religion, it is instructive to note that 'sometimes come-outism was countered by "push-outism"'.[4] In other words, the increased radicalism and refusal to be in submission to ecclesiastical authority of any kind, forced some churches to expel ministers when they proved incorrigible. Coming out and being pushed out were two sides of a common issue. For the come-outer, being pushed out was something to glory in. It demonstrated the righteousness of their cause and witnessed to the path of life.

> When we are turned out of the synagogue and all the forces of hell are turned loose on us, we may rest assuredly [sic] our preaching is pleasing to God and that we are stirring the devil and his gang. When we preach true Holiness, the devil will howl and groan. I had rather enjoy the Holiness of God than to burn in hell forever.[5]

For the come-outers the time had come to define the true church of God, to enact an even greater reformation of Christianity than had been accomplished either in the sixteenth century or in the age of revivals in the early nineteenth century. Among the distinguishing features of the come-out movement was the conviction that all church denominations had been founded, and continued to exist, in gross error. There was only one true community of the body of Jesus Christ and that was

---

[2] Synan, *The Holiness-Pentecostal Movement in the United States*, p. 46.

[3] Quoted in Graham, *Cosmos in the Chaos: Philip Schaff's Interpretation of Nineteenth-Century American Religion*, p. 76. See Graham's treatment of 'Religious Freedom and the Threat of Sectarianism', in *Ibid.*, pp. 1-43.

[4] Frederick A. Norwood, *The Story of American Methodism* (New York and Nashville: Abingdon Press, 1974), p. 298.

[5] 'Letters from the Folk', *The Pentecostal Advocate* (14 May 1908). Cited in Jones, *Perfectionist Persuasion*, p. 90.

the single 'Church of God'.

I. Origins of the Church of God

> Like a mighty army moves the Church of God;
> Brothers, we are treading where the saints have trod;
> We are not divided; all one body we,
> One in hope and doctrine, one in charity.[6]

♣ ♣

Well before the age of the come-outers and the profusion of groups called the 'Church of God' was a man and a chapter of American religious history which would exert no mean influence over the career of Daniel Warner, one of the premier figures in American come-out religious history. That man was John Winebrenner (1797-1860).

Winebrenner cannot be detached from his historical context. He lived through the mighty religious upheavals of the first half of the nineteenth century. His religious experience was moulded by the democratizing principles which took hold within the structures of American Christianity. His religious thinking was shaped in the fiery furnace of reform and renewal. Early nineteenth-century America witnessed great fervor in the attempt to regain original Christianity. Biblicism, the contravening of traditional authority, volunteerism, revivals, missionary efforts and ecumenism must be numbered among the salient features of the American religious experience. Winebrenner inherited those emphases. As a parish minister, in the course of the 1820s, Winebrenner fell into conflict with his denomination; the German Reformed Church. Winebrenner's departure from that communion was not precipitated by any sudden or dramatic event. It was, rather,

---

[6] Sabine Baring-Gould, 'Onward Christian Soldiers' in *Inspiring Hymns*, no. 177.

a process which took several years to come to fruition.[7] Chief among the problems Winebrenner initially encountered within his denomination was their reluctance to endorse his revivalist tendencies. Winebrenner had no qualms about preaching in other churches not belonging to the German Reformed Church. This did not pass unnoticed. Moreover, he had also invited non German Reformed preachers to fill his pulpit. This had proven shocking to some. Beyond this there was an increasing number of complaints about elements of revivalism in worship services presided over by Winebrenner. This was explicated in terms of noise and confusion. His prayer meetings and 'experience meetings' were extraordinarily lengthy, sometimes lasting until four in the morning. According to Winebrenner, 'this is the way to fan the chaff from the wheat.' His denomination did not agree. These meetings, then, were held in opposition to the vestry of the church.[8] Early on Winebrenner maintained contacts with both the Methodists and the Brethren,

---

[7] J. Harvey Gossard, 'John Winebrenner: Founder, Reformer, and Businessman', in *Pennsylvania Religious Leaders*, eds., John M. Coleman, John B. Frantz and Robert G. Crist [Pennsylvania History Studies, No. 16] (University Park, PA: The Pennsylvania Historical Association, 1986), p. 87. See also Richard Kern, *John Winebrenner: Nineteenth Century Reformer* (Harrisburg, PA: Central Publishing House, 1974), pp. 32-3 and C.H. Forney, *History of the Churches of God in the United States of North America* (Harrisburg, Pa: Publishing House of the Churches of God, 1914), pp. 3-141. Kern remains the definitive study of Winebrenner.

[8] See Gossard, *Ibid.*, p. 88 and Richard Kern, *John Winebrenner: Nineteenth Century Reformer*, p. 5. The German Reformed Church hierarchy had problems with Winebrenner holding camp meetings. Kern, *Ibid.*, p. 33. In October 1822 the synod heard ten complaints against Winebrenner: failing to consult the vestry in church affairs, encouraging church members to attend other congregations if they were not receiving benefit from the German Reformed Church, holding prayer meetings, anxious meetings which involved 'groanings' and speaking out 'Amen Amen', calling people out publicly for healing, holding lengthy meetings, openly condemning people, forging ties with other congregations outside the German Reformed Church, inciting dissatisfaction to the point where funerals in families of church members excluded him, extending church membership to 'suspect' persons without consultation and, being remiss in visiting parishioners. Forney, *History of the Churches of God in the United States of North America*, pp. 13-14.

usually in the context of the camp meeting.[9] These contacts must surely have stimulated Winebrenner's thinking along revivalist lines. Notwithstanding, Winebrenner steadfastly refused to adhere to the authority of the vestry and this persistent insubordination eventually caused Winebrenner's departure from the church.[10] When barred from his own church, Winebrenner commenced preaching in the villages, school-houses, private homes and out-of-doors.[11]

The protracted conflict between Winebrenner and the vestry of the German Reformed Church came down to five issues which the former insisted upon without negotiation.[12] First, Winebrenner appealed to the final authority of the Bible in matters of faith and practice. In a series of correspondence with a professor of theology at the German Reformed Seminary at Mercersburg, Pennsylvania, John W. Nevin, Winebrenner's consistent final appeal was to the scriptures as he interpreted them.[13] Second, Winebrenner began to stress that regeneration was absolutely essential for one to become either the member of a church or indeed a Christian. His reaction to the perceived unregenerate lives of Christians may reflect the realities his opponent John Nevin wrote of in his characterization of the state within the German Reformed Church in the early nineteenth century.

> To be confirmed and then to take the sacrament occasionally was counted by the multitude all that was necessary to make one a good

---

[9] On this see especially William A. Sloat, II., 'The Role of the Methodists and the United Brethren in the Formation of John Winebrenner's Church of God' *Evangelical Journal* 10 (No. 2, 1992), pp. 55-64.

[10] See the argument in favor of this thesis in Kern, *John Winebrenner: Nineteenth Century Reformer*, p. 33.

[11] Forney, *History of the Churches of God in the United States of North America*, p. 23.

[12] The issues are conveniently outlined in Gossard, 'John Winebrenner: Founder, Reformer, and Businessman', pp. 89-90 and in some detail in Kern, *Ibid. passim*.

[13] There is an excellent discussion of this correspondence, together with edited extracts of those letters in Kern, *John Winebrenner: Nineteenth Century Reformer*, pp. 57-73.

Christian, if only a tolerable decency of outward life were maintained besides, without any regard at all to the religion of the heart. True, serious piety was indeed often treated with open and marked scorn. In the bosom of the church itself it was stigmatized as miserable, driveling Methodism. The idea of the new birth was treated as a pietistic whimsey. Experimental religion, in all its forms was eschewed as a new fangled invention of cunning imposters, brought in to turn the heads of the weak, and to lead captive silly women. Prayer-meetings were held to be a spiritual abomination. Family worship was a species of saintly affection, barely tolerable in the case of ministers (though many of them gloried in having no altar in their houses), but absolutely disgraceful for common Christians. To show an awakened concern on the subject of religion, a disposition to call on God in daily secret prayer, was to incur certain reproach. . . . The picture, it must be acknowledged, is dark, but not more so than the truth of history would seem to require.[14]

It is possible to find in Winebrenner's formative years an influential factor in the matter of regeneration. From Samuel Helffenstein, the German Reformed pastor in Philadelphia, Winebrenner came to understand the importance of personal regeneration as the *sine qua non* of Christian faith.[15] In time this led Winebrenner to assume a posture of judgment. He was later accused of denouncing people publicly from the pulpit and on one occasion was reported in the midst of a funeral sermon to have declared that from his understanding of scripture the majority of those already buried in the church cemetery were in hell. Such comments did not

---

[14] Nevin, 'The Heidelberg Catechism', *Weekly Messenger* (10 August 1842). Cited in Kern, *John Winebrenner: Nineteenth Century Reformer*, p. 35. It is difficult not to regard Nevin's bleak and somewhat shocking assessment as exaggerated. In light of known periods of revivalism and emphases of piety within the German Reformed Church in the eighteen and nineteenth centuries, one must conclude that Nevin's statements are overdrawn and perhaps generalizing from a specific context. A selection of Nevin's works can be found in *The Mercersburg Theology*, ed., James Hastings Nichols (New York: Oxford University Press, 1966).

[15] Winebrenner received his theological training under Helffenstein's tutelage between 1817 and 1820. On the matter of Helffenstein's influence on Winebrenner *vis-à-vis* regeneration, see Kern, *John Winebrenner: Nineteenth Century Reformer*, p. 17.

endear Winebrenner to his parishioners.[16] However, in distinction to the Holiness movements, Winebrenner did not always espouse radical standards of holiness. The use of tobacco was fairly widespread among Winebrenner's later group and in the 1840s the Mt. Joy Church in Pennsylvania had this sign attached to the back of its pulpit for the benefit of those preaching from that spot: 'No spitting of tobacco juice from this pulpit.'[17] Holiness preachers and the adherents of come-out Christianity would have been appalled at the need for such a sign. Nonetheless, theatres were referred to as 'Synagogues of Satan' and *The Gospel Publisher* denounced play houses as 'cradles of vice, schools of scandal; yea trap-doors of hell.' Being Christian and frequenting theatres, ball-rooms and other such places was thought inconceivable.[18]

Rooted in his conviction of the necessity of personal regeneration was a related belief in the innate ability of humankind to turn to God in repentance. With this stance, Winebrenner was casting off the Calvinist doctrines of election, predestination, providence and perseverance. Fourth, Winebrenner assailed the sacramental theology of his tradition. He came to understand the Lord's Supper and Baptism as ordinances rather than sacraments, setting aside the idea that they were channels of grace in favor of regarding them as symbolic. He rejected infant baptism and in time came to believe, on the basis of his reading of the New Testament, that immersion was the only acceptable biblical pattern. Additionally, he adopted the practice of foot washing and in 1829 declared that the practice was obligatory as a 'positive command'. Finally, he redefined the nature of the church. In 1829, near the height of his struggle with the German Reformed Church,

---

[16] Forney, *Ibid.*, p. 14. The veracity of these charges, of September 1822, submitted to the synod of the German Reformed Church, were acknowledged by Winebrenner.

[17] Quoted in Kern, *John Winebrenner: Nineteenth Century Reformer*, p. 175.

[18] Forney, *History of the Churches of God in the United States of North America*, pp. 65 and 118.

Winebrenner published his views on ecclesiology.[19] At this point the dissenter was becoming the reformer. Winebrenner suggested emphatically the only appropriate name for the church was the 'Church of God'. Deploring the chaos, so characteristic of American Christianity at the end of the third decade of the nineteenth century, Winebrenner presented his book as a possible solution.

> These unhappy and deplorable circumstances, under which thousands are placed, should excite our tenderest sympathies, and prompt us to speedy and energetic efforts, to ameliorate their condition and bring about a salutary reformation in regard to these ecclesiastical matters, so manifestly wrong, and so much confused.[20]

It has been argued that Winebrenner's insistence on the use of the name 'Church of God' alone as the sole viable and useable designation for the church was his only original doctrine, one which distinguished him from all other contemporary religious movements.[21] The culmination of these events and doctrinal formulations throughout the 1820s and the early 1830s resulted in the formation of a new religious movement: the Church of God. As Richard Kern makes clear, ' . . . the Church of God could not be catalogued with any one of the major streams of American Protestant Christianity.'[22] Other apologists affirmed that the 'movement by Winebrenner was not schismatic. It was reformatory.'[23] As far as Winebrenner was concerned the Church of God was not just another denomination or church

---

[19] Winebrenner, *A Brief View of the Formation, Government, and Discipline of the Church of God* (Harrisburg, PA: Montgomery and Dexter, 1829).

[20] Winebrenner, *A Brief View of the Formation, Government and Discipline of the Church of God*, p. iii.

[21] Gossard, 'John Winebrenner: Founder, Reformer, and Businessman', p. 90.

[22] Kern, *John Winebrenner: Nineteenth Century Reformer*, p. 52.

[23] Forney, *History of the Churches of God in the United States of North America*, p. 19.

among others. Indeed, the Church of God was the true, apostolic body of Christ.[24] His perception of his independent church is revealing and deserves to be quoted at length in his own words.

> The name or title, Church of God, is undeniably the true and proper appellation by which the New Testament church ought to be designated. This is her scriptural and appropriate name. This, and no other title, is given to her by divine authority. This name or title, therefore, ought to be adopted and worn to the exclusion of all others.
> There are those, who have pled for the use, and for the exclusive use, of some other appellations: such as the name of Christian: others for that of Disciples; and others, again, for the name Brethren, &c. But it ought to be recollected, that not one of those is a proper noun, or a patronymic, and, therefore, none of them is ever used in the Scriptures as an appellation for the church. The individual members of the church are, and may be, very properly so called; but not so with regard to the church herself. We nowhere read of the 'Christian Church,' or of the 'Disciples' Church,'nor of the 'Brethren's Church,' &c.[25]

In other words, Winebrenner had no qualms about appointing his church as the true representative of a restored apostolic Christianity. This conviction would feature among the leading articles of the Winebrennerian movement. 'As to the origin of the Church of God, we maintain, and truth compels us to say, that she justly claims priority to all evangelical churches.'[26]

At the first General Eldership meeting of the 'Church of God' in October 1830, Winebrenner preached a sermon on the significance of a proper ecclesiology based on the text Acts 5:38-9. According to Winebrenner churches ought to be formed of Christians or believers only, without a sectarian or human name, having

---

[24] This meant that the apostolic constitution had to be adopted: no creeds, laws, human name, and each congregation was to be independent. Kern, *John Winebrenner: Nineteenth Century Reformer*, p. 85.

[25] This in Winebrenner's contribution to the *History of all the Religious Denominations* . . . . , p. 171.

[26] Winebrenner, *Ibid.* , p. 170.

no creed or discipline save the Bible, be subject to no extrinsic or foreign jurisdiction and be governed by their own officers chosen by the majority of the members of each individual church.[27] A meeting thereafter confirmed the following resolution:

> ... there is but one true church, namely: the Church of God . . . . it is the bounden duty of all God's people to belong to her, and none else . . . . it is 'lawful and right' to associate together for the purpose of co-operation in the cause of God.[28]

Moreover, Winebrenner claimed that Christ had founded the Church of God. Winebrenner responded to his critics that the name 'Church of God' had been selected on the grounds of reason and revelation, not for the purpose of magnifying its adherents.[29] It comes as no surprise to learn that Winebrenner's contemporaries regarded this position as presumptuous and arrogant. Despite the reaction, Winebrenner forged ahead and the result was the establishment in 1830 of perhaps the first church organization in America to use the title 'Church of God'.[30] At the 1830 meeting Winebrenner was elected 'speaker' and elsewhere referred to as

---

[27]   Winebrenner, *Ibid.*, p. 173.

[28]   The relevant part of the resolution appears in Winebrenner, *Ibid.*, p. 173 and is quoted in C.H. Forney, *History of the Churches of God in the United States of North America*, p. 313.

[29]   'As a religious community, therefore, we claim to stand identified with, and to be a part of, the one true Church of God, of which Jesus Christ is the founder and head.' Winebrenner, *History of all the Religious Denominations* . . . , p. 172.

[30]   Kern draws this conclusion from his own research while noting accurately and appropriately the fact that there were prior to Winebrenner several independent churches in eastern Pennsylvania, unrelated to each other, who used the title. *John Winebrenner: Nineteenth Century Reformer*, p. 52. According to Winebrenner, the end of the protracted struggle with the German Reformed Church led to reform. 'Thus originated the Church of God, properly and distinctively so called, in the United States of America; and thus, also, originated the first eldership.' This is Winebrenner's conclusion in his later book, *History of all the Religious Denominations* . . . . , p. 173.

'bishop'.[31] The title 'Reverend' became anathema in the Winebrennerian communion and was replaced with the Scriptural term 'Elder'.[32] Rather than seeing his stance as schismatic, Winebrenner encouraged unity in the true Church of God.[33]

By 1844 the Church of God had summarized its doctrines in a series of twenty-seven articles. In that articulation, Winebrenner affirmed the authority of scripture, doctrine of the Trinity, depravity of humankind, redemption through Christ, the gifts and work of the Holy Spirit, free, moral, agency of all persons, justification by faith, regeneration, the ordinances of baptism (by immersion), eucharist (received frequently, in a sitting position and only in the evening) and obligatory foot washing. The Lord's day was declared a day of rest, songs, prayers and preaching should characterize Christian worship, evangelistic outreach became essential, and Christian benevolent causes were deemed worthy of support. Alcohol was immoral, slavery unchristian, civil wars unholy, but Christians ought to be subject to the government save in cases where the authorities obviously deviated from the law of God. Furthermore, the Church of God affirmed the necessity of holy living, the unity of the church, the second coming of Christ, the resurrection of the dead, the creation of a new heaven and new earth, immortality of the soul, judgment and everlasting rewards and punishments.[34] Interestingly, despite the excessive emphasis on eschatology current in the 1830s and 1840s, there seems to

---

[31] Winebrenner, *History of all the Religious Denominations* . . . , pp. 172 and 187. Article 5 of the 'Constitution of the General Eldership of the Church of God in North America' defines the function of 'speaker'. 'The Speaker shall be the presiding officer of all the meetings of the Eldership . . . . He shall conduct the business thereof . . . he shall endorse all orders on the Treasurer . . . . ' *Ibid.*, p. 183.

[32] Forney, *History of the Churches of God in the United States of North America*, p. 78.

[33] His paper, *The Gospel Publisher*, begun in 1835, was a principle organ in the attack against schism. Winebrenner made good use of it. Forney, *History of the Churches of God in the United States of North America*, p. 52.

[34] Winebrenner, *History of all the Religious Denominations* . . . . , pp. 176-81.

have been no preoccupation with such matters even during the height of the Millerite enthusiasm. On matters of social concern in the mid-nineteenth century, it is instructive to note that Blacks were converted into the early Church of God and Winebrenner's position on slavery was that the institution and practice was indeed sinful but not necessarily intolerable. His position curiously shifted in the late 1830s from 'the sin of slavery' to the 'sinfulness of its abuse'.[35] Winebrenner considered the Church of God a peace church. When forced to choose between war and slavery, though being opposed to both, Winebrenner asserted that war was a greater evil than slavery.[36]

In 1844 I. Daniel Rupp published a book on American religious groups. By 1848 Winebrenner had acquired the rights to that work and issued an enlarged, illustrated second edition.[37] Winebrenner included himself among the fifty-three eminent authors and included a portrait of himself in the work. Previous to this, Winebrenner had been carrying on a literary debate with John Nevin. The latter published in 1848 his analysis of the problem of sectarianism in America.[38] In brief, Nevin, along with his colleague Philip Schaff, regarded the rise, spread and proliferation of sectarian religion as the worldly, physical embodiment of

---

[35] On this see Kern, *John Winebrenner: Nineteenth Century Reformer*, pp. 97, 112 and 138 with references to the sources. See also Gossard, 'John Winebrenner: Founder, Reformer, and Businessman', pp. 93-5. By comparison, Peter Cartwright also opposed slavery but likewise refused to lend any support whatsoever to the cause of the abolitionists. *Autobiography of Peter Cartwright*, p. 94.

[36] See the outline in Kern, *John Winebrenner: Nineteenth Century Reformer*, p. 144.

[37] *History of all the Religious Denominations in the United States: containing authentic accounts of the rise, progress, faith and practice, localities and statistics, of the different persuasions: written expressly for the work, by fifty-three eminent authors belonging to the respective denominations* (Harrisburg, PA: John Winebrenner, 1848).

[38] John W, Nevin, *Anti-Christ; Or the Spirit of Sect and Schism* (New York: John S. Taylor, 1848).

John Winebrenner and the 'Come-Out' Movement   173

antichrist.[39] The Winebrennerians were included in Nevin's study. At the same time as Nevin's *Anti-Christ* appeared, Winebrenner had reissued the *History of all the Religious Denominations* . . . . Nevin wrote a lengthy review of that work in the *Mercersburg Review* in 1849. The book was deemed important if only in a negative way as a valuable commentary on the dire religious situation in America at mid century. Nevin critiqued it thoroughly, especially those parts concerned with the Church of God and the portrait of Winebrenner himself.

> Last, though of course not least, deserves to be mentioned the full bust and particularly speaking face of John Winebrenner, V.D.M., the present publisher of this book himself; to whom we are indebted for the idea of these 'splendid portraits of distinguished men,' and who has the honor besides, as we here learn, of being the originator of a sect styling itself the 'Church of God,' (about the year 1825), one of the heros thus of his own book; to say nothing of the distinction which belongs to him as the historiographer of his sect, one of the 'fifty-three eminent authors,' as before noticed, to whose united paternity the book before us refers itself on the title page. Mr. Winebrenner's portrait may be said to go beyond all the rest, in a certain self-consciousness of its own historical significance and interest. It has an attitude, studied for dramatic effect; an air of independence; an open Bible in the hands; in token, we presume, that Winebrennerism makes more of this blessed volume than any other sect, and that it was never much understood till Mr. Winebrenner was raised up at Harrisburg, in these last days, to set all right, and give the 'Church of God' a fresh start, by means of it, out of his own mind.[40]

Nevin's sarcasm was unmistakable. His attitude was shared by his Mercersburg colleague Philip Schaff who regarded the sects in a negative light even if later he

---

[39] According to Nevin there were at least twelve marks of antichrist: no mediation between God and humans was necessary for salvation, an undervaluing of the mystery of Christ, a conviction that the church is not a divine institution, a low view of the ministry and the sacraments, contempt for history and authority, emphasis on individual freedom, hyperspiritualism, arbitrary dualism between God and nature, fanaticism, endless division, finds its summation in the flesh (here Nevin gave the examples of the Anabaptists at Münster in the 1530s and the Mormons at Nauvoo), and finally, false theology. Nevin, *Anti-christ; or the Spirit of Sect and Schism*, pp. 48-68.

[40] See Kern, *Ibid.*, pp. 74-8 for extracts from Nevin's review of Winebrenner's book. The initials V.D.M. signified 'minister of the word of God' in its Latin form.

grudgingly came to admit that they did stimulate interest in religion.[41] Notwithstanding this criticism, the book proved to be Winebrenner's most profitable publishing venture.[42]

In 1849 Nevin renewed his attack on Winebrenner and the issue of sectarianism with the publication of 'The Sect System'.[43] Nevin regarded the *History of all the Religious Denominations* . . . as a prime example of the most serious dilemma facing American Christendom in the nineteenth century. He attacked the strict *sola scriptura* doctrine as espoused by Winebrenner. 'The narrowness and tyranny of the sect spirit, unfriendly to all generous christian life, is of fatal force in particular against the cultivation of *theology* . . . .'[44] Nevin linked together in devastating fashion the rise of sectarian tyranny on the foundations of a pure biblicism which presented itself as an absolute authority. Nevin was adamant that sects such as the Church of God offered nothing other than a perverted gospel fashioned in the image of its own dominant personalities. 'The sect calls all men . . . to take refuge in her communion. She does not simply offer them the Bible. . . . She is not content to make them christians, but seeks to make them also [of herself].'[45] Nevin accused the various sects of assuming their own inherent infallibility in the rôle of interpreter of both Christian tradition and scripture. If the keys were originally given to Peter and the apostles, in these last days they have been handed to the guardians of sectism and, according to Nevin, were being used to chaotic ends. 'Sects . . . are disposed to stand upon the right

---

[41] Schaff's opinion reflected in Graham, *Cosmos in the Chaos*, pp. 16-17 and *passim*.

[42] Gossard, 'John Winebrenner: Founder, Reformer and Businessman', p. 97.

[43] 'The Sect System', in *Catholic and Reformed: Selected Theological Writings of John Williamson Nevin*, eds., Charles Yrigoyen and George H. Bricker (Pittsburgh: The Pickwick Press, 1978), pp. 128-73.

[44] Nevin, 'The Sect System', pp. 137 and 159.

[45] Nevin, *Ibid.*, p. 167.

of private judgment and individual freedom . . . .'[46] In the end, Nevin concluded that the rhetoric and the reality were two separate issues and the sects simply propounded innumerable inconsistencies as they contributed to the shattering of Christian unity.[47] Winebrenner's attitude to Nevin's criticism was arrogant and abrasive. He insisted on continuing the polemic even in the face of Nevin's obvious reluctance to do so. The extant correspondence bears this out.[48]

Enthusiastic disciples of the Winebrennerian tradition tended to hold their founder in high regard. 'Had he lived to the present no name on the American pulpit could have shone with more splendor than his.'[49] He was the 'sainted and immortal Winebrenner.'[50] 'Winebrenner was the incarnation of integrity and honor.'[51] Richard Kern has argued that despite the polemics and the influence he clearly wielded over the early history of the Church of God, Winebrenner cannot be regarded in the category of the 'traditional image of the ecclesiastical autocrat.'[52] Be that as it may, it seems implausible to agree with the conclusion that Winebrenner was opposed to come-outism.[53] He had left the German Reformed Church for, in his own words, the church was ' . . . a sect—and withal a mal-

---

[46] Nevin, *Anti-christ; or the Spirit of Sect and Schism*, p. 55.

[47] Nevin, 'The Sect System', pp. 166 and 169.

[48] A good deal of relevant extracts have been included in Kern's study, *passim*.

[49] The *Harrisburg Daily Topic* in its issue of 30 June 1870 paid this tribute to Winebrenner. The entire text appears in Kern, *John Winebrenner: Nineteenth Century Reformer*, pp. 191-2.

[50] Forney, *History of the Churches of God in the United States of North America*, p. 131.

[51] Forney, *Ibid.*, p. 134.

[52] Kern, *John Winebrenner: Nineteenth Century Reformer*, p. 177.

[53] Kern, *Ibid.*, p. 209 n. 55.

practising sect . . . . a Synagogue of Satan.'[54] He had come out and pointed the way to the true Church of God. In one of the ironies of nineteenth-century American religious history, a Church of God pastor in the West Ohio Eldership, in the decade following Winebrenner's death, caused a schism in the Winebrennerian Church and led a movement for a reformation of the church. That man was Daniel Warner, one of the preeminent leaders of the come-out movement.

II. 'A narrower way'

> There are people almost ev'rywhere,
> Whose hearts are all aflame
> With the fire that fell at Pentecost,
> Which cleans'd and made them clean;
> It is burning now within my heart;
> All glory to His name!
> And I'm glad that I can say I'm one of them.
>
> [Refrain]   One of them, one of them
> I am glad that I can say I'm one of them;
> [Sanctified, sanctified].
> I am glad that I can say I'm [sanctified].
>
> Tho' these people may not learned be,
> Nor boast of worldly fame,
> They have all received their Pentecost
> Thro' faith in Jesus' name;
> And are telling now, both far and wide,
> His pow'r is yet the same,
> And I'm glad that I can say I'm one of them.
>
> They were gathered in the upper room,
> All praying in His name,
> They were baptized with the Holy Ghost,
> And pow'r for service came;
> Now what he did for them that day

---

[54]   Winebrenner published these comments in his paper, the *Gospel Publisher*. The relevant extracts appear in Kern, *John Winebrenner: Nineteenth Century Reformer*, pp. 59-60.

He'll do for you the same,
And I'm glad that I can say I'm one of them.

Come, my brother, seek this blessing
That will cleanse your heart from sin,
That will start the joy-bells ringing
And will keep the soul aflame;
It is burning now within my heart;
All glory to His name,
And I'm glad that I can say I'm one of them.[55]

♠ ♠

There are four main factors in the development of religious sectarian movements: ecclesiological concerns, social and/or moral issues, theological emphases, and the influence of charismatic personalities.[56] The community of the faithful which became the inheritance of men like Daniel Warner was a community built upon a shared experience. That shared experience was founded on the basis of nineteenth-century American religion, especially in its revivalist context. The experience encompassed the impulses of holiness and the religious culture it engendered. The narrower way added a third component, that of separation, or come-outism. This common, shared experience provided the essential parameters for a new movement. For the come-out movement, their chief concern was a reformation and renewal of the church, the experience of entire sanctification and the gaining of perfection. A plethora of charismatic leaders pointed the way to the chosen land. In 1877 John P. Brooks addressed two Holiness conferences in Cincinnati and New York City. In those addresses Brooks identified six weaknesses within the Holiness movement; weaknesses which continued to hamper

---

[55] Isaiah Guyman Martin, 'I'm Glad I'm One of Them' in Edwin P. Anderson, ed., *Melodies of Praise* (Springfield, MO: Gospel Publishing House, 1957), no. 12. Words in brackets are an alternative version.

[56] Norwood, *The Story of American Methodism*, p. 292.

the movement. First, Brooks decried the idea that every possessor of holiness should teach. This had led to the problem of imperfect teaching. Second, he identified the issue of 'unthorough experiences', that is that certain persons thought representative of the Holiness cause lived lives which were unholy bringing much reproach. Third, Brooks condemned the lack of aggression in the propagation of holiness. Fourth, the matter of misleading testimonies wherein converts sometimes claimed not to be capable of temptation, sin or any failing. Fifth, the tendency to be completely unconnected to any church affiliation and sixth, 'excessive and extravagant experiences.'[57] The come-out movement sought to transcend these problems by breaking new ground apart from the fallow soil of denominationalism.

Daniel Warner and other leaders of the come-out movement were the inheritors of a powerful and pervasive religious tradition. That tradition was Holiness. For two generations it had challenged and confronted American culture. Now it mounted yet another offensive in its curious detachment. The central experience of the come-out movement was 'entire sanctification, the second blessing, Christian perfection, perfect love, heart purity, the baptism with the Holy Ghost, the fullness of the blessing, full salvation, and Christian holiness . . . .'[58] This variously designated experience was prerequisite to authentic Christianity. Denominational Christianity eschewing the idea were ridiculed. Those who achieved it were lauded. For example, when John Cookman died in 1871, at his funeral Randolph Foster declared: 'The most sacred man I have ever known is enshrined in that casket.'[59]

The reforming element within the holiness principle precipitated the rise in a 'Church of God' ideology. Winebrenner had definitely decided for the use of the term as the only acceptable biblical designation. Now in the latter years of the

---

[57] The substance of Brooks' address appears in Dieter, *The Holiness Revival of the Nineteenth Century*, pp. 222-3.

[58] Jones, *Perfectionist Persuasion*, p. 83.

[59] Cited in Smith, *Called Unto Holiness*, p. 18.

nineteenth century, the notion began to acquire significant momentum. Between 1880 and 1923 no fewer than 200 groups adopted some version of the name 'Church of God' to designate their churches.[60] There were the radicals among the come-outers like Daniel Warner who eschewed all form of church polity and denominational structure. The idea of organization was abhorrent to Warner and he carried the ideas of John Winebrenner and the 'Church of God' ideology to their extreme limit. Extremism was not limited to the 'Church of God' mentality. Indeed, the old hard line standards of holiness emerged yet again within the come-out ranks. S.B. Shaw reported the beginnings of a 'narrower way'. 'Gold watch chains, gold cuff buttons and even bows on a hat went for Jesus' sake' and many were slain in the spirit as they came out for Christ's sake.[61] Now that apostate Christendom had been thrown off and the way was clear of hindering forces, Christian perfection could once again flourish. In 1887 S.B. Shaw announced the Michigan State Camp Meeting with this call: 'come come-outers, come everybody . . . and let us all get melted down before God, so we will not have any feelings toward each other in opposition to perfect love. May God save us from narrow-minded selfishness and bigotry, save us from sin of all kinds.'[62] Implicit in Shaw's invitation was the suggestion that the paradox of religious democracy had pervaded the ranks of the come-out Holiness movement.

Men like Daniel Warner and Solomon B. Shaw perceived themselves as divinely commissioned to unite all true Christians. But the task proved too great for Warner and Shaw and indeed no one stepped forward in the nineteenth century equal to the herculean task. In the end, the come-out movement itself shattered into a thousand pieces of perfection. Though Warner would found a tradition which would last, and others wrote stirring apologies for come-outism, the 'narrower

---

[60] Vinson, *The Pentecostal Movement in the United States*, p. 77.

[61] Quoted in Smith, *Called Unto Holiness*, p. 34.

[62] Quoted in Smith, *Ibid.*, p. 33.

way' produced no lasting unity, the calls of Shaw fell on deaf ears and the history of the come-out movement spawned its own prodigy of step-children, into what Philip Schaff called the expanding American 'wilderness of sects'.[63] As much as any other tradition in American religious history, the come-out movement underscored the paradox of religious democracy.

---

[63] Warner's following of course became the Church of God (Anderson, Indiana). Among the notable defences of the come-out movement see John P. Brooks, *The Divine Church* (New York and London: Garland Publishing, Inc., 1984). Originally published in 1891.

CHAPTER 4

Daniel Warner and the Battle Against 'Babylon'

As a matter of historic fact, D.S. Warner stood rather in the historic tradition of radical Christianity, extending from the dissidents from Roman Catholicism in the eleventh century down through the Anabaptists into the radical Christianity of modern times.[1]

♠ ♠

One hundred years have contributed to the making of the image of Daniel Warner. Born in 1842 in the midst of religious and social upheaval, he became a player in the drama of late nineteenth-century American religion. Regarded in some quarters as a 'radical reformer-restorer' Warner assumed prominence in the last fifteen years of his life.[2] Though later perceived as 'an utterly sincere and undogmatic man',[3] Daniel Warner emerged at the forefront of the come-out movement and almost from the beginning was regarded as a premier spokesman for that cause.[4]

---

[1]   Charles E. Brown, *When the Trumpet Sounded: A History of the Church of God Reformation Movement* (Anderson: Warner Press, 1951), pp. 83-4

[2]   Barry L. Callen, *Contours of a Cause: The Theological Vision of the Church of God Movement (Anderson)* (Anderson: Anderson University School of Theology, 1995), p. 35.

[3]   Brown, *When the Trumpet Sounded*, p. 56.

[4]   'He [Warner] is generally recognized as the universal leader of this total reformation movement.' Charles E. Brown, *When Souls Awaken: An Interpretation of Radical Christianity* (Anderson: Gospel Trumpet Company, 1954), p. 105.

182 *Daniel Warner and the Battle against 'Babylon'*

In the overall historiography of the Church of God Reformation Movement '...
the most articulate exponent of sanctification as the remedy for division was Daniel

Figure 6   Daniel Warner as he appeared *c.* 1887 (with his son Sidney). Courtesy of Warner Press and the Archives of the Church of God, Anderson University

Warner . . . .'[5] Sanctification was not an option for Warner, but an absolute necessity. If he were undogmatic in other areas of theology he certainly was not when it came to the issue of holiness. 'Gentle, meek, loving, and thoroughly unselfish, he was an example of Christliness that those who knew him will always remember. And yet when it came to the execution of judgment against sin and religious apostasy, his tongue or pen was a mighty sword in the hands of God.'[6] As an instrument in the hands of God for renewal, reformation and restoration, Warner's career was 'marvelous.'[7] So compelling, ostensibly, was the man Daniel Warner and his work, that witnesses arose to claim that anyone who ever met the man, and embraced his teachings, would forever 'reverence his memory almost beyond bounds. . . .'[8] 'He was a holy man and his life was without spot or blame.'[9] Decades after his death, there were those within the Church of God come-out legacy who readily identified the days of Warner as standard.[10]

The details of Warner's life have been set forth comprehensively elsewhere.[11] The purpose of this chapter is to briefly sketch the life of Warner to

---

[5] John W.V. Smith, 'Holiness and Unity' *Wesleyan Theological Journal* 10 (Spring 1975), p. 32.

[6] A.L. Byers, 'Pioneers of the Present Reformation' *Gospel Trumpet* (5 February 1920), p. 19.

[7] *Ibid.*, p. 18.

[8] Brown, *When the Trumpet Sounded*, p. 108.

[9] *Life Sketches of Mother Sarah Smith* (Anderson: Gospel Trumpet Company, n.d.), p. 36. Sarah Smith (1822-1908) was a member of Warner evangelistic company in the 1880s known as the 'Flying Messengers'.

[10] Callen, *Contours of a Cause*, p. 185.

[11] There are a number of standard sources. The most important include the writings of Warner himself. His diary (1872-1880) is extant in six volumes in the D.S. Warner papers. Archives, Anderson University. The journals have never been published, but are available in typescript form. Hereafter, referred to as *Journal*. Significant autobiographical details can also be found in a collection by Warner published as *Poems of Grace and Truth* (Grand Junction, MI: Gospel Trumpet Publishing House, 1890).

provide a biographical context for an analysis of his rôle in the paradox of religious democracy in nineteenth-century America. Daniel Sidney Warner was born on 25 June 1842 in Bristol, Ohio [now called Marshallville]. The following year his family relocated to Crawford County near New Washington, not far from the town of Bucyrus, Ohio. The entire area had a rather dismal reputation, from a religious perspective. According to frontier evangelists, 'Ohio was . . . a land of moral desolation' while neighboring Indiana fell considerably below the standard of civilization.[12] With such reputation it is not surprising that frontier religion had pushed its way through the Ohio territory before Warner's birth. The revival at Cane Ridge in the summer of 1801 had a greater influence overall in Ohio than any other state save Kentucky.[13] From New York to Ohio the dominant religious presence was that of Methodism.[14] Warner's parents were not particularly religious

---

Among the most important secondary sources are Andrew L. Byers, *Birth of a Reformation or The Life and Labors of Daniel S. Warner* (Anderson: Gospel Trumpet Company, 1921) reprinted (Guthrie, OK: Faith Publishing House, 1966); Charles E. Brown, *When the Trumpet Sounded: A History of the Church of God Reformation Movement* (Anderson: Warner Press, 1951) and John W. V. Smith, *The Quest for Holiness and Unity: A Centennial History of the Church of God (Anderson, Indiana)* (Anderson: Warner Press, 1980). Smith treats Warner's biography more fully in his *Heralds of a Brighter Day: Biographical Sketches of Early Leaders in the Church of God Reformation Movement* (Anderson: Gospel Trumpet Company, 1955) though without the benefit of references. More recently John A. Morrison and Joseph Allison published a biographical treatment of Warner in successive issues of *Vital Christianity* (9 June 1974 – 19 January 1975). The *Vital Christianity* series was intended for a popular audience and has little scholarly value. More recently, Barry L. Callen, *It's God's Church! The Life and Legacy of Daniel Sidney Warner* (Anderson: Warner Press, 1995). The Church of God historian, Merle D. Strege has agreed with Warner Press to write a critical biography of Warner, one which will situate him in the larger context of the Holiness movements and American Protestantism. Such a work is much needed and it is to be expected that Strege's book would supersede the aforementioned.

[12] James B. Finley, *Autobiography of Rev. James B. Finley; Or, Pioneer Life in the West*, p. 330.

[13] Conkin, *Cane Ridge: America's Pentecost*, p. 175.

[14] Edwin Gaustad, 'Regionalism in American Religion', in *Religion in the South*, ed., Charles Reagan Wilson (Jackson: University of Mississippi Press, 1985), p. 160.

and Daniel was more or less a skeptic of religion until 1865. In February of that year Warner attended a Winebrennerian service and made a decision to become a Christian. The event was a decisive turning point in Warner's early life. The next month the Civil War invaded his life and he became Private Daniel S. Warner, Company C, 195th Ohio Volunteer, Infantry Regiment.[15] The war ended a month later and Warner's brief military career was over.

Following his discharge from the army, Daniel Warner entered Oberlin College as a student. Oberlin had long been a center of holiness teaching and American revivalism. The leading personalities at Oberlin were Asa Mahan and more importantly Charles Finney, though by the time of Warner's arrival was in his final, active years. There is little doubt that the young Daniel Warner heard the old, great revivalist.[16] In the 1860s Oberlin was still a leading center of holiness-perfectionist teaching and revivalism. Extant records are silent with respect to any relation or influence between Finney and Warner. All that can be ascertained with any certainty is that both men were at Oberlin at the same time, Warner owned at least one of Finney's books, both held certain similar ideas about health, both diverged from the other on the subject of holiness.[17] On the basis of Warner's career it is accurate to state that Oberlin and Finney did not find support in the young Warner.[18] Despite two separate stints at Oberlin College, Warner did not complete his studies and became for a time a school teacher.

On Easter night, 1867 Warner preached his first sermon in a Methodist Episcopal meeting in a school house and by October of the same year had been granted a preaching license by the West Ohio Eldership of the Winebrennerian

---

[15] Merle D. Strege, *Tell me the Tale: Historical Reflections on the Church of God* (Anderson: Warner Press, 1991), p. 46.

[16] John W.V. Smith, *Heralds of a Brighter Day*, p. 24.

[17] There is essentially no material for a study of Finney and Warner. But see Harold L. Phillips, 'Warner and Charles Finney' *Vital Christianity* (6 October 1974), pp. 7-8.

[18] Brown, *When the Trumpet Sounded*, p. 56.

Church at its eleventh annual session at Findlay.[19] This marked the formal beginning of Warner's religious career, a career which would span nearly three decades leaving an indelible mark on the shape of American Christianity. An unrequited love affair, followed by the death of his first wife, a pastoral assignment at Mount Blanchard, several administrative positions with the West Ohio Eldership, led up to Warner's departure from Ohio for the wilderness of Nebraska as a frontier missionary.[20] At this point in his life, Warner began writing a journal which is extant and which remains a valuable collection of documents for any study of Warner's life and career up to 1880.

This early association with the tradition of John Winebrenner proved influential in the development of the movement Warner later led. With Winebrenner, Warner was especially keen to witness the emergence of the primitive church *redivivus* in the American context. To that end, Winebrenner had attempted to reform his own denomination along strictly biblical lines. The adoption of the name 'Church of God', a rejection of all creeds save scripture, baptism by immersion, and foot-washing are a few of the characteristics embraced by both men. These features were considered among those distinguishing characteristics of the New Testament church and were regarded as essential components of a truly apostolic community. In due course, however, Warner and the Winebrennerians clashed over what the former considered to be the latter's unfaithfulness to biblical principles. Nevertheless, the early 1870s were a fruitful time of ministry for Warner. Only six years into his ministry with the Winebrennerians he reported having preached in excess of 1200 sermons resulting in more than 500 conversions.[21] The career of Daniel Warner as a religious reformer and leader of a popular movement reveals a persistent preoccupation with

---

[19] A.L. Byers, *Birth of a Reformation or The Life and Labors of Daniel S. Warner*, pp. 41, 49.

[20] Callen, *It's God's Church!*, pp. 52-3.

[21] *Journal*, 27 April 1873.

preaching and a firm belief in its efficacy in the process of leading men and women to God, to salvation, and of course, later, to entire sanctification and the true church.

Late in 1872 Daniel Warner, despite his almost certain exposure at Oberlin College, remained a professed opponent of the doctrine of sanctification. He records his attitude on attending a Holiness meeting.

> Evangelic. meeting. Brother Waid preacher—heard a great noise, but to the congregation it appeared as a tinkling silver and sounding brass, evidently having no effect. Nearly all blowed loudly the horn of sanctification—but manifested but little of its fruits such as travel [sic] of soul for the sinner—and sympathy for the one soul at the altar, to whom none gave a word of encouragement, but each in turn arose and boasted of their holiness. O, the delusions of Satan how manifold they are.[22]

What Warner denounced as 'delusions of Satan' later became, for him, the power of God. His early journal entries also underscore a preoccupation which he may have gleaned from Oberlin and the Winebrennerians in part. 'The M.E. Church had a festival—I and a few members of the same church (who repudiated these follies and inconsistencies) met for prayer and the Lord was with us: These brethren were much dissatisfied with their Church relation.'[23] Here, Warner demonstrated his early and abiding distaste for worldliness and denominationalism. It has been pointed out correctly that confronting these matters would remain a lasting element of Warner's ministry.[24]

On 25 June 1873 Warner left Ohio to take up his appointment as a home missionary in Nebraska. Four days before his trip west, Warner records receiving a letter 'from a <u>kind friend</u>.'[25] This was a reference to Sarah Keller of Upper Sandusky, a woman who plays a crucial rôle in the analysis of the paradox of

---

[22] *Journal*, 11 November 1872.

[23] *Journal*, 8 November 1872.

[24] Callen, *It's God's Church!*, p. 54.

[25] *Journal*, 21 June 1873. The underlined words are Warner's.

religious democracy in the next chapter. Warner's first year on the Nebraska frontier was full and eventful.[26] The next spring he made his way back to Upper Sandusky and on 4 June 1874 married Sarah Keller.

> This is the happy day to which my mind has so often soared ahead of time to embrace in sweet anticipation. Thank God that the onward flight of time has brought the day in which my Angel Sarah and self shall be joined in holy wedlock. . . . At 4 the ceremony was performed. . . . Now a new leaf is turned, a new era begun in the history of my life. O Lord, how can I thank thee enough for the great gift of my own pure, amiable, fair and lovely Sarah? May God assist me to make her life happy as far as it is in the power of man to do so. God bless our union and make us together happy and useful.[27]

Warner was right. A new era had begun. In time his wife and her family proved to be the instrument for changing Warner's mind about holiness and his acceptance of that teaching fuelled the direction of his religious career. Beyond that, Sarah eventually forced Warner to come to terms with himself, his ministry, his theology and ultimately with his perception as a religious leader. It would take a full decade but the leaf had turned, a new era had begun, the history of Warner's life was irrevocably influenced by the events of this 'happy day.'

In August, Daniel and Sarah Warner returned to the Nebraska outpost. The following year was difficult both on personal and ministerial grounds for the Warners. By the fall of 1875, Daniel Warner ostensibly had decided to leave Nebraska. His journal entries break off at 3 June and with the exception of a few minor fragments there are no extant, substantial records until 10 December when we find Warner back in Ohio. His mission to Nebraska was over, as it turned out, for good. Warner seems to have taken up leadership capacities in Ohio and his journal bears out the details of his work. In 1877 he returned to formal studies,

---

[26] In addition to his journal, one may also consult with profit his lengthy poem 'Meditations on the Prairie' in Warner, *Poems of Grace and Truth*, pp. 33-116 for his thoughts and experiences while laboring south of the Platte River between Lincoln and Grand Island.

[27] *Journal*, 4 June 1874.

enrolling at the Presbyterian Vermillion College at Hayesville. Like his tenure at Oberlin this was to be a short stay. But 1877 proved to be the first major turning point of Warner's career. Reports from Nebraska indicated that Warner was badly missed. The Nebraska Eldership Standing Committee reported in 1877 that 'the churches of God at Wayland and Pleasant Hill have suffered greatly on account of the resignation of D.S. Warner two years ago.' Another report assessed Warner very favorable. 'D.S. Warner is a model young man, of deep piety and superior courage and means business in the work of the ministry, and if he continues he will make his mark in the church.'[28] The mark Warner eventually made on the Winebrennerian fellowship was unexpected. In that same year, Warner repudiated his opinion on the 'Satanic delusions' of sanctification and whole-heartedly embraced the holiness teaching and ethos.

As mentioned earlier, Daniel Warner's initial, positive, encounter with the idea of holiness came through the mediation of Sarah and the Keller family. The Kellers had previously become affiliated with a Holiness group in Upper Sandusky.[29] By April 1877 Sarah had professed the experience of sanctification. Warner's entries in his journal from April through July chronicle in part his own struggle and gradual acceptance of the teaching. By July Warner was personally seeking sanctification publicly. His journal provides witness of his own life-changing experience. On 7 July Warner testified to his reception of sanctifying grace. Warner described this experience as a passage from wilderness to the promised land. 'O glory to God once more I was a little child. I felt the blood of Jesus flowing through my entire "soul, body, and spirit." Heaven on earth, "Hallelujah it is done: I believe on the son, I am saved by the blood of the crucified one."'[30] Scholars who have made Warner the subject of an in-depth analysis agree

---

[28] Both reports are quoted in Callen, *It's God's Church!*, p. 68.

[29] Brown, *When the Trumpet Sounded*, p. 67.

[30] *Journal*, 7 July, 1877.

that from this time onward Warner was a committed Holiness preacher.

While the Kellers, Sarah, and the close Warner circle all rejoiced in the experience of entire sanctification, there were grave reservations also expressed from other quarters. Within two months Warner came face to face with the West Ohio Eldership. The Winebrennerians did not hold to the teaching of holiness. John Winebrenner had insisted on the necessity of regeneration and evidence of a genuine Christian faith in the lives of professing believers. He opposed sectarianism and the use of alcohol but did not accept the holiness emphases or doctrine of entire sanctification. The Winebrennerian Church of God may with some justification be regarded as a Methodist type church, but lacking the holiness dimension.[31] When Warner persisted in following the Holiness tradition, verbal exchanges ensued in the course of worship services and a direct confrontation was not long in coming. Following an evening service wherein Warner had been forced to hear a sermon attacking and denouncing the holiness message, he was handed a folded sheet of paper by the minister. Warner records its contents in his journal.

> The following charges are preferred against Elder D.S. Warner
>
> First, for inviting a sect of fanatics calling themselves the Holy Alliance band to hold meetings in the local Churches of God without consulting the Elders or trustees or myself,
> Second, for joining in with these said band and bidding them Godspeed and thereby has brought schism and division among these churches,
> Third, for the accommodation of this professed Holy band that he invited to hold a meeting of ten days in the Church of God Chapel in Mansfield, Elder D.S. Warner did on the evening of the 8 of July in less than one hour had the ordinances of washing the saints feet and the Lord's Supper attended to.

---

[31] See Richard Kern, *John Winebrenner: Nineteenth Century Reformer* (Harrisburg: Central Publishing House, 1974), *passim*.

Fourth, for stating publicly in Shenandoah about the 26 of Aug. that he had been preaching his own doctrine prior to seeking his so-called holiness.

W.H. Oliver[32]

Warner had incurred the wrath of his church and unless he was prepared to recant, submit to ecclesiastical authority, the path to dissent was already being marked out. In due course the charges formally came before the West Ohio Eldership and were sustained. Notwithstanding, his ministerial license was renewed with the proviso that he refrain from bringing Holiness groups into the Church of God. To this Warner agreed and the crisis appeared past.[33]

This incident reveals the divergence of the Winebrennerians and Daniel Warner. John Winebrenner had stepped out of the German Reformed communion seeking the path to authentic ecclesiastical reformation and Biblical Christianity. To his satisfaction that had been achieved in the developments between 1830 and 1860. The tradition of the Church of God accepted Winebrenner's direction and interpretation. While he may have not been a dictator, as Richard Kern has suggested, his authority was respected and obeyed by the subsequent generation.[34] In 1877 the West Ohio Eldership had no wish to break from tradition, adopt the innovations of the Holiness movement, or follow the direction suggested by Daniel Warner. Their identity was intrinsically related to the stable structure of the Church of God as it had evolved to the mid-nineteenth century. Warner was part of that same tradition and had been for more than ten years. But now he had

---

[32] *Journal*, 16 September 1877. Oliver was characterized as a 'hard-working evangelist' and was appointed 'traveling missionary' by the 17th West Ohio Eldership Conference in 1873. He labored more than forty years in the Winebrennerian Church of God. C.H. Forney, *History of the Churches of God in the United States of North America* (Harrisburg, PA: Publishing House of the Churches of God, 1914), pp. 113, 564 and 582.

[33] Forney, *History of the Churches of God in the United States of North America*, p. 567.

[34] Kern, *Ibid.*, p. 177.

accepted the radical ideas of the Holiness movements and embracing the doctrine of entire sanctification perceived the reformation of the church and the path to authentic Biblical Christianity going beyond where the Winebrennerian tradition had stopped. This provoked serious conflict and a dramatic confrontation between institution and potential reformer.

Warner's pledge to refrain from allowing Holiness groups in the Church of God was in fact a wavering commitment. Two months later, he stepped down from his appointment and returned to Upper Sandusky. This was an indication of Warner's growing discontent with the Winebrennerian Church. In December 1877 Warner preached a revival in Findlay and the results were published in the Winebrennerian *Church Advocate*: twenty testified to the blessing of entire sanctification. The pastor of the Church of God congregation where the revival had been held added his prayer that everyone would seek for this experience. In the same month, in the same venue, Warner reported that the aforementioned Church of God pastor had been personally 'sanctified through the blood of the Lamb.'[35] It did not take long for the West Ohio Eldership to move into action. Warner stood trial on 30 January 1878. He faced three primary charges. First, that he had transgressed the rules of the church, second that he was in violation of the rules of cooperation, and third, that he was party to dividing the church. Warner was unrepentant. He was summarily expelled from the West Ohio Eldership and forbidden to publish further with the Church of God. Warner interpreted his troubles by writing a special heading in his journal: 'Trial and Expulsion from the West Ohio Eldership of the Church of God for Preaching full salvation, for following the Holy Spirit, and helping to save over 150 souls in this place.' The following day, as he later recorded in his journal, Warner received a revelation from God to follow a narrower way, to join together the doctrine of holiness and all truth outside the parameters of traditional Christianity.[36] The events of January

---

[35] Both accounts are quoted in Callen, *It's God's Church!*, pp. 76-7.

[36] *Journal*, 7 March 1878.

cannot be dismissed as coming to bear upon Warner's revelation. He was finished with the West Ohio Eldership unless he was prepared to submit to their authority. To do so would be to shift the holiness message from the center of his ministry. This, Warner could not do. His expulsion prepared the way for a new commission; a mandate which would come to him within hours of hearing his suspension. From this point on, Warner was prepared neither to listen to the voice of human authority, nor submit to any ecclesiastical structure. Now, more than ever before, Daniel Warner was preeminently interested in seeing souls saved and sanctified. That he had to separate from his church in order to fulfil this divine commission was a small price to pay. Despite this momentous step his dissent was not yet complete.

Warner continued his ministry as an itinerant evangelist and Holiness preacher. As detailed in the next chapter he became involved in publishing and moved to Indiana where for a time he continued in fellowship with the Northern Indiana Eldership of the Winebrennerian Church. All along, however, Warner continued with his holiness preaching and emphases and as time went by increasingly came to despise what he called sectarianism. Three years had now passed since Warner proclaimed having a new vision and divine commission. The events from early 1878 through late 1881 are both intriguing and puzzling. If Warner believed so ardently that God had raised him up to join holiness and truth in a reformation of the church, apart from sectarianism, why, then, did Warner delay so long in making his final and decisive break? Why did it take nearly four years for Warner to accept his destiny and 'come out'? At length Warner began to question his relationship with the Holiness Association. There were several indications that Warner was about to 'come out' from all human organizations and serve God in God's one, true church. Warner was coming to terms with the implications of status quo American religion and in this coming to terms, *ipso facto* rejected it.[37]

---

[37] Merle D. Strege, *Tell Me Another Tale: Further Reflections on the Church of God* (Anderson: Warner Press, 1993), p. 96.

He ran into conflict with the Holiness Association at Terre Haute, Indiana in May 1881 after failing to get a resolution passed wherein recognition of denominations would no longer be valid for affiliation. In October 1881 at Beaver Dam, Indiana he attempted to persuade the Northern Indiana Eldership to accept his vision of radical holiness and unified non-sectarian Christianity. Warner proposed that a complete Biblical pattern of ecclesiastical polity be adopted, to wit, eliminating ministerial licenses and foregoing all formal church membership requirements, allowing the evidence of regeneration to function as the sole criterion for partnership in the body of Christ. The Eldership rather firmly declined to adopt Warner's resolution. Yet again he had failed to sell his vision. If he had imagined up to that point that the Winebrennerian Church of God was not a sect, Warner had no option now but to disclaim them along with the rest of Christendom and come out. He threw down the gauntlet. Declaring that every sectarian division of the church was sinful, Warner announced that he could no longer persist in supporting open sin. Of the less than thirty people in attendance five responded to his challenge, sided with Warner, and shook off the dust of their feet against the spiritual Babylon of the Winebrennerian fellowship.[38]

A similar occurrence in the same month at the annual meeting of the Northern Michigan Eldership of the Church of God marked the rise of come-outism associated with Daniel Warner. Warner had already been to Michigan preaching his vision of holiness and unity. His efforts met with popular support. But at the meeting on 15 October at Carson City the Eldership were considerably less receptive to the vision and commission of Daniel Warner. They rebuffed his efforts at reform. Anticipating that the Northern Michigan Eldership would differ little from its Indiana counterpart, the Michigan come-outers drew up a series of resolutions. In this statement the come-outers affirmed their sense of living in the last days, in the eschatological moment when, in the tradition of the Hebrew apocalyptic Book of Daniel, God's true saints would be delivered and the true

---

[38] Smith, *The Quest for Holiness and Unity*, p. 44.

house of God built yet again. With this consciousness firmly motivating their stance they resolved to live a life of holiness in anticipation of the end of the world, to join themselves to no organization save the 'church of God', to be led by the Holy Spirit, organized by the same spirit and governed by the Bible. The Michigan saints further resolved to abandon the practice of ministerial licensing and to recognize true ministers of the gospel on the basis of their 'fruits.' Fellowship was declared withheld from all ministers not demonstrating a godly life or whose teachings were at variance with the Word of God. Finally, it was resolved that fellowship would be extended to all Christians who were truly regenerated, who endeavored to forsake 'the snares and yokes of human parties' and who were willing to join with the single community of the faithful, built on Christ and the Scriptures and in the unity of the Spirit.[39]

There were those within American Christianity who perceived the rise of post-revolutionary America as the prelude to the millennium. Warner was not among them. For him, the experience of entire sanctification was the quintessential key to the Kingdom of God. Holiness denied and decried the world. Nothing in the secular realm had any relation to the transformation holiness effected in the lives of men and women. If Massachusetts Bay Colony was the city on a hill giving light to the world for those expecting America to lead the way to the millennium, then the beauty of holiness was the city on the hill for the come-outers. This city, not made by human hands, was the work of God and had been prepared to lead the remnant of true Christianity out of spiritual, sectarian Babylon into the light of a final reformation.

Eschewing all forms of human ecclesiastical organization, Warner resolved to belong to God's church in the biblical way. He could not agree with the opinion of Philip Schaff who insisted that true union in the end was essentially inward and

---

[39] The resolutions are set forth in Byers, *Birth of a Reformation*, p. 269.

spiritual.[40] For Warner this view had validity. But it stopped well short of the biblical ideal. In his first book Warner outlined this new vision of the Church of God and Christian union. First, the historic divisions of Christendom into denominational structures had been the work of the Devil and the cause of many souls being destroyed. Second, the sin of sectarianism must be borne by those belonging to the various sects. Third, the sole antidote for the disease of sectarianism was the personal experience of sanctification. Fourth, the formation of a non-sectarian body of believers was required by God's Word and constituted both a spiritual and visible union. Fifth, all those belonging to the true Church of God must be washed and cleansed from the iniquity of sectarianism.[41] At last, after nearly four years, Warner had taken that momentous step toward implementing the divine vision and commission he had received. According to Warner, no longer would Christians devise their own standards for church membership. Human control over entrance to the body of Christ was thereby eliminated. In this way the church could once again function visibly within the world as the true church of God. This community could now be the gathered body of Christ, dwelling together as the Church of God, belonging only to God.[42] With this step Warner helped to inaugurate a new era in American church history. But between the rhetoric and the reality, a familiar chasm began to open. The climate of religious democracy made it possible for Warner to disassociate himself from the formal Holiness movements, the Winebrennerian Church of God, and denominational Christianity altogether. That religious culture also allowed Warner, unhindered, to commence what he termed a final reformation of the church. But dissent, once again, was not tolerated by

---

[40] Schaff affirmed this view in his inaugural address as professor at Union Theological Seminary in 1871. Graham, *Cosmos in the Chaos: Philip Schaff's Interpretation of Nineteenth-Century American Religion*, p. 227.

[41] Warner, *Bible Proofs of the Second Work of Grace* (Goshen: E.U. Mennonite Publishing Society, 1880), pp. 431-2.

[42] Callen, *Contours of a Cause: The Theological Vision of the Church of God*, p. 35.

dissenters. Warner disliked theological controversy intensely and in fact did not permit it.[43] His vision and confidence in his divine commission by natural consequence led to his posture at the head of a dynamic movement. Warner's authority was promoted in a variety of ways: through preaching, editorializing, publications, and personal mediation at various junctures in early Church of God 'come out' history. Disruption of his divine commission could neither be ignored nor tolerated. On one occasion Warner physically threw a man out of a meeting for constantly disrupting the proceedings.[44] The validity of the assertion that '[n]o responsible leader of this movement has dared to assume (in theory at least) that she or he has the last word biblically or theologically' can be tested only in the fiery furnace of conflict and confrontation.[45] Warner eliminated conflict in two ways. As editor of the official Church of God publication, the *Gospel Trumpet*, he regularly used that medium to control opinion. Whenever conflict persisted Warner appealed to his calling and the Truth which had been entrusted to him. Loyalty to this transcended all other issues.[46] The future hymnologist Barney E. Warren was hand-picked by Warner in 1886 when the former was still a teenager. Warren's father objected to his son going off with Warner's evangelistic company. The protracted confrontation posited God against the sin of rebellion. The issue came to a head on one occasion with the following eye-witness account.

> As I recall the circumstances, Brother Warner stood pleading for the boy, but Tom [Warren, the boy's father] was obstinate. Suddenly Brother Warner seemed to be changed into another man. His eyes flashed as if with a sort of piercing fire; he stepped up close to the rebellious father, but did not touch him, and cried out: 'Tom Warren, you are fighting against God, and you cannot get away with it.' That strong man, a former wrestler,

---

[43] Strege, *Tell Me Another Tale*, p. 85.

[44] Axchie A. Bolitho, *To the Chief Singer: A Brief Story of the Work and Influence of Barney E. Warren* (Anderson: Gospel Trumpet Company, 1942), pp. 37-8.

[45] The assertion respecting authority is that of Barry Callen, *Contours of a Cause*, p. 45.

[46] Strege, *Tell Me Another Tale*, pp. 85-6.

trembled and sank to the floor, while Brother Warner stood over him and said: 'God has smitten you, and you cannot get up until you let Barney go.' After a while he yielded, and said: 'Barney is the Lord's.' Then Brother Warner said: 'Now you can get up'–and he did.[47]

Daniel Warner could not be deterred from his commission and his calling. Warner's adherence to his heavenly vision would eventually cost him his second wife.[48] According to some interpretations, Warner had no other choice but to take the path he did. It was the only course open to him on account of the fact that he was 'under the burden of an historic mission.'[49] But no matter the cost, Warner was driven by a force which gave him the ability to ignore all else, sacrifice everything else, and never be distracted for any length of time. Only death could distract Warner from his God-appointed course.

Following the failure of his second marriage in 1884 Warner established the 'flying messengers' who travelled the countryside more interested in promoting their Holiness Church of God message than they were in actually establishing churches. Warner, Sarah Smith, Nannie Kigar, Frances Miller and Barney Warren were the 'flying messengers.' This contingency—three women and two men, none married to each other—travelling around in a wagon was gist for the rumor mills in the four years (1884-8) they constituted the 'flying messengers'.[50] From Michigan to Mississippi, from Missouri to Pennsylvania, and as far afield as eastern Canada, the 'flying messengers' proclaimed Warner's vision.[51] Though this guerrilla evangelism had its obvious deficiencies, covering much ground but often

---

[47] This account was told by F.G. Smith and is in Bolitho, *To the Chief Singer: A Brief Story of the Work and Influence of Barney E. Warren*, pp. 12-13. Bolitho later says that the stand-off between Warren and Warner lasted two hours! *Ibid.*, p. 32.

[48] Byers, 'Pioneers of the Present Reformation', p. 19.

[49] Brown, *When the Trumpet Sounded*, p. 114.

[50] Strege, *Tell Me the Tale*, pp. 30, 39.

[51] Smith, *The Quest for Holiness and Unity*, pp. 59-80.

leaving little by way of substantial or permanent impression, the adventures of this extraordinary itinerant holiness band merits further attention in the context of the expansion of come-out Christianity and late nineteenth-century revivalism in the midwest.[52]

Two other novel ideas for evangelism marked the early come-out movement. Warner had attempted to put into service a 'salvation car'. In 1881 Warner came up with the idea of securing a rail road car and fitted out as a mobile evangelistic center. The cost proved prohibitive and despite direct appeals for funding in the pages of the *Gospel Trumpet* the project was never realized.[53] The second project, the *Floating Bethel* did succeed. In 1893 an idea was set forth for a floating meeting house to be launched on the Ohio River where it could float down to the Mississippi and on to the Gulf of Mexico. *Floating Bethel* would stop at every possible landing place and dock for meetings. A large river barge was secured, living quarters and a chapel constructed on board and in early 1894 *Floating Bethel* left Pittsburgh on its floating evangelistic tour south. Warner made this his base for the fall and winter of 1893. Though in service for nearly five years the innovative church was destroyed in a fire while docked at Moundsville, West Virginia.[54]

Another means of spreading the message of holiness and non-sectarian Christianity was through the medium of the camp meeting. Warner enthusiastically lent his support by participating in regular camp meetings.

> It was a marvel of divine power and glory last year, and we expect the coming meeting to exceed in glory, all others, as the redeemed hosts have

---

[52] Valorous B. Clear, *Where the Saints Have Trod: A Social History of the Church of God Reformation Movement* (Chesterfield, IN: Midwest Publications, 1977), pp. 85-7. 'The record of the travels and work of this company are worthy of a book.' Brown, *When the Trumpet Sounded*, p. 126.

[53] Smith, *The Quest for Holiness and Unity*, pp. 60-1.

[54] Smith, *Ibid.*, p. 74. There are photographs of *Floating Bethel* in Smith, *Ibid.*, p. 281 and Callen, *It's God's Church!*, p. 124.

been much increased in numbers, and advanced in the power and fire of the Holy Ghost. Make your arrangements to come with a tent.[55]

Between 1892 and 1895 there were established at least twenty-five annual grove meetings, fourteen camp meetings, along with several general assemblies in association with the Warner movement of come-out holiness.[56] Through the ministry of the 'flying messengers', itinerant holiness preaching, camp meetings, and the religious press, Daniel Warner promoted incessantly the cause and message of entire sanctification and non-sectarian Christianity. His evangelistic tours took him as far west as Los Angeles and by the early 1890s Warner's bi-monthly paper the *Gospel Trumpet* was printing between six and ten thousand copies per issue.[57]

In 1893 Warner married for the third time. His bride on this occasion was Frances 'Frankie' Miller one of the former 'flying messengers.' As he approached his fiftieth birthday, Warner seemed to age rapidly and appeared elderly. Photographs reveal his weak constitution, haggard features and the use of a cane. Warner expressed his hope to undertake a world tour, but his declining health made that an impossibility.[58] In May 1894 the Warner's took up residence in a new house on the edge of the camp grounds in Grand Junction, Michigan. Here, Daniel Warner spent most of the remaining eighteen months he had left to live. In the fall of 1895 Warner composed what was almost certainly his last poem. Perhaps he sensed the faint, but quickening steps of the Grim Reaper.

> After the Battle
>
> Lo, they are gone; that armored host
> Whose feet have daily pressed

---

[55] An announcement for a camp meeting at Bangor, Michigan in 1886 in Warner's paper the *Gospel Trumpet* (15 April 1886).

[56] Callen, *It's God's Church!*, pp. 140-1.

[57] Brown, *When the Trumpet Sounded*, p. 163.

[58] Byers, *Birth of a Reformation*, pp. 419-21.

> And all is hushed to rest.
>
> But hark! the leaves upon the trees
>   In echoes lisp their song,
> And on the wings of every breeze
>   Salvation floats along.
>
> But they are gone, those heralds strong,
>   Who stand within the sun,
> And all that army dressed in white
>   To other fields have run:
> And from this holy battle-field
>   New waves of glory roll,
> And these, in turn, will others wake,
>   To spread from pole to pole.[59]

On the first day of December Warner preached a sermon in the school house on the camp grounds at Grand Junction. It was to be his last discourse. Over the course of the next several days his health declined rapidly and on the night of 12 December 1895 at his new home in Grand Junction, Michigan, Daniel S. Warner succumbed to pneumonia and died at the age of fifty three. While the legacy he engendered does not always and openly acknowledge it, Warner is to be rightly regarded as the founder of the Church of God Reformation Movement (Anderson Indiana).[60]

Accolades poured in from around the come-out movement in tribute to the slife and legacy of Daniel Warner. According to his followers, he had fought a good fight, he had finished the course, he had kept the faith. The historical legacy of the come-out Holiness movement is witness to the nature of that faith.

> He was evidently chosen of God as a great reformer. While he was meek, mild, and gentle, he was heroic and fearless as a Martin Luther. We shall

---

[59] These two stanzas have been extracted from the larger poem quoted in Byers, *Birth of a Reformation*, pp. 423-5.

[60] Strege, *Tell Me Another Tale*, p. 7 points out the obvious facts that it is Warner's name which is mentioned far more frequently than any other among the early pioneers, that Warner's name has been memorialized in institutions, publishing houses and churches.

do well to preserve his words of writings and to remember his example, for we shall thereby be worth more to God and souls.[61]

---

[61] The words of Barney Warren quoted in Byers, *Birth of a Reformation*, p. 441.

CHAPTER 5

Conflict and Crisis in the Kingdom of God in Ohio

On the last Sunday of the meeting, in the morning service, when the hour of preaching arrived, Brother Warner leaped into the pulpit and cried, 'Fire, *fire, FIRE*'. . . . His subject was The Consuming and Destroying of Apostate Christianity—the consuming fulfilled in the present reform work, and accomplished 'with the spirit of his mouth' (the flaming truth accompanied by the fire of holiness) . . . . For three and one half hours the message came forth like mighty thunder-peals. People sat spell-bound during all that time. I trembled under the mighty power of God. Under such preaching, it was not difficult to find the highway that leads to Zion.[1]

♠ ♠

In the archives of the Otto F. Linn Library of Warner Pacific College in Portland, Oregon there is a book which has on the frontispiece these words penned by the author: 'To the students of Warner Pacific College. May you keep the Warner message ever relevant.'[2] There is of course sufficient room for ambiguity about the phrase 'the Warner message.' The reference may be directly to Warner himself or the author may have had in mind the mission statement of Warner Pacific College. Even if the reference were clearly to the latter there must surely

---

[1] This at the camp meeting in Perryville, Pennsylvania in August 1893. Recounted in Herbert M. Riggle, *Pioneer Evangelism* (Anderson: Gospel Trumpet Co., 1924), pp. 59-60.

[2] Valorous B. Clear, *Where the Saints Have Trod: A Social History of the Church of God Reformation Movement* (Chesterfield, IN: Midwest Publications, 1977).

be some relation between the Warner of history and an institution of higher learning named after him, particularly when the volume in question is a history of the movement Warner inspired.

Daniel Warner has been dead for one hundred years. Who was he and what was his message? There has never existed a *communis opinio* for either of these questions. In many ways Warner continues to exist today, much as he did during his own lifetime, as an enigmatic religious itinerant. Certainly Warner was a product of nineteenth-century American revivalism. His life was both a lamp and a mirror of that evolving religious and cultural context. He illuminated that fascinating plethora of religious enthusiasm, piety and experimentation surging through the uneven halls and crowded rooms of the beleaguered house of American religion. At the same time Warner's career reflected the eager expectancy, unbridled enthusiasm and restless ferment of the social, cultural and philosophical contours of religious innovation in America during a time he called 'the evening light.'[3] In some ways his message was the same as every other religious prophet, in others it was profoundly different. Between the lamp and the mirror lies the intrigue of Warner. A distinctive product of religious democracy he was prominent among those to underscore the paradox of that development.

Today Warner's name is well known, at least in certain American religious circles, but the man and his message remain shrouded behind the institutions and churches erected in his name. In the main, the historiography of the movement he inspired has, for the most part, reflected one particular interpretation and analysis of the man and his message. There have been very few serious dissenters to that portrait. While there is much that is valid, worthy and worthwhile in those interpretations of Warner, the focus of this chapter is essentially a re-opening of

---

[3] See for example his hymn, 'The Evening Light,' in *Songs of the Evening Light*, eds., Barney E. Warren and Andrew L. Byers (Grand Junction, MI: Gospel Trumpet Publishing Co., 1897), no. 1. The first stanza is representative: 'Brighter days are sweetly dawning, oh, the glory looms in sight! For the cloudy day is waning, and the evening shall be light.'

the case of Warner's most famous, or perhaps infamous, detractor. Sarah Ann Keller became Daniel Warner's second wife in 1874. Ten years later she abandoned her marriage vows, denounced her husband publicly, and thereafter obtained an uncontested divorce. Sarah Warner has never been taken seriously. In the paradox of religious democracy in nineteenth-century America, as it relates to Warner, it is worthwhile to look again at her involvement in early Church of God history and particularly at her decisive break with Daniel Warner. She is likely not the key to deciphering the mystery of the man and message of Warner, but quite clearly she does provide an important clue toward increased understanding. While her rôle certainly does not count as a major dimension in American religious history, she is one of those small, but important, pieces of information that helps add a little more detail to the puzzle that remains of some aspects of the life and thought of Daniel Warner.

I. Denouncing 'Come-Out' Christianity

> There has sprung up among us a party with holiness as a watchword; they have holiness associations, holiness meetings, holiness preachers, holiness evangelists, and holiness property. Religious experience is represented as if it consists of only two steps, the first step out of condemnation into peace and the next step into Christian perfection . . . . we deplore their teaching and methods in so far as they claim a monopoly of the experience, practice, and advocacy of holiness, and separate themselves from the body of ministers and disciples.[4]

♠ ♠

---

[4] The bishops of the Methodist Episcopal Church, South addressing the General Conference in 1894. Quoted in Charles E. Jones, *Perfectionist Persuasion: The Holiness Movement and American Methodism, 1867-1936* (Metuchen, N.J.: The Scarecrow Press, Inc., 1974), p. 63.

Daniel Sidney Warner (1842-1895) was the preeminent founder of the Church of God Reformation Movement. He rose from virtual obscurity to the forefront of the expanding Holiness movements. The circumstances surrounding his relationship to Sarah Keller are of importance for the purpose of this chapter. Sometime prior to 1867 Warner was engaged to Frances Stocking who later succumbed to insanity.[5] On 5 September 1867 Warner married Tamzen Ann Kerr, probably one of his students. She died on 26 May 1872. Sometime in 1873 Warner met the Keller family who lived in Upper Sandusky, Ohio. A romantic relationship between the thirty-one year old Warner and the eighteen year old Sarah Keller soon ensued. Within a few months Warner was affectionately referring to her as 'my darling Sarah.'[6] Before the month had passed, Warner was speaking of Sarah in the context of imminent matrimony.[7] A marriage license was issued on 2 June 1874 with the wedding occurring two days later. As we have already seen, at the time of his second marriage Daniel Warner was an itinerant preacher affiliated with the West Ohio Eldership of the Winebrennerian Church.[8] Committing matrimony did not sidetrack Warner's ministry routine for long. Two days after his marriage Warner was in Toledo attending a grove meeting. Warner's frequent and prolonged absences from Sarah and their itinerant lifestyle later had serious repercussions. Within three weeks Sarah was 'much troubled and depressed.' Six

---

[5] *Journal*, 11 June 1874.

[6] *Journal*, 17 March 1874.

[7] See for example, *Ibid.*, 30 March, 9-10 April, 1874.

[8] Warner served as First Clerk at the thirteenth West Ohio Eldership Conference on 15 October 1869 held at Kirby, Wyandot County. Warner held the same position at the fourteenth conference on 14 October 1870 at Hopewell, Seneca County and similarly at the fifteenth conference on 13 October 1871 at Findlay, Hancock County. At the sixteenth conference of the West Ohio Eldership on 11 October 1872 at South Bridgewater, Williams County, the young Daniel Warner gave the opening sermon. See C.H. Forney, *History of the Churches of God in the United States of North America* (Harrisburg, PA: Publishing House of the Churches of God, 1914), pp. 562-3.

months later Warner noted that his absence 'seems to rob her of all the happiness of life.' Warner may have been moved by her despondency, but for him, there was nothing he could do. 'It was nearly enough to break my blessed wife's heart to have me leave her. O Lord comfort her heart. Were it not that "necessity is laid upon," I could not leave her.'[9] The profound and heart-wrenching difficulty of being married to a man like Daniel Warner is apparent and has been noted already.[10] However, Warner's absolute commitment to his calling did not gladly abide being surpassed by any other obligation, responsibility or interest.

Marital dissatisfaction in the Warner household was exacerbated by the untimely death of their three-year-old daughter, Levilla, in 1878 and potentially by Warner's developing Holiness theology which, in the words of the Winebrennerian historian C.H. Forney, '. . . gave the brotherhood considerable trouble.'[11] Essentially, Warner's association with certain Holiness factions had influenced him toward adopting the theological premise that sanctification functioned in the lives of Christians as a distinct second work of grace. This doctrine did not find wide acceptance within the Winebrennerian fellowship. After repeated warnings by the West Ohio Eldership and Warner's persistence he was, in 1878, ultimately expelled.[12] Warner promptly declared his complete separation from denominational Christianity and forthwith pursued wholeheartedly his theological leanings. There is no evidence to suggest that at this time Sarah had any theological

---

[9] On this see Warner's comments in his *Journal*, 27 June 1874, 27 January 1875, and 16 February 1875, and *passim*.

[10] See for example Robert H. Reardon, *The Early Morning Light* (Anderson: Warner Press, 1979), pp. 17-18.

[11] Forney, *History of the Churches of God*, p. 561.

[12] A result of the Daniel Warner case prompted the committee on resolutions to submit the following statement to the twenty-second West Ohio Eldership Conference in 1878: 'That any minister of this body that may presume to preach the dogma of a second work for sanctification shall be deemed unsound in the theology of the Church of God, and should not hold an ecclesiastical relation as a minister in this Eldership.' *Ibid.*, p. 567.

reservations.

Warner's new commission as the leader of a radical, separatist movement apparently was of divine origin.

> On the 31st of last January the Lord showed me that holiness could never prosper upon sectarian soil encumbered by human creeds and party names and he gave me a new commission to join holiness and all truth together and build up the apostolical church of the living God. Praise his name I will obey him.[13]

Late in 1880 two Holiness papers, the *Herald of Gospel Freedom* and *The Pilgrim* merged to form the *Gospel Trumpet*. Within six months Warner emerged as the sole editor. From 1881 onwards the *Gospel Trumpet* had as its main mission the promotion of Warner's newly discovered ideas about holiness and God's true church.[14] The paper proved to be an integral component in the Warner campaign, joining the ever-increasing stream which sustained the culture of religious print. Beyond the paper, the movement began publishing alternative hymnals with their purpose clearly stated: 'It is a fact well known . . . that the hymns of the past fail to express the glorious light and liberty, Grace, Truth, and Power the Free and Holy Church has attained in this blessed evening light.'[15] The new hymnody of the Warner movement proposed to augment the glow of the evening light.

During this time of transition and renewal there is evidence to suggest that

---

[13] *Journal*, 7 March 1878. There is an inexplicable five-week interval between the commission and the diary notation.

[14] See John W. V. Smith, *The Quest for Holiness and Unity*, pp. 44, 55-8, and p. 452 n. 3. The history of the *Gospel Trumpet* is recounted in Harold L. Phillips, *Miracle of Survival* (Anderson: Warner Press, 1979). See pp. 19-47 for the Warner era. In June 1962 the *Gospel Trumpet* changed its name to *Vital Christianity*. The periodical continued to publish regularly until August 1996, a history of 115 years.

[15] Preface, *Songs of Victory*, ed., Joseph C. Fisher, 4th Edition (Grand Junction, no publisher listed, 1885). See also the preface to *Echoes from Glory*, eds., Barney E. Warren and Daniel S. Warner (Grand Junction: The Gospel Trumpet Publishing Co., 1893), 'The book will be found to sing nearly all the precious themes of the gospel, especially the "Present Truth," in which the saints are established.'

Sarah Warner had moved into a quasi-leadership rôle. During services she sometimes 'testified boldly to the second work and admonished the church.' On other occasions Sarah opened the meeting and provided spiritual leadership. In 1878 Sarah actually functioned in leadership capacities apart from Warner. She was instrumental in the leadership at a revival in Mansfield, Ohio in March of that year and in fact had been called specifically for that purpose. Even Warner reluctantly came to admit that the Holy Spirit had confirmed Sarah's call to him.[16] During the period 1883-1884 there were no fewer than twenty-four letters published in the *Gospel Trumpet* addressed to both 'Brother and Sister Warner.'[17] While she did not in any way begin to rival her husband in leadership ability or popularity the foregoing is significant to suggest that Sarah had recognizable leadership qualities.

Unknown to Warner, but clearly looming on the horizon, was a gathering storm of crisis for Warner's fledgling Holiness movement. In the eye of the impending storm was the leadership of Sarah Warner. At the height of the tempest Sarah was catapulted into an even further conspicuous leadership rôle. It became a test of religious democracy; a confrontation with theological absolutism.

A peculiar episodic incident brought Warner to his first major test. Sometime before 1883 a young minister, R.S. Stockwell, joined the Warner effort. Stockwell received the highest praise from Warner and was enthusiastically endorsed and promoted by the *Gospel Trumpet*. 'Brother R.S. Stockwell, of Ada, Ohio expects to devote himself to the holiness evangelistic work. He is full of the Spirit, and the light of God's awful present truth. A mighty man of God. Send and get him to work for souls wherever the Lord wills.' Elsewhere, Stockwell was

---

[16] For Sarah's activities see Warner's *Journal* entries for 9 September 1877, 16 November 1877, and 23 March 1878.

[17] See *Gospel Trumpet* issues for 1 October, 15 October, 15 November, 1 December, and 15 December, 1883, and 15 April 1884. Too much should not be made of this. Many letters in the same period were addressed exclusively to 'Brother Warner.' Nonetheless, her inclusion with Warner as 'co-leaders' of the new Holiness movement, at least in the minds of some, is not wholly without significance.

regarded as 'blessed with the gift of healing, and of prophecy' and 'the Lord wonderfully used . . . [him].'[18] Not long thereafter, in early 1884, a small movement of discontent arose against Warner guided by the 'super-papal authority of Stockwell.'[19] In the first instance Stockwell began promoting a teaching known as 'marital purity.' Marital purity, or marital celibacy, was a teaching which insisted upon sexual abstinence even within a marriage relationship. It was in fact considered part of the sanctification experience and constituted a third work of grace.[20] Contrary to some opinion Stockwell was not the originator of this idea. Indeed, the teaching represented a unique strand in the Holiness movements and was centered in Cincinnati. Without ever explicating her reasons, Sarah accepted Stockwell's teaching. This must have placed an additional, tremendous burden on an already strained marriage. In the second confrontation with Warner, Stockwell, an associate named Rice, together with Sarah, attempted to talk Warner into turning over his controlling interests in the *Gospel Trumpet* to someone else. Warner withstood them and the crisis seemed past.[21] Stockwell disappeared from the stage of history as abruptly as he had appeared never to be heard from again. Nothing further is known of Stockwell's life before his sudden appearance in Bucyrus, Ohio, and no trace of him thereafter has ever been disclosed. His brief encounter with Daniel Warner, however, had lasting effects. Shortly after

---

[18] Editorial, 'Ready to go for Jesus,' *Gospel Trumpet*, (1 December 1883), editorial, 'Glorious Meeting Near Dixon, O.', *Ibid.*, and unsigned, 'The Assembly Meeting,' *Ibid.*, (15 November 1883). Stockwell was mentioned in the *Gospel Trumpet* as early as the previous year. See the unsigned article, 'Our Tour in Ohio,' *Ibid.*, (22 September 1882). Pagination in the *Gospel Trumpet* did not begin until the first issue of 1898.

[19] One of Warner's later designations for Stockwell in his, 'A Fallen Woman,' *Gospel Trumpet*, (15 July 1884).

[20] The notion of a third work of grace was denied by the Warner camp in an unsigned article titled, 'Is There a Third Grace?' *Gospel Trumpet*, (1 November 1883).

[21] For the Stockwell incident see Byers, *Birth of a Reformation*, pp. 292-295. It is possible that 'S. Rice' referred to by Warner in 'Our Tour in Ohio,' *Gospel Trumpet*, (22 September 1882) is the same individual.

Stockwell vanished, Sarah followed suit. The difference in their departures was that Sarah would be heard from again rather dramatically.

There is sufficient evidence to cast doubt upon the thesis that Sarah had simply been duped by the 'fuddled prophet,' the 'grumbling prophet,' the 'whimpling prophet,' the 'abominable false prophet.'[22] Indeed, Stockwell clearly may have been the trigger which forced Sarah forward in coming to terms with her own profound marital discontent and nagging doubts about the direction of the movement. Within weeks of abandoning Warner and depriving him of his three-year-old son Sidney, Sarah Warner moved to the offensive. In the 1 May 1884 issue of the *Christian Harvester* she systematically denounced the Warner movement in an article titled, 'Come-Outism Renounced.' The *Christian Harvester*, based in Cleveland, was a rival Holiness paper edited by Thomas K. Doty which had already denounced the tenets of 'come-outism.'[23] The previous year the *Gospel Trumpet* had referred to the *Christian Harvester* as an example of the 'babylon works' of those who are outside the truth,[24] and an editorial in the *Gospel Trumpet* sarcastically referred to Doty as 'that dear little man of the Harvester . . . .'[25] A month after Sarah Warner published her critique of Warner's holiness doctrine the *Gospel Trumpet* condemned the *Christian Harvester* together

---

[22] Warner, *Poems of Grace and Truth*, pp. 66-67 and 'A Fallen Woman,' *Gospel Trumpet*, (15 July 1884). These are terms Warner used to express his contempt for Stockwell.

[23] Aubrey L. Forrest, 'A Study of the Development of the Basic Doctrines and Institutional Patterns in the Church of God (Anderson, Indiana),' unpublished Ph.D. dissertation, University of Southern California, 1948, p. 41. John W.V. Smith has stated that through letters to rival holiness papers Sarah denounced Warner and criticized his teachings. *The Quest for Holiness and Unity*, p. 65. Apart from the aforementioned article no other writings by Sarah Warner have been uncovered.

[24] Unsigned article, 'Dead Works,' *Gospel Trumpet*, (15 October 1883).

[25] *Gospel Trumpet*, (1 June 1884).

with a number of other papers as being imbued with the spirit of antichrist.[26] The Sarah Warner article created an immediate sensation.[27] No sooner had the article been released but that it took on a life of its own. Whatever Sarah Warner intended with its composition was certainly overshadowed by the wide-ranging responses to it. Deplored by the Warner circle, it was eagerly seized upon and taken up by Warner's opponents and *Gospel Trumpet* rivals. Because of its fundamental importance for the topic at hand, and its relevance for early Church of God history and an analysis of Warner within the paradox of religious democracy, the text is produced here in its entirety.

Come-Outism Renounced

The following communication pretty fully explains itself. It was written by Sister Warner, the wife of D.S. Warner, the Come-out leader, and editor of the Gospel Trumpet. Those who know Sister W. generally, among the straight holiness people, have confidence in her integrity. God bless her, and may she save her husband from his strong delusions. She desires the holiness papers to copy her article:

Dear Brother Doty: My soul praises God today for a perfect salvation in Jesus. He sweetly abides in my heart, and I do know that his Word is true. His promises to save from all sin and keep in perfect peace are most wonderfully verified in my case; praise his name! Salvation is sweeter to my soul every day I live.

'And how sweetly Jesus whispers,
Take the cross, thou needst not fear;
For I've trod this way before thee,
And the glory lingers near.'

Yea, praise God for the cross, and the glory that always follows.

I feel it my duty to say to all God's children, that he has opened my

---

[26] Editorial, *Gospel Trumpet*, (1 June 1884).

[27] In addition to appearing in the *Christian Harvester* (1 May 1884) it was also printed in the *Michigan Holiness Record* 2 (July 1884). It is here produced from the text published in Byers, *Birth of a Reformation*, pp. 297-299. Searches thus far have failed to produce an extant copy of the *Christian Harvester*. Volume two of the *Michigan Holiness Record* is available at Asbury Theological Seminary and at the Bentley Historical Library in the University of Michigan at Ann Arbor. In both instances, however, the relevant pages are missing from the microfilm copy.

eyes to see the evils of come-outism. I am free from it, and forever renounce it and praise God that he has so completely delivered me from the spirit of it. I am thoroughly convinced that this effort to unite God's people by calling them out of the churches is not God's plan of unity. It simply cuts off a few members by themselves, who get an idea that none are clearly sanctified unless they see as 'we' do; and, then, they have a harsh grating that is the very opposite of love. I have found that the predominant spirit of the come-out movement is the same self-righteous, pharisaical spirit that Christ rebuked when he was here on earth. They hold and teach that no one can be entirely sanctified and belong to a 'sect.'

It is not necessary for me to speak of the fanaticism and absurdities connected with this movement; but I am not at all surprised to hear of men losing their minds after passing through such a meeting as the assembly at Sulphur Springs last November. I have seen more Babylon confusion outside the churches than in. I know whereof I speak, for I have been connected with the movement from its beginning, and as you all know, at the very head of it. And while I believe it my duty before God to renounce it, and stand aloof from it, I have all charity for those connected with it. I am confident that I have nothing in my heart but love toward them all, and love to my husband; nor do I reject him, but I can not endorse either the movement or its organ, the Gospel Trumpet. I must obey God, and walk in the light he has given me, or forfeit salvation, which I can not afford to do. I have suffered the loss of all things, but rejoice to know that I am counted worthy to suffer for Jesus' sake.

In taking this step for God I have not been hasty. I have been convicted of this duty for some time. Circumstances and the manifestations of the spirit of this movement have been such for several months past that I fear further delay on my part would be disastrous to the cause of Christ and my own soul. I humbly ask the prayers of all God's children that he will keep me firm and sweet while passing through the furnace.

Mrs. S.A. Warner

Upper Sandusky, Ohio, Apr. 22, 1884.

One does not have to speculate long to imagine what sort of impact Sarah's renunciation had upon rival Holiness camps, the popular piety of Warner's followers and not less upon Daniel Warner himself. Warner's protracted struggle over this unprecedented upheaval is well documented.[28] He posed a rebuttal, then continued as before.[29]

Why did Sarah Warner write this article? Doubtless she was fully cognizant of the embarrassment and lingering humiliation it would bring to Warner like salt on the open wound of her departure. There are several possibilities. The obvious and sometime popular option is the influence of R.S. Stockwell. However, as alluded to earlier, the very content of the *Christian Harvester* article seems to point away from that direction. Any hint of improprieties with Stockwell, manifested in their common thrust to wrest control of the *Gospel Trumpet* away from Daniel Warner, together with their subsequent simultaneous rejection of him is offset by their common profession of adherence to the notion of 'marital purity.' Furthermore, an argument against this thesis is strengthened by the total lack of hard evidence and the complete absence of even a suggestion of any inappropriate behavior or subsequent relationship. Another commonplace in most discussions of Sarah Warner tends to regard her and her denunciations of Warner in the proverbial 'axe to grind' category. However, the components one might expect to find in the article to document such a premise are entirely lacking. She does not mention the unhappiness in her marriage we clearly know existed. There are no allusions to the sort of despondency which characterized the early years of her marriage. She does not argue in any way for the doctrinal proposition *vis-à-vis* marital purity even though she had clearly accepted the tenet earlier in the year. Her tone is neither hostile nor abusive. The argument is coherent without excessive rancour. It is not characterized by anger or by an unreasoning agitation. Though one might clearly expect it, there is no direct attack upon the person or character of Daniel Warner. While it would be possible to argue otherwise there is not a

---

[28] *cf.* Warner's own emotions in *Poems of Grace and Truth*, pp. 61-116 and the narrative account in Byers, *Birth of a Reformation*, pp. 295-301.

[29] 'A Fallen Woman,' *Gospel Trumpet*, (15 July 1884). The document is reproduced in Appendix A. and is treated below.

detectable overtone of spiritual imperialism or superiority in the article. There does exist, however, within the text a number of rationale which Sarah Warner sets forth as the motivating factors in her departure from the 'Come-Out' movement and her separation from Warner.

An analysis of 'Come-Outism Renounced' yields a number of provocative arguments against the radical, separatist movement affiliated with Daniel Warner. First, Sarah drew attention to 'the spirit of it [come-outism].' The context would indicate that by this she had specific concerns about the attitude being fostered and projected by the movement. Second, there is some hesitation concerning the end result of the movement's quest for Christian unity. The ' . . . effort to unite God's people by calling them out of the churches is not God's plan of unity.' Sarah Warner suggested that rather than producing unity the Come-Out movement was breeding division. Third, she asserted that the Warner group linked true sanctification to their own peculiar interpretation and understanding of Christian life. In other words, the Warner faction insisted that ' . . . none are clearly sanctified unless they see as "we" do . . . .' The implication Sarah advanced clearly drew a line of demarcation understood by Warner and his associations between the truth of their position and the rest of professing Christians. Fourth, Sarah drew attention to the correlation between seeing as 'we' do and an air of self-righteousness. 'I have found that the predominant spirit of the come-out movement is the same self-righteous, pharisaical spirit that Christ rebuked . . . .' Her implication was that Warner and his followers had laid an exclusive claim to spiritual insight and truth and were now the guardians of religious revelation on earth. Fifth, she proposed on the basis of the foregoing points that the Come-Out movement had obtained a superior spiritual plateau above the mass of denominational Christianity, derogatorily referred to as sects.' 'They hold and teach that no one can be entirely sanctified and belong to a "sect."' Here, Sarah attributed to the Come-Out movement the key to entire sanctification. The implication was that by belonging to the Come-Out movement one may be entirely sanctified, an experience not possible elsewhere. Sixth, and finally, Sarah accused her former colleagues of 'fanaticism and absurdities.' She made vague reference to an incident at Sulphur Springs, Ohio in November 1883. She clearly alleged that the movement was guilty of extremism and excess.

The foregoing synopsis of 'Come-Outism Renounced' would appear to suggest that the author was engaged in a philosophical/theological dissent rather than simply lashing out in an emotional reaction. Her theses are both provocative and problematic. They are provocative because they force us to take a new and different look at Daniel Warner. They are equally problematic in that they run counter to the point of contradicting the pervasive portrait of Warner painted so compellingly and consistently on the canvas of Church of God historiography. One may either accept Sarah Warner uncritically or one may reject her out-of-hand equally uncritically. The only reliable method for testing her allegations against the early Come-Out movement is through an analysis of the works of Daniel Warner which will surely either corroborate or refute her ideas. Before embarking upon such an investigation it will be helpful to briefly peruse the expressed opinions held concerning Daniel and Sarah Warner in the early history of the Church of God.

II. Creating the Warner Myth

> In my estimation, there never lived a more holy or godly man than he. I doubt whether any other reformer was any more devoted to the cause of Christ than he, or ever preached sermons that were more deep or soul-stirring than his. He lives in the hearts of the people today, and in his writings will be heard until the end of time.[30]

♠ ♠

---

[30] The testimony of Julia Cheeseman as quoted in Byers, *Birth of a Reformation*, pp. 430-1.

Almost always the disciples pervert the masters: Jesus, Paul, Augustine, Luther, Calvin, Wesley, Barth and on and on. Without fail they suffered the metamorphosing tendencies of their followers. On the other hand, the disciples predictably romanticize the masters. The intention in this study is not to deal with the former issue, but a consideration of the latter is unavoidable. Sarah Warner's contentions do not square with the commonly held conceptions of Daniel Warner. By all accounts Warner was a charismatic and effective communicator. Three précis illuminate Warner's staying power as a preacher. Jacob W. Byers reported that at a camp meeting in Los Angeles in 1892 Warner preached three sermons of three hours each in a single Sunday service![31] In the archives of the Church of God there is an unpublished paper titled 'The Meeting at Sycamore Chapel' by D. Sidney Warner, the son of Daniel Warner. It recounts a particular event which took place in the summer of 1886 in the vicinity of Beaver Dam in North-Central Indiana. The Sycamore Chapel belonged to the Campbellites. Alfred B. Palmer was preaching on the subject of miracles when in mid-sermon he was accosted by a skeptic who produced a glass of water and urged Palmer to turn it into wine. This unexpected challenge de-railed Palmer and left him momentarily stunned. Palmer was rescued by Warner who happened to be sitting on the platform. Warner leaped to his feet with the dominical words recorded twice in the Gospel of St. Matthew: 'An evil and adulterous generation seeketh after a sign; and there shall no sign be given to it but the sign of the prophet Jonas.' The sign of the prophet Jonah in Sycamore Chapel was decisive. Warner then continued.'"I command you in the name of the Lord, to go and sit down." The man returned to his seat, and then for more than an hour Bro Warner poured out the Word of God and people sat spellbound.'[32] Palmer's sermon on miracles had taken an unforeseen turn.

---

[31] Cited in Barry L. Callen, ed., *A Time to Remember: Beginnings* [Church of God Heritage Series, Vol. 1] (Anderson: Warner Press, 1977), p. 91.

[32] D. Sidney Warner, 'The Meeting at Sycamore Chapel.' typescript, Archives, Anderson University.

218   *Conflict and Crisis in the Kingdom of God in Ohio*

Attached to the same document is an account of the first camp meeting at Grand Junction, Michigan in June 1892 as recalled by Frank Smith wherein Warner preached a lengthy sermon. Apparently Warner had been preaching on the scattering and gathering of God's people for two hours when the dinner bell sounded. Warner had only completed his homily on the scattering of God's people. He asked the congregation whether or not he ought to stop for dinner or should he proceed. The audience urged him on. Whereupon he departed on a two hour and ten minute discourse on the gathering of God's people. These incidents demonstrate Warner's captivating presence in the pulpit.[33]

However, while Warner clearly was a superb communicator one must also take into consideration the historical context. The personality was significant, but the popular mind-set should not be minimized. Long sermons, extended revivals and all-night prayer meetings were common during this period in history.[34] The church functioned as a social center in a way it does not in late twentieth-century America. Warner was not, then, unique in nineteenth-century America for protracted pulpiteering. His pre-occupation with preaching, though perhaps excessive, was likewise illuminating both of the Holiness movements and the nineteenth century in general.[35]

---

[33]   The down side of the aforementioned source lies in the fact that the events Sidney Warner recounts occurred at a time when he was all of five years old. Its recollected value has either been augmented by sources unnamed or its accuracy must be questioned. The four hour and ten minute sermon is attested to also in Byers, *Birth of a Reformation*, p. 437. According to Gale Hetrick, the first camp meeting at Grand Junction began on 14 June 1892. *Laughter Among the Trumpets: A History of the Church of God in Michigan* (Lansing: Church of God in Michigan, 1980), p. 60.

[34]   Francis Asbury reported in his journal for 1 June 1800 the details of a meeting in Delaware. '. . . we began our love feast at half-past eight; meeting was continued (except for one hour's intermission) until four o'clock, and some people never left the house until nearly midnight . . . .' *The Journal and Letters of Francis Asbury*, volume 2, p. 234.

[35]   Warner's obsession with preaching is revealed early on in his career when he wrote of being nearly beside himself at the prospects of staying home to care for Sarah and Levilla who were ill instead of preaching. '. . . I dare not spend the Lord's day

In 1880 a council was held in Indianapolis concerning the as yet unborn *Gospel Trumpet*. The conviction was expressed in that context that Daniel Warner was called by the Holy Spirit through divine providence to promote salvation through the vehicular organ of the *Gospel Trumpet*.[36] Warner, quite naturally, was regarded by his disciples as an instrument of the Holy Spirit.[37] Warner's work constituted an 'historic mission'[38] and in that remarkable constitution became for his followers the 'final reformation' of the church in the same spirit as the European reformations of the later Middle Ages and early modern period. The

---

without doing something for Christ, but I failed to get a place to preach . . . . this is the second Sabbath in eight years that I have not preached the word of God . . . . Felt ill at ease that I could not be preaching somewhere.' *Journal*, 27-28 March 1875. On another occasion Warner wrote that due to sickness in the family ' . . . was compelled to stay home . . . . O how wretched I felt all day . . . . I know there were crowded houses to hear the Gospel. O how I longed to preach to them.' *Journal*, 31 December 1876. There are no Warner sermon texts extant. Indeed, Warner never mentioned in his journal studying for, or preparing sermons. Much of Warner's preaching was probably extemporaneous, similar to his unexpected hour-long discourse at Grand Junction referred to above. This was not all that uncommon. In his journal dated 18 August 1853 John Humphrey Noyes wrote: 'In the evening I preached a written sermon, and resolved never to do so again unless by absolute necessity.' Quoted in *Religious Experience of John Humphrey Noyes Founder of the Oneida Community*, ed., George Wallingford Noyes (New York: The MacMillan Company, 1923), p. 60.

[36] The note and some details of the Indianapolis meeting may be found in a manuscript book vaguely catalogued in the Anderson University Archives as Book 07: Scratch Book. D.S. Warner papers. Archives, Anderson University. Indeed, Warner was convinced that the *Gospel Trumpet* was God's paper. Phillips, *Miracle of Survival*, p. 23. Elsewhere, Warner wrote a hymn titled, 'The Gospel Trumpet' which alluded to the destruction of Babylon. In *Songs of Victory*, no. 80.

[37] See for example the sympathetic treatment by Ethan Henry Waller, 'The Doctrine of the Holy Spirit in the Preaching and Teaching of Daniel S. Warner,' unpublished B.D. Thesis, School of Religion, Butler University, 1954, *passim*.

[38] Brown, *When the Trumpet Sounded*, p. 114. Brown notes that 1842 was a 'year of decision,' a turning point in American history for, among other things, it was the year of Warner's birth. *Ibid.*, pp. 42-43.

difference this time was the unique 'elements of finality.'[39]

The rôle of Daniel Sidney Warner in this final reformation is nowhere better expressed than in the words of Andrew Byers: '. . . Daniel S. Warner, destined to be one of the principal instruments in God's hands to produce a shaking in the ranks of spiritual Israel, and to lead the hosts of the Lord back to Zion from their wanderings in the wilderness of denominationalism.'[40] Warner was, then, '. . . a remarkable example of a man possessing the Christian spirit and the Christian graces wonderfully developed.' He was 'Christ-like' in thought, word and deed.[41] On the basis of this presupposition it is little wonder that Byers, in his prolific citing from Warner's journal, carefully edited out those sections which did not support the accepted thesis nor contribute to the creation of myth.[42] Notwithstanding this claim, Charles E. Brown has maintained that Warner '. . . never allowed his preconceptions to blind him to a present truth . . . .'[43] Others reported

---

[39] Byers, *Birth of a Reformation*, p. 19. The early hymn books of the movement reflect this conviction. The preface to *Echoes from Glory* makes reference to 'this present and last reformation of divine truth . . . .' The preface to *Songs of the Evening Light* refers to 'this great and last reformation.'

[40] Byers, *Birth of a Reformation*, p. 30.

[41] *Ibid.*, p. 29.

[42] This was observed after reading Warner's *Journal* and subsequently the work of Byers. In some instances Byers omits portions of lines or entire sentences altogether, without any indication. The observation is, as it turns out, not original with this research. 'Significant portions of the journal have been edited out by Byers when he uses them. Many of these are passages which show a very human side of Warner.' Kenneth Lee Watts, 'Journal of D.S. Warner Typescript Copy, footnoted and together with notes,' unpublished paper, 1983, p. 384. This annotated version of Warner's journals is kept in the Anderson University Archives. It is possible that Byers did not present a portrait of Warner representative of the movement. He may have been reflecting a narrow mentality. Byers was a 'creator of myth.' For these latter remarks I am indebted to the late Dr. Milo Chapman, President Emeritus of Warner Pacific College. Chapman knew Byers personally. Personal interview, 24 November 1994.

[43] Brown, *When the Trumpet Sounded*, p. 67.

that 'Warner was a holy man of God; his life was without spot or blame.'[44] One individual even had a vision wherein he saw a ship being guided by a man at the helm. That man was Daniel Warner.[45] Since the vision had come by divine inspiration there can be little doubt regarding what that ship symbolized and what function had been assigned to Warner. These kinds of enthusiastic sentiments fostered the romanticizing of the memory of Warner and brought him to the very brink of attaining a cult-like status of 'saint' within the popular religious dimension of the movement he inspired. Andrew Byers has collected a considerable number of memoirs regarding Warner's popular conception. The following serve as representative. Herbert M. Riggle asserted that the influences of Warner's life and ministry had universal, historic significance.[46] Others compared him to the fearless heroism of Martin Luther and applied to Warner the stirring epitaph Philip Melanchthon wrote of the Wittenberg reformer: 'He being dead yet speaketh!'[47] 'Brother Warner was a humble, godly man . . . . His humility, zeal, and power with God, and ability to expound the Word of God, fitted him to be classed in the role of reformers . . . .'[48] '. . . D.S. Warner had fine illumination in some respects, the finest and most glorious ever received since the Apostolic Age . . . .'[49] Warner apparently possessed either supernatural powers or had a remarkable relationship with God. It is alleged that on one occasion Warner had

---

[44] Henry C. Wickersham, *A History of the Church* (Moundsville, WV: Gospel Trumpet Publishing Co., 1900), p. 313.

[45] Joseph C. Fisher, '"Vision and Interpretation" by the Lord' *Gospel Trumpet* (1 September 1884).

[46] Cited in Byers, *Birth of a Reformation*, p. 443.

[47] Cited in *Ibid.*, p. 441.

[48] Enoch E. Byrum, *Life Experiences* (Anderson: Gospel Trumpet Company, 1928), p. 146.

[49] Charles E. Brown, *When Souls Awaken: An Interpretation of Radical Christianity* (Anderson: Gospel Trumpet Company, 1954), p. 109.

a rainstorm delayed interminably. On another, he was successful in stopping a moving train through prayer.[50] There were also instances where he escaped physical harm during brutal attacks.[51] His apparent affinities with Christ once caused him in Carthage, Missouri to be the recipient of words formerly applied to Jesus: 'What manner of man is this that even the winds obey him?'[52] In the estimation of others, 'Brother Warner was one of the most godly men I ever met; he was so consecrated . . . .'[53] Daniel Warner was in the vanguard of those who preached the evening light.[54]

Perhaps the most striking and startling dimension to the myth of Warner lies in the enthusiastic conviction that he succeeded where all other reformers failed. That success lay in the all-important ability to transcend time, history and culture and return to the ethos of primitive Christianity as an authentic part of the cast of the *dramatis personae* in the tradition of the apostles and prophets. According to some, the historical Warner transcended his own time and stood in the authentic tradition of apostolic witness. 'Daniel S. Warner was the boldest, most radical, most liberal thinker on Bible lines since the days of the apostles. At

---

[50]   Cited in Byers, *Birth of a Reformation*, pp. 431-2.

[51]   In a report detailing evangelistic efforts in August and September 1884 in Mercer County, Pennsylvania, Warner relates being beaten by a drunken man. 'He soon struck me with all force in the forehead, but through God his blow was not more than a ball of cotton. . . . [then] He seized a large rocking chair and slammed it down on us with all vengeance, but through the Lord Jesus Christ our uplifted hands turned it off with ease . . . . The infuriated man grabbed a common wood-bottom chair by the back and struck down twice or three times at our head, which was safely shielded by the hand of the Lord . . . . There was not a hair of our head hurt, not a scratch or mark upon our body. The next morning we felt our right wrist was slightly sprained by stopping the blows, but it soon disappeared . . . .' The report appears in Byers, *Birth of a Reformation*, pp. 316-18.

[52]   Cited in *Ibid.*, p. 431.

[53]   Cited in *Ibid.*, p. 431.

[54]   Della J. Green, 'In Memory of Bro. D.S. Warner,' *Gospel Trumpet*, (19 December 1895).

one sweep he stepped clear out into the very glory and simplicity of early Christianity and he pointed out the only way to church unity.'[55] According to this, Warner quite clearly fulfilled the words of his own song: 'Now are many running to and fro, spreading holiness around; and the evening light begins to glow. . . .'[56]

Between the image and the reality lies a chasm. There are in fact two Daniel Sidney Warners: the Warner of history and the Warner of myth. The problem is, categories such as truth and fiction, authenticity and romanticism, history and hagiography cannot necessarily be neatly assigned to tightly patrolled parameters. The Warner of myth is not falsehood and deception. On the other hand, the Warner of history is not objective truth. Both are the subjective creations of time and interpretation. After the battery of accolades noted above, there is the distinct possibility that Daniel Warner might not have recognized himself.

As noted earlier, this portrait of Warner does not coincide with the 'Come-Outism Renounced' by Sarah Warner. Unless one is prepared to simply dismiss her as a 'crackpot' this glaring discrepancy has not caused as much concern as one might expect. It is difficult to see why this potential *faux pas* does not disturb Church of God historiography more than it seems to do. Before turning to the corpus of Warner's works it may be useful to assemble a brief portrait of Sarah to juxtapose over against the one just noted of Daniel Warner.

III. Demonizing the Angel Sarah

> Last night I had a dream of meeting my Angel Love Sarah. O how happy I was to return . . . and embrace with a sweet kiss my precious companion . . . with whom my soul longs to be. . . . O Lord preserve our lives and health until my arms shall encircle and my lips press the sweet lips of my beloved Sarah, the fairest, purest and most lovely of all the virgins of earth

---

[55] Robert L. Berry, *Golden Jubilee Book* (Anderson: Gospel Trumpet Company, 1931), p. 9.

[56] 'Are You Ready Waiting for the Lord?' in *Echoes from Glory*, no. 209.

.... whose constant and ardent love is worth more to me than all the treasures and honors of earth. O could I hold converse with that bright luminary whose bright beams and gentle rays are falling so graciously upon the earth today, I would ask if the revolving earth brought another creature under his shining light so pure, fair and lovely as my own blessed Sarah .... she is the fairest and most lovely piece of God's creation .... I should be happy and a grateful man, having such a rich treasure .... my Angel Sarah ....[57]

♠ ♠

Unlike her husband Sarah Warner neither inspired a movement nor even a devoted band of followers. Indeed, insofar as we know, not long after she published her denunciations of Warner and the Come-Out movement, Sarah Warner disappeared from the stage of American religious history. Hence, any portrait of her must be largely drawn from mainly hostile sources, namely Warner himself, the followers of Warner, and those she possibly vilified and scandalized in her dramatic departure from the Warner campaign. The portrait, then, may not have the same benefit of integrity that Warner's does. Nevertheless, the portrait that does emerge performs a valuable function in the attempt to come to terms with the man and the message of Daniel Warner. At the time she wrote 'Come-Outism Renounced' Sarah Warner was twenty-eight years old. We have already alluded to her forays into leadership activities of the burgeoning Holiness movement. If Daniel Warner was called by the Holy Spirit it is worthwhile noting that he stated clearly that his marriage to Sarah was the work of God. 'O Lord what a blessing thou hast here bestowed on thy unworthy servant .... O Lord this is thy doing ....'[58] In his early poetry Warner spoke of Sarah with great affection and referred to her with terms such as ' . . . modest, pure, of guileless piety . . . graceful . . .

---

[57] Daniel Warner, *Journal*, 30 March, 10 April, 5 May, 26 May, 4 June 1874.

[58] *Journal*, 30 March 1874.

her face rare charms of beauty wore' and 'sweet tempered innocence.'[59] After the traumatic loss of Tamzen, and amid the rigors of frontier evangelism, 'the fair and affectionate creature' became Warner's 'angel love Sarah.'[60]

Figure 7 Sarah Ann Warner as she appeared in the 1880s.
Courtesy of Warner Press and the Archives of the Church of God, Anderson University

---

[59]   Warner, *Poems of Grace and Truth*, p. 48 *et al*. Facing page 48 there is an engraving of the young Sarah Keller. For similar sentiments see Warner's *Journal* entry for 3 May 1884 and *passim*.

[60]   *Journal*, 24 and 30 March 1874.

Prior to 1884 Sarah enjoyed the unmitigated praise of the movement. 'Sister Warner was a splendid woman and had been a faithful companion to her husband.'[61] Beneath the glowing exterior of being the 'constant companion' of an important religious reformer there is evidence to suggest that Sarah was not as thoroughly committed to the consuming agenda of raising up the authentic Church of God through preaching, writing, publishing, and polemicizing as Warner quite clearly was. Apparently unnoticed heretofore are some inscriptions in Sarah's hand among the papers of Daniel Warner in the Anderson University Archives.[62] These are an invaluable glimpse into the inner emotional life of Sarah Warner. From Warner's journal we know of her sometime despondency and loneliness. Apart from these annotations in an accounting ledger, catalogued as Book 15, we have no other first-hand source of her inner feelings. She expressed her devotion to Warner, but one senses that something is missing.

> In this album I do impart
> The lasting friendship of my heart
> That you may have to look upon,
> Perhaps when I am dead and gone.
>
> Let me in these unsullied lines
> Some offerings leave to <u>thee</u>
>
> That when you read in after times
> Will make <u>you</u> think of me.[63]

---

[61] Byers, *Birth of a Reformation*, p. 292.

[62] Book 15: Accounts and Other Notes. D.S. Warner papers. Archives, Anderson University. One-half of this particular book is an accounting ledger from the year 1881 in Rome City, Indiana. The second half of the book is largely comprised of annotations and poems written by Sarah Warner. Inside the back cover there is stamped three times the name, 'Mrs. D.S. Warner' along with the autograph, 'Sarah Ann Warner.' Inside the front cover the name, 'Sarah' is written. The book is unpaginated and references and quotations will simply refer to the book.

[63] The emphasis in the poem noted by the underlined words is Sarah's.

Quite clearly Sarah's devotion to Warner remained as the following citation demonstrates:

> Forget thee? Oh never.
> While throbs in my breast
> The heart that forever
> With thee seeks to rest
> Thou to me art a treasure
> That hallows each spot
> Life has little pleasure
> Where thou art not.

Below the verse Sarah's name is printed. While she loved her husband Sarah also had experienced the 'dark night of the soul' and she prayed, 'O Jesus, lead me Lord, through any dark and subterranaen [sic] way of sorrow or pain . . . .' Her own struggles in the 'dark night of the soul' led her to think of perhaps the happier days of her youth.

> And up and down the whole creation
> Sadly I roam
> Still longing for the old plantation
> and for the old folks at home.
>
> All round the little farm I wandered
> When I was young
> From many happy days I squandered
> many the songs I sung
> When I was playing with my brother
> happy was I
>
> Oh take me to my kind old mother
> there let me live and [. .]
> One little hut among the bushes
> One that I love
> Still sadly to my memory rushes
> No matter where I [. .]
>
> When will I see the bees a humming
> All round the court
> When will I hear the banjo humming

down in my good old home.[64]

These personal sentiments, charged with emotion, reflect a common theme throughout, beginning with the first annotation written on the inside of the cover.

> Remember me my constant friend
> Remember me till life shall end
> And if the grave be first my lot
> Remember me and forget me not.

There is little point in producing here all of the verses and annotations in Sarah's hand from Book 15. There is much thematic repetition. Perhaps the most poignant of all is this final selection which does indeed evoke within the reader a profound sense of empathy at her deepening quiet despair. The poem is titled 'Hope and Memory.'

> The soul may long with fervent hope
> For worlds of future bliss
> But Oh! how saddening to the heart
> To be forgot in this.[65]

The poem bears the signature, 'Mrs. S. A. Warner.'

It is regrettable that Sarah Warner wrote no memoirs before her untimely death at the age of thirty-seven. Investigations have uncovered no extant correspondence. She kept no journal and wrote no books. Unless further documents should be uncovered the historian is left with her article published in the *Christian Harvester* and these rough notes previously cited.[66] At least seven and

---

[64] Line 12 of the poem breaks off in mid sentence. Line 16 of the poem has one word at the end of the line which I was unable to transcribe.

[65] As elsewhere in Book 15 the emphasis in the poem, noted by the underlined words, is Sarah's.

[66] Not all of the books in the personal library of D.S. Warner, now held in the Anderson University Archives, belonged to Warner. An examination of the 341 volumes comprising the personal library of D.S. Warner revealed that five books belonged to Sarah. Two of the books are medical, two others are theological, and the fifth is a hymn book. There are occasional marginal lines and underlining throughout. Regrettably, there are no annotations. All five volumes have the name, 'Mrs. Sarah A. Warner,' or some

a half pages have been cut out of Book 15 in the 'Sarah section.' It is quite impossible to speculate with any certainty about what may or may not have been written on those pages. The historian is left with more questions than answers, more ideas than data.

Daniel Warner clearly knew of Sarah's struggle. Undoubtedly he cared deeply and was not unmoved. It is equally clear that he was unprepared to modify his involvement in his 'historic mission.' Warner's primary concern was his work, not Sarah. He was prepared to pay any cost to succeed. Unfortunately Sarah became part of the cost.[67] Following the debacle of 1884 the portrait of the 'splendid woman' and 'faithful companion' changed dramatically. From here on it was as if Satan had entered into Sarah. ' . . . the devil made a desperate effort' against Warner and '. . . succeeded in turning Bro. Warner's wife against him.'[68] The idea of deception as the primary motivating factor in Sarah abandoning the Come-Out movement was first advanced by Daniel Warner in his public response to her. In that delineation Warner asserted that the work of the devil was responsible for tearing Sarah away[69] and elsewhere that her contentions set forth in the *Christian Harvester* were 'vile slanders that [S]atan had sent.'[70] The deception motif was taken up by Warner's followers and has become part of the legacy of Sarah Warner.[71] Once deceived, the angel Sarah fell from grace becoming victim to the commonplace association of heretics and sexual

---

variation thereof written in her hand.

[67] See for example Reardon, *The Early Morning Light*, p. 18 and Hetrick, *Laughter Among the Trumpets*, p. 9.

[68] Wickersham, *A History of the Church*, p. 442.

[69] 'A Fallen Woman,' *Gospel Trumpet*, (15 July 1884).

[70] Editorial, 'Persecutions of John Bunyan,' *Ibid.*, (1 July 1884).

[71] Byers, *Birth of a Reformation*, p. 293 is but one example.

perversion.[72] By 1887 she was denounced as having joined a sexually promiscuous sect associated with Henry Raub of Bucyrus whom Warner affirmed 'is possessed with free-love quaker devils, and has been for years.'[73] Warner claimed that Sarah fell in among this group, 'continued in their fellowship, and doubtless still does.' He charged all the 'babylonian' papers, who had printed Sarah's denunciation of the come-out movement, with having 'gloried in the works of the devil'.[74] More than being simply deceived and given over to the lusts of the flesh, Sarah was also transubstantiated into a personification of evil. 'O hath those eyes, with love sparkling once so bright, Beheld the fabled gorgon's monstrous sight? Which seeing, as the ancient legends run, Quickly turned its beholder into stone.'[75] The demonizing of Sarah was complete and Warner was pitied to the end of his days as the victim. 'Bro. Warner has virtually become a widower for the Cause of

---

[72] In medieval and early modern Europe (and to a certain extent in early America), heresy and sexual deviance were linked. *Ketzerei* in south Germany could mean either heresy or sodomy. The terms 'bugger' and 'buggery' have their origins in the Middle Ages associated both with the rise of heresy in Latin Christendom and general sexual immorality. Defenders of social order and guardians of official Christianity worked hard at demonizing heretics by engaging in propaganda campaigns aimed at scandalizing the community. Stock accusations against dissenters in late medieval and early modern Europe quite frequently were a combination of charges relating to heresy, sexuality and witchcraft. The extant records of the witchcraft trials in Salem Village, Massachusetts in 1692 reflect a similar mentality. To be a heretic was to be a sexual pervert, and to be sexually immoral meant one was also guilty of heresy. In this way it is not at all surprising to find references in late medieval Europe alluding to the idea of 'committing heresy with one's body.' I developed this at some length in my 'Image Breakers, Image Makers: The Rôle of Heresy in Divided Christendom', presented at the World Congress of the Commission Internationale d'Histoire Ecclésiastique Comparée in Lublin, Poland in September 1996, forthcoming.

[73] Warner, 'Note' *Gospel Trumpet* (15 September 1887). 'They also preach that they are so pure they can kiss each other promiscuously. A man can kiss another man's wife, and the woman can kiss the men whenever they feel like it.' John N. Slagle, 'Stumbling Stone Fruits' *Gospel Trumpet* (15 September 1887).

[74] Warner, *Ibid*.

[75] Warner, *Poems of Grace and Truth*, p. 88.

Christ . . . .'[76] Hereafter, Warner consistently viewed Sarah to the end of her life as an outcast.[77] The angel of light was now an angel of darkness, a minister of the Devil, an ensign of hell. As for Stockwell, after the devastating appearance of the 'leprous spots' of his 'plague', the silence accompanying his disappearance was punctuated only once or twice by vague, but ominous reports. ' . . . that poor deceived man Stockwell, who was means in the hands of the devil in over throwing Mrs. Warner. God used the *Trumpet* last winter to "condemn" that tongue, and cut off his pernicious works, since which he too has dropped off the devil's mask, and no longer professes to be a child of God. The Lord have mercy on him, and save him.'[78]

Warner's followers continued to vilify Sarah as a heartless woman, especially when she gave up her son Sidney.[79] Warner attempted to win Sarah back without success, and even went as far as to give letters he had written to Sarah to others to read apparently to demonstrate his desire to be reunited with her.[80] Two years after their separation Sarah returned Sidney to the custody of his father. She obtained an uncontested divorce on 9 April 1890. Sometime thereafter, in 1892, she remarried.[81] Occasionally articles in the *Gospel Trumpet* referred to Sarah

---

[76] Joseph C. Fisher, '"Vision and Interpretation" by the Lord' *Gospel Trumpet* (1 September 1884).

[77] See his poem to her titled, 'To the Alien,' in *Ibid.*, pp. 175-181.

[78] The words denoting disease are Warner's and appear in his poem 'Meditations on the Prairie' in *Poems of Grace and Truth*, pp. 61-2. The report on Stockwell may be found in Joseph C. Fisher, '"Vision and Interpretation" by the Lord' *Gospel Trumpet* (1 September 1884).

[79] Byers, *Birth of a Reformation*, pp. 296, 303.

[80] See the letter of Elizabeth Walter in *Ibid.*, pp. 428-429.

[81] Smith, *The Quest for Holiness and Unity*, p. 65. Smith is misleading in his articulation of the events. Perhaps unwittingly, Smith has all of these events occurring within two years when in actuality they are spread out over eight years. Brown says she obtained a divorce by 1886. *When the Trumpet Sounded*, p. 113. The copy of the divorce

generally in a negative light.[82] In the spring of 1893 a terse communication was published throughout the *Gospel Trumpet* world: 'Sarah died this morning in Cincinnati.'[83] Paradoxically, her memory remained fresh enough that a casual reference to her first name was sufficient for identification. Immediately, overtones of divine judgment on her wickedness reverberated throughout the movement. The aforementioned *Gospel Trumpet* editorial alleged that she had forsaken not only Warner, but God. Her death clearly was linked to her wickedness, heresy and open sin. The demonizing of Sarah Warner was *de facto* taken for granted.

It is apparent that Sarah generally was considered only an unfortunate episode in Warner's life. She has not been dealt with apart from the Stockwell incident by Church of God historiographers ostensibly because she constitutes an embarrassment to the movement and brings little that is favorable to the person of Daniel Warner. Most books on Warner or early Church of God history gloss over her life. Some omit her altogether.[84] It is remarkable that there is no photograph of Daniel and Sarah Warner together in the Church of God Archives. There are photographs of Daniel and Tamzen and Daniel and his third wife, Frankie. The

---

decree in the Anderson University Archives is dated 9 April 1890.

[82] See for example, an article by E.J. Hill, 'A Visit to Grand Junction,' *Gospel Trumpet*, (7 January 1892).

[83] Warner, 'A Sad and Sudden End of This Life,' *Gospel Trumpet*, (1 June 1893). The date of Sarah's death was 24 May 1893. The telegram had been sent by Sarah's brother, L.F. Keller.

[84] Brown, *When the Trumpet Sounded*. Brown indexes references to Warner's first wife, Tamzen, and Warner's third wife, Frances 'Frankie' Miller. There is no reference to Sarah even though Warner was married to Sarah longer than the other two combined and was the mother of Warner's son. She is mentioned in the narrative of the book. Harold Phillips never refers to Sarah by name in his *Miracle of Survival*.

absence is conspicuous.[85] The current historian of the Church of God, Merle Strege, has commented informally that on the whole Sarah has been dealt with unfairly by the church.[86] Strege's published opinion comes to the heart of the matter: Warner sacrificed his second marriage on the altar of what he called the Truth.[87]

Sarah had once written, 'Remember me and forget me not.' Daniel Warner never forgot her. In the year of his death, Warner told Curtis Montgomery again how Sarah, being deceived by the enemy had forsaken him.[88] Twenty years earlier Warner had been adamant that God had brought him and Sarah together. On the eve of his death surely he questioned that youthful confidence.

As previously noted Warner's portrait remained constant. Its glow only intensified with the passage of time. On the other hand, the image of Sarah presents a striking contrast. As time went on, after 1884, she became increasingly tarnished in the popular view until she fell into oblivion altogether.[89] Her essential humanity became sacrificed on the altar of the evolving Warner myth. If, as suggested earlier, Warner might fail to recognize his own image among his followers, one wonders if Sarah might likewise not recognize her portrait.

---

[85] There are however more single photographs of Sarah than the others. There are three separate portraits of her in the Archive holdings in addition to the engraving noted earlier. Among the papers of D.S. Warner in the Anderson University Archives there is a photograph of Sarah. On the back Warner has written: 'Make a cut of this picture with hair, collar, & dress, plain like the accompanying lady but show more of the bust.'

[86] Interview at Anderson University, 8 November 1994.

[87] Strege, *Tell me Another Tale*, p. 86.

[88] See Montgomery's letter in Byers, *Birth of a Reformation*, p. 441.

[89] Some responding to her article deliberately omitted her name. 'Sister-- . . . . assumes for the *Gospel Trumpet*, almost infinitely, more than it is entitled to or its editor claims.' R.W. Lyman, 'Idolatry Exposed,' *Gospel Trumpet*, (1 June 1884).

IV. God, the Devil and Warner's Books

All sectarians are warped by their creeds, and blinded by their sect idols, so that they cannot see, nor walk in the straight line of God's truth. Every sect name and creed becomes an idol, which perverts the judgement, and corrupts the conscious, and induces the practice of wresting the scriptures for the sake of the sect god. Entire sanctification, and the Holy Spirit destroy the sects and denominations, therefore all that adhere to, and defend these organized schisms are without the Holy Spirit. 'From such turn away.'[90]

♠ ♠

The opinions expressed by Sarah Warner in the *Christian Harvester* have already been noted in terms of their provocative and problematic character. The articles are potentially too significant to be set aside without proper consideration. The only reliable and responsible method of dealing with them is to analyze their content and implication in the corpus of Warner's writings. By the testimony of his own pen Sarah Warner's allegations will either be silenced or substantiated.

Initially, Sarah Warner denounced 'the spirit' of the movement. It seems sensible to take points one, three and four from Sarah's articles, noted above, and deal with them together. What sort of spirit and attitude did Warner display towards others; Christians and non Christians? The Come-Out movement insisted that all denominational Christianity was in error. There is only one authentic church, that is the Church of God. All true Christians must 'come out from among them and be separate' from denominationalism and join the one Church of God. Daniel Warner clearly identified himself as the representative of the Church of God. While this was not unique it did provide evidence of a new identity forged in the fires of the social, cultural and religious upheaval which characterized so

---

[90] Daniel Warner, untitled article, *Gospel Trumpet* (1 February 1885).

much of the nineteenth century. In order to understand Warner's apparent narrow definition of the church one must realize that there was an organic ecclesial concept within Warner which yielded the notion that the church is exclusive. The context of the times is equally all important for understanding Warner's radical insistence on the ideas of separation and perfection. However, it is essential to acknowledge the polemical nature of writing in the nineteenth century. Scathing language and caustic denunciations were common, particularly in religious debates. Hence it is not surprising to find Warner condemning other Christians. What is surprising is the frequency and vitriolic language used. But even here Warner is more representational than anomalous. Nevertheless, it is possible to conclude that some of the persecution encountered by Warner was self-inflicted. 'I have talked to B. E. [Barney] Warren who told me that when lying under a house in Alabama beside D.S. Warner as they hid from the mob, he had a very clear conviction that Brother Warner had brought on the persecution by the rash language which he used in his preaching.'[91]

Such 'rash' language targeted much of American Christianity. The Methodist Episcopal Church was denounced for its 'follies and inconsistencies' and Warner noted that the 'M. E.' Church was successful in producing backsliders.[92] The Church of the United Brethren was assailed.[93] 'Vile' Catholics and the 'corrupt Roman Catholic Church' destroyed moral good.[94] Elsewhere Warner referred to the adherents of Rome as 'fiendish,' 'sect idolators, and wicked sinners.'[95]

---

[91]   Cited in Charles E. Brown, *When Souls Awaken*, p. 84.

[92]   *Journal,* 8 November 1872, 25 January 1877, and 27 January 1879.

[93]   *Ibid.,* 13 November 1872.

[94]   *Ibid.,* 24 November 1872, 6 May 1876, and 17 April 1878.

[95]   'News from the Field,' *Gospel Trumpet,* (1 November 1886). For the view of Catholicism see Robert E. Koeth, 'A History of Anti-Catholicism in the Church of God Reformation Movement,' unpublished M.A. Thesis, School of Theology, Anderson

Lutherans were often referred to as 'blind' and '... too ignorant on all [spiritual] matters to talk intelligently ....'[96] The Spiritualist religion sometimes caused insanity and destroyed its adherents '... morally, mentally and physically.'[97] Alexander Campbell and his followers betrayed 'their spiritual ignorance' which Warner attempted to '... show those poor souls who had been gulled with [the] false doctrine of Campbellism .'[98] The fate of 'poor, silly Adventist[s]'[99] Warner found pitiful to contemplate. Several of his books are diatribes against the Adventist faith. 'The "darkness of Sinai" hangs over all their writing,' they compose the 'modern pharisees and sadducees' and Warner found himself compelled to '... renounce the Advent creed and spirit as positively antichrist ....'[100] Their teachings are 'dark leaven,' they are characterized by 'blindness,' an 'utter absence of spiritual knowledge,' 'foolish minds' and great 'delusion.' 'Oh, the blindness and thick darkness of Adventism .... They read the Bible with such idolatrous devotion to their own inventions ....' Even their morality is suspect because of their alleged doctrinal deviance.[101]

College, 1983.

[96] *Journal*, 8 January 1873, and 1 August 1874.

[97] *Ibid.*, 11 June 1874.

[98] Warner, *The Sabbath; or Which Day to Keep* (Moundsville, WV: Gospel Trumpet Publishing Company, 1899), p. 109 and *Journal*, 19 March 1876.

[99] '... Mr. Keneston, a poor silly Adventist (who has not more sense than a man of his doctrine would be supposed to possess) arose and harangued some moments. What pity the poor creature has such deficient mental vision. How confused the wretched Adventist doctrine.' *Journal*, 27 December 1874.

[100] Warner, *The Sabbath; or Which Day to Keep,* pp. 51, 110, and 184.

[101] D.S. Warner and H. M. Riggle, *The Cleansing of the Sanctuary* (Moundsville, WV: The Gospel Trumpet Publishing Company, 1903), pp. 74, 79, 80, 95, 156, and 177. Riggle finished writing this book after Warner's death. The references to the Adventists cited here are drawn from Warner's portion of the book only. In his hymn, 'The Hand of God on the Wall,' Warner again subtly linked denominationalism with immorality. 'O

Conflict and Crisis in the Kingdom of God in Ohio 237

Methodism, as noted earlier, constituted the heart of early American revivalism and was the dominant Christian influence in the Ohio of Warner's youth. The grand tradition of Wesley, Whitefield, Asbury and Cartwright did not escape the censure of Warner's pen. 'It is a painful thing to record that the name Methodism has become most commonly to mean opposed to truth' and Warner accused certain Methodists of bigotry.[102] Confusion reigned among the Baptists,[103] the Disciples sensed the error of their ways when confronted by the Church of God.[104] The Dunkers were called 'sects' and Warner used the word 'sin' in reference to them when their theology was at odds with his,[105] and did not hesitate to adjudicate other theologians as wrong.[106] Warner rejoiced when denominational Christians acquiesced in the truth he proclaimed.[107] The Quakers held to 'ridiculous position[s]' and their 'heresy' he deplored.[108] Even the Winebrennarian Church did

---

the sin and confusion, O the vanity and pride of the multitude of Sodom, who in Babylon abide . . . .' *Anthems from the Throne*, eds., D.S. Warner and Barney E. Warren (Grand Junction: Gospel Trumpet Publishing Company,1888), no. 70.

[102] *Journal*, 10 April 1875, and 2 April 1876. The emphasis, through the use of underlined words, is Warner's.

[103] *Ibid.*, 26 November 1876.

[104] *Ibid.*, 24 January 1877 and 12 March 1877.

[105] Warner, *Salvation Present, Perfect, Now or Never* (Moundsville, WV: Gospel Trumpet Publishing Company, n.d.), p. 63.

[106] See for example his passing reference to Nikolaus Zinzendorf (1700-1760), founder of the Herrnhuter Brüdergemeinde and Moravian leader, whose theology of regeneration cannot be reconciled to scriptural truth as understood by Warner. *Bible Proofs of the Second Work of Grace* (Goshen, IN: E.U. Mennonite Pub. Society, 1880), p. 162.

[107] In this instance the convert had been a Universalist. *Journal*, 28 February 1873.

[108] Warner and Riggle, *The Cleansing of the Sanctuary*, p. 275 and *Gospel Trumpet*, (1 May 1883). Elsewhere Warner denounced the Quakers as being as much a sect as anyone else. This in response to a letter inquiring about whether or not the Quakers were part of sectism. *Gospel Trumpet*, (1 November 1883). See also Warner, 'A New-Spun

not escape the fiery denunciations of Daniel Warner. While he admitted that John Winebrenner had been an honest man of God, Warner noted that the Winebrennerians did not ' . . . possess sufficient light to avoid the formation of another sect.' Hence, ' . . . they are now received in peace in the Babel sisterhood.'[109]

In a remarkable poem titled 'Soul-Cripple City' Warner likened practically all of Christendom to unfortunates who must employ the aid of crutches in order to walk. The crutches are of course the varieties of denominational Christianity. This litany of deception is bold, sweeping and unsparing. To protect himself from the danger of the 'filthy streets' Warner noted that he was 'taking disinfectives plenty' against the 'bigots' and 'whoredom spirit' in 'Soul-Cripple City.'

> The oldest crutches in the market are the Roman Papal brand . . . .[Then came] Luth'ran crutcheries . . . . Next appeared the English crutches, and the High Episcopal . . . . Wycliffe crutches, Calvin crutches, Quaker, Shaker, Mennonite, Wesley crutches, in twelve branches, M. E. crutches, black and white. Methodism, Afric, German, Methodism Protestant, Methodism labeled 'Calvin,' both M. E's. north and southern brand. 'Free' and 'Union' Methodism, and the ism 'Primitive.' All these horns of beast division, on their stilted crutches live . . . . In the nude, and lude [sic] and dev'lish Methodism takes the sway . . . . Then there are Baptist crutches, . . . 'Free-will' Baptist, Bond-will Baptist, . . . There are Baptist called 'Ephrata'. Saturnarian Baptist too. 'Anabaptist' . . . . Three-dip Dunkers, new and old, 'Primitive', 'Progressive', factions. . . . Satan cooped a reformation in the key stone-land of Penn. Eldershipped it, with ovation, down the river to this den. In the harbor of Soul-Cripple, cast her anchor

---

Line of Lies,' *Gospel Trumpet*, (1 November 1887).

[109] Warner, *An Exclusive Christ* (Anderson: Gospel Trumpet Company, n.d.), pp. 7-8. Elsewhere Warner refers to the 'Winebrennerian sect.' *Questions and Answers on the Church* (Grand Junction: Gospel Trumpet Publishing Company, n.d.), p. 10 and in an article titled, 'Holiness Triumph over Dragon Zeal, *Gospel Trumpet*, (1 November 1883). For Winebrenner see Richard Kern, *John Winebrenner: Nineteenth-Century Reformer* (Harrisburg, PA: Central Publishing House, 1974) and chapter 3 in this book. Of the remaining books in Warner's library only one remains from the pen of John Winebrenner. *History of all the Religious Denominations in the United States*. . . . There is considerable evidence that this book and Winebrenner's thought influenced Warner profoundly.

Conflict and Crisis in the Kingdom of God in Ohio 239

> in the mud, on her main-mast hung the devil the misnomer, 'Church of God.' O! ye Presbyterian crutches, . . . 'English', 'German', 'Kirk of Scotland', 'Cumberland', 'Associate', and 'seceders' from the Bible, 'Covenanters' and Reformed . . . wooden legs deformed. There are props United Brethren, all disjointed out of Christ, Glassite, Hicksite, and Socinian, Rotten Universalist. There are crutches labeled Christian . . . . There are crutches Unitarian, Omish [sic?], dull of sale and rust. Also Supralapsitarian [sic], a few Landisites in dust. There are crutches 'Congregational', and 'Associate Reform'. And all dark 'Evangelical', God-forsaken and forlorn . . . .

Warner then went on to ridicule as spiritual cripples the lying prophet, William Miller, and the Adventists, William Booth, the rival of Jesus Christ, and the 'hollow-drum religion' of the Salvation Army Movement, Lyman Johnson, the 'Lie-man' Quaker,[110] Charles Taze Russell and the Jehovah's Witnesses 'on a hellward leaning "Tower,"' among others. The entire 'Soul-Cripple City' are all singing 'O my crutch! my crutch!! . . . glory to our crutch.' Later Warner adds, 'Farewell all ye sordid cripples, nay, how can we say farewell, "Fear, the pit, and snare, upon thee", must attend thee down to hell.' Warner then breaks off from the hell bound throng to accompany the 'righteous' to salvation and heaven in the dawn of evening light.[111] He cannot possibly remain with those who 'vainly' trust in their 'dark creeds.'[112] Standing at the edge of the great American experiment in

---

[110] Elsewhere Johnson is referred to by Warner in 'Note,' *Gospel Trumpet*, (15 September 1887) and in his 'A New-Spun Line of Lies,' *Gospel Trumpet*, (1 November 1887).

[111] Warner, *Poems of Grace and Truth*, pp. 119-174. Elsewhere, Warner rejoiced that the '" . . . ites" are destroyed . . . .' See his hymn, 'In the Holy Land,' in *Anthems from the Throne*, no. 54. 'Soul-Cripple City' is set forth in a poetic form which has not been followed here. See the complete text in Appendix B. That adherents of denominations were expected to go to hell is not to be doubted. 'I said in a revival meeting that I never expected to see an M.E. nor a U.B. nor an Evangelical in heaven.' *Life Sketches of Mother Sarah Smith*, p. 13.

[112] Warner, 'The Church Triumphant,' in *Echoes from Glory*, no. 185. The idea was repeated by his followers. 'But sects are full of sinners. There is no identity whatever between the Church that Christ built and sect-Babylon.' Herbert M. Riggle, *The Christian*

religious democracy, Warner reiterated the message scrawled across the wall of the king's palace in Babylon during the feast of King Belshazzar: 'Mene, Mene, Tekel, Parsin . . . . weighed in the balances and found wanting.'[113] Though he was a product and a beneficiary of the democratic principle there was in Warner the tendency to adjudicate the righteousness of his cause and the unrighteousness in the remainder of American Christendom.

The *Gospel Trumpet* likewise supported Warner's convictions. 'They sit trembling upon their lofty but narrow Methodist, Baptist, United Brethren, or Presbyterian plank, while with one hand they try to hold onto the walls of God's church.'[114] Both Roman Catholicism and Protestantism constituted apostasy and '. . . the whole business of Roman and Protestant babel have left Christ and have gone over to the gods of Baal.'[115] Having eschewed the experience of entire sanctification and refusing to yield to the divinely ordained path to Christian unity, Christendom, according to Warner, must be considered spiritually bankrupt. To the come-outers, it was clearly a sign of the end of time.

In fairness to Warner there are some positive references toward denominational Christianity. Warner referred to a 'Christian' in the Methodist Episcopal Church and later to a 'Free Methodist sister.'[116] He was grateful to others, not of his particular persuasion however, when their scholarly erudition

---

Church: Its Rise and Progress (Anderson: Gospel Trumpet Company, 1912), p. 366.

[113]   The story is told in the Hebrew Bible in the book of Daniel, chapter 5.

[114]   'The Shaft Giving Way,' *Gospel Trumpet*, (1 November 1881) and (15 August 1883). By this later date the purpose of the *Gospel Trumpet* had been more clearly delineated. The new masthead statement read: 'Edited and Published semi-monthly in the Name of the Lord Jesus Christ. For the Purity and Unity of His Body, the defense of ALL His Truth, and the ABOMINATION of Sect Babylon.'

[115]   Warner and Riggle, *The Cleansing of the Sanctuary*, pp. 37 and 268. '. . . both the Cotholic [sic] and Protestant churches profess the Christian religion . . . .' *Bible Proofs of the Second Work of Grace*, p. 377.

[116]   *Journal*, 20 October 1877 and 17 October 1879.

could be utilized for the promotion of his ideas.[117] Warner referred to the Mennonites as his 'beloved brethren' and in reference to three specifically named Mennonites Warner asserted '. . . they are gloriously saved and definite for Jesus.'[118] The Mennonites appear to be the only religious group referenced by Warner of whom more positive is said than negative.

Clearly, Warner deliberately distanced himself from the vast majority of Christian adherents. Some of his followers insisted that God had selected Warner specifically to preach against denominationalism.[119] If there appears to be some substantiation to Sarah's allegation that the 'spirit' of the movement, at least as personified in Warner, was a 'self-righteous, pharisaical' one, this again must be tempered by keeping in mind the acerbic context of nineteenth-century polemics. One could simply assume that the corollary allegation that everyone must 'see as "we" do. . . ' naturally follows. However, it will be safer to test that assumption against the witness of Warner's own writings. This is the crucial test for determining where Warner ought to be placed in the paradox of religious democracy in nineteenth-century America. At this juncture, Warner's posture determines whether or not he might reasonably be considered a dictator disguised as a democrat.

Kenneth Scott Latourette has noted that Warner's followers recognized God's people in all denominations.[120] Alexander T. Rowe maintained late in the

---

[117] 'Many thanks to Dr. [Daniel] Steele and others for the precious truths they have brought out of the original text.' See this note in his *Bible Proofs of the Second Work of Grace*, pp. 356-357. Steele was a Holiness evangelist and a professor at Boston School of Theology.

[118] *Journal*, 5 December 1879 and 6 August 1879. The journal is especially useful for understanding Warner's 'very soul . . . to know him intimately and to capture the spirit of his work.' Smith, *Heralds of a Brighter Day*, pp. 26-27.

[119] *Life Sketches of Mother Sarah Smith*, p. 33.

[120] Kenneth Scott Latourette, *Christianity in a Revolutionary Age*, Vol. 3, *The Nineteenth Century Outside Europe* (Grand Rapids: Zondervan Publishing House, 1961),

nineteenth century that people could be saved in denominational Christianity.[121] Charles W. Naylor defined the Church of God as 'part of the church.'[122] Frederick G. Smith articulated the Church of God as a '. . . movement within the universal church . . . .'[123] Finally, Albert F. Gray noted that the Church of God was comprised of all Christians.[124] Latourette was not part of the movement. Rowe, Naylor, Smith and Gray were. If this later view is the same as Daniel S. Warner's then Sarah Warner's argument collapses.

In Warner's mind the Church of God and denominational Christianity were of separate origins. The former was founded on Christ and the apostles upon the foundation of Scripture. Warner's poem 'The Crusades of Hell', part four 'Satan's Third and Last Crusade' was Daniel Warner's explanation for the existence of denominational Christianity. According to this poem, Satan conspired with the demonic host to subvert the faith. The first crusade, apparently, had been an attempt to defeat the church in open warfare. In the second crusade the devilish throng had proposed to join the community of faith. Both crusades had suffered ignominious defeats. Now was the time for the third and final crusade. The subversion of the faith would be achieved through the creation of denominationalism.[125] '[A]ll . . . ites, are really the devils organized forces against

---

p. 117.

[121] 'What We Believe,' *Gospel Trumpet*, (6 January 1898).

[122] 'Heart Talks: Some Questions About the Church,' *Ibid.*, (28 February 1929), p.11.

[123] Cited in Barry L. Callen, ed., *A Time to Remember: Teachings,* [Church of God Heritage Series, Vol. 3] (Anderson: Warner Press, 1978), p. 83.

[124] 'Distinctive Features of the Present Movement,' *Gospel Trumpet*, (23 February 1922), p. 5.

[125] Warner, *Poems of Grace and Truth*, pp. 248-9. See also pp. 10-11 and 27-8. Denominationalism is the wife of Satan, '. . . her chief founder was the devil.' *Ibid.*, p. 121.

Conflict and Crisis in the Kingdom of God in Ohio 243

the Lord and His Christ, against thorough bible holiness which destroys all sects and denominations; all ites and isms.'[126] This conviction led Warner to adamantly assert that 'all . . . sects are of the devil.'[127] Given that every sect is demon inspired there is no way any sect can be the church or even part of the one true Church of God.[128] Since all sects are not part of the church there is every reason to forsake the broad road and join the narrow way of come-outism. Indeed, the movement could sing the refrain, 'Ev'ry human structure 'round us, crumbles into gen'ral wreck . . . .'[129] The alternative is clear. 'All our meetings are salvation and praise meetings, and all Babylon confusion is cast back into the fire of the burning. Hallelujah! Amen and amen!'[130] Against this third great crusade was set the armies of God, clothed in white, riding on 'holiness steeds.' While the horses have a 'heavenly neigh' the 'campaign of fire shall sweep over the land,' destroying the beast and his army.[131] The Come-Out movement had assumed its own image of warfare. Church of God sociologist Val Clear has stated that this motif was probably the main *raison d'être* for the Church of God movement in its earliest years. 'God repudiates all denominations, wants his children to leave all denominations and relate only to the church which Jesus founded.'[132] Amid the confusion of

---

[126] Unsigned, 'Dead Works,' *Gospel Trumpet*, (15 October 1883).

[127] Warner, *No Sectism; or a Review of a Tract Bearing the Above Title Written by A. Sims* (Moundsville, WV: Gospel Trumpet Publishing Company, n.d.), pp. 6-7.

[128] Warner, *An Exclusive Christ*, pp. 6-7 and *The Church of God; or, What is the Church, and What is Not* (Moundsville, WV: Gospel Trumpet Company, 1885), p. 2.

[129] Warner's hymn, 'The Golden Morning' pointed this out. *Echoes from Glory*, no. 208.

[130] Warner, *Questions and Answers on the Church* (Grand Junction: Gospel Trumpet Publishing Company, n.d.), p. 21.

[131] See Warner's hymn in *Echoes from Glory*, no. 197.

[132] Val Clear, *Where the Saints Have Trod: A Social History of the Church of God Reformation Movement*, p. 8.

'Babel' Warner could sing of the freedom from the bondage of the 'sects.'[133] At the Council at Indianapolis in 1880 the decision to '. . . separate ourselves from all human sects, abandon all party names, and reject all man made creeds . . . .' was made.[134] The decision was based on the conviction that ' . . . every intelligent reader of the Bible knows that . . . sects . . . are not the church of God. . . .'[135] With this conviction as the foundation of his vision and commission, Warner was able to declare confidently that his come-out form of Christianity was the authentic biblical, apostolic, single Church of God. The basis was the experience of entire sanctification; the result was a new identity.

The doctrine of entire sanctification alluded to earlier was the difference between apostate denominationalism and the truth of the Come-Out movement. Those who were entirely sanctified could understand truth more fully than an 'unsanctified soul.'[136] The sanctified are victorious in everything.[137] Indeed, individuals '. . . will be more apt to find God if they utterly disregard . . . [all sects].'[138] Christians must beware of 'sectarian' preachers and their teachings which stray afield from the message being trumpeted by Warner since '. . . Satan . . . has in his employ . . . many professed ministers of the gospel, all well trained in Sinumust College.'[139] These gospel charlatans are 'corrupt and self-aggrandizing

---

[133] See for example his hymns 'Who Will Suffer for Jesus?' in *Echoes from Glory*, no. 169, 'The Evening Light' in *Songs of the Evening Light*, no. 1. and 'Beautiful Zion' in *Salvation Echoes*, eds., Barney E. Warren, Andrew L. Byers, C.E. Hunter and D. Otis Teasley (Moundsville, WV: Gospel Trumpet Publishing Company, 1900), no. 55.

[134] Book 07: Scratch Book, D.S. Warner papers. Archives, Anderson University.

[135] Warner, *The Church of God*, p. 32.

[136] Book 07: Scratch Book, D.S. Warner papers. Archives, Anderson University.

[137] Warner, 'I'm Reigning in this Life,' in *Anthems from the Throne*, no. 74.

[138] Warner, *Altar and Mercy Seat* (Grand Junction: Gospel Trumpet Publishing Company, n.d.), p. 17.

[139] Warner, *Salvation*, p. 43.

shepherds' who have contributed to these divisions and spiritual malnutrition of God's people.[140] Charles Naylor later asserted that Warner believed a time would come when God would no longer extend salvation into the 'sect' configuration. Those who failed to come out would go to hell and be lost.[141] However, those who joined Warner and the Come-Out movement could be assured of 'walking on his [Christ's] holy plain . . .' and living 'upon the mount of holiness . . . in heaven's view . . . .'[142]

In the fall of 1884 after the annual assembly Warner made it quite clear why people should join his movement. Using the words of Scripture Warner made a dramatic personal application: '. . . we know that we are of the truth . . . we know that we are of God, and he that heareth us not is not of God.'[143] This attitude, consistent with the times and manifested in a variety of ways, caused Warner to claim a direct, intuitive understanding of Scriptural truth. He further believed steadfastly that his views when brought into maturity constituted the 'light of the Lord.'[144] Barton Stone may have defended his decision to allow Methodists to preach at Cane Ridge in 1801 on the basis of Christian unity rather than facilitating the seeds of theological difference, but Warner's approach to holiness and unity revolved around his self-understanding as God's specially appointed prophet. In

---

[140] *Bible Proofs of the Second Work of Grace*, p. 380. Elsewhere, Warner referred to other ministers as 'dum [sic] dog[s]' and 'priests of Babylon' who serve in 'idol temple[s].' 'Sin in High Places,' *Gospel Trumpet*, (15 September 1883). The article is unsigned but is clearly from Warner's pen.

[141] Charles W. Naylor, *The Teachings of D.S. Warner and his Associates* (Privately published, n.d.). No pagination. Naylor's assertions are none too far afield. One has only to recall Warner's poem, 'Soul-Cripple City,' discussed above.

[142] *cf.*, Warner's songs 'Everlasting Joy,' in *Anthems from the Throne*, no. 20 and 'The Angel Choir' in *Salvation Echoes*, no. 181.

[143] Warner's declaration is cited in Byers, *Birth of a Reformation*, p. 319.

[144] Forrest, 'A Study of the Development of the Basic Doctrines and Institutional Patterns in the Church of God (Anderson, Indiana),' p. 53.

other words, Warner claimed special insight into spiritual matters.[145] Consequently, he could affirm that the '. . . Church . . . is required to have but one mouth, which means perfect harmony in all her teachings.'[146] Like many nineteenth-century religious reformers, Warner perceived himself as the principle organ through which God spoke truth and perfect pure doctrine. Herein, Warner exemplified the paradox of religious democracy. Having that conviction he equated attacks on himself with the work of antichrist. As a servant of God, to oppose Warner was to oppose Christ, to 'antagonize the *Gospel Trumpet*' was to 'abide the consequences of fighting against God's Word'[147] since '. . . the *Trumpet* . . . reports more real salvation than any [other] paper. . . .'[148] Up to the end of his life Warner spoke passionately of how God had called him to lead the faithful out of error and that God had revealed to him '. . . the sect Babylon of the Revelation . . . .'[149] Naylor later affirmed that only Warner and his closest associates were the ones to

---

[145] Koeth, 'A History of Anti-Catholicism in the Church of God Reformation Movement,' p. 75. Koeth has noted that Warner, in a 'special manner' claimed to have received insight into spiritual matters, in this case with regard to holiness.

[146] Warner, *The Church of God*, p. 19. Or, as Mother Sarah Smith put it, '[t]here never was a sectarian preacher that could preach the whole Bible, and there never will be.' *Life Sketches of Mother Sarah Smith*, p. 12.

[147] Warner, 'To Our Contemporaries,' (16 January 1882). In his 'New Year's Greetings,' *Gospel Trumpet*, (1 January 1882) Warner attacked George Watson and his views expressed in an 'antichrist sheet' wherein Watson apparently had spoken disparagingly of Warner. The latter called it '. . . a thrust at Jesus Christ.'

[148] Warner, 'Note,' *Gospel Trumpet*, (15 September 1887). This opinion was also expressed elsewhere. 'Many people who reject the truth must soon after suffer the terrible consequences. I desire to sound a warning to the *Trumpet* readers, and especially those who have it sent to them free of charge. The truths it contains are a savor of life unto life or death unto death.' *Life Sketches of Mother Sarah Smith*, p. 66.

[149] See the account cited in Byers, *Birth of a Reformation*, p. 441. In 'Soul-Cripple City,' Warner most surely associated himself with the 'angel of Jehovah' and the 'holy heralds' who, 'with Trumpet loudly sounding,' proclaim the eternal gospel and call sinners to repentance. *Poems of Grace and Truth*, pp. 155 *et al.*

see the light of truth.[150] While Naylor may be indulging in hyperbole he should not be dismissed too readily especially when it is clear that Warner on numerous occasions publicly attacked rival Holiness movements and their publications. The *Christian Harvester* was dismissed as representing '. . . silly . . . babylon works . . . . ' An editorial in the *Gospel Trumpet* lumped together the '"Harvester," "Highway," "Gospel Banner," "Fire and Hammer" and other editors . . . . ' with the spirit of antichrist. Further, the publication 'The Fathers Love' in Oakland, California was labelled 'a publication of Satan.'[151] Warner went so far as to issue a warning that one read the publications of Babylon at their own spiritual peril. 'You are not in condition to read papers, containing error without great danger to your soul, unless you have the Holy Spirit, the Comforter and discerner. And having Him you have no need, desire, nor time to read such.'[152] Warner, of course, had to read such literature. He was, after all, endowed with an 'historic mission'. The power of God had been given to him to discern truth from error, to unite holiness with all truth and to lead the gathering of God's people together into the Church of God in the time of the evening light. Theology may well have been democratized but spiritual authority among the prophets of the Christian faith had neither been taken away nor diminished. The Bible was the provenance of all but dictators disguised as democrats continued to interpret the word of God. These same leaders pointed unerringly to the path of truth. To do so it was necessary to identify the works of the enemy, warn the faithful of the pitfalls which yawned just outside the ark of safety. For perilous times such as these, God had raised up men

---

[150] Naylor, *The Teachings of D.S. Warner and his Associates*.

[151] Unsigned, 'Dead Works,' *Gospel Trumpet*, (15 October 1883), Editorial, *Ibid.*, (1 June 1884) and Warner, 'The Devil's Love,' *Ibid.*, (15 October 1885). There are numerous unsigned articles in the *Gospel Trumpet*. John W.V. Smith has authoritatively assigned some of them to Warner. There are no established criteria for this. However, since Warner had close editorial control over the paper it is reasonable to assume that he probably wrote or certainly endorsed all unsigned articles.

[152] Warner, untitled article, *Gospel Trumpet* (1 February 1885).

of discernment, men and women of the Spirit, leaders who could navigate the masses through the dangerous straits of life's passages and, in the end, to the harbor of salvation on the other side. The voyage was too treacherous to be taken alone. Only the foolhardy would even make such an attempt. The risks of destruction were too great to be undertaken without a reliable guide. Without a divinely-inspired captain at the helm the chances of crossing successfully the great divide were virtually nil. One of those individuals in the ordered confusion of late nineteenth-century American Christianity who knew the proper route to salvation was Daniel Warner.

All of Warner's polemicizing was entirely consistent with religious editorializing in nineteenth-century America. While it may be unfair to denounce Warner as megalomaniacal, it may be argued that he did situate himself as an arbiter of truth. However, in fairness to him there have been few reformers indeed who have not so perceived themselves. The context of the nineteenth century clearly bears this out and it is consistent, in the main, with ecclesiastical history. The dilemma caused by the encounter of democracy with dictatorship could never escape the Gordian knot it tied.

Warner's hymnody also reflected these same pervasive views which became in time characteristic of the Warner movement. The heavenly voice called, 'Come, my people from confusion . . . .' Warner urged that all should flee, 'Taking not a babel stone . . . . [while] . . . myriad souls are sleeping, soon to wake in judgment fires!'[153] Warner likened denominational Christianity to the festive orgy held by King Belshazzar in the royal palace in Babylon narrated in the book of Daniel in the Hebrew Bible. The 'great king of Babel' throws a feast in the 'lofty steeple hall' prior to 'Babel's utter fall . . . . Babel's kingdom now is finished.' Those who have 'come-out' are saved from its destruction.[154] Elsewhere, Warner

---

[153] 'The Holy Remnant' in *Echoes from Glory*, no. 182.

[154] 'The Hand of God on the Wall,' in *Anthems from the Throne*, no. 70.

called for true Christians to stand '. . . from sin babel aloof . . . . clad in the armor of light and Omnipotent truth . . . . as . . . creeds and divisions . . . fall to demerit . . . .'[155] Warner's hymn, 'Angels Gathering the Elect,' placed the Come-Outers as God's servants in a prophetic rôle in the time of the evening light. The song cogently expressed Warner's sense of his own mission and thus several verses should be quoted here.

> Mighty messengers are running
> Shouting, flee from Babel's doom!
> For her plagues are swiftly coming,
> Her destruction will be soon.
>
> Popish reign of bloody terror,
> Passed around–an awful night–
> Now the cloudy day of error
> Breaks away in evening light.
>
> Hark! The shouts of joyful freedom,
> 'Tis the captives coming home;
> From each name of sect confusion,
> Made complete in Christ alone.
>
> Out of Sodom's desolation,
> Out of mystic Babel's fog;
> In the light of full salvation,
> We are coming home to God.[156]

Many of the dominant motifs of the early Come-Out movement find expression in this hymn.

Robert Reardon has acknowledged Warner's negative sentiment toward sects and ecclesiastical organization. Reardon has suggested two sources for this. First, it originated from theological convictions. Second, it was an emotional reaction stemming from his controversy with the West Ohio Eldership of the

---

[155] 'The Evening is Glorious,' in *Ibid.*, no. 58.

[156] *Ibid.*, no. 90.

Winebrennerian Church which climaxed in 1878.[157] The Achilles heel of Reardon's apology is that Warner had moved into an acerbic denunciatory rôle against other Christians long before he ran amiss of the West Ohio Eldership. Reardon's argument, however, does help to put Warner's post 1878 career into perspective. John W. V. Smith has touched on Warner's rôle as the leader of a religious movement. Smith, however, demurred from the suggestion that Warner was an autocrat, '. . . inflexible or . . . had ultimate control regarding what the movement believed, taught, and practised.'[158] Smith's thesis should not be accepted without qualification given Warner's insistence upon uniformity, unanimity, and perhaps conformity; characteristics of practically all reformation movements. While Warner obviously perceived God as the fount of all authority and the final standard for truth, he seemed never aware of the apparent contradiction in the exercise of his own authority. To call Warner an autocrat may be too strong. But that he did not escape the paradox of religious democracy can scarcely be denied. Warner denounced the following jingle in unrelenting terms.

> We must agree to disagree,
> We mortals can not hope to see
> The Word of God just all the same,
> Until we reach a higher plane.[159]

For Warner, only one great truth existed and there was little point in agreeing to disagree about that. Heralds of new revelations need no earthly verification achieved through debate and theological consensus. Convinced as he was of the veracity of the divine vision and commission he had received in 1878, Warner was in no position to compromise, even if he had wanted to. Thus, Warner's attitude

---

[157] Reardon, *The Early Morning Light*, pp. 20-21.

[158] Smith, *The Quest for Holiness and Unity*, pp. 183 and 206.

[159] Cited in Warner and Riggle, *The Cleansing of the Sanctuary*, p. 251.

is one of increasing rigidity throughout the period 1875-1895[160] and his rôle as an authoritative personality figured heavily into the configuration of the Come-Out movement.[161]

Judging from the views expressed earlier by Latourette, Rowe, Naylor, Smith and Gray it would seem that the views of the Church of God after the death of Daniel Warner deviated significantly from those of its founding father. Based on the evidence presented it would seem difficult to draw an equation between the two. While Sarah Warner's exegesis is arguable, the writings of Daniel Warner lend themselves in many instances in many ways to the sort of interpretation that she derived from them: a 'spirit' of self-righteousness and pharisaism, one which demanded that all must see 'it' the way 'we' do. Again, one must not divorce Warner from his historical context and judge him anachronistically by the

---

[160] For evidence of this see his successive articles, 'Do Ministers of God See Eye to Eye?' *Gospel Trumpet*, (14 December 1893), 'The Ministers of God See Eye to Eye' *Gospel Trumpet*, (21 December 1893), and 'The Ministers of God Must See Eye to Eye' *Gospel Trumpet*, (28 December 1893). By contrast Milo Chapman, an elder statesman of the church remarked to me in private conversation, that Warner's attitude was Christian and generous towards everyone. The negative reaction came later in the post-Warner years. Personal Interview, 24 November 1994. It is difficult to find a correlation between this statement and the foregoing and reconcile the two.

[161] Warner is not generally regarded today by descendants of the Come-Out movement as an authoritative voice despite the fact that it has been noted ' . . . history must label him as founder and guiding light of the early fortunes of both the Church of God Reformation Movement and the publishing work so closely allied to it.' Phillips, *Miracle of Survival*, p. 49. There were, however, churches named after him. The First Church of God in Vancouver, Washington, begun in 1926, originally was named 'Warner Memorial Church'. G. Samuel Dunbar, *Truth Along the Trail: A Centennial History of the Church of God in Oregon* (Salem: Publications Commission of the Association of the Churches of God in Oregon and Southwest Washington, 1993), p. 124. One can only speculate on how Warner might have viewed this. During the early years of the come-out movement, Warner's followers were sometimes called 'Warnerites'. 'Such a designation defies all that Warner and the movement stands for.' Barry L. Callen, *It's God's Church! The Life and Legacy of Daniel Sidney Warner* (Anderson: Warner Press, 1995), p. 10. On the relevance and relativity of Warner *vis-à-vis* the nature and application of authority see Merle D. Strege, *Tell Me the Tale: Historical Reflections on the Church of God* (Anderson: Warner Press, 1991), pp. 120-22.

standards of another era. But the portrait of Warner extrapolated earlier from his followers does seem to hang askew on the structure of his literary endeavors. Contrary to the stated motives of the Come-Out movement, but corresponding to the dissent of Sarah Warner, the attempt at the unification of the church and Christianity paradoxically seemed in danger of creating further division. Sarah seemed aware of the dilemma, Warner saw only the forward march of truth and to that end he gave his energies.

According to Daniel Warner the movement designated the 'Come-Outers' had Christian unity as its primary focus and goal and was not a rival church or sect among the others. 'The Christians branded "come-outers" have founded no church or sect, nor do they intend to; but, on the contrary, they have abandoned all sects to live in the one church that Christ founded, and into which we were inducted by regeneration.'[162] As we have seen, the Come-Out Movement, as associated with Warner, formally began on 1 October 1881 at Beaver Dam, Indiana, and on 15 October of the same year in Carson City, Michigan.[163] The message of holiness had preceded Warner. Oberlin and Methodist perfectionism had cast deep roots in Michigan.[164] The way of the Lord had been prepared. The fallow ground had been broken up and the Warner vision could take root. Christendom was spiritually bankrupt. As previously noted, in elongated fashion, Daniel Warner clearly accepted this premise. In fact, Warner declared that the commandment of God was for all believers to come out of the false churches.[165] At this point Warner included the Winebrennerian Church among the true fellowship of the faith. The 'come-out'

---

[162] 'Questions Answered,' *Gospel Trumpet*, (15 August 1881).

[163] The circumstances, details, and implications of these events have been well documented. See for example, Smith, *The Quest for Holiness and Unity*, pp. 44-5.

[164] Timothy L. Smith, *Called Unto Holiness: The Story of the Nazarenes: The Formative Years* (Kansas City, MO: Nazarene Publishing House, 1962), p. 33.

[165] *Journal*, 8 June 1873.

view was predicated upon the assumption that the false churches followed the 'system of Antichrist doctrines' and were hopelessly steeped in 'spiritual ignorance.'[166] All 'sects' and 'churches' were not of God. 'If therefore, the holiness movement lays waste some churches in its course, it is simply because they are composed, in general, of sinners.'[167] Indeed, they are frauds whose end is death. 'For your soul's sake cast away your religion . . . .' and be saved from churches.[168] However, it was not enough to simply forsake one's 'sect.' Warner seemed to infer that merely leaving a sect was in itself without meaning. The true efficacy lay in the Come-Outers joining with him.[169] Indeed, Warner noted early in his career that those who finally forsook denominational Christianity confessed that they had been wrong and that Warner and his associates had been correct.[170] Warner's confidence in the essential truth and integrity of his position was so unshakeable that ostensibly he declared that all true Christians would be gathered into the movement within a single generation.[171]

Into what were these Come-Outers being gathered? Already we have heard Warner submit that it was not into a new church or sect. Instead authentic Christians were gathering into the 'Church of God . . . the only proper appellation

---

[166] Warner, *What is the Soul* (Anderson: Gospel Trumpet Company, 1908), p. 67 and Warner and Riggle, *The Cleansing of the Sanctuary*, p. 273.

[167] Warner, *An Exclusive Christ*, pp. 6-7 and *Bible Proofs of the Second Work of Grace*, pp. 404-5.

[168] Warner, *Salvation*, p. 55 and *Bible Proofs of the Second Work of Grace*, p. 416. Religion, for Warner, was detrimental to salvation. His hymn, 'A Solemn Charge,' noted that 'millions lost today have stumbled downward o'er religion, blent [?] with shades of night . . . .' in *Salvation Echoes*, no. 64.

[169] Naylor, *The Teachings of D.S. Warner and his Associates*.

[170] *Journal*, 13 November 1872.

[171] Naylor, *The Teachings of D.S. Warner and his Associates*. Naylor asserts, 'This I know from his own lips . . . .'

... and true church.' Those who joined themselves to any other body called by any other name were by consequence '. . . guilty of the sin of division.'[172] The Church of God had no human founder and was organized by Christ alone.[173] Historically, Warner's group has eschewed any reference to themselves as a denomination and have preferred the designation 'movement'.[174] Following the conviction expressed by John Winebrenner, Warner was certain that the Church of God was not simply another denomination. Instead, it represented the true, apostolic body of Christ. It is here in his ecclesiology where perhaps Warner's single theological novelty can be detected. Unlike many before him, Warner equated the visible and the invisible church. By stripping away all semblance of human organization and denominationalism and abiding solely in the true Church of God, authentic invisible Christianity was made visible.[175] The question remains, how could Warner be so certain that he represented the one true 'Church of God' and that all others were in error? The query has already been broached. According to Warner, God had revealed to him the truth and had called Warner to proclaim that same truth with unflagging insight.[176] In a discussion in 1880 on why the

---

[172] Warner, *The Church of God*, p. 21.

[173] Warner, 'Church of God,' in *Songs of the Evening Light*, no. 197.

[174] This is not the context in which to address the issue of the Warner movement and its relation to denominationalism or its affinities to the sect-church schema set forth by Ernst Troeltsch in his seminal opus, *Die Soziallehren der Christlichen Kirchen und Gruppen* (1911) translated by Olive Wyon as *The Social Teachings of the Christian Church* (1931). However, an American religious historian as eminent as Mark Noll has referred to Warner's movement as a denomination. *A History of Christianity in the United States and Canada* (Grand Rapids: William B. Eerdmans, 1992), p. 379.

[175] Brown, *When Souls Awaken*, pp. 63-4.

[176] Apparently some of Warner's songs were the result of divine verbal dictation. See the editorial note appended to Warner's hymn, 'Perishing Souls,' which stated: 'These verses were suggested by the Savior appearing to a brother in a vision, with a banner containing the words of the first line,' in *Echoes from Glory*, no. 125. Precedent for this idea goes back to the hymnal *Anthems from the Throne*, wherein the editors in a preface stated ' . . . both words and music were marvelously inspired by the Holy Spirit.' Warner

Gospel Trumpet should be an independent paper Warner noted the following. First, that the work assigned to him by God should be subject, not to humankind, but to the Spirit. Second, because 'whatever work God gives a man to do naturally receives more light on that subject and work than others.'[177] Warner could refer to his own work as a faithful '. . . contending for the truth & salvation that heaven sent to earth.'[178]

Hence, the Church of God as defined and described by Daniel Warner was the true church. Indeed, Warner reported in his journal of how he '. . . made him [a fellow named Mumpers] confess that the Church of God was the only scriptural church. . . .'[179] Since 'Christ is an exclusive Christ' and the Christian faith 'is an exclusive faith' and the 'truth of God is exclusive' then the true church 'is also exclusive' and all who are saved are in the Church of God.[180] Despite Warner's intentions and the basic philosophy of the Come-Out movement, Sarah suggested that the call for unity ultimately became a cause for division. In the first instance, Warner assumed the primary teaching rôle. His doctrines became commonplace ideas in the Come-Out movement and in early Church of God history. With the inevitable flood of human problems within any social configuration there arose a need for some kind of political ordering. Again, this largely became Warner's lot.

---

had also claimed, in his first book, that he had written in the very presence of God. *Bible Proofs of the Second Work of Grace*, p. 16.

[177] Book 07: Scratch Book, D.S. Warner papers. Archives, Anderson University.

[178] Letter from D.S. Warner to William Ryland, 21 May 1889. D.S. Warner papers. Archives, Anderson University. The letter is extant in typescript only and is therefore an unsubstantiated correspondence. The tone and the language however seem consistent with Warner's style.

[179] *Journal*, 22 April 1874 and 20 November 1876.

[180] Warner and Riggle, *The Cleansing of the Sanctuary*, p. 265.

He stated clearly that 'the polity of the Church of God is [the] Bible.'[181] The rhetoric was sound but the reality was that someone had to provide the interpretation. Warner articulated the biblical principles through expository writing on the 'polity of the Church of God.'[182] Warner took full advantage of the culture of religious print which by the 1880s was still expanding. On later occasions Warner preached on church political matters and castigated those who dissented from his views,[183] in the same manner as other reformers. Warner's Winebrennerian views on church polity and Christian exclusivism remained unchanged despite his expulsion from the West Ohio Eldership. As noted previously, Warner later came to regard the Winebrennerians as simply another 'sect.' This became their lot due to their resistance to the truth of entire sanctification and their insistence upon following the 'godless' pattern of organization. The truth of Winebrennerian Christianity went with Warner in his departure. Later it became fully developed and brought to maturity under the careful supervision of Warner apart from the hierarchical oppression of the West Ohio Eldership.

Sarah Warner insisted that Come-Outism 'simply cuts off a few members' of God's people by themselves. For her this was divisive. Her insinuation was that the few members cut off by themselves became unwittingly a rival 'sect,' with good intentions but nonetheless adding to the splintering of the body of Christ. Church of God historiography has consistently reacted to this suggestion with strong denials. The issue becomes contentious. Buildings were erected for Come-Out meetings, pastors were appointed upon Warner's directives, teachings were

---

[181] *Journal*, 3 January 1875. This conviction, at least in theory, did not undergo alteration in the transition from the Winebrennerian Church to the exclusive 'Come-Out' position. Warner also affirmed the Bible as 'the rock of everlasting ages' in his hymn, 'Precious Bible,' in *Echoes from Glory*, no. 62.

[182] *Journal*, 1 December 1874.

[183] *Ibid.*, 16 August 1876. Warner referred to H.S. McNutt as a 'poor foolish creature . . . [who] has showed a bad and fatal spirit' for speaking out against Warner's views.

formulated, church polity developed and organization inevitably occurred. It is difficult, then, to avoid situating the Warner movement within the sect configuration as he articulated it.

The unity proposed by Warner resembled more a uniformity than a unanimity. Complete agreement in matters of doctrine became mandatory for full acceptance and the total realization of unity within the movement.[184] It has already been noted by others that '. . . radical departures from accepted teaching was considered heresy and loss of group approval and ostracism were controls used to combat such departures.'[185] Of course, the by now traditional commonplace of ridiculing other Christians with epithets such as 'the mark of the Beast' persisted.[186] Warner continued to view denominational Christianity as 'Babylon,' 'schools of vanity,' 'hotbeds of pride and false religion,' and 'worldly gatherings.'[187] For him the alternative quite clearly was 'Come-Outism.'[188] For Sarah that option became ultimately intolerable and untenable. Its propensity for division surpassed its promise for unity. Her convictions were supported by other Holiness groups. Their protests and admonitions to Daniel Warner, however were not considered valid on account of their persistent affinity to 'sectarianism'. Warner's group suffered unnecessary ostracism in the sense that they lost vital

---

[184] Naylor, *The Teachings of D.S. Warner and his Associates.*

[185] Forrest, 'A Study of the Development of the Basic Doctrines and Institutional Patterns in the Church of God,' p. 162.

[186] In this case the object was a Dunker preacher at Bucyrus, Ohio, around 1881. See the account in Enoch E. Byrum, 'Customs and Traditions,' *Gospel Trumpet*, (1 July 1915), p. 3.

[187] *Gospel Trumpet*, (1 December 1885).

[188] 'That Ye Break Every Yoke,' *Ibid.*, (1 June 1881). See also his other arguments in 'Square Come-Outism,' *Gospel Trumpet*, (1 June 1881), 'Questions Answered,' *Gospel Trumpet*, (15 August 1881), and 'The Shaft Giving Way,' *Gospel Trumpet*, (1 November 1881). All of these articles are largely reproduced in Byers, *Birth of a Reformation*, pp. 261-6. See also his 'Propping up the Walls,' *Gospel Trumpet*, (1 December 1884).

contact with other groups who shared similar or identical views on holiness.[189] Had Warner's ecclesial ideal been realized then obviously the hope for unity would likewise have come to fruition. When it became apparent that not all Christians would rush into the movement in a single generation, as Warner apparently anticipated, then the quest for unity had to steer its course through the treacherous straits between the Scylla of accommodation and the Charybdis of sinful division. Daniel Warner despised the very notion of accommodation. In his mind it was this 'sin' which had destroyed the Winebrennerians. Sarah Warner, evidently, was unprepared for the division she perceived as the result of Warner's attitude and theology. Her criticism was clearly subjective, but perhaps not without foundation.

The movement headed by Daniel Warner turned, not only on the idea of abandoning sects but also, on the notion of entire sanctification. The two ideas were organically related. As Sarah put it, 'They hold and teach that no one can be entirely sanctified and belong to a "sect."' Interpreters of the Church of God movement essentially have been unanimous in their assessment that the early main teachings included the doctrine of entire sanctification.[190] Earlier in his career, Warner had shied away from the notion. However, in 1878 he gave his assent to the idea and became perhaps its leading proponent in late nineteenth-century America. While Sarah was later to repudiate the cult of the wholly-sanctified Come-Out Movement this stance created one of the great ironies of the Warner saga. Initially it was her relatives, the Keller family, and the Holiness band in Upper Sandusky that exerted a compelling influence upon Daniel Warner during

---

[189] The sociological effects of this marginalization within American religious history is a topic for another study. For the perhaps inadvertent separation from other Holiness groups see Charles E. Jones, *Perfectionist Persuasion: The Holiness Movement and American Methodism, 1867-1936*, (Metuchen, NJ: The Scarecrow Press, Inc., 1974), p. 60.

[190] Clear, *Where the Saints Have Trod*, p. 8. For a good overview of the 'Church of God' concept, together with the understanding of radical holiness see Melvin E. Dieter, *The Holiness Revival of the Nineteenth Century* (Metuchen, NJ: The Scarecrow Press, Inc., 1980), pp. 245-95.

'the holiness agitation of 1877-78 . . . .'[191] The Holiness movements, of course, preceded Warner by several decades and its influences extend back even further. The teachings of John Wesley (1703-1791) and his brother Charles Wesley (1707-1788) are often referred to as the watershed for the Holiness emphasis, though the notion can be found in Jacob Arminius (1569-1609). Wesleyan teachings were disseminated in America in part in the eighteenth century by George Whitefield (1714-1770) and later into the nineteenth century by Francis Asbury (1745-1816) and others. Oberlin theology, as articulated by its main representatives, Charles Finney (1792-1875) and Asa Mahan (1799-1889) stressed the idea of 'Christian perfection.' Phoebe Palmer and her sister Sarah Lankford were leading lights of the Holiness movements in the 1830s and beyond. By the late 1860s organizations such as the 'National Camp Meeting Association for the Promotion of Holiness' were founded and together with the Keswick revivals in England after 1875 also played a rôle in the formation and shaping of American holiness.

By 1878 when Warner declared himself for sanctification there were numerous contemporary Holiness bodies, periodicals, and leaders proclaiming the doctrine of sanctification: George D. Watson, an Illinois Holiness leader, J.A. Wood, Walter C. Palmer, John S. Inskip, William MacDonald, Daniel Steele, George Hughes, editor of the *Guide to Holiness*, Isaiah Reid, editor of *The Highway*, Thomas K. Doty, editor of the *Christian Harvester*, L.B. Kent, and John P. Brooks, editors of the *Banner of Holiness*, and others.[192] Among the radical

---

[191] Warner referred to the general context in these terms in his *Bible Proofs of the Second Work of Grace*, p. 287.

[192] In addition to the *Gospel Trumpet*, and the aforementioned there were a plethora of periodicals in the nineteenth century devoted to the message of holiness. The following is a sample of titles: *Advocate of Bible Holiness, Advocate of Christian Holiness, Beauty of Holiness, Christian Advocate and Journal, Christian Perfection, Christian Spectator, Christian Standard and Home Journal, Church Advocate, Divine Life, Earnest Christianity, Good Way, Herald of Gospel Freedom, Herald of Holiness, Highway of Holiness, Holiness Messenger, Michigan Holiness Record, Northern Christian Advocate, Pacific Herald of Holiness, Pentecost, Pentecostal Herald, Texas Holiness Advocate, The*

Holiness leaders could be numbered John P. Brooks of Bloomington, Illinois, Hardin Wallace of Texas, later of Southern California, Solomon B. Shaw of Lansing, Michigan, and Daniel S. Warner. Warner, however, began to distinguish himself in the areas of Come-Outism, entire sanctification and perfection. As noted above, Sarah also acquiesced for a time in these emphases. Byers has asserted that Sarah '... also was sanctified, and the change in her was a test that he [Warner] had no words to gainsay.'[193] Thereafter she '... testified boldly to the second work and admonished the church.'[194] Her admonitions later were directed toward Warner and his followers.

After 1878 Warner's personal library began to show signs of its owner's preoccupation with the Holiness message.[195] He began to read many books on the topic. To the end of his life this interest never waned. The message of sanctification, for Warner, was both a 'divine' teaching and constituted the 'perfect way.' Those who received sanctification were likewise 'made perfect.' This idea of perfection became one of the distinctives of the Come-Out movement. Warner could 'bid all sin adieu' and further proclaim, 'There can be no failure

---

Christian's Pathway of Power, and *The Way of Life.*

[193] Byers, *Birth of a Reformation*, p. 103.

[194] *Journal*, 9 September 1877.

[195] John Alan Howard, 'The Chronology of the Development of Daniel Sidney Warner's Belief in Holiness and Sanctification With Special Attention Given to His Library and Reading Concerning the Subjects of Holiness and Sanctification Plus a Section Including Bibliographical Listings and General Observations Regarding the D.S. Warner Private Library Collection,' Unpublished paper, Church of God Archives, Anderson University, 1970. As noted earlier, not all of the books belonged to Warner. Some were Sarah's, others belonged to Frankie Miller. Still other books were added to the collection after Warner's death. Several belonged to Sidney Warner. There were even further volumes which have not survived. We know that Warner's library once was lost in a fire in Tiffin, Ohio. *Bible Proofs of the Second Work of Grace*, p. 394.

....,'[196] Moreover, the insistence revolved around freedom from sin in this life and a return to the original state of perfection.[197] Indeed the idea of sanctification became the center for both Christian life and ministry[198] and was the will of God.[199] Accordingly, the basis for the unity which Warner strove after so ardently is to be found in the experience of 'entire sanctification, or perfection,' for the experience 'heals all divisions' and produces perfect Christian unity.[200] In this posture, Warner reflected ideas which had been advanced a generation earlier by Phoebe Palmer and others who had taught that sanctification was the pre-requisite for the final reformation of the church and the sole basis for Christian unity. In his teaching of holiness it is entirely possible to fail to find any trace of innovation. Warner simply reflected the doctrine as historically developed and articulated.[201] Beyond repairing

---

[196] Warner's hymnody, again, played a key rôle in the proclamation of this conviction. 'Farewell to Sin' and 'How Often I've Pondered' in *Echoes from Glory*, nos. 153 and 192. Further see *Ibid.*, no. 6, 'Oh, Praise the Lord,' no. 51, 'This is Why I Love My Savior,' no. 67, 'Salvation is Flowing,' and no. 195, 'Tell me Pilgrim.' See also *Anthems from the Throne*, no. 67. The conviction of sinless perfection was boldly stated by the editors in their preface to *Songs of the Evening Light:* 'As the brilliant light of full salvation shines within us, and we realize that we are given "power over all the power of the enemy," enabling us to live free from all sin . . . .'

[197] See particularly his *Bible Proofs of a Second Work of Grace*, pp. 26, 83, 462, and *passim*.

[198] See Warner's entries in his *Journal* for 23 October 1877, 13 January and 11 August 1878 and his *Innocence: A Poem Giving a Description of the Author's Experience from Innocence into Sin, and from Sin to Full Salvation* (Grand Junction: Gospel Trumpet Publishing Company, 1896).

[199] 'Fill Me with Thy Spirit,' in *Echoes from Glory*, no. 172.

[200] Warner, *The Church of God*, p. 23. 'Here we say is secured to us the essential and all-sufficient means of producing perfect unity in all the body of Christ . . . . Entire sanctification heals all divisions by removing the cause . . . .' Warner and Riggle, *The Cleansing of the Sanctuary*, p. 260. Sanctification results in the cessation of 'party names and discord . . .,' and produces '. . . order, and harmony out of Babylon confusion . . . .' *Bible Proofs of a Second Work of Grace*, p. 238.

[201] This is the conclusion reached by Charles E. Brown in his *When Souls Awaken*, p. 58.

the breach of division Warner equated sanctification with salvation. His Sunday sermon for 19 May 1878 at Beaver Dam, Indiana, identified the promise made to Abraham with the inheritance of sanctification.[202] According to Warner sanctification was salvation and full salvation equalled sanctification,[203] so that heaven was gained through holiness.[204] Those who had been endowed with the blessing of entire sanctification, as understood by Warner, were then given a special gift of discernment. Those sanctified could in fact determine who among them were not. '. . . It was of no use for anyone to claim to be sanctified when not; for all who had the experience could at once detect them. Glory to God this is generally true.'[205] With this assurance of both truth and spiritual discernment Warner, like other reformers, perceived himself as the arbiter of truth and error in theological matters. Those who refused to 'come-out' of denominational Christianity '. . . are not thus made one . . . are not sanctified [and are] not in possession of the glory.'[206] Resistance to this truth was a demonstration of the lack of sanctification and was by consequence a forfeiting of salvation. Negotiation on this article was

---

[202]   'Identified this inheritance [salvation] with the promise made to Abraham. Gen[esis] 12 & 17.' *Journal*, 19 May 1878. Warner formally made this connection in his *Bible Proofs of a Second Work of Grace,* p. 85. Further, Christ died to secure the reality of holiness. 'We Must Be Holy,' in *Echoes from Glory*, no. 76, and also the 'true objective end of Christ's atonement and shed blood' is the experience of sanctification. 'New Year's Greeting,' *Gospel Trumpet*, (1 January 1882).

[203]   'Perfection of Christian character is then a present experience, and is the result of salvation . . . [Hebrews 10:14]. It is here declared identical with entire sanctification, and sanctification is salvation.' Warner, *Salvation*, p. 46.

[204]   On this see Warner's hymns, 'Will You Go with Us to Heaven?' in *Echoes from Glory*, no. 73, especially verse three: 'We are going thro' to glory by the Bible, See the way-markers, "be ye holy thro' the blood . . . ."' and 'Who Shall Dwell with Christ?' in *Songs of the Evening Light*, no. 201, especially verse four: 'You must be holy, white as snow, none but the pure shall dwell with Christ.'

[205]   This was Warner's comment on a statement made by a 'Bro. James Young' at a house meeting held in Canton, Ohio on 13 November 1877. *Journal*, 13 November 1877.

[206]   Warner and Riggle, *The Cleansing of the Sanctuary*, p. 262.

impossible for Warner. Any notion of agreeing to disagree was repugnant. The divine mandate was clear. 'All sons of God must holy be . . . [and] . . . unless you're sanctified, you can never, never 'bide in the presence of the heavenly throne.'[207] 'To agree to disagree . . . is babel confusion. To know the truth is our privilege; to teach the truth, our duty . . . .'[208] Not only did resistance to Warner's message result in salvation lost, it likewise procured for the unbeliever the fellowship of Satan gained. 'God is on the side of perfection, and Satan and his cursed unbelief stand against it. Reader, this fact will help you to determine whether you are of God or of the devil. God's truth teaches and his saints live out Christian perfection.'[209] So profoundly convinced was Warner of these premises, of 'come-outism' and entire sanctification that he devoted his first major literary effort to their articulation.[210] Warner seemed adamant that one could not possibly be entirely sanctified and remain outside of the one true Church of God connected to a 'sect' which by definition was contrary to Christian unity and inherently antagonistic to the teaching and leading of the Holy Spirit. To deny the second work of grace motif was, for Warner, tantamount to opposing God.[211] This Warner knew for certain, the Bible told him so.

---

[207] Warner's hymns made this very clear. 'What Manner of Love' in *Anthems from the Throne*, no. 68, and 'We're a Happy Pilgrim Band' in *Echoes from Glory*, no. 107. The conclusion was not unique to Warner. His followers pursued the same line of argument with consistency. The following remark makes the point in representative fashion: 'Remember, there are but two ways spoken of in the Bible, one is *the narrow way, the way of holiness which leads to heaven*; the other is the broad road that leads to eternal destruction.' *Life Sketches of Mother Sarah Smith*, p. 76 emphasis mine.

[208] Warner, *The Church of God*, pp. 25-6.

[209] Ibid., *Salvation*, pp. 42-3.

[210] Ibid., *Bible Proofs of a Second Work of Grace*. The book is a clear exposition of the doctrine of the second work of grace. In this volume Warner declared sanctification to be an 'instantaneous' work (p. 48) and declared the notion of sanctification as a process to be a 'fatal delusion of satan.' See pp. 30, 324 and elsewhere.

[211] Ibid., p. 232.

Despite her quite apparent early enthusiasm Sarah Warner now found herself at odds with the spirit of the movement so much so that she arrived at the conviction that the combining of 'come-out' philosophy with the teaching of entire sanctification led to a *reductio ad absurdum*. She took her stand against it just as adamantly as Daniel Warner assumed a position for it. The ensuing result was her public attack published in the *Christian Harvester*. In the end, Sarah became convinced that it was Warner's movement which needed reforming, more than the church the movement sought to reform.

Appended to her critique of the spirit of the movement, its divisive nature, narrow insistence on uniformity, self-righteousness, and untenable theological conclusions was a reference to apparent 'fanaticism and absurdities connected with this movement . . . .' Sarah Warner then made reference to a meeting held in Sulphur Springs in November 1883. In some ways the Sulphur Springs scenario was an example of the sort of dangers and extremism which sometimes gestate and come to fruition in radical, separatist movements like the one energized by Warner. Sulphur Springs was a small community near Bucyrus, Ohio. From 9-12 November 1883 Daniel Warner had called for a general assembly of the true church to gather. He had sent out an invitation drawing attention to 'spiritual gifts,' 'the power of the Spirit,' 'perfect consecration,' freedom from the 'bondage of sect captivity' and the opportunity to be 'stirred up and strengthened' and 'sharpened' in the faith once delivered to the saints.[212] The response to Warner's announcement was overwhelming. Religious eccentrics, deviants, and those seeking a platform from which to trumpet their peculiar ideas came flowing out of the hills like water into a rain barrel. On Friday, 9 November the first gathering convened in Conlay Bethel. Immediately, as it were, the place was filled with fanatics some preaching their message that the wearing of 'collars, collar buttons, lace, eye glasses' and

---

[212] 'First General Assembly in Ohio,' *Gospel Trumpet*, (15 October 1883). The Sulphur Springs incident is reported in some detail in Byers, *Birth of a Reformation*, pp. 288-92.

other accessories was sinful. All of this was entirely consistent with the long-standing holiness war against worldliness. On Saturday the meeting shifted to Sulphur Springs. More fanatics appeared. All were decidedly anti-sectarian, but many, probably to Warner's horror, were also anti-sanctification. The confusion and discord became so great that the Sunday meeting was held in a private house with some secrecy. In an attempt to thwart the fanatical faction the meeting for the last day of the assembly was moved again, this time to another private residence. The plot failed. Word leaked out of the whereabouts of Warner and his gathering and the crowd followed. Even more fanatics joined in. The final day proved to be the most tumultuous. There were reports of 'jerking,' 'crying out,' and possible demon possession.[213] One woman claimed to be possessed by a devil. Evidently she attempted to spit upon and claw anyone who came near. Warner later reported exorcisms. In a sense the assembly had degenerated into a debacle.

Warner did not perceive the Sulphur Springs meeting as a disaster. In a long article[214] Warner spoke of the gathering as 'a great turn out of the true saints.' He admitted that 'legions of devils [had rushed] into the community' and that a great conflict had ensued before the dragon and his angels had been cast out. But in the main, the work of God had been accomplished. That scoundrel Stockwell, before his fall from grace, had been at Sulphur Springs and had facilitated the move of God witnessed there. According to Warner's report, 'the Lord

---

[213] Jerking, of course, had been a prominent feature at Cane Ridge and in later revivals and camp meetings throughout the nineteenth century. Warner, however, was opposed to such demonstrations of the spirit. Axchie A. Bolitho, *To The Chief Singer: A Brief Story of the Work and Influence of Barney E. Warren* (Anderson: Gospel Trumpet Company, 1942), p. 52. Commenting on meetings in the summer of 1887 in Crawford County, Missouri, Warner expressed his unequivocal condemnation of the practice. 'A terrible nervous jerking had seized upon many in the meetings . . . . jerking is not mentioned in the Bible as a manifestation of God's Spirit, but is ascribed to a malignant spirit . . . . We renounced that working as of the devil. . . .' Warner's report is quoted in Byers, *Birth of a Reformation*, pp. 353-8.

[214] Unsigned, 'The Assembly Meeting,' *Gospel Trumpet*, (15 November 1883).

wonderfully used . . . Brother R.S. Stockwell, from Ada.' God used Stockwell at Sulpher Springs, the Devil would soon use him for other means.

The fanaticism and absurdities which Sarah Warner pointed out were in a sense a natural, although unintended, consequence of the 'come-out' teaching. For some, 'Come-Outism' was an opportunity to escape from religious control, order and structures of teaching, polity and religious expression. In other words, those attracted to the emotional, phenomenological, and alternative forms of religious expression, without the restraint of discipline were in this instance, drawn to a movement which on the surface appeared to allow them the greatest possible latitude. The type of behavior exhibited by some at Sulphur Springs was sufficient evidence for Sarah to equate their fanaticism and absurdities with insanity. Sulphur Springs was not an isolated instance. Indeed, similar radicalism was fairly characteristic of revivalist religion in the nineteenth century and consistent with the early history of the Come Out movement. For leaders such as Daniel Warner, radicalism could not detract from the work of God.

The issue of fanaticism is a bedevilling problem, fraught with the cloud of bias and subjectivity. Clearly there were 'absurdities' and 'fanaticism,' by almost any definition, within the Warner movement just as there always have been in virtually every other movement. One form of possible fanaticism was the on-going holiness wars of competition. The doctrine of sanctification sometimes gave rise to contests of godliness aimed at demonstrating spiritual superiority evidenced by tangible 'dos' and 'don'ts.' Warner and his followers, on one occasion, were challenged by rivals to put off their collars, cuffs and other superfluous accessories on the grounds of pride. Not to be outdone the challenged demonstrated their sanctified spirituality by removing the offending items and throwing them into a stove.[215] On a different occasion a Free Methodist challenged Warner to another

---

[215] Enoch E. Byrum, 'Customs and Traditions,' *Gospel Trumpet*, (1 July 1915), pp. 3, 11. The event took place in Bucyrus, Ohio, around 1881.

test. The former was willing to give up his church membership if the latter would give up his necktie. Warner took off his tie and the Free Methodist came out.[216] From this time on, and for a number of years, neckties were anathema in the Church of God; condemned as a symbol of pride. Is this not an example of the authority wielded by Daniel Warner? Does it not, even in a small way, underscore his participation in the paradox of religious democracy? On other occasions salvation was equated with setting aside social and cultural convention. One Holiness adherent boldly, and with great thanksgiving, testified: 'I was saved from sectism, horse-racing, ball playing, secret orders, fairs, shows, picnics, dances, worldly amusements of all kinds, jestings, light and foolish talking, immodest apparel, superstition, etc. Now, I can see plainly that if I go back to any of these things, I make myself a transgressor.'[217] Reflecting on fanaticism, Charles E. Brown cogently summarized the concern with non-conformity. ' . . . worldliness was not defined as the actual behavior of men, but rather as whatever was the common custom of the times, especially within the ranges of art, music, beauty, and the enjoyment of life.'[218]

The other charge of fanaticism centered more in attitude, theology and matters of piety. Warner's attitude in this regard has already been examined. Contending views and their holders were routinely condemned in keeping with the ethos of the times. It seemed that Warner believed sincerely that no true Church

---

[216] Charles E. Brown recounts the incident in his, *When Souls Awaken: An Interpretation of Radical Christianity* (Anderson: Gospel Trumpet Company, 1954), p. 77. Brown cites as his authority the witness of Barney Warren who was present at the time of the challenge.

[217] From the last years of the nineteenth century and into the present century the line of holiness deepened and the aforementioned quotation demonstrates the prevailing spirit of the times. Charles E. Orr, 'Self-Examination,' *Gospel Trumpet,* (29 November 1906), p. 7.

[218] Brown, *When Souls Awaken*, p. 88.

of God had existed between the days of the apostles and his own lifetime.[219] Basking in the glow of the evening light the editors of the *Songs of the Evening Light* hymnal could enthusiastically state: 'The pure gospel is shining now as it never has shone since the days of primitive Christianity. The ransomed of the Lord are returning from their apostatized condition . . . .'[220] In other minor areas, the movement tended toward extremes and what some could refer to as fanaticism. The 'Come-Out' term itself was predicated upon the apocalyptic words of Revelation 18:4: 'Then I heard another voice from heaven saying, "Come out of her, my people, lest you take part in her sins, lest you share in her plagues . . . ."' Warner did not need a multiplicity of Scripture, nor an extended argument in order to develop a particular theological understanding. 'One clear, unequivocal passage of Scripture is sufficient to establish any doctrine . . . .'[221] Warner could also adopt seemingly extreme positions by asserting that 'there are no sinners in the church' and those who do sin are clearly not Christian.[222] His biblical exegesis further reflected in some instances, a tendency toward extremism and fanaticism, though in fairness to him the spirit of his times frequently tended in the same direction.[223]

---

[219] Naylor, *The Teachings of D.S. Warner and his Associates.*

[220] Preface, *Songs of the Evening Light*. The comment is entirely consistent with Warner's own personal conviction and the ethos of the movement.

[221] Warner, *Bible Proofs of the Second Work of Grace*, p. 15. For the 'Come-Out' Movement it has already been noted that Warner held the spiritual discernment to understand which passages were 'clear and unequivocal.' Warner's method of exegesis consisted largely of proof-texting. See Waller, 'The Doctrine of the Holy Spirit in the Preaching and Teaching of Daniel S. Warner,' p. 38.

[222] Warner, *The Church of God*, p. 9 and *Salvation*, p. 23.

[223] In 1883 Warner wrote an article titled 'Babylon Leaders and Dragon Authority.' His exposition centered on Revelation 13. Warner identified the first beast as Roman Catholicism. He then turned his attention to the identity of the second beast. 'Now who will tell us what this second beast is? There is absolutely nothing on earth that corresponds with it, but protestant sectism. The sects are closely related to Rome their mother. So is the second beast allied with the first. They exercise the same kind of authority, namely that which [sic] conferred by the dragon, an ecclesiastical authority

At other junctures Warner got himself into trouble and found himself the object of ridicule. After praying for a black woman in Dunkirk the woman was miraculously healed. A few days later she died. Warner was summoned from Upper Sandusky for the funeral. Her relatives believed that the woman could be raised from the dead. Warner admitted that miracles were a permanent factor within the true Church of God. However, after an indeterminate length of time spent in prayer and in commanding the deceased to arise, Warner had finally to preach a funeral sermon. Stories circulated stating that Warner had stood the corpse on its feet and had commanded it to walk to no avail.[224]

Warner looked upon his faith and ministry with utmost seriousness and took it very personally when others did not share his sense of urgency and intensity.

> Started early for Polk Co. Stopped at Bro. Ogden's. Bro. H. Hoffer brought us some letters, one from Father and Mother Keller. All are well but seem to have no sympathy for us here on the frontier. Not even a disposition to do justice by us. Lord forgive them. We will suffer all things for thy sake. O God my heart is bruised and crushed. We seem to meet with no sympathy from friends or brethren. Many have grown cold. Bros. Hoffer & Ogden would not go to meeting. Went on to the Bense Sch. House, preaching time no one there. Two neighbors came, no member of the Church of God. None seen coming. O Lord God the waves are rolling over me. All things against us. Some are offended because we will not recognize the Devil's secret gods with which they have been polluted. Others are backslidden. Lord the troubles of my heart are enlarged. It is more than I can bear. I cannot restrain my grief, for the desolation of Zion. The people are now gathering but my tears prevent the reading of a hymn.[225]

---

constituted by humanly created offices,' *Gospel Trumpet*, (15 October 1883).

[224] The incident is reported in Byers, *Birth of a Reformation*, pp. 156-8. The latter story is undoubtedly propaganda. However bizarre the propaganda, there is generally some basis in fact. In this case the story is likely factual that Warner did pray for healing and subsequent resurrection. The dramatics noted were likely sensational details added later.

[225] *Journal*, 12 September 1874.

Warner's piety sometimes gave way to extremism and fanaticism. Warner was occasionally so consumed with the work of ministry that he simply had neither time to eat properly nor even bathe.[226] His religious experience transubstantiated itself into his identity. He consistently signed his name with the accompanying phrase, 'Your saved brother.' Even in non-religious books he owned Warner would sometimes make reference to his religiosity.[227]

Warner believed, and evidently stated in 1895, that Jesus had told him he would live until the second advent. Naylor asserted that Warner had said this several times previously.[228] Even at the time of his death fanatical tendencies seemed to surround Warner. William G. Schell preached the funeral when Warner died and claimed that God had told him that Warner had been taken out of this life, by God, as a rebuke upon the unfaithfulness of the church.[229] In the context of her allegations regarding fanaticism and absurdities the point Sarah Warner seemed to make was that the Come-Out movement provided a context for extremism,

---

[226] *Ibid.*, 7 March 1878. Here again, Warner is not unique. One has only to think of Martin Luther who had not made his bed in over a year, let alone bothered to wash the bedding. He gave as his reason for this his commitment to the work of the gospel. Roland H. Bainton, *Here I Stand: A Life of Martin Luther* (Nashville and New York: Abingdon-Cokesbury Press, 1950), p. 290.

[227] For example, Warner owned a book titled, *Poems* by Dinah Maria Mulock. On the inside cover Warner wrote:
D.S. Warner's Book
Saved in Jesus
Bought Auburn, Ind. Dec. 2, 1889
The book is in the private library of D.S. Warner in the Anderson University Archives.

[228] Naylor, *The Teachings of D.S. Warner and his Associates*. Also noted by Smith, *Heralds of a Brighter Day*, p. 47.

[229] William G. Schell, untitled memorial article, *Gospel Trumpet*, (19 December 1895). '. . . God showed me that he had removed Bro. Warner for a rebuke upon the church for their unfaithfulness. Set this down in your hearts, beloved brethren, for it comes from God. The standard of God's truth must be lifted higher by the Lord's ministers; and devils and all manner of sins must be more furiously rebuked than ever before . . . . Brethren, we must pay heed to this rebuke, or God will doubtless send us more fearful ones.'

however unintended, and once the flood-gates were opened control, apart from autocratic rule and censure, was virtually impossible.

Sarah Warner's charges are easily dealt with in the context of Warner's writings. However, the opening of historical documents such as these amounts to an opening of a literary Pandora's box. Obviously there are many sides to the person and thought of Daniel Warner. If Warner was as divisive as Sarah alleged, how then can history account for the development of an entire movement in the conviction of unity? Perhaps it is here where context is most vital. The opening of Pandora's box amounts to a collision of portraits. The portrait of Daniel Warner is juxtaposed to the portrait of Sarah. Ultimately these portraits must be juxtaposed against history. The immediate context of their situation cannot simply be dealt with in that narrow corridor. The larger context of history must also be explored. The colliding fragments of myth, historicity, the politics of personality, the existential fusion of horizons, and the varieties of subsequent interpretive methodologies cannot be reduced to an objective exegesis of shifting texts to satisfy an unshifting agenda. In short, one contextual interpretation may be entirely correct, but untenable in another context. In other words, Sarah's contentions may find legitimate substantiation depending upon the criteria used and the factors present, while a new set of criteria and prevailing conditions may entirely alter their viability. This does not allow Warner's interpreters to sidestep his detractors. Despite the ambiguity of interpretation the witness of Sarah Warner can neither be denigrated nor dismissed. Sarah must remain a serious component in the legacy of Daniel Warner. To ignore her is to run the risk of failing to take Warner seriously. Anything less yields caricature and misunderstanding.

V.   Shout at the Devil

Hitherto we have permitted all these babylon comforters to fly through the land, in silence, longsuffering and patience. Knowing that while hell was in much jubilee over them, God would have all the enemies of His truth in derision, and would destroy the works of the devil. . . . This work of the devil which has . . . brought a reproach upon the cause of holiness . . . has filled all hell with a jubalee [sic]. . . . it is received in hell with thanksgiving . . . .[230]

♠ ♠

Two and a half months after the appearance of 'Come-Outism Renounced' Daniel Warner publicly responded.[231] The title, 'A Fallen Woman' makes clear the direction and essential conviction Warner had in this public *apologia pro vita sua*. The tone is emotional and quite clearly was produced under great duress. Warner does not, surprisingly, address any of Sarah's specific allegations except her concern regarding the spirit of the movement. He is able to reduce the quarrel to its lowest common denominator: 'So we have the matter reduced to this conclusion, namely "several months past" an evil spirit either entered into ourself, or into our dear wife.' Since Warner is emphatic that 'God's pure spirit in our heart . . . ' is evident to all, it is manifest then that '[t]he fact is, the poor woman fell a victim to the seducing spirits, that rushed into the country last fall.' Here, Warner certainly must have in mind the 'abominable false prophet,' Stockwell, under whose influence Sarah clearly succumbed to such an extent that 'she has not forgotten the poor fallen brother . . . .' The evil spirit, then, resided in Sarah. She had changed, not Warner. '. . . the only change manifest in us, is that of deeper humility, more charity, and more meekness and wisdom in avoiding harsh and

---

[230] Warner, 'A Fallen Woman' *Gospel Trumpet* (15 July 1884).

[231] 'A Fallen Woman,' *Gospel Trumpet*, (15 July 1884). The article occupies nearly five and a half long columns in the paper and has been reproduced in its entirety in Appendix A.

unbecoming language.'[232] More than that, Warner's defence has the significant reinforcement that '. . . God had given us, by His Spirit one intimation after another, that the trouble was in wife. . . .' Operating under the powerful conviction of divine guidance, Daniel Warner may have been utterly incapable of objectively reflecting on the larger picture of his marriage to Sarah and on the implications of his efforts to promote holiness and unite a fragmented Christendom. He did waver on that tumultuous night when Stockwell and his associates pressed him. But once Warner had regained his composure and refused their advances he became convinced for all time in the essential truth of his own position. When Sarah departed and published against him, Daniel Warner could see not only a personal affront but an attack upon God and the truth of the gospel of Jesus Christ. The Stockwell confrontation and Sarah's surprise departure amounted to a shot across the bow of the Warner reformation. But the shot only appeared to come from Stockwell and Sarah. Warner was convinced it was the conniving work of the Devil designed to destroy Truth.

The rest of Sarah's article was dismissed as 'indefinite insinuations' and regarded as illegitimate since Sarah had failed to marshall any '. . . bible argument against the doctrine we teach. . . .' Warner, in several places accused Sarah of regarding him as evil. He quoted her as saying she 'shrinks from [him] as from a deadly serpent.' There is no allusion or quotation of this sort in the *Christian Harvester* article. Warner does make reference to 'her letters' to various editors and asserted that he had in his possession no fewer than eleven papers, and knew

---

[232] Warner's claim comes as somewhat of a surprise. His obstreperous tone has already been documented. Calculation of the sources referred to in this study, in this regard, show the following. If July 1884 is the line of demarcation there are in actuality more instances of 'harsh and unbecoming language' in the post-July 1884 period than in the pre-July 1884 period. Admitting the difficulty of definition it seems fair to submit that Warner's position on this issue remained unchanged. He never escaped the polemical terminology of the nineteenth-century context. The testimony of Barney Warren, with respect to Warner's language, cited above is instructive.

of others, in which he had been defamed for his 'bad spirit.'[233]

Sarah's article was, for Warner, part of 'the last days of deception.' The 'infernal legions [and] . . . awful hosts of hell' had been unleashed. Sarah was the 'heartless foe . . . under the hallucinations [and] delusions of the devil . . . .' Sarah had become 'the unfortunate woman,' the 'poor deluded wife,' the 'poor guilty woman,' the 'poor fallen woman,' and 'my poor deceived wife.' For Warner, 'she is in league with hell.' 'Had the arch deceiver of souls, left sufficient womanly modesty and discretion, to keep out of the public prints, this duty, we trust, would not have been encumbent [sic] upon us.' But '. . . the malignity of such conduct' could not be overlooked. Indeed, to ignore this attack would be to fail to take the Devil seriously, but Daniel Warner never underestimated his enemy and on this occasion he claimed to have intimate knowledge.

Only about one third of Warner's article dealt with Sarah's argument. The remaining two thirds of his response centered on domestic issues. For example, '[w]e were often surprised at wifes [sic] usurpation of authority over us . . . .' Warner then went to some length to demonstrate Sarah's inhospitable demeanor to strangers, lack of spiritual discernment, insubordinate behavior, unethical conduct, constant faultfinding, unreasonableness in their marital relationship, duplicity, apparent laziness and unwillingness to share in domestic responsibilities, her lack of respect toward her husband and her unrepentant attitude toward her sins. As noted above, Warner later asserted that Sarah had given her allegiance to a promiscuous 'free love' sect.[234] According to Warner, it was all 'pure

---

[233] Warner did not indicate which papers these were. The fact that more than eleven papers sided with Sarah is some indication of the immediate effect of her article on the constituency of the Holiness movements. At least one paper, the *Vanguard*, criticized Sarah for going into print and condemning the *Gospel Trumpet*. Warner noted this in his response. It is unlikely there were others. Had there been, it seems that Warner certainly would not have failed to call them to his defense.

[234] Warner, 'Note,' *Gospel Trumpet*, (15 September 1887). This assertion follows the report of John N. Slagle, 'Stumbling Stonefruits' in *Ibid.*, wherein the behavior of the 'free-love' group was outlined.

deviltry'[sic] and a far cry from the former 'angel love Sarah' and 'splendid woman' portrait noted earlier. 'O my God! we shall never forget the coldness, confusion and treachery we felt in that heart, and saw in that face . . . .' 'Come-Outism Renounced,' according to Warner, 'was received in hell with thanksgiving.'

Warner mentioned only the *Christian Harvester* and the *Highway of Holiness* in his article. But clearly all those who participated in Sarah's transgression did so from within the 'babylon scaffolding.' The following year Thomas K. Doty and the *Christian Harvester* were again denounced.

> . . . he [Doty] and his Chicago committee of fellow babylonians . . . . [and their counsel] is also by inspiration of the devil. It betrays utter darkness of soul and ignorance of God's present work in this world. Surely 'night has come to the prophets,' 'the sun has gone down over' poor Doty's soul and the mists and fogs of babylon have shut out the whole luminous realm of God's present truth.[235]

Daniel Warner's thesis, 'A Fallen Woman,' cannot rightly be considered a response to the charges set forth by Sarah. Rather than answering her contentions, Warner attacked her character and thus engaged in an *ad hominem* argument which has been singularly unhelpful in terms of understanding her strong reservations toward the movement. What Warner spends the majority of his article dealing with may be, in fact, entirely truthful and accurate. Nonetheless, it raises two issues. First, there is at present, no way to substantiate Warner's argument. We have no access to Sarah's side of the story. Second, even if Warner's dissertation could stand without modification, it remains irrelevant. Whether or not Sarah was indeed the sort of woman Warner alleged, has little to do with the contentions she raised against the Come-Out movement. Setting forth the argument that Warner simply refused to respond to something demonically inspired is less

---

[235] Warner, 'Harvester Twisting,' *Gospel Trumpet*, (15 November 1885). Long gone were the days when Warner gave thanks to God for Doty. *Journal*, 1 January 1878.

than satisfactory. While it remains a possibility, it seems highly improbable when we know he consistently wrote against, and engaged, others he firmly viewed as outside the house of truth and beyond the gate of salvation. In the full glare of the evening light, Daniel Warner opted to turn his face from 'the fallen woman' under the clearly stated proviso of vindicating 'the cause of Christ' and the 'Truth of God.' Shielded by his divine commission and faithful to the heavenly vision, Warner stood vindicated.

VI. Shadows in the Evening Light

Free from babal, in the Spirit,
Free to worship God aright;
Joy and gladness we're receiving,
O how sweet this evening light![236]

♠ ♠

The Church of God Reformation Movement was thought to be the final reformation of the church. At the apex of his influence Daniel Sidney Warner called attention to this remarkable rapprochement of cosmic and eschatological time. '"Three days and a half," the Spirit interprets to us as 350 years of protestantism, beginning 1530, and ending with the beginning of the evening light in 1880. In the evening light the two witnesses rise up again in power.'[237] Three years earlier Warner had identified the two witnesses as the Word and the Spirit.

---

[236] Daniel Warner, 'The Evening Light' in Joseph C. Fisher, *Songs of Victory* (Williamston, MI: Gospel Trumpet Company, 1885), no. 58.

[237] 'Questions Answered,' *Gospel Trumpet*, (15 September 1887). Earlier, Warner was not as certain that his own time was the evening light.'The army that the Lord brought up from the valley of dry bones, shall bury in the grave of spiritual night all who do not pass through the fire and adore the God of holiness. The "seven months," that are required to bury Gog and cleanse the Church, it is probable, is prophetic time-"a day for a year"- making 210 years; but whether the Wesleyan reformation, or the present more general movement be the point to reckon from, I am unable to say . . . .' *Bible Proofs of the Second Work of Grace*, p. 386.

Their mission was to witness to the 'great holiness reformation.'[238] Warner's preoccupation with eschatology was rooted squarely in the apocalyptic traditions of the nineteenth century.[239] Simultaneous with the 'coming-out' of Daniel Warner was the evening light of human history. The day of the world was drawing to a close. But the evening light lingered over the final reformation of the church and the Come-Outers could sing, 'Oh rejoice forevermore . . . . in this blessed evening light.'[240] There were indeed two witnesses to that final reformation. One gave forceful testimony to the transforming power of Christian unity via 'come-outism' and the second work of grace. The other gave equally powerful testimony to the divisive reality of the same movement via fanaticism and the spirit of self-righteousness. These two witnesses in the evening light were Daniel and Sarah Warner.

The relevance of the Warner message was that of holiness and unity. John W. V. Smith's centennial history of the movement is appropriately titled, *The Quest for Holiness and Unity*. Perhaps the Warner message can be most relevant when tempered through the critique of Sarah. Nowhere in her renunciation of 'Come-Outism' did she denounce or deny the basic message of holiness and unity. Her critique essentially fell on deaf ears. The movement was bending its collective ear toward Warner, not his detractors. Daniel Warner claimed an authority which Sarah did not, and never would possess. The pervasive view held of Warner drowned out whatever merit Sarah might have had in her public stand. She was marginalized to the point of scorn and her witness became lost. Clearly her witness

---

[238] 'The Two Witnesses,' *Gospel Trumpet*, (1 June 1884) and (1 July 1884).

[239] On the Church of God controversy over the interpretation of biblical apocalyptic literature and possible relations with nineteenth-century Adventist methodology and exegesis see John E. Stanley, 'Unity amid Diversity: Interpreting the Book of Revelation in the Church of God (Anderson)' *Wesleyan Theological Journal* 25 (No. 2, 1990), pp. 74-98.

[240] Warner, 'Rejoicing,' in *Echoes from Glory*, no. 98.

was tarnished and she cannot stand blameless. Any tendency toward romanticizing the image of Sarah Warner must be suppressed. Her abandonment of Sidney is a curiosity, one which can only be speculated upon. Her acceptance of the 'marital purity' doctrine, after a decade of marriage, is likewise an oddity which should not simply be brushed aside. Warner's scathing review of her character should likewise not be summarily dismissed. Furthermore, it should not be forgotten that prior to 1884 she did not, insofar as we know, have any substantial reservation about the content or direction of the movement. There are questions, serious questions, about Sarah which cannot be answered. But unanswerable questions need not be ignored or dismissed. Still, Sarah Warner knew Daniel Warner as well as anyone. She had stood with him for ten years, which included the struggles of the formative and tumultuous years from 1878-1881. Her witness cannot be set aside arbitrarily. She deserves to be taken seriously. Perhaps in the end she helps us understand Warner and his message better by forcing us to go beyond the myth to obtain a fuller, more complete view. In this way she helps present the enigmatic aspect of Daniel Warner. Her witness tempers his basic message and in this she does the movement service though neither she nor the movement probably realized it.

The issues raised in the *Christian Harvester* in the spring of 1884 have been presented and examined: the spirit of the movement, the viability of Come-Outism for Christianity, an extreme holiness ideal, and a tendency toward fanaticism. These concerns have been tested in the context of Daniel Warner's own writings as surely as Sarah tested them in the fiery furnace of the Come-Out movement in Ohio. One of the possible conclusions which emerge suggest that irreconcilable differences in personality, attitude, and theological understanding forced Daniel and Sarah Warner into different directions in their spiritual quests. Perhaps their marital and religious divorce were two sides of the same coin. Ultimately it is impossible to assign absolute guilt or absolute innocence to either party. For too long Sarah has been written off as merely having 'an axe to grind.' She probably did. That, however, does not necessarily negate her thesis. This does not *ipso facto* mean that Warner is thereby invalidated. On the contrary. If anything, this study should be understood as less an attack upon Daniel Warner and more a rehabilitation of Sarah. This study addresses a chapter of Warner's life which hitherto has been ignored or deemed irrelevant. The analysis and subsequent interpretations presented here are clearly not the only possible conclusion and, one would hope, certainly not the final word. Indeed, Daniel Warner was sincere and committed to his understanding of truth, church renewal and the leading of the Holy Spirit. He was characterized by the ideas of a second work of grace, entire sanctification, sinless perfection, an imminent eschatological expectation and an intolerance toward the 'error' and 'heresy' he perceived in the 'sects.' Therefore all denominational Christianity was in error. There existed but one authentic church—the Church of God. All true Christians must 'come-out' of the sects, be separate and join the Church of God. Warner's agenda was governed by this ideal. But between the ideal and the reality lay the chasm. Warner's focus on division blinded him to the possibilities of restoration and unity that clearly were current around him. Benighted by his own vision he ignored the evidence of his own quest which lay around him. Convinced of the truth of his own position he was unable to recognize truth elsewhere. The evening light belonged to him and his perspective on American religion around him seems tied up almost exclusively with that 'darker view of a hopelessly divided Christendom.'[241] The tendency among his followers to accept uncritically this view turned pioneers into settlers. The come-outers witnessed what they perceived to be a religious transfiguration. Like the impetuous St. Peter of old they decided to erect dwellings. Such action had its own consequences. The principle of openness and wholeness was not matched by the practice. If Warner's voice can be understood as prophetic in any sense, certainly in the prevailing dilemma of the paradox of religious democracy it became trapped

---

[241] Merle D. Strege, *Tell me Another Tale: Further Reflections on the Church of God* (Anderson: Warner Press, 1993), p. 11. Strege asserts that the Church of God has tended to follow Warner uncritically in its acceptance of this view of American ecclesiastical history.

frequently in its own isolationism and arrogance.[242] Caught on the horns of an inescapable dilemma, Warner unwittingly exemplified the struggle of dictators disguised as democrats. The paradox of religious democracy is once again underscored.

Warner looked too high up and too far away for his ideals and in his attempts to realize them he destroyed some of what he hoped to save. His zeal cannot be questioned. His wisdom can. Warner succumbed to some of the very things he tried to combat. His quest for unity sometimes gave way to division. Possibly Warner's ideals were too naïve, simplistic and reductionistic. Change necessarily came after his death. By the time Warner died there were more than twenty-five grove meetings, fourteen camp meetings and several general assemblies. Warner had written most of the books and periodical literature. He had composed many of the songs and had spoken at most of the general meetings. His works quite naturally became the standard for teaching and church polity. There was no successor of equal stature waiting in the wings in late 1895. No one other than Warner was ever able to wield absolute authority.[243] So a change of emphasis began.[244]

Two of these changes can be seen in the person of Enoch E. Byrum. Prior to his death Warner had entertained the idea of establishing a school for the training of ministers at Grand Junction. A meeting was called for December 1895. Death intervened in the life of Warner and the meeting was never held. Warner's successor, Enoch E. Byrum, answered a reader's inquiry in the *Gospel Trumpet* about the proposed school with the terse response that there was neither a school

---

[242] This forthright assessment is both valid and helpful, neither negating nor extolling Warner. Barry L. Callen, *Contours of a Cause: The Theological Vision of the Church of God Movement (Anderson)* (Anderson: Anderson University School of Theology, 1995), p. 8 n. 3.

[243] Brown, *When Souls Awaken*, pp. 105-6.

[244] Forrest, 'A Study of the Development of the Basic Doctrines and Institutional Patterns in the Church of God,' p. 54.

nor would there ever be one.[245] The second area of change related to supernatural intervention in human affairs. While Daniel Warner certainly held to the idea of divine healing, Byrum made the idea the flag-ship of his ministry. His quarters in the *Gospel Trumpet* office were filled with crutches, canes, orthopedic devices and other evidences of healing.[246] A photograph of Byrum shows him seated beneath a large sign holding a Bible and a poised pencil. On the walls are the aforementioned evidences of healing. The sign reads: 'These crutches are from people who have been healed and who have left them as trophies of faith.'[247] So convinced was he of the power of divine healing that at age eighty-one while he lay dying, Enoch Byrum was unable to reconcile his ideas and the focus of his ministry with his own illness and impending death.[248]

Two months before his death Warner had written in the *Gospel Trumpet* his conviction that certain types of medicine might be used.[249] Byrum wasted no time upon assuming the editor's chair at Grand Junction in denouncing that concession.[250] 'During our absence in October an article was published in the *Trumpet* in which the brother who wrote it lowered the standard below the Bible line . . . .'[251] Byrum claimed that if he had been in Grand Junction at the time Warner made his ruling on the use of medicine, the article would never have gone

---

[245] *Gospel Trumpet*, (26 December 1895).

[246] Reardon, *The Early Morning Light*, p. 36.

[247] Callen, ed., *A Time to Remember: Testimonies* (Church of God Heritage Series, volume 2) (Anderson: Warner Press, 1978), p. 69.

[248] Reardon, *The Early Morning Light*, p. 37.

[249] *Gospel Trumpet*, (24 October 1895).

[250] 'Before Warner was cold in his grave, E.E. Byrum moved naturally occurring remedies to the forbidden list . . . .' Strege, *Tell me the Tale*, p. 121.

[251] *Gospel Trumpet*, (2 January 1896).

to press.[252] There is considerable reason to question Byrum's stout assertion vis-à-vis editorial control over the *Gospel Trumpet*. Nonetheless, time would show that neither Enoch Byrum nor any of his successors could wield the same authority as Daniel Warner.

At the height of research, by natural course the work of the aforementioned Charles W. Naylor, was discovered.[253] If Andrew Byers was the principle myth

---

[252] Clear, *Where the Saints Have Trod*, p. 69.

[253] Charles Wesley Naylor (1874-1950) is best known for his song writing and contributions to Church of God hymnody. See Robert H. Reardon, 'Charles Wesley Naylor', in *Worship the Lord: Hymnal of the Church of God—Hymnal Companion*, eds., Lloyd A. Larson and Frank Poncé (Anderson: Warner Press, 1991), pp. 29-38 and David L. Neidert, 'Reformation's Song', unpublished MS. Anderson University, 1985, pp. 26-31. Naylor's book referred to above represented a negative element toward Daniel Warner. While Naylor was very popular he was not a theologian of the church. In later years he became somewhat embittered with his rôle in the movement. It is unclear what led to his marginalization. There are at least two possibilities. Relatively early in his life Naylor suffered a debilitating accident in which he was seriously injured and from then on remained greatly incapacitated. In April 1908 while helping to take down a tent after a meeting in Sydney, Florida Naylor suffered internal injuries including a dislocated left kidney. In June 1909 he was injured again in a traffic accident. From 28 June 1909 he was confined to his bed. As time went on and Naylor was not healed, people wondered whether or not he really had faith. It is likely such an experience led to Naylor's embitterment. There were also rumors about Naylor's actual condition. 'Steele Smith commented to some that when the blinds were down he [Naylor] could be seen moving about his room.' Private letter from Robert H. Reardon, 18 October 1997. Enoch Byrum is quoted as having once said, 'Naylor would have been healed but he never *claimed* his healing.' Cited in Reardon, *The Early Morning Light*, p. 36. Naylor died on 21 February 1950, still in his bed after nearly forty-one years. For an overview of his life see Brown, *When the Trumpet Sounded*, pp. 180-2. A second possibility is that Naylor led to his own marginalizing through his largely negative assessment of Warner. It has been suggested that his book, *The Teachings of D.S. Warner and his Associates*, was received mainly in a negative light which could have led to his separation from the mainstream. A reflection twenty-five years after its publication described its general reception as ' . . . the storm that swirled around . . . .' Harold L. Phillips, 'Editorial' *Vital Christianity* (9 June 1974), p. 7. Milo Chapman contended that the undated book appeared sometime in the 1930s. Robert Reardon definitively dated it to around 1942. See his essay 'Charles Wesley Naylor', pp. 33-4. I pressed Reardon on the dating and it seems based entirely on recollection. Private letter, 6 January 1998. On the other hand, Merle Strege has asserted that Naylor's book appeared in the post World War II years and this seems to be the common opinion. The discovery of an unpublished manuscript among the A.L. Byers Papers in the Archives of the Church of God throws considerable doubt on the Chapman and Reardon recollections. The Byers manuscript has a cover letter attached to it, signed

Conflict and Crisis in the Kingdom of God in Ohio   283

maker behind the shadowy figure of Daniel Warner then Charles Naylor became the principle de-mythologizer. Much of what Naylor presented in his controversial booklet has unwittingly been sustained by this study, though again the relevant qualifications concerning context should continue to be applied.[254] While Naylor

---

by Byers, dated 9 July 1950. The document itself begins by stating that Naylor's booklet had been published 'some months ago.' Presumably the booklet was published the previous year. Byers' reaction to it and the nature of his response suggests that little time had elapsed between the Naylor publication and the writing of the Byers manuscript. The precise dating of the book is essential for determining what rôle the book had on Naylor's attitude in later years. If the book was published in 1949 as opposed to the 1930s one may safely rule out the suggestion that Naylor's bitterness can be put down to a negative backlash to his assessment of Daniel Warner. Controversy undoubtedly surrounded Naylor's work. This may be evidenced by the existence of the Byers manuscript, who was later described as 'highly incensed over what he felt was a one-sided and unnecessarily harsh attack on the memory of Warner.' Phillips, *Ibid.*, p. 7. There are, however, two other clues about the general reaction to the booklet. First, a statement printed in the Naylor volume by a 'Committee on Distribution' makes clear that 'about thirty representative ministers have read this paper and it has been judged to be of sufficient importance to warrant a wider study . . . .' This would indicate some type of ministerial opinion within the Church of God. The identity of this committee is a matter of speculation. According to Harold L. Phillips, 'that "committee" had no official standing and no connection with [the] Gospel Trumpet Co. It was a "self-formed" group that assisted Naylor in getting his ms. into print. I do recall that there was much speculation at the time over who the members were.' Private letter, 20 October 1997. Secondly, a copy of the Naylor booklet in the Otto F. Linn Library of Warner Pacific College contains this handwritten annotation on the title page: 'Read Carefully, thoughtfully, Prayerfully. In my opinion a much-needed admonition to Our People - C.S.M.' This copy of the book was at one time in the possession of the Church of God in Everett, Washington. It was also in the possession of Albert F. Gray (1886-1969) until the late 1960s when it became part of the Warner Pacific College library collection as a gift from Gray (11 March 1966). It was processed into the collection in 1968. I have not been able to identify 'C.S.M.' Nonetheless, it may be suggested that there was a not inconsiderable support for Naylor, thereby effectively mitigating the second possibility for his marginalization. With respect to Naylor and Byers, it must be pointed out that while both had met Warner and had some association with him, both had to rely considerably on what others told them about Warner. Phillips, *Ibid.*, p. 7. Both men would have been in their early 20s when Warner died. Many have speculated on Naylor's alleged bitterness. However, Reardon who knew Naylor personally over the course of a number of years told me that even though 'he was pretty much shunned by the establishment in his later years', he [Reardon] 'had never detected bitterness in Naylor.' Private letter, 18 October 1997. Charles Naylor remains a compelling enigma.

[254]   In 1950 a formal rebuttal against Naylor's work was launched by Andrew Byers. The fragment which was to constitute the initial stage of this rebuttal was never

has played virtually no rôle in these conclusions, he was, undoubtedly one of the first in the Church of God movement to articulate a reasoned critique of Warner and for that he should be acknowledged.

To the extent that Warner's ideals percolated down to the grass roots level may be gauged from his prolific song-writing. There is little doubt that few people read Warner's books. His pamphlets would have received wider circulation due to the energetic outreach activity of the Gospel Trumpet Publishing Company.[255] Again, there is no way to ascertain readership. Probably his editorials and articles in the *Gospel Trumpet* were fairly widely perused. But certainly the more than two hundred hymns he wrote and published in the hymn books of the movement became commonplace.[256] So while the adherents of 'Come-Out' popular religion were likely unfamiliar with Warner's arguments as a writer, they were more than cognizant of them through his songs, as noted earlier, and his preaching.

For Daniel Warner everything revolved around the will of God and humanity's response to it. Near the end of the year 1877 Warner drew up his

---

published and Byers died before he could make any further serious progress on the project. The manuscript fragment, 'In Vindication of D.S. Warner and his Work' is among the A.L. (Andrew L.) Byers Papers, Archives of the Church of God, Anderson University, Anderson, Indiana, B620 1995. The text appears in Appendix D. Why the Byers response was not published by the *Gospel Trumpet* remains a matter of speculation. I put the question to Harold L. Phillips who assumed the office of editor-in-chief less than a year after Byers submitted his paper. 'Unfortunately for the historical record . . . the answer to that question went to the grave with the death of Dr. [C.E.] Brown. (I think I know the "probable" answer, but of necessity it would have to be conjecture even though in my mind highly probable, so I will maintain silence on that one.' Private letter, 20 October 1997. When pressed, Phillips declined to express his opinion.

[255] Warner's pamphlets were circulated widely, sometimes in more than one edition. Translations into Spanish, German, French, and modern Greek were also published by the Gospel Trumpet Publishing Company.

[256] The first hymnal *Songs of Victory* appeared in 1886 and was followed by *Anthems from the Throne* (1888), *Echoes from Glory* (1893), *Songs of the Evening Light* (1897), and *Salvation Echoes* (1900) all published by the Gospel Trumpet Publishing Company. *Songs of Victory*, as noted above, circulated before being reissued under the auspices of the Gospel Trumpet Company. Appendix E contains a list of more than two hundred hymn titles written by Warner.

famous 'Covenant With God.'[257] This covenant accounted in large measure for Warner's intensity. He regarded it with utmost seriousness. It is noteworthy to look at the inclusion of his daughter and his wife in it. Warner turned both of them over to God.

> Levilla Modest whom we love as a dear child bestowed upon us by thy infinite goodness, is hereby returned to thee if thou wilt leave us [to] care for her and teach her [of] her true Father and Owner; we will do the best we can by thy aid to make her profitable unto thee. But if thou deemest us unfit to properly raise her or wouldest have her in thy more immediate presence, behold she is thine, take her.

When Levilla died six months later Warner sadly, but with full confidence, surrendered her to God.[258]

It is somewhat of a contrast to note his attitude regarding Sarah in his covenant to the events thereafter. 'She whom I call my wife belongs forevermore to God; Use her as thou wilt and where thou wilt, and leave her with me, or take her from me, just as seemeth good to thee and to thy glory.' When, after more than six and a half years later, Sarah departed, Warner did not, and could not, say as he had when Levilla died, 'Thy will be done' and 'we felt a calm and sweet resignation to the will of God, to whom. . . [she] belonged.' Sarah had fallen. There was little need to respond systematically and in detail to her charges in the *Christian Harvester*. Warner could accept God's will in the death of his three year old daughter. He could not see Sarah's public stand of dissent in the same light. Perhaps Sarah Warner's life is both a lamp and a mirror of Warner himself.

The story of religious history is a tale of rise and fall; a saga filled with myth, legend, inspiration and the extraordinariness of divine presence in the ordinariness of human history. In the end, both heros and villains are the same flesh and bone. The Hebrew prophet Zechariah first noted: 'It shall come to pass, that at evening time it shall be light.' Warner applied the idea to himself. The

---

[257] *Journal*, 13 December 1877.

[258] *Ibid.*, 24 June 1878.

evening light of the 1880s has faded. But in their own unique ways both Daniel and Sarah Warner are indispensable witnesses to that evening light, each adding a little more detail to the flickering shadows which hide from us the past.

CHAPTER 6

Democracy and Dictatorship: A Gordian Knot

A horrid thing pervades the land,
The priests and prophets in a band,
   (Called by the name of preachers,)
Direct the superstitious mind,
What man shall do his God to find,
   He must obey his teachers.

They are directed to obey,
And never tread another way,
   All others are deceivers;
All those who do dissent from this,
Are not within the road to bliss,
   Nor can be true believers.[1]

♠ ♠

     The dilemma of dictatorship constitutes the reality which lies at the heart of religious democracy. Christian equality presupposed by the cross in theory has proven to be more difficult in reality in the drama of religious history. Official old world religion was dominated by the clergy—bishops, popes and patriarchs—and the structures of Christianity. The patterns of piety in the new world, though not

---

[1]   Joseph Thomas, *Life, Travels and Gospel Labors of Elder Joseph Thomas* (New York, 1861), pp. 173-4.

unconnected to the history and traditions on the other side of the Atlantic, found their earliest expressions in the liberty of an unexplored, undeveloped context. In theory this allowed for radical forms of experimentation. The triumph of the American Revolution provided frontier religion both opportunity and crisis. That opportunity consisted in the spread of democratic principles into the circles of religion and religious expression. Such principles were eagerly seized upon by new and burgeoning movements and resulted in a theologizing of democracy. The wildfire of enthusiasm which followed had also to contend with a crisis which pervaded the parameters of opportunity. That crisis was a broad unsettling of authority which accompanied the turn of the nineteenth century in general and seems to have precipitated an attack upon the traditional categories of moral and social order.[2] Growing apprehension concerning the viability of pre-revolutionary social order also revealed an all too apparent lack of confidence in the structures of official Christianity. A solution, in the form of religious democracy, came to the fore and presented itself to American religion. The nineteenth century constituted a long harvest of religious innovation, enthusiasm, and expression produced from the planting of the democratic seeds. The soil of the new world had been most fruitful. The problem with authority remained, however, and the precipitous crisis brought about by the American Revolution deepened as the century progressed. Very quickly this became the enduring dilemma of religious democracy. When the lion and the lamb lie down together, the lion has little to fear; but the lamb ever remains in danger of being devoured.

Among the flocks of sheep grazing in the several green pastures of democratized Christianity were wolves and lions. These wolves and lions had not entered the sheep fold to scatter the sheep. Indeed, in the absence (or banishment) of the traditional shepherds, they had come to protect the innocent lambs from the

---

[2] David D. Hall, 'The Uses of Literacy in New England, 1600-1850', in *Printing and Society in Early America*, eds., William L. Joyce, David D. Hall, Richard D. Brown and John B. Hench (Worchester, MA: American Antiquarian Society, 1983), p. 43.

ravages of the world and godless culture. If acquisitiveness, materialism, competitiveness, lust, disorder, selfishness, tyranny and social inequalities were among the cultural identities of nineteenth-century America,[3] these stronger beasts took up the responsibility of protecting the flocks and giving guidance to the sheep in order to avoid the pitfalls of this new, but dangerous world. While this was generally true, the more germane issue lay in the assumption that divine truth and authentic Christianity could be rediscovered absolutely. Free from the chains of tradition these regulators among the sheep saw the advantage in securing the walls of the sheep fold. Transgression of these boundaries was not permitted. A brief consideration of the boundaries of a medieval town makes the point. The walls or ramparts identified the social autonomy of a city or community. Troops maintained perpetual watch. Throughout the night, the walls glimmered with the light of torches. The gates were shut from nightfall until morning. No one was permitted either to enter or leave during this time without permission. Climbing the walls was severely punished. To even approach the walls during the night was considered a criminal offence. The walls symbolized security and identification. They formed a boundary between the community and the rest of the world. Walls kept the world out and the community in.[4] In some respects it was as difficult to break out of a walled city as it was to break in. A narrowing of the ranks ensued. The walls were carefully patrolled, the gates of entrance strictly monitored, while inside the fold, a new order began to emerge. This new order was of divine origin, sent directly from God to this emerging caste of shepherds for the instructing and guidance of those within the fold. Accompanying this new religious order were

---

[3] Dorothy C. Bass, 'Sex Roles, Sexual Symbolism, and Social Change: A Study in Religious Popular Culture of Nineteenth-Century American Women' *Radical Religion* 4 (No. 1, 1978), p. 25.

[4] See Robert Muchembled, *Popular Culture and Elite Culture in France 1400-1750*, trans., Lydia Cochrane (Baton Rouge: Louisiana State University Press, 1985), pp. 110-11.

new patterns of beliefs and practices, both of which applied equally to all adherents.

The shattering of Christianity and the continuous fragmenting of religion in nineteenth-century America only exacerbated, in the minds of some religious leaders, the chaos of a disintegrating world. Their spirits vexed by the sectarianism which engulfed the American churches they turned their hearts to God and the result was visions of reform and renewal. Men like Joseph Smith, William Miller and Daniel Warner were certain that God had given them a means and a mandate for a general reformation of the church. More than that, they were convinced that their vision was the correct one. Guided by their visions, driven by their divine commissions, such leaders did everything in their power to convince their followers and persuade the world that salvation and Truth could be found with them. Endowed with such an historic mission there could be little room for compromise. They were divine spokesmen and the fate of Christianity was within their hands. Their development from Christian pilgrim to spiritual dictator is entirely understandable.[5] For religion, the offspring of the American Revolution had been twins: democracy and dictatorship. Democracy spawned a veritable explosion of churches and new religious movements. With this dramatic increase the potential for dictators also increased exponentially. Between the Revolutionary War and 1845 the population of America increased from two-and-a-half million to twenty million. The ratio of clergy tripled from one minister for every fifteen hundred people to one minister for every five hundred inhabitants.[6]

Daniel Warner preached a message of Christianity unity. But unity proved

---

[5] 'A body which thus claims to be *a* Church, independently of all the rest of Christendom, is bound indeed, in inward consistency, to hold itself as *the* Church . . . .' John W. Nevin, *Anti-christ; or the Spirit of Sect and Schism* (New York: John S. Taylor, 1848), p. 78.

[6] Nathan O. Hatch, *The Democratization of American Christianity* (New Haven and London: Yale University Press, 1989), pp. 3-4.

inimical to nineteenth-century American religion. Warner's view of unity was extreme and it has been argued that the Warner vision could never exist in this world.[7] This conclusion was not one Warner could gladly abide. 'The *Trumpet* will go on . . . . We feel that the gates of hell cannot stop the truth . . . .'[8] Daniel Warner represented truth. In his efforts to win the world he exemplified the paradox of religious democracy. He was a comet in the religious world of the later nineteenth century, streaking across the skies of sectarianism, burning brightly, securing a great deal of attention, before disappearing in the light of another day.[9] The movement inspired by the visions of Daniel Warner was a result of this paradox of democracy and dictatorship. Warner's 'come-out' brand of Christianity was an alternative to the disorder of democracy, the self-centeredness of American culture, and the worldliness of Christianity in general. He was convinced that he represented the one sure path to salvation, Godliness, Truth and authentic Christianity. The problem with such an approach becomes readily apparent. Clearly, all truth claims are potentially divisive.[10] Laying down the boundaries of religious truth and creating an orthodoxy has as an immediate and unavoidable consequence the purely arbitrary invention of heresy. When lines are drawn to indicate truth, whatever falls beyond the scope of those lines comes to constitute heresy and in this sense, heresy may be described as a purely arbitrary, though perhaps unintentional, invention of religious authorities. Such authority might be

---

[7] C.W. Naylor, *The Teachings of D.S. Warner and his Associates* (Privately published, no date).

[8] *Gospel Trumpet*, (15 November 1881).

[9] Lorenzo Dow, on account of his far-ranging exploits and travels in eastern United States, was described as a 'comet in the religious world.' Melvin E. Dieter, *The Holiness Revival of the Nineteenth Century* (Metuchen, N.J.: The Scarecrow Press, Inc., 1980), p. 189 n. 4.

[10] Jan Shipps, *Mormonism: The Story of a New Religious Tradition* (Chicago and Urbana: University of Illinois Press, 1985), p. 27.

identified as the governing body of a particular denomination or a single, charismatic, popular religious leader. The founder of Christianity may have said that in his Father's house were many rooms, but his followers have persisted in the conviction that they should all live in the same one.[11] There can be little doubt that Daniel Warner acquiesced in the conviction that all the followers of Christ ought to reside not only in one house, but within that house in a single room of doctrine and experience. Of the many rooms available in God's house, Warner was able to decide which room contained truth and security. His dictatorship in attempting to direct all believers to the one room must be understood in this context and within this conviction. There were consequences for Warner's posture. The most serious error he made was the association of organization with sin and evil. This unwittingly produced individualism.[12]

Among the many religious entrepreneurs of the nineteenth century it is instructive to note several of their common characteristics. Many of them lacked formal education—Barton Stone, William Miller, Francis Asbury, John Leland, Richard Allen, Joseph Smith—and were frequently contemptuous of education.[13] In the words of James Finley, education often occurred in the backwoods.[14] 'In Spirit-filled American religion, charismatic figures can sometimes go from the

---

[11] Robert I. Moore, *The Origins of European Dissent* (London: Penguin Books Ltd, 1977), p. 1.

[12] Charles E. Brown, *When Souls Awaken*, p.112. Brown also explicated the tension between the 'leader principle' and the 'democratic principle' noting that the transition from the former to the latter constitutes the greatest change to have occurred within the historic constituency of the Church of God Reformation Movement. *Ibid.*, p. 105.

[13] Nathan O. Hatch, *The Democratization of American Christianity*, p. 13. Despite Warner's brief periods of formal study at Oberlin College and Vermillion College he cannot accurately be regarded as formally educated and certainly not as theologically trained.

[14] 'My place of study was the forest . . . .' *Autobiography of Rev. James B. Finley or, Pioneer Life in the West* (Cincinnati and New York, 1853), p.196.

ecstasy of new birth or new revelation to the pulpit in a matter of days.'[15] Methodist circuit riding preachers studied very little and their libraries were slight as Peter Cartwright attests.

> It is true we could not, many of us, conjugate a verb or parse a sentence, and murdered the king's English almost every lick. But there was a Divine unction attended the word preached, and thousands fell under the mighty power of God, and thus the Methodist Episcopal Church was planted firmly in this Western wilderness, and many glorious signs have followed, and will follow, to the end of time.[16]

Many of these same leaders denigrated religious creeds and confessions and mocked the systematic theologies of historic Christianity. Casting aside all such encumbrances they encouraged their followers to disdain traditional forms of authority and heed the prophetic voice. Rather than formal religious catechism such popular leaders emphasized the Bible, exhorted their hearers to read that august volume and rather than joining churches and religious societies were further encouraged to make personal decisions concerning their own salvation and spirituality. As previously noted, popular religious leaders like Warner derived their power in the first instance from a professed religious experience and divine calling. In practical application of that authority, however, they gained immeasurably from personal identification with common people. Their style of preaching was attractive to many. Their methodologies reflected popular culture and their charisma was sufficient to mobilize entire groups of people. American Christianity had never been united. Oneness was an ideal never realized. The upshot of revivalism was an almost complete, and probable, permanent fragmenting of American religion. Born in the womb of democracy the struggle for identity followed the tortured paths of religious experimentation and innovation and

---

[15] Charles E. Hambrick-Stowe, *Charles G. Finney and the Spirit of American Evangelicalism* (Grand Rapids and Cambridge: William B. Eerdmans, 1996), p. 22.

[16] *Autobiography of Peter Cartwright* (Nashville: Abingdon Press, 1984), p. 12.

the signposts along the way indicated the creation of a new identity and religious culture. Those signposts included the theologizing of democracy, revivalist preaching, camp meetings, circuit riding preachers, religious experiences, the culture of religious print, the Bible, and of course, the rise of the popular and powerful individual in the 'pulpit'. To those within such a culture God was present. The view from beyond the culture suggested godless pandemonium.[17]

The fabric of American religion was not cut from a single cloth. The nature of the evolution of religion demonstrates the common denominator of social and political democracy but how the varieties of American Christianity developed was both diverse and in some cases unexpected. The nature of religious culture—camp meetings, revivals, voluntary societies, regional differences—all reveal fundamental differences, which, while rooted in a sense of religious democracy, produced Christian pluralism. In the bewildering riddle of pluralism with its concomitant sense of chaos and confusion dictators disguised as democrats seized the wheel of the religious world and sought, single-handedly, to turn history toward their version and understanding of the Kingdom of God. The reaction of revivalism to traditional forms of European Christianity was a turn of the wheel. Evangelicalism was then outdone by the Holiness movements which represented a further turn of the wheel. Daniel Warner and the Come-outers were responsible for yet another direction as American religious history struggled with its own sense of democratic freedom and with the perils of its own implications. Driven by a restorationist focus as well as apocalyptic angst, Daniel Warner was responsible for a seismic event within the American Holiness tradition. Charles Naylor affirmed that Warner probably received significant theological impetus from the Holiness Alliance and the Seventh Day Adventists with respect to his conviction of the imminent second coming of Christ. His preoccupation with prophecy may likewise be traced to

---

[17] Steven D. Cooley, 'Applying the Vagueness of Language: Poetic Strategies and Camp Meeting Piety in the Mid-Nineteenth Century' *Church History* 63 (No. 4, 1994), p. 574.

Newton, Adam Clarke, Alexander Campbell, William Miller and Uriah Smith.[18] From these sources Warner was convinced that the second advent was soon to be unfolded precipitating the end of the world and human history. Standing at the brink of eternity Warner's mission was intensified. Perishing souls were being ushered out in the waiting arms of eternity. Without the experience of entire sanctification and a forthright repudiation of 'sect Babylon' their souls were destined for everlasting damnation. The democratic religious leader fully cognizant of this fact could ill afford not to become a spiritual dictator. If Warner never perceived himself as a dictator then this might be explained as a legitimate blindness created by his zeal to fulfil the task laid upon him by God.

To speak of a religious democracy does not necessarily mean assuming that people ever really thought or acted for themselves. Even in the context of revivalism when personal decisions were freely made, did people really think and act for themselves? To what extent were they manipulated into certain responses and psychologically prepared for a reception of the message, whatever that might have been? The potential for the abuse of spiritual power and authority was immense. Fear tactics supplemented the message. Hell-fire and brimstone accompanied the visions of the prophets. Meetings, revolving around the charismatic power and presence of the preacher, were engineered to produce predictable ends. That charlatans and imposters could work such contexts to their own ends is well known and documented. Elmer Gantry types were not uncommon in the nineteenth century and the literary creation of such individuals cannot be considered purely imaginary.

> I use a get the people jumpin' an' talkin' in tongues, an' glory-shoutin' till they just fell down an' passed out. An' some I'd baptize to bring 'em to. An' then—you know what I'd do? I'd take one of them girls out in the grass, an' I'd lay with her. Done it ever' time. Then I'd feel bad, an' I'd pray and pray, but it didn't do no good. Come the nex' time, them an' me was full of the sperit, I'd do it again. I figgered there just wasn't no hope

---

[18] Naylor, *The Teachings of D.S. Warner and his Associates.*

> for me, an' I was a damned ol' hypocrite. But I didn't mean to be . . . . Here's me preachin' grace. An' here's them people gettin' grace so hard they're jumpin' and shoutin'. Now they say laying' up with a girl comes from the devil. But the more grace a girl got in her, the quicker she wants to go out in the grass. An' I got to thinkin' how in hell, s'cuse me, how can the devil get in when a girl is so full of the Holy Sperit that it's spoutin' out of her nose an' ears. You'd think that'd be one time when the devil didn't stand a snowball's chance in hell. But there it was.[19]

Warner would have been appalled at this sort of behavior which has considerable substance in the camp meeting, revivalist context. Getting full of the 'spirit' and indulging in promiscuous behavior might be seen as one form of negative response to the passionate preaching and instigation of dictators disguised as democrats. But were there other responses? In the midst of a context saturated with religious fervor and millenarian expectations does not the preaching of eternal destruction, coupled with a message of certain salvation for those who accept the 'plan of salvation' being offered, carry with it the suggestion of appropriate response? Under the sway of religious demagoguery can it be reasonably asserted that the majority of common people, even in a context of democracy, think and act for themselves? What in one instance may be called the work of the Holy Spirit may likewise be attributed to charisma, manipulation, emotionalism or sheer coercion. Obviously the outsider may be predisposed to see it completely other than those on the inside. The difference between the movements of divine presence and a spiritual mêlée may only be in the eye or heart of the beholder.

Religious democracy held within itself several common elements including Jeffersonian egalitarianism, an aversion to Calvinism, anticlericalism, revivalist preaching and, despite that anticlericalism, a trend toward spiritual dictatorship. When examining this phenomenon it is perhaps essential to categorize such an investigation in terms of an historically specific democracy. That is to say,

---

[19] The Reverend Jim Casy confessing to Tom Joad in John Steinbeck, *The Grapes of Wrath* (New York: P.F. Collier & Son Corporation, 1939), pp. 29-30. See also Sinclair Lewis, *Elmer Gantry* (New York: Harcourt, Brace and Company, 1927).

democracy is different in diverse contexts based upon such factors as time, place, context and major prevailing influences. Thus, nineteenth-century American religion placed emphasis upon human cooperation as a defining factor in the Kingdom of God.[20] This human cooperation and response was essential to the program of Daniel Warner. Men and women were free to come out of the sects of 'Babylon', seek for and receive the empowerment of entire sanctification, to then perfect holiness in the fear of God, to belong only to the one true 'Church of God' and to faithfully follow the directions of God as mediated through the vision and commission of Daniel Warner. The historically specific democracy of the Holiness movements was tempered into a carefully crafted freedom of response and behavior. Of course this conflicted with competing religious visions and social culture in general. There were also several other serious exclusive truth claims being trumpeted by groups not so far removed from Warner. It constituted a battle for the minds of believers, a struggle with eternal implications and cosmic significance. The battlefield was the theatre of the mind. Colliding divine commissions prompted bloodless religious wars with the salvation of souls hanging in the balance. Ritual and authority defined such contests. For Daniel Warner that ritual amounted to prayer, Bible reading, the assembling together of believers and seekers, protracted preaching, an invitation to decide for oneself, the perfecting of holiness, admonitions to the lost, wicked, and the adherents of every strand of 'Babylonian' Christianity. These rituals repeated inexorably constituted the work of God in the lengthening shadows of the evening light. The dilemma of this ritual remained in its consistent dependence upon the authority of the 'man of God.' Ritual and authority both came under the persuasive and pervasive provenance of the popular leader, the individual endowed with power from on high, who while utilizing the principles of democracy and democratic culture could not be other

---

[20] James H. Moorhead, 'Between Progress and Apocalypse: A Reassessment of Millennialism in American Religious Thought, 1800-1880' *The Journal of American History* 71 (No. 3, 1984), p. 528.

than a dictator. By the end of the nineteenth century the development and expressions of the American religious experience reveal the social uses of religion and the religious uses of history, politics and culture.

Between the extremes of spiritual disorder and ecclesiastical imperialism lay the challenge of religious reform and renewal for Daniel Warner. In order to avoid both the aforementioned pitfalls Warner declared a vision constituting a *via media*.

> It is, indeed, my honest conviction that the great holiness reform cannot go forward with the sweeping power and permanent triumph that God designs it should, until the Gospel be so preached, and consecration become so thorough, that the blood of Christ may reach, and wash away every vestige of denominational distinction, and *'perfect into one'*—yea, *one* indeed and in truth—all the sanctified.[21]

The dilemma was that Christian unity and the perfecting of the body of Christ could only be achieved through the vision given to Warner. Men and women had the freedom to seek after God, to strive for holiness, to come out from the denominational configuration into the light of God's truth and grace. Each of these steps was predicated upon the social and political forms of democracy current in America in the nineteenth century. Warner never hesitated to declare the truth and non-negotiable nature of these individual freedoms. Where democracy, as a religious and social principle, ceased was in the exclusive claim by Warner to truth and divine sanction. Individual freedom was acknowledged for the believer to seek God, strive for holiness, to come out of all the forms of Christian apostasy, and to make decisions regarding salvation, spirituality and God. But this liberty was attended consistently by a single prescribed path leading to a common destination. Warner seems to argue every bit as vigorously for this understanding as he does for the aforementioned freedom of individual Christians.

---

[21] D.S. Warner, *Bible Proofs of the Second Work of Grace* (Goshen, IN: E.U. Mennonite Publishing Society, 1880), p. 436.

Babylon was to be 'threshed.' This idea led to great extremes and bitter attacks on other movements and all who were members of them. The idea of unity was limited to one group. All must come to that group. Just leaving a sect did not avail anything. People must come to *us*. . . . Unity meant, not so much unanimity as uniformity. It meant all must see 'eye to eye' and 'speak the same thing.' This left no place for individual thought. A few leaders formulated the doctrines, and all perforce must agree with them or be adjudged 'crooked in doctrine.' Complete doctrinal agreement was held necessary for acceptance or unity. . . . Since only Brother Warner and the few associated with him 'saw the light,' upon them was laid the responsibility of proclaiming it and bring about 'the reformation' of the church . . . . Since those who accepted the call 'Come out' formed the nucleus of this 'reformation movement,' it naturally resulted that they felt and taught, directly or by implication, that all other Christians should and must leave their sects and come to this 'one body' and become a part of this group exclusively.[22]

Charles Naylor claimed to speak from a personal experience of more than fifty years within the tradition inspired by Warner. That reflection and summation may be measured against the writings of Warner himself in order to establish the veracity or error of Naylor's observations. His detractors perceived Charles Naylor's comments as constituting an attack upon Warner '. . . and the message he gave his life for [was] being unworthily trampled under foot.' Naylor was posthumously confronted with having written 'perverse things about the church . . . [and turning] his back on the reformation truth he had always upheld.' Beyond that, Naylor was alleged to have set his mind to 'discolor and misrepresent' the message and motives of Daniel Warner. In the aforementioned attack '[t]his poor man [Charles Naylor] lost his way and his flounderings have only brought error and confusion to his position.'[23] Since both these documents have been reproduced in appendices there is little point in engaging Naylor and Andrew Byers in a

---

[22] C.W. Naylor, *The Teachings of D.S. Warner and his Associates*.

[23] Andrew Byers, 'In Vindication of D.S. Warner and His Work', unpublished manuscript, 1950, pp. 1-2. The A.L. (Andrew L.) Byers Papers, Archives of the Church of God, Anderson University, Anderson, Indiana, Archives B620 1995.

debate. There is surely truth and error on both sides and something to be learned from each perspective.

Nevertheless, the career of Daniel Warner between 1878 and 1895 underscored the paradox of religious democracy in the nineteenth century. There was the way, the truth and the life. Holiness and unity were two sides of the common coin of the authentic Christian faith. Warner understood this and save in the momentary struggle with Stockwell in 1884 never wavered in his acceptance and self-understanding of his rôle as God's instrument for revelation and salvation in the waning glow of the evening light. The message continued to reverberate.

> Your craft best thrives
> Where virtue dies,
> By festives nude,
> And frolics lewd.
> By games of chance,
> And pious (?) dance,
> Obtaining pelf,
> By lies and stealth
> By jockey-joles,
> And sale of souls.
> By taking in
> The secret sin,
> Your sect may swell,
> And prosper well;
> And keep apace
> In Babel's race,
> Of ri-val-ry,
> And jeal-ous-y.
> Till lightnings flash
> The coming crash,
> Of Heaven's ire,
> 'In flaming fire,'
> And ruin smite,
> The works of night.
> And hell possess
> Your 'Churchliness.'[24]

---

[24] 'Lines, at the close of an article reproving some sectish idolatry'. D.S. Warner, *Poems of Grace and Truth* (Grand Junction: Gospel Trumpet Publishing House, 1890),

The great crash would be the last judgment; a judgment at once rewarding the 'Church of God' and punishing severely all 'Babylonian' Christians. The former would be admitted to heaven and eternal bliss, the latter consigned to hell and everlasting damnation.

Benjamin Franklin once was asked to provide a pre-publication comment on a book dealing with religion.

> . . . the consequence of printing this piece will be, a great deal of odium drawn upon yourself, mischief to you, and no benefit to others. He that spits against the wind spits in his own face. . . . I would advise you, therefore, not to attempt unchaining the tiger, but to burn this piece before it is seen by any other person; whereby you will save yourself a great deal of mortification by the enemies it may raise against you, and perhaps a good deal of regret and repentance.[25]

Through his preaching and writing, Daniel Warner consciously and deliberately unchained the tiger of ecclesiastical wrath. The thought of suppressing his work, either oral or literary and especially the principle organ of the Come-Out message, the *Gospel Trumpet*, would have been a repulsive thought to Warner. Furthermore, he would have regarded such advice as that proffered by Franklin as treason against God and a betrayal of the covenant he had made with God. Beyond that he would be remiss in the execution of his divine commission and in active violation of transgressing the integrity of the vision given exclusively to him. There is little indication in the extant records of Warner's life that he ever seriously considered abandoning the quest for unity and holiness. The rhetoric of American religion and the reality of his movement poised no dilemma for Warner. He may have eschewed the traditional authority of the theologians, but his followers valued the words of his mouth and the ink of his pen to an extent that his authority was legitimated. He

---

p. 223.

[25] This letter, dated around 1786, was possibly directed to Thomas Paine. *The Complete Works of Benjamin Franklin*, ed., John Bigelow (New York and London: G.P. Putnam's Sons, 1888), volume 9, pp. 354-5.

may never have suggested that the word of Warner was the word of God, but in the carrying out of his commission there was little difference and indeed there was little reason to draw discernable lines of demarcation.

The dilemma of religious democracy is perhaps a bit more subtle in the case of Daniel Warner insofar as he neither sought legitimation in the eyes of the world in general nor in the perspective of Christianity specifically. There was little personal ambition, it seems, to gain intellectual recognition for his work or his books. Moreover, Warner appears never to have been afflicted with the urge to attain widespread social sophistication. In this, Warner stands apart from many of his fellow religious leaders. 'Dissenting paths have often, in America, doubled back toward learning, decorum, professionalism, and social standing.'[26] Warner's path did not follow this fairly well-worn circular route. Neither did his path deviate from its original course. He refused to sell the birthright of the Come-out movement to any and all bidders at any cost. He was a dissenter and a reformer, utterly committed to what he understood as the call of God and the truth of the gospel for America in the last decades of the nineteenth century. Warner was no transitional figure. He did not perceive himself in the rôle of the forerunner, a type of John Baptist. He was the herald of the end of time, the culmination of religious history, the ingathering of the true church in holiness and unity as the Church of God. As committed as he was to the centrality of the Bible, Warner recognized the limits of democracy and his career reflected the conviction that it was unreasonable to promote the truths of scripture, encourage his followers to read those truths, and then turn them over to their own devices in the matter of understanding, interpretation and application. So the man of one book wrote many books to explain and clarify the one book and adjudicated his mission in gathering the true church together to include instructing the masses on the meaning of that single all-important book. This necessitated a certain degree of marginalization. Warner's levelling of the 'come out' field in the true Church of God had as an immediate

---

[26]   Hatch, *The Democratization of American Christianity*, p. 202.

response his gradual elevation as leader, prophet and preacher. It may not have been his intention, design or desire, but it remained and underscored an unavoidable and undeniable aspect of religious democracy; the paradox of democratic dictators.

APPENDIX A

Warner's formal response to Sarah Warner's article 'Come-Outism Renounced' was published in the *Gospel Trumpet* on 15 July 1884, two-and-a-half months after Sarah's essay had appeared in the *Christian Harvester* and other Holiness papers. There are undecipherable words in the text which have been noted [..].

'A Fallen Woman'

We now take up our pen to perform the most painful duty that the providence of God has yet called us to perform in the journalizing work. To a heart of deep and fervant [sic] affection, and of fine sanguine nervous sensibilities, nothing can be more crushing and trying to the soul than to have the one who has been 'one spirit,' with us, and who is 'one flesh,' turn away and become a heartless foe, under the strong delusions of the deceiver. This Satan has seen, were his most hopeful plan to overthrow our soul, and but for the infinite mercy and grace of God, he had succeeded. O how our heart flows with love to our Almighty Deliverer, from the awful hosts of hell that were determined to crush and destroy our soul. O dear Jesus do thou unite all they [sic] saints in heaven and earth, in shouts of triumph, and holy praises to God for our escape from the infernal legions of hell. 'Bless the Lord Oh my soul and all that is within me, praise his holy name!['] And shall we shrink from doing the will of our God, whose amazing mercy brought our soul up out of the jaws of hell, after we had, through subjection to satans [sic] wiles, well nigh been lost? Nothing but eternal trueness to God and a clear conviction of His will could, by any means, induce us to publish abroad the following record. Had the arch deceiver of souls, left sufficient womanly modesty and discretion, to keep out of the public prints, this duty, we trust, would not have been encumbent upon us. But having in our possession no less than eleven papers and having heard of others, in which we are denounced as having very bad spirits, etc., it becomes necessary that the children of God scattered abroad should know something about this. When a woman rushes into the public prints, and sounds over the country that she 'shrinks from'—such as her husband—'as from a deadly serpent,' either he must be a very bad man, or she is lead [sic] by a devilish spirit. But if the parties so renounced are such bad men their works must correspond, and it were the duty of that person to publish those evil deeds, that all may see the proof of the bad character she has ascribed to them. No honest man or woman will renounce God's professed children, without specifying the 'manifestation of those spirits,' by which they are proved to be evil. For the last two months our name, with many of God's saints, have been blowed [sic] abroad in many papers under vague and suspicious coloring, leaving every body to fill up the picture with his own surmisings. All of which bears upon its face marks of the crafty works of the devil. The wiley 'old serpent,' always keeps in the dark, throws out indefinite insinuations, to raise blind fancied suspicions, for the consolation of such as are condemned by the truth.

I wish to be understood as making a distinction between satan and the victims he has blindfolded and harnessed to do his service; while we hate the former, we only pity the latter and we only expose his works for the purpose of delivering their souls. Hitherto we have permitted all these babylon comforters to fly through the land, in silence, longsuffering and patience. Knowing that while hell was in much jubilee over them, God would have all the enemies of His truth in derision, and would destroy the works of the devil. But consistancy [sic] demands that we speak. It is known that my wife renounces us. Therefore, one or the other must be wrong. Had she attempted bible argument against the doctrine we teach, we would be under necessity to defend that; but she has made no appeal to the word of God, no attempt to try the doctrine by the scriptures, neither has any sect defending paper ever done so though they have condemned us, neither she nor they that glory in her fall, have made any attempt to try us by the Bible. This is another mark of satans [sic] leading. With him it matters not what the Bible says; he takes the liberty to renounce whatever he does not like; simply because of his aversion to it.

It is then wholly a question of bad spirits. Well spirits are good or bad just as their manifest works are good or bad, just as they act in harmony with, or in opposition to the Word of God. And if our enemies cannot accuse our teaching before the Bible, we are ready to appear with them before the same tribunal to test what spirits we are of: for we know no other standard by which to 'try the spirits.'

In *Harvester* of May 1st my wife says 'The manifestations of the spirit of this movement, have been such for several months past,' etc. So you see ni [sic] her eyes this movement has manifest a different spirit for several months past than heretofore. This proves [..] either [..] or us with whom she has been associated, have several months past fallen under the control of a different spirit. And since she refers to the place where she has been connected with the movement, 'we cheerfully take the insinuation upon oursel [sic]. If we have fallen under the power of an evil spirit several months ago, of course we would appear evil in her sight; and if the evil spirit entered her at that time then also our fellowship must cease, and we appear evil in her eyes. For she has not forgotten the poor fallen brother that frequently came to our place, and confidently asserted that we had all changed, when we both knew that the change had taken place in him. So we have the matter reduced to this conclusion, namely 'several months past' an evil spirit either entered into ourself, or into our dear wife. But two things now remain to dispose of the case; first to find out which it was, and second, to have the disturbing element ejected. Now it must be apparent to all, that a change of tenants, will soon make a change in the appearance about a house; especially when there is so much contrast between the former and present occupant as between the Spirit of God, and a spirit of the evil one. We therefore appeal to all the readers of the Trumpet, whether they have marked any change in the paper that would indicate that God's pure spirit in our heart had been supplanted by the devil. God knows, we know, and all the thousands of our readers know very well that the only change manifest in us, is that of deeper humility, more charity, and more meekness and wisdom in avoiding harsh and unbecoming language. But with this improvement, thank God! we have not departed from our fidelity to God in warning, reproving, and rebuking, with all longsuffering and doctrine, both in print and by the word of mouth, as God has required of us. But need I tell the reading, religious world that a sudden and awful change has taken place in our wife? Do they not all see it? Yea do not so many of the pure saints feel it? Even some who had never seen her, but felt perfect fellowship in the Spirit, realized by the Spirit of God, when at a throne of grace, that she had dropped out of the fellowship, before they heard a word about the awful works of the enemy of souls. Though the editor of *Vanguard*, through his sectarian education, thinks us in error, he is not so far intoxicated on the wine of babylon, as many others, hence can see the inconsistency of her conduct. 'We think.' says he, 'his good wife [such she has been, and we trust will be again] could have found some more consistent way to win him, than to rush into print with such raw repudiation of his paper.' No one but persons utterly blinded by sectarian idols can fail to see the malignity of such conduct. That a change has taken place in our wife, and that by the reception of pernitious [sic] and inconsistent spirits, even such as are predjudiced [sic] against us may see, much more all the impartial. The fact is, the poor woman fell a victim to the seducing spirits, that rushed into the country last fall. Shortly after the assembly, this intruder into our family began to crop out. A fallen brother and wife came to our office, on business. It was late and they lived eleven miles in the country. We invited them to stay all night, brought them to the house as soon as they entered the door, wife said with an expression and tone that made my heart ache and which caused them to leave very suddenly, 'you dont [sic] expect to stay here all night, do you?' Then feeling ashamed of the abruptness of the expression she said. [sic] 'you would be welcome to stay but our beds will be full with the company we have.' It is true we were quite full, but a comparison of the word 'welcome' with the terrible spirit manifest in the first expression, was to us a surprising and shocking evidence of hypocrisy, and inconsistency.

 A loss of the gift of discerning spirits, which she had had very clearly, was the next indication that something was wrong. She pronounced 'grandly saved,' and had perfect rellowship [sic] with such as soon proved to her, as was known to us to be a graceless hypocrite.

We were often surprised at wifes [sic] usurpation of authority over us, we could not understand why she had no concience [sic] in reference to the many scriptures that command wives to be in subjection to their husbands, and those that forbid their usurpation of authority over them. The Lord bids us to give a sample of her guardianship over us. A letter from Bro. Isaac Kee, whom we dearly love in the Spirit, addressed to ourself, was first read by her, which she then put into her pocket; when we wished the same, it was refused, and though we humbly besought her to let us read it, she said it would not do us any good. Well we had to humbly submit, and deny ourself the right of reading our own mail, because, as the poor deluded creature says in the *Harvester*, 'I love my husband' so intensely, that she volunteered to be our guardian, and inspect, and decide for us, what we had, and what we had not ought to read. How would all you editors that have been so much comforted concerning your babylon scaffolding, by her letters, like such an extremely kind wife? Or how would you like a wife that loved you so well that, behind your back, she would write to parties with whom you had business that was no concern of hers whatever, and interfere with the same, warning them that you were not capable of attending to your own business. If any one would like to see such a piece of poor deviltry jus [sic] call and see us. Thanks to the brother in the west, who thought a husband should see such communications, and returned the same to us. We pass over a record, written in God's book, that were difficult to portray; and that would make you shudder if we were to attempt it. An experience with legions of devils, through which we passed, by the amazing mercy of God, which we never can recall without our heart being filled with gratitude to the Allmerciful [sic] God of our deliverance. We may, if the Lord will, so far as we are able, some time in the future, put the whole matter, upon record in a tract. For the present we would just say that we held our wife in such high esteem, that it was natural every time there seemed a discrepancy, between us, to suspect ourself, rather than her. We have many witnesses to prove that we regarded her almost as an angel of heaven. But notwithstanding our extravagant idea of her purity, and the knowledge of our own entire consecration to God, and constant witness of the Spirit of the Lord, to a pure heart, there was a want of perfect unity in our spirit. There was a picking at, and finding fault with us, yet nothing specified wherein we were wrong. This lead [sic] us to a severe heart searching, to find out the trouble. Finally, in our own house, after one of those general combings, we dropped upon our knees, and asked wife to point out what she saw wrong in us, and we would get right if it took our life. She made no attempt to do so. We were determined to have sweet fellowship and harmony of spirit in the family if possible.

For the first time in nearly seven years, we allowed satan to put an 'if' between our faith and the cleansing blood. Through that little 'if' the enemy entered, robbed our soul of the river of peace, and brought confusion into our mind. O may God keep us from the presumption of a doubt, [..] reference to the promise of God. The next evening in family worship the Lord swept away the confusion, reentered His temple, and sweetly assured our heart of His perfect love.

The next day we went to a meeting at Jerry City, Wood Co. Saturday eve. and sabbath morning our soul was as clear as heaven, but that day and night and Monday, the 'mystery of iniqity' [sic] worked again in wife and Stockwell, until the devil got our eyes off of Christ upon them, when confusion and doubts came in again, and we humbled ourself down before the whole Church at their feet like a little child; but as neither they nor the Holy Spirit, pointed out any defect in our heart or consecration we looked right to the Lamb of God and was again blessed with assurance and peace. Glory to God! We must necessarily pass by much of the dealing of God, man, woman and the devil with us, for the want of space. In a meeting at a private house in Bucyrus Ohio, Stockwell filled the little ones with an hours harangue, principally of the devil's stuff. The delusive powers of the devil were greatly manifest, we were victimized by the same; and in our intense eagerness to be right with God and have the blessing of fellowship restored in our family, we once more humbled ourself under the super-papal authority of Stockwell, backed by wife and others, under the hallucinations of the devil, (we know just what we say, and shall gladly give an account to God for the same) and we actually agreed to walk in their light and obey their orders, even though God should reveal to us before it could be done that we should not do it. This demand was directly made by Stockwell, and God is witness to it, with all the people there assembled. If any man will go farther than that to have harmony with his wife, we would like to hear from him. O the infinite mercy of God, that did not send us to hell that night, for having sold Christ, out of deference to our wife and her abominable false prophet. O my soul and all that is within me give everlasting thanks to God that we are alive to-day and out of hell. We think if our poor deluded wife would humble herself once, before God and let us test her consecration by the standard of the Bible, we could soon have the discordant element removed without her denying God's sovereignty, as we did in an extreme attempt to cleave to her.

Though God had given us, by His Spirit one intimation after another. [sic] that the trouble was in wife, and once we were constrained to tell her so, we nevertheless allowed the 'Old serpent, the devil and satan' to accuse us, rather than entertain the unpleasant conclusion that an evil spirit had entered her. But after suffering the most terrible punishment until morning, the Lord Jesus broke the devil's power, filled my soul with an infinite depth of peace, cut off all fellowahip [sic] with wife and Stockwell, and enlightened our understanding of the devilish powers that had been seeking to crush onr [sic] soul. Glory to God forever! But then began the awful conflict with swarms of devils that surged around us, and sought to drive us from our proclimation [sic] of freedom from all men and women, to serve the Living God only.

One woe is past. And behold there followes [sic] another quickly. The day we packed our things at Bucyrus, O. and hauled them to the car, wife went to the post office in the forenoon and got the mail, which she always took the liberty to open, and if necessary, use means if any was found. At noon Bro. Horton, from this place, and ourself were summing up the several amounts, necessary to cover our debts, and moving expences [sic]. Knowing that wife had gone in debt some at the store, we asked her how much it was. She replied that it was paid. Presently we asked her who had sent us money. She said sister McKee, of Goffs Kansas. We asked her how much? Ten dollars was the reply. This was in the presence of Bro. Horon [sic] and Wm. Shields. About one week after arriving here, we received a card from her, containing the following statement, 'I found sister McKee's letter in my pocketbook, after I got here. It contained $60. I wanted to talk to you about it but did not have a chance.' Now you all see that the poorfallen [sic] woman told a positive falsehood as tothe [sic] amount of money the letter contained, and another one about her desire to communicate with us in reference to the matter. The facts are we worked together all the afternoon, packing household things, and she could have spoken to us at any moment, if she had wished to do so. About ten o'clock at night there was a train going west, and though it was raining we were very weary she was very anxious to go to Upper Sandusky that night yet. A kind neighbor and self barely prevailed upon her to stay until morning. We arose early the next morning and took her trunk to the station then returned and helped her and the child to the train. As soon as we had reached the depot she suggested that we better return immediately. Did not the poor guilty woman have a chance to speak to us about the money? Nay does not her conduct show that she was disturbed with fears lest some question might be asked about the kind sister's letter? O my God! we shall never forget the coldness, confusion and treachery we felt in that heart, and saw in that face that evening and morning. Is such conduct becoming to holiness? Is it Christlike to treat a husband in that way and then publish him abroad as an evil spirit to be shunned as a 'deadly serpent?' Do not all men and women of honest heart see why she shrinks from us? Is it to be wondered at? See the case explained in Psalm 101:3,4,7. No wonder she shrinks from such as walk honestly with God, and finds more congenial association with such as abide in the 'holds of nuclean [sic] spirits.' The woman cannot truthfully say that she was driven to that shameful conduct by any extreme circumstances. No circumstances can justify lying, nor any stealthy act. God is witness that we never refused her any means she wanted when we had it, and could possibly appropriate it to her wishes. Shortly after she turned away from us, and that too without a single unkind word or act, on our part, and took Stockwell for her oracle, we gave her about $20. at one time. We kept a woman most of the winter to do housework, hired our washing done, and by the help of God filled wifes [sic] daily orders for the house, and table. Let us consider one circumstance. After Bro. Horton had taken the train and left we recolected [sic] an item of our expense that we had overlooked: this cut us short about $8.00. We saw no way to do but withhold that amount from a neighbor that we owed about $20. until we could send it to her. And though we told this fact to wife, and she knew very well, that that person would spare no oppertunity [sic] to report us as dishonest rascal etc. she would rather disobey the plain injunction of God's Word, weich [sic] forbids any 'offence' that would occation [sic] the 'ministry blamed.' She would rather have her husbanb [sic] evil spoken of, and that too with an apparent ground, and rather have the cause of Christ suffer, than act like an honest woman, confess and turn over the mouey [sic] that was not hers, ask for what she needed, and save the cause of Christ a reproach, and our heart, pangs of untold grief. How does this agree with the declaration in the *Harvester*, 'I love my husband.' How much would you appreciate such love? But I do not charge this upon the unfortunate woman. Nay it is the doing of those evil spirits that have deceived and entered her heart, and which now so influences her eyes, that we appear to her as 'deadly serpent.'

The pure and sacred reverence with which we had so recently regarded our dear wife caused these direct lies, and extreme selfishness, to fill our soul with horrer [sic] and amazement. O my brethren we tasted the real sufferings of Christ. 'Horror hath taken hold upon me because of the wicked that have forsaken thy law.' Yea 'my heart is sore pained within me; and the terrors of death are fallen upon me, and horror hath overwhelmed me. And I said, O that I had wings like a dove! for then would I fly away and be at rest. I would hasten my escape from the windy storm and tempest.' God has bottled the tears of those sleepless nights. So keenly we felt the pure law of God set at naught by 'bone of my bone, and flesh of my flesh,' that we suffered as with Christ upon the cross for the sins of the world. O dear Jesus, we have tasted of thy awful suffering, it seem, to the full extent of our ability to endure. Our flesh consumed away up on our body, and life drew nigh to the very shadow of death. Over veneration and surrounding religious organs our hair became well mixed with white. Just now we remember, and ask sister McKee's pardon for not having written her an acknowledgement of her kind donation to the Gospel of Christ. Our prolonged baptism of suffering, rendered us scarcely able to answer correspondence.

In the midst of our heart agonies we wrote a solemn and earnest reproof to wife, but her concience [sic] not being awakeued [sic] to her sin as ours was, satan only used it to make us appear of an evil spirit, in her eyes. She made no answer to the awful sin of lying, but coolly suggested that we owed her an apology for having rebuked the same. Some weeks later she did confess that she erred, and gave back $15. of the money. But even before that confession, which does not apply at all to the direct sin of lying, which still remains unrepented of, and unconfessed, she publishes her testimoney [sic] abroad that she was more sweetly saved than ever. And this is the kind of holiness the sectarian sheets have auch [sic] a jubalee [sic] over. This work of the devil which has at present broken up a family, brought a reproach upon the cause of holiness, robbed us our sweet child for over three months past, and which has filled all hell with a jubalee [sic], the *Highway of Holiness*, says 'should be received with thankfulness.' Yes it is received in hell with thankfulness, and just to the extent that babylon glories in the same, she proves that she is in league with hell. But we must draw to a close. While our heart is sad for the sake [of] our dear companion, we have great reason to give everlasting thanks to God for the glorious fruits of these furnace flames. O

how our weaknesses have been searched out, and our patience perfected. Glory to the name of our God!
>
> We would not cast away the gold,
> We've gathered in the furnace flame.
> Neither wish again the dross,
> Here purged in our Redeemers name.

A fallen woman? Yes, but not from a profession of Godliness, not from prayers, pretentions to piety, and forms of religion. That were contrary to the devils [sic] present policy; he would far rather that all hearts that backslide from God, and the love of truth should keep up a profession, and the more lovely, and pious they can appear the better deceive souls. These are the last days of deception. Try the spirits by the Word of God. Evil spirits will always be detected by the spiritual minded, because of their lack of reverenc [sic] for the Word of God, and an unfeeling conscience, for the transgression of the law of Christ. Notwithstandiug [sic] the very dark conduct, of my poor deceived wife and her deliberate story telling to cover it, she writes us June 30, these words, 'I can say all the way through, that I was inocent [sic], and done all for the best.' O the blinding, and conscience-killing power of the devil toward the vital present truth of God. Bless God we daily shout His praises because we know that all things work together for good to us and to the cause of Christ. Though 'satan hinders' as the word acknowledges, yet God is able to over run all to His final glory. While we take pleasure in reproaches for Jesus sake, and have no disposition to write in personal defense, we dare not shrink from this vindication of the cause of Christ. This, and the restoration of our dear wife, have been our only objects. And when the subject of this article reads it, she will know that were our object to injure her, several things would not have been passed over in silence. But we hope that God will spare us from any farther duty in this direction, and that for Christ's sake He will answer our night and day prayers, for her restoration to Himself and to us. Amen!

Daniel

APPENDIX B

Warner's poem 'Soul-Cripple City' encapsulates his mature thought on American Christianity in the nineteenth century. The text was published in *Poems of Grace and Truth* (Grand Junction, MI: Gospel Trumpet Publishing House, 1890), pp. 119-74. Due to the relative obscurity of the book the entire text appears in this appendix. This volume was the first cloth-bound book published by the Gospel Trumpet Publishing House. Due to faulty stereotyped plates a number of passages are almost unreadable. Words and phrases which could not be transcribed have been indicated [..]. The use of punctuation throughout the poem is inconsistent and at times appears to follow no known convention. No attempt has been made to standardize punctuation.

'Soul-Cripple City'

Not a mere imaginary
Object, born on fancy's wing,
Is the city of this story,
But a real historic thing.
Though by tropes and proper figures
We delineate her fame,
Though she has some mystic features,
She's an entity the same.

She's a city, but not local,
A disorder wide diffused,
Or a system-cursed confusion,
By each system more confused.
So we'll briefly trace her hist'ry,
And inspect her filthy streets,
Taking disinfectives plenty,
For the morbidness she keeps.

In the book of Revelation,
And in prophesy we learn,
An apostate generation
From the truth astray would turn.
Would forsake the Holy City
Wherein dwelleth righteousness,
And from Zion's mount of beauty,
Wander in the wilderness.

And, like Cain who slew his brother,
Fled into the land of Nod,
From the country of his father,
'From the presence of his God,'
And there built him a city,
These apostates from the Lord,
Were to think them wise and mighty,
Far above the written Word.

So of them it was predicted,
That a city they'd devise,
And her deeds so foul and wicked,
Were to reach unto the skies.
Also those 'confounded builders'—
An insult to Wisdom's Son—
Were to call their bedlams churches.
But God named her 'Babylon.'

Tis fulfilled. They've built the babel
On the sands of sectish strife.
Her chief founder was the devil,
Though disguised, she is his wife.
Filth and all abominations
Lodge in her these latter days.
Her six hundred babel nations
Tread six hundred crooked ways.

Each one leads direct to heaven,—
So the bigots all declare—
If you'll take the sectish leaven,
And each quarter pay your fare.
Neath a great and tow'ring steeple,
At the head of every street,
There the mixed and 'mingled people,'
Both to play and worship meet.

There they throng to sell and gamble,
Crying, 'all done, twice and thrice.'
Souls are bartered for a trifle,
Trifles bring the highest price.
There are ladies sold at auction,
To the highest bidding fool.
Money is the mighty unction,
That inspires the pulpit tool.

So a thousand shoddy trinkets,
Dolls and monkeys, pop and ale,
Make the merchandise of babel,
And insure a pious sale;
For in buying every member
Gets a ticket he conceits,
That will pass the door of heaven,
And secure the highest seats.

There are shows and lewd carousals,
Where the members whoop and laugh,
And with wicked men and devils,
Dance around the golden calf.
Most conspicuous in the revel,
Is the hypocritic priest
Who thus serves the very devil,
'Neath the livery of Christ.

Now they stand in line of battle,
Mimic war, and muster brooms:
For their pastor's bread and butter,
They must soften to buffoons.
'Shoulder arms', 'there, hold them level'—
Even women take a part—
'Broom brigades' won't sweep the devil
Nor his cobwebs out their heart.

New inventions, strange and silly
Always find a ready sale.
Money begging without scruple,
Please the prophets, 'head and tail.'
So they welcomed in the devil,
Heard him lie to gender fun,
Put him up and sold at auction,
Just to help the cause along.

How it did surprise the devil.
That the cripples bid so fast.
All the town was in a rival,
Nick to have at any cost.
As the sale ran high and rapid,
Satan hollowed loud and gruff,
'We have legions for your market,
And you all can have enough.

So the prince of diabolians
Took the undisguised control;
For he needed now no longer

Wear a mask in Cripple-Soul.
To his children who could enter
Only in the rear by stealth,
Now the gateway standeth open,
If they'll only bring their pelf.

Note that heard and tell, if able,
Which are sheep, and which are goats,
It would even puzzle Gabriel
To assort them by their notes.
Why should sheep, if any present,(?)
All adopt the goatish bleat?
Playing goat will not be pleasant
At the final judgment seat.

Well denominated babel,
Such she is in very deed,
A confused and drunken revel,
Killing souls for mammon greed.
Yet we've named her by Soul Cripple,
A cognomen justly due.
And you'll set it to her credit
As her customs we review.

But whereunto shall we liken,
Or with what similitude,
Paint this foolish generation?
Foolish children, sinful brood!
All within that mystic city
Walk not upright on their feet
But on crutches play the cripple,
'Tis a custom they must keep.

Not a man in all Soul-Cripple,
Not a woman, girl or boy,
But must go it on quadruple,
Must the wooden legs employ.
Not one ever tried it walking
On created feet alone,
Not on crutches to be stalking
Were a scandal to the town.

Strength and speed their limbs are losing,
Although God had made them sound.
But for want of proper using,
Hang they limpsy to the ground.
Their backs are bent, and shoulders gibbous,
Thus they mope as quadrupeds.
[..] it happens
Some collide protruding heads.

But why go they thus a hobbling,
Rich and poor, and young and old,
On their wooden members shuffling?
That's the right way, they are told.
From that city's first conception,
There went forth a firm edict,
None in her municipation
Dare in soundness walk erect.

So they hold the old tradition,
As a law in Cripple Soul.
Each succeeding generation
Muster crutches in the roll,
Each teach the stupid notion
To their children as divine,
On their stilted locomotion
Make them cripple into line.

Now the useless legs they're sporting
Are of varied stamp and kind,
Each one takes his own assorting,
To the fancy of his mind.
O'er six hundred fact'ries humming
Keep the market in supply.
All in competition running,
All in style and numbers vie.

The oldest crutches in the market
Are the Roman Papal brand.
They in human blood are painted,
And the highest price command.
All these antiquated relics

Bear inscription, Nicene date
And a trademark, dame of harlots,
Myst'ry babylon the great.

This firm held exclusive patent,
And monopolized the trade
For twelve hundred years unrivaled,
Until Luther haply made
The discov'ry that their charter
Was without authentic seal.
So he blazed abroad the matter
By his thunder and his quill.

Many cast the bloody crutches
From their galled arms away.
Then an angel hell dispatches,
Feign-lly a son of day.
And he hailed the reformation,
Bid them quickly organize:
Mostly on the old foundation,
Built they Luth'ran crutcheries.

This is now the eldest daughter
Of the harlot mother great,
Oath bound prison, souls to slaughter,
Cursed and degenerate.
And her trade-mark is the second
Two-horned beast that did appear,
Speaking like unto a dragon.
And a foaming keg of beer.

Next appeared the English crutches,
And the High Episcopal.
Thence the mania fast increases,
Every style conceivable.
Wycliffe crutches, Calvin crutches,
Quaker, Shaker, Mennonite,
Wesley crutches, in twelve branches,
M.E. crutches, black and white.

Methodism, Afric, German,
Methodism Protestant,
Methodism labeled 'Calvin,'

Both M.E.'s. north and southern brand.
'Free' and 'Union' Methodism,
And the ism 'Primitive.'
All these horns of beast division,
On their stilted crutches live.

A dozen clan of Methodism
Crying here is Christ, and there.
All in lively opposition,
Compass earth to sell their ware.
Entertain the base and funny,
Lie and steal, to pious end.
Any rook to raise the money,
That's the way to raise the wind.

In the nude, and lude and dev'lish
Methodism takes the sway.
Steeple-houses tall and stylish,
Mesh and milk the goats to pay.
Festive 'tables full of vomit'
Is the trademark of this name.
She's a black and smoking comet,
And her glory is her shame.

Then there are Baptist crutches,
Hard-shell, and inflexible
'Free-will' Baptist, Bond-will Baptist,
[..]'xi Principle.'
There are Baptist called 'Ephrata.'
Saturnarian Baptist too.
'Anabaptist,' and some later
Baptist crutches we'll undo.

First there are the tri-crutched baptist,
Three-dip Dunkers, new and old,
'Primitive,' 'Progressive,' factions,
All spewed out, 'twice dead' and cold.
They believe in three immersions,
Rising filthy from the flood,
But think not of one submersion,
Neath the precious cleansing blood.

In this mart of vain religions
You will find on Water street,
And at all her river stations,
Crutches vaunted as complete.
But the clubs that they are vending,
Are as hollow as a horn:
They that buy need no repenting,
In cold water they are born.

All that ride upon their notion,
Think they're valiant in dispute;
Water, river, lake and ocean,
Here salvation they impute.
'Deny the power' and take our patent,
Come and join our empty wells.
Note our trade-mark, 'tis a camel
Feeding empty oyster shells.

Satan cooped a reformation
In the key.stone-land of Penn.
Eldershipped it, with ovation,
Down the river to this den.
In the harbor of Soul-cripple,
Cast her anchor in the mud,
On her main-mast hung the devil
The misnomer, 'Church of God.'

Here she places on the market
Her new crutch in Cripple Soul.
Fills the measure of a bigot,
In the sacred name she stole.
Her weak crutch is highly varnished,
And her trade-mark is a cloak,
With a name in amber tarnished,
And a camp befogged with smoke.

Then she raked the earth for money
To erect a factory,
In the gassy town of Findlay,
Where her preacher dudes could be
Caught to ape and mimic others,
Over nicely mince and nod.
So they dote upon their Athens,
She's their pride inflating god.

All these bapto 'sociations
Have a god of water made,
Leaving fire and salvation,
And the blood without the trade.
More than all the sect who clamor
Just to make the sinner wet,
Who have swallowed down a Campbell
And are straining at a gnat.

True, to follow Christ's example
Is sublime, and very good.
But to dip a trembling sinner,
Is to set at naught the blood.
Dead to sin and self forever,
We immerging, testify,
But to plunge and raise a rebel,
Is to dip him in a lie.

While a drop or two to sprinke,
That is but a popish rite,
Catered to the flesh and devil;
Born in superstition's night.
Yet the drop betrays its meaning,
Snapped into the sinners face,
That on sponsors he is leaning,
Hoping for a drop of grace.

Since to bury in immersion
Presupposes we are dead,
Then repent and get salvation
E'er into the stream you're led.
But if candidate is filthy,
And to sin he will not die,
Then the smallest bit of water
Will but tell the lesser lie.

O! ye Presbyterian crutches,
All of dozy timber made,
'English,' 'German,' 'Kirk of Scotland,'
'Cumberland,' 'Associate,'

And 'seceders' from the Bible,
'Covenanters' and Reformed;
Each priestism is a charnel
And your wooden legs deformed.

There are props United Brethren,
All disjointed out of Christ,
Glassite, Hicksite, and Socinian,
Rotten Universalist.
There are crutches labeled Christian,
All the better to deceive:
And an earth-born 'Christian Union,'
That would all together weave.

Materialistic crutches
Also occupy a stand.
And some tables spread with clutches,
Hop as devils play their hand.
There are crutches Unitarian,
Omish, dull of sale and rust.
Also Supralapsitarian,
A few Landisites in dust.

There are crutches 'Congregational,'
And 'Associate Reform.'
And all dark 'Evangelical,'
God-forsaken and forlorn.
River Brethren, Shaw's young Missiou,
Unswathed, out of season born.
all the bundles we can't mention,
A confusion multiform.

'Twas in eighteen four and forty,
William Miller set the day,
That he would, with all his party,
Spread his wings and fly away.
So they robed themselves all ready,
And assembled in the town.
Though their faith was strong, yet steady
Gravitation held them down.

As the sun his race was running,
All with upward gazing eye,
Waited for the Savior's coming,
To confirm the prophet's lie.
But their flapping was a failure.
O'er them waned the evening light,
Leaving all the dupes of Miller
In confusion's darkest night.

But they'd started out to travel
On some new discovered route,
So, assisted by the devil,
They must never turn about.
Then they met in general council
For to hit upon a creed,
Which of all the lies in Cripple,
Their's must take the very lead.

So the devil searched the record
Of the meanest lies he'd thought,
Then he moved, and Miller second,
And 'twas carried by vote;
'These two crutches, in Soul-Cripple
We will place upon the roll,
That 'neath Sinai we must tremble,
And deny we have a soul.'

Then this craft, in falsehood shapen,
And conceived in very sin,
Their infernal business open,
And to bondage gather in.
Use the law to till their coffers,
And to spread their lies abroad.
At salvation they are scoffers,
Keeping Saturday's their god.

But the city council issued
An injunction on their trade,
For that market, 'twas decided,
Just for Cripple Soul was made.
O ye Advents ye can never
In this market hold a stall,
From Soul-Cripple you must sever,

For ye have no soul at all.

Then the foolish Millerism
Fell to looking very brown;
Having pitched so far from Zion
Were not fit for Cripple Town.
So they made a new edition
In the 'wilderness of sin,'
There to vend their blue religion,
And to spread their legal gin.

'Twas a waste and desert region,
Once possessed by Sadducees,
Who denied both soul and angel,
For the fleshly mind to please.
So did Ebionites inhabit
This parched wild in later years.
In the smoke of burning Horeb,
There they groped in legal fears.

They were 'wanting understanding,
'Poor in sense,' Origen said.
The epistles all rejecting,
On the pentateuch they stood.
The Galatians were so lawish
Once to think of moving there,
But the 'postle cried, ye 'foolish,'
Flee from that satanic snare.

So these tramontanian deserts
Lay for many ages waste,
Till the Non-soul-legal-ventists
Out of Cripple Soul were cast.
Here in 'blackness and the tempest,'
And beneath the thundering curse,
All these bondage sons of Hagar
Gathered up their babel force.

Here they walled about their region,
To exclude all angels' stroll,
And so fear all apparitions
That they carnify the soul.

And, lest God should make them trouble,
Say they're only flesh and wind,
Knowing he will never bother
With the lower cattle kind.

Satan had the city courted,
And to marry they agreed.
When the nuptials celebrated,
They were rudely *charivarid*
Marched a brigade, all red shirted,
General Booth in chief command,
Proudly o'er them banners flaunted,
An imposing martial band.

Then they broke the grave-yard silence
Of the city, lost in dreams.
Drums were beating loud and vig'rous,
Others thumping tambourines.
All the town awoke in panic.
Teams took fright and ran away.
Nervous men were seized with frantic,
And the devil was to pay.

Day and night they kept the racket
Of the drumming round the town.
Seeing they would never stop it,
Council met to shut them down.
But the loud noisation army
Said their mission was from God.
Booth, they thought more wise than Jesus,
Had supplanted Him as head.

Christ had lacked the special wisdom,
Money raking to demand
Of the preachers he comissioned,
As they traveled o'er the land.
Booth preeminence obtaining.
On his financiering tact,
Now asserts his lordship standing,
Filling out what Jesus lacked.

Jesus even was so simple
That He sent His heralds forth.
Without drum or tinkling cymbal,
Nor a tambourine; for-sooth
Taught, if He but be uplifted,
And His love the people saw,
Through the melting of His Spirit,
Then to Him all men would draw.

This the Gen'ral thought a failure,
'Christ alone will never do,
If the world we hope to capture,
We must march with pomp and show.
A 'kingdom not with observation,'
Will not take in our day;
Ten to one will join religion,
If we make a fine display.'

Christ, we read is 'head' and 'captain,'
Of His Church and kingdom pure,
Booth presumed himself commission,
Into rival office swore;
As it proved a speculation,
One Moore, thought he'd share the spoil
So they split the clatteration
In two armies on this soil.

Now they plant their rival forces,
Fronting each in battle line.
Each to each lift up a 'war cry,'
Bravely smite the tambourine.
Moore, the traitor, seized the barracks,
And command in chief assumes.
So they fire on each other,
With their painted 'Quaker guns.'

But the safety of Soul-Cripple
Was endangered by their din.
Drumming, thumping like a rabble
Nuisance, a shocking sin
'Gainst the sacredness of Sabbath,
And against all common sense.

All a hollow-drum religion,
Like the Pharisee's pretense.

So this racketation army
Was ejected from the town,
And they formed a new edition,
To the city of renown.
On a dry and desert common.
Joining on to Quaker street,
Here they serve the god of mammon.
And their martial glory beat.

Here they drum men out the kingdom
Of the devil, in their ranks,
Who but glorify the bedlam,
Lavish on it all their thanks.
Here they spread the banquet table,
Spend the night in revelry
Mixing Christ in all their babel,
Hell approved profanity.

Drunkards leave their whiskey guzzling,
Join the army, loud and brave,
To the pious 'tis so puzzling,
Drums and tambourines can save
Time soon proves it no salvation,
An enthusiastic spell.
Soon the shallow weak sensation
Leaves the soul enroute for hell.

While the business of Soul-Cripple
Made its wanted daily round,
And her crutches selling rapid
All along her market ground,
And her merchants waxing wealthy,
By the 'bundance of her trade.
Suddenly there rose a sturdy,
Who no little trouble made.

All the people of the city
Were much startled by a sound,
That proceeded from a speaker,

And re-echoed all around
In the chiefest convocation,
At the corner of the street,
On a store-box elevation
Spake the man with zealous heat.

So the crippled soulians hearkened,
Horror stricken into mutes;
For that voice so loud and hollow
Seemed to come up from his boots.
Yea it rattled; 'gainst the buildings,
Like an angry threatening row.
So the people came together,
Wond'ring what was coming now.

And behold! it was a preacher,
In a deep and gutt'ral tone,
Crying, 'put away your crutches,
Stand complete in Christ alone.
There's no use of all this hobbling
On your sinful sectish props,
They're inventions of the devil,
And their merchants gaudy tops.

'Your divisions are all wicked,
They engender only strife;
Jesus prayed that His disciples,
Should be one here in this life.
Not His Word, but your inventions,
Have begotten party lines.
Therefore burn up all your crutches,
And repent of all your sins.'

This was now an awful message,
In the ears of Cripple-Soul.
'He's a mover of sedition,
And a sacriligious fool.'
Cried the people in a clamor,
Neath the smarting of his scourge.
Though much truth was in his hammer,
Not a coal was in his forge.

But the fierce intrepid scolder
Was not eas'ly driven out.
So that night he took his corner,
And resumed his pouring out.
Hail and grapeshot on the crutch'rics,
Quite to break the business up.
So he made the bab'lon merchants
Swallow down a bitter cup.

When the loud discourse was over,
And the benediction bowed,
Round the speaker there did gather
Quite an indignation crowd.
'Why inveigh against our crutches'
One and all began to cry,
On them we have leaned for ages
'And we'll ride them till we die.'

Nay, but answered Lyman Johnson—
For that was the speakers name—
Christ is all we need to lean on,
But your crutches make you lame.
One then gave this quip rejoinder,
'Inconsistency you show,
While you smite us with your hammer,
You yourself on crutches go.'

This provoked a burst of cheering.
When the laughter did subside,
And the stranger had a hearing,
he vehemently denied.
But rejoined again the other,
'Do not lie, for it is true,
'Since you left the lap of mother,
You have rode on crutches too.'

'Not a man in all Soul-Cripple
More than you on crutches ride.
Like your spine your creed is crooked,
As if satan sat astride.
We have all some kind of crutches,
And we think it no disgrace,
'But the man that keeps his covered

Best be scarce about this place."

At this Lyman grew more chafy,
And in loud defence he cried,
'It is false, I have no hobby,
On no hackneyed props I stride.
Christ is all I want I tell you,
All your crutches I disdain,
'They're a curse to all this city,
They dishonor Jesus' name.'

Then they, pressing round him, rudely
Raised his sacerdotal gown,
When, behold! to his confusion,
there the man was hanging down
'Twixt the same old Quaker crutches
On their market long had stood.
Then great laughter and derison
Burst from all the multitude.

This exposure drove the pester
In confusion out the town.
Now there was a Quaker common,
Held by them and Booth alone;
North and westward from the city;
On that bleak and dreary site
He took squatter's right to settle,
And to carry on the fight.

'Twas a slightly elevation,
From the great confusion town,
Which advantageous position
'Nabled him to scatter down
Hail and all annoying missiles
To molest the devotees.
Riding yet his anti-naggy,
He'd assail their crutcheries.

Then this Cripple Soul tormenter,
Struck upon this new device;
Built a great refrigerator,
That would manufacture ice,
Which, by summer and by winter,

With an enginery of war,
He threw on the fated city
All their restless peace to mar.

O what torment and what sorrow
From that north edition came,
Hail-stones now and ice tomorrow,
Tripped and stumbled all the lame.
Blood and fire he never mingled,
All a frigid aspect wore.
So the chilly blasts of Lyman
Froze their dead religion more.

Just what adverse moulding forces
May have stamped their dire effect
And mishaped the mind of Russel,
We are not prepared to state.
But it seems that some misfortune
Sat upon his embryo,
Hence it was, the Holy Bible
He could not believe was true.

On that Book he sat in judgment,
Holding it much under par,
By the standard of his wisdom:
For he thought, 'twere better far,
Had it been confined to heaven,
And that all must on it dwell;
But, O dear that dreadful larum
Of an everlasting hell!

Tho' 'twill do on earth to' prison
Men who thirst for human blood,
All should freely stalk in Heaven,
Thief and villain, bad and good.
Since the Word gives faithful warning,
That the wicked must depart
If they slight complete salvation,
And so demonize their heart.

Russel said he would not stand it;
Unless God revised the Book,
To the wisdom of his ethics

He'd drop on the skeptic hook.
Since the Scriptures verse his reason,
And declare there is a hell,
He kicked out of Heaven's traces,
And became an infidel.

But to be a skeptic merely,
Did not meet the devil's plan,
That is stale and out of season;
So, said he, 'my faithful man,
You've been bravo 'gainst the Bible,
And abhorred the thoughts of hell,
But you'll curse the place still louder
When with us a while you dwell."

'Now I know you love promotion,
And I've found a place for you,
We've devised, in hell's convention,
Something altogether new.
Or, at least, we've dresed it over,
So it cannot help but take,
For the restless hearted sinner
Wants a cooler for the 'lake.'

'Once we did a thriving business
On the universal bate,
But the thunderbolts of heaven
Knocked it wholly out of date.
So we gave it a new dressing,
And confessed that hell is right.
But its flames would work redemption,
And just burn the sinner white.

This was also soon exploded
And it fell in disrepute;
For in spite of all precaution,
It showed up in hellish fruit.
So we've now revised the system
And will make another run
With the same old lie tucked under
This new garb, 'the age to come.'

We bestow on you the honor
To be head of this new plan.
Many seen would jump the offer,
But we think you are the man.
Therefore publish to all nations
That a favored age is near,
That will scoop all up to Heaven
Who have served the devil here.

Need not tell them to be wicked,
They'll attend to that no doubt,
When you promise them our patent
Coming age to help them out.
For the works I've planted in them
Will propel them right along,
Into evry line of sinning
When the fears of hell are gone.

Mr Russel bowed politely
And expressed no small surprise
That, amid his numerous fam'ly,
He should so conspicuous rise.
'Since,' said he, 'it's fallen on me
To be head and patentee
Of this latest shift infernal,
I'll accept it cheerfully.'

So they made a new edition
To the town of every craft,
'Till too late deferred redemption;
And for joy the demons laughed
All the sinner's lust unbridled,
Who believe the soothing lie,
'Now's the time to dance and revel,
And get pious by and by.

'Your good tidings, Mr. Russell,
Suits our wishes very well;
For we love to serve the devil,
But kept back for fears of hell.
The Old Bible has salvation
Forced upon the people 'now,'
But I like your new edition,
Where the future age will do.

'What's the use to be Religious
Where it makes the devil rage.
Just keep back, he won't disturb us
In the Russelsonian age.
And its nice to have his favor,
In this world where he's at home,
So we'll serve him till he leaves us,
In the happy age to come.

'The old Bible's far too narrow,
All its hope must here begin.
So we'll stretch it to another
Age, to have more time for sin.'
On a hellward leaning 'Tower,'
Russel and the devil sit,
While their falsehood loving army's
Mar hang downward to the pit.

While the populace of Cripple
But corrupted all their way,
God beheld in sovereign pity,
Some within her prisons lay,
Who were citizens of Zion,
And were of another heart.
These all heard a voice from heaven,
Come 'my people' thence depart.

Yea, arise, depart 'my people,'
'This is not at all your rest,'
For, alas! it is polluted,
T'will thy soul in tophet cast,
And destroy with sore destruction.
Lest her plagues upon thee fall.
Flee ye out the midst of bab'lon
And deliver now thy soul.

Jesus Christ the awful 'Breaker'
Then came up before their face,
To assemble all of Jacob,
And redeem them by His grace.
So He opened up a passage,
Through the gateway led them out.
As their King passed on before them,

All the multitude did shout.

When the Lord evacuated,
Left her empty, desolate,
Forth He called the honest hearted,
He Himself without her gate.
'Come,' O come all ye 'my people,'
Or my face no more you'll see,
Hear my voice no more in babel,
Hasten out and come to me.'

Yet within her meshes lingered
Some who were of 'double mind.'
Who loved God, but knew not whether
They could leave all else behind.
Then, with Trumpet loudly sounding,
Messengers Jehovah sent,
Preaching the Eternal Gospel,
And commanding all repent.

Robed in spotless white of Heaven,
Glory shone upon their face.
And their words, an awful hammer,
Fell like hail-stone on the place.
But there was yet with it mingled
Flaming fire, and the blood;
These they cast upon the people,
And extoled the Son of God.

Hail destroyed their false religion,
While the blood and fire combined,
Cleansed and purged unto perfection,
All who were of willing mind.
Soon the wood, and hay and stubble,
Caught on fire all around,
And their fact'ries were in danger
To be leveled to the ground.

For these heralds spake in power
Awful burning words of God.
Preaching Christ and full redemption,
Through His all atoning blood.
Each one had a golden censer,

Filled with Heaven's holy flame,
Which they cast upon the city,
In their King's Almighty name.

Then all they who sighed for freedom,
And abhorred the city's deeds,
Wept for joy to hear the tidings
And renounced their dwarfing creeds.
'Long,' said they, 'we have been waiting
For the light that shines to-day,
'Tis the truth we have been seeking,
And we'll tread its golden way.

But now came the days of trouble
For that city of ill fate;
For the Lord arose to judge her
In her wicked Sodom state.
So 'their faces gathered blackness,
And 'they gnawed their tongues for pain,'
For her merchandise was perished,
Dead and gone her hope of gain.

They were 'mad upon their idols,'
And they strove against the Lord.
Even gnashed upon His servants,
Just because they preached His Word.
Each began at once extoling
His own hobby very much.
Crying, 'Great is our Dianna,
And all glory to our crutch.

If you burn up all our crutches
And consume our factories,
You will leave us stripped and wasted;
For what have we else but these?'
But the holy heralds answered,
'We are come to do you good,
Even turn you from these idols,
To the true and living God.'

Then spake one for wisdom noted,
In his town an honored sage,
'That crutches do have God's approval
Is evinced by hoary age.'
'Nay, by fruits we know each system,
Not by mere antiquity,
Else would sin, the source of factions,
Yet present the stronger plea.'

Then stepped up one Mr. Simple,
By him-self reputed wise.
In a centumacious wrangle
Labored loud to 'pologize
For the City's superstition.
He alleged it indiscreet
For a living man to venture,
Walking only on two feet.

'For, said he,' a pond'rous body
Can't - a scientific fact -
Rest securely on two proppings,
Hence our crutch is what we lacked.
If by casting two legs from us,
We could better get about,
Would we not be yet more [..]
Less two more and do without.'

But they answered, 'O ye people,
'Ye ask counsel at your stocks.'
And ye 'say your staff declareth.'
So ye lean upon your props.
Erring in your whoredom spirit,
Egypt is the staff you trust,
And while on it you are leaning,
It doth in your vitals thrust.

'They do 'break and rend thy shoulders,'
Sorely pierce within thy 'loins,'
Yet ye make these your inventions,
Equal to your flesh and bones,
And as needful as the members
Of the body, all complete,
God created, standing perfect,

Unencumbered on its feet.

'Is there life within your crutches?
Have they veins and coursing blood?
'As if the staff should lift up,' bravely
Yea, 'as if it were no wood.'
I, the Lord create the body,
But your props I can't endure,
They insult creative wisdom
And exalt the creature more.

'With the God-created body
You these timbers classify.
Yet you know they're late inventions,
And your claim for them a lie.
Long before these cripple trappings,
Was the body Heaven made,
And on it you cast dishonor
By your counterfeiting trade.'

'You've deformed and dwarfed the system,
By your clumsy headed rails,
And reduced its locomotion,
To the crawling of the snails.
And you're taxed and drummed to paupers
To support your crutcheries,
In return you're hanging empty,
Like a scare-crow in the breeze.'

But again rejoined the cripple
In conceit and bigotry,
'Look out over hill and valley,
Those green waving fields you see,
Reaching into foreign missions,
Were all planted, watered tilled
By man leaning on their crutches,
Would you blast their goodly yield.'

'Nay,' replied the herald of Heaven,
'I'd not blast, but much improve,
And enlarge the fruits of labor.

Those poor crops can never prove
That your crutch is an advantage:
They obstruct your arms and hands,
As you labor in the vineyard,
As you hobble o'er the lands.

'If some products have been gathered,
By weak cripples hung on poles,
How much greater were the harvest,
And the vintage of poor souls,
Had you cast off all encumbrance,
And like men, erect and strong,
Swiftly gathered in abundance,
While on props you've moped along.

'O ye foolish generation!
All [..] blind and dumb!
How unfit for distant nations,
All divided here at home.
You have compassed land and ocean,
See [..] ostensibly;
But have shamed the very heathen,
Each with rival crutchery.'

Then arose another zealot,
Who averred his crutch the best,
Said he'd not exchange for any
Other patent on the list.
But the herald answered quickly,
'God cares not to have you swap,
But flee out this cursed city,
And give all her business up.'

Lo, this caused the man to shudder,
Filled with horror and amaze.
'O my crutch! my crutch!! my city!
Rather let the orient blaze,
Never light again my vision;
Let my tongue forbear to move,
And my hands forget their cunning,
If my crutch I cease to love!

'Should I cast away my "Method.'

O what could I lean upon?
I should have to seek another,
Or soon break and topple down
So to give up all our crutches
Would but lead to other kind
And, alas! there're now too many,
They confuse and craze the mind.'

'You would take away our leanings
And you bid us walk erect,
But this would be unbecoming,
And a thing we can't expect.
There's none perfect, no none perfect!
So we can't, *we can't be straight*
Till we quit this life of sinning,
And we enter Heaven's gate.'

Then the angel answered, 'Cripples,
You deny the power of God.
You ignore the great Physician,
Who hath shed His precious blood.
Thee to save in perfect soundness,
And respine you by His might,
Put you walking upright, soaring
Like the eagles sunward flight.

'In His name, the Great Jehovah,
We must blow this awful blast,
Judgment, ire and full destruction
On this wicked place is cast.
Therefore all your crutches, idols,
Gather in a gen'ral heap,
And t'appease the wrath of Heaven
Burn them, burn them in the street.

'This thy cup that God has given,
Cup of wormwood and of gall.
Ye must drink it all ye nations,
'Drink, be drunken, spue and fall.'
So they drank the cup of fury,
And were 'moved and mad and fell.'
'On their glory shameful spewing,'
Filled the place with fumes of hell.

Then those fac'tries where the crutches
Were turned out in great supply,
Soon were wrapped in red destruction;
And the people raised a cry,
O my crutch'ry! O my crutch'ry!
Woe is me this evil day.
O my great and noble fact'ry,
In its ashes soon must lay!

When they saw their pride was burning,
And their merchandise had fled,
Far at sea her merchants weeping,
Casting dust upon their head,
Loud bewailed her sudden ruin.
Saying, 'O alas! alas!!
Our great city clothed in purple,
Lies a burning smoking mass.

Then the angel of Jehovah
Said to all the holy ones,
'Rejoice Apostles, and ye Heavens
Over her, as judgment comes.'
And they shouted, Alleluia!
Now is come salvation pure,
And the Kingdom and the glory
Of our God forever more!

Then the city was divided:
All the good and pure and blest.
Deeper into God [..]
And attained His holy rest.
Even 'mid the wild commotion
Of the city's utter fall,
They resolved to go to [..]
And their King was all in all.

These all cast away their crutches,
And began to walk erect.
But the children of confusion,
Though more num'rous, were deject.
For it grieved them sore that many
Had ignored their wooden gods.

So they gnashed upon the pilgrims,
Beat them with their stilted hobbs.

And, behold! when Quaker Lyman
Saw his ice was melting down,
Yet defamed the holy remnant,
More than all in Cripple Town.
In so much that justice ordered,
That his name and deeds befit,
This due change should be recorded,
Namely should be *'Lie-man'* writ.

Now had come the separation
'Twixt the cripples and the sound,
'Twixt the joyful in salvation,
And abject on crutches found.
Those set out for true Mount Zion,
With a bright and joyful hope.
These still linger in the ruins,
'Mid the dust and ashes grope.

Yea they are so mad confounded,
And unto their city's fame
Are so blindly yet devoted,
That amid the very flame,
They do weary them with building
Structures that the flames consume:
And they close their eyes from seeing
Babel's judgment and her doom.

Fallen! Fallen! is the city,
And an habitation, drear,
Of each foul and hateful spirit.
Yea of demons thronging there.
Satyrs dance amid her revels
Doleful beasts, and birds unclean,
Goats and imps, and fools and devils,
Mixing up, combine the scene.

All her priests divine for money,
Cater to the pride and sin
Of the carnal minded many.
Whom their net hath taken in.

While the blind lead on the blinded,
All deceived, deceiving all,
Satan smiles upon the business,
Death and hell cast on the pall.

Here on her we drop the curtain,
And shut out the od'ous scene.
O, thou filthy bloody harlot;
Hell is straitened with thy sin.
Farewell all ye sordid cripples,
Nay, how can we say farewell,
'Fear, the pit, and snare, upon thee,'
Must attend thee down to hell.

But adieu for we must travel
With the remnant who return,
Fleeing from the fall of babel,
To the New Jerusalem.
Hark! a noise like many waters!
'Tis the captive's jubilee.
Like the voice of mighty thunders.'
Hallelujah! we are free!

For, behold! with joyful wonder,
Just out side the crumbling wall,
Of that hold of craft and plunder,
There the pilgrims found withal,
First a highway, then a higher,
'Called the way of holiness.'
Here the God of love and power,
Raised them up to righteousness.

Here they gained eternal safety,
From the prowling beasts around.
Lions, vultures, beasts of raven,
Never shall thereon be found.
But there walk the holy people,
'And the ransomed of the Lord
Shall return and come to Zion,
On this highway of His Word.

Now the host in joyful freedom,
And sweet order move along.

Filled with everlasting glory,
Sounding loud the victor's song.
Nearer, nearer, to Mount Zion!
Sorrow, sighing flee away.
And the strains of angels harping
Fall upon them all the day.

More and more the light of Heaven
Drove the shadows from the day.
Grace and truth were richly given,
All along the shining way.
Till the pure 'beloved City,'
Burst in grandeur on our sight,
That was hid in captive ages,
Till the dawn of evening light.

Hallelujah! Glory! Glory!
We have found a sweet release
From the straps and yokes of babel,
From her lords and gruff police.
Free [..] from all confusion!
Rent the chains of servitude.
Free [..] O great salvation!
Through the blood, the cleansing blood!

Saved from clamor sect and ism.
From the mold of every creed.
From the curse of strife and schism,
Dead to all her mammon greed.
We defy the hold of devils,
And despise her patent rules,
Not a terror in her councils,
Not a horn upon her bulls.

No Tobiah in the temple,
To defile the holy fane.
And consume the meat oblations
That unto the priests pertain.
All his stuff's cast out the chamber,
And the cleansing is complete.
No more wedding with Sanballat,
Nor can hell again defeat.

All the breaches in salvation.
Round about Jerusalem,
Are closed up against the nations,
'Gainst the ites of Babylon.
Moabs, Arabs, Gog and Geshem,
Egypt, Sodom, Horonites,
Half-bred Ashdods, Sabbath trader
Canaanites and Ammonites.

So the saints are free forever,
From the fear of beast control.
To the Kings beyond the river
Pay no tribute, custom toll.
Free from foreign intervention,
Circuit tax and revenue,
From Sanballat's sect convention
In the valley of 'Ono.'

Free from conf'rence machinations,
From committee's round of trash.
From preambles, and discussions,
From the speaker's carnal lash.
Free from making, and revising,
Laws for Babel's stupid god.
Free from voting, wire-pulling,
'All a pompous empty fraud.'

Priest credentials—a deception
Only needed by the quack,
Void of Holy Spirit unction,
Trusting in a musty stack
Of old sermons garb'ed and stolen—
And Soul-Cripple lesson leaves,
All were bound and left consuming,
With her thorn and brier sheaves.

Not a stone for a foundation,
Nor to lay a corner down,
Did the ransomed carry with them,
From old fallen Cripple town.
For their 'city hath foundations,'
And her builder God alone,
Pure as Heaven, whence descended,

And returning to His throne.

But who is this Holy City.
As the moon so bright and fair,
Looking forth in all the glory
Of the morning sun so clear?
Ah! she is the Bride of Jesus.
His own Church, arrayed in white.
Lo: His beauty is upon her,
And Himself her crystal light.

God is in her hallelujah!
And she never shall be moved!
Jesus Christ is her foundation,
And her righteousness, approved.
All her law is love; and freedom
Is her balmy atmosphere.
Far more sweet and blest than Eden,
Is her walk with Jesus here.

All her music is Celestial,
Sang by angels round the throne,
And then wafted by the Spirit
To this border-land of home.
All the ransomed sing together,
In angelic harmony,
By salvation made a unit,
As in Heaven all agree.

Not a spirit of dissension.
Nor discordant voice we hear.
For no alien ever entered,
Nor can ever enter here.
Christ the door, and His salvation
Is the way to enter in,
And through Him there's no admission,
Without leaving every sin.

Jesus is our Head and Ruler,
And his Word our only guide.
And His gentle Spirit leader.
Be our peace, a constant tide,
Flowing in our tranquil bosom,
Where is reared the mystic throne
Of the King of Peace Eternal.
Where He dwells and reigns alone.

O the glorious hope of Zion!
O the riches of her grace!
Ever happy are the people
Who abide in such a place.
God is over all in Glory,
And is through them great and small,
And He's in them by His Spirit,
Jesus! Jesus! All in all!

APPENDIX C

The following extracts are from Charles Naylor's booklet, *The Teachings of D.S. Warner and his Associates*. This undated work was privately published. It was likely published in 1949. It constitutes a critique of the thought of Warner from the perspective of a man who spent his life within the movement generated by Daniel Warner. The booklet is unpaginated.

The Teachings of D.S. Warner and his Associates
A Survey and Analysis by C.W. Naylor

OCCASION FOR THIS PAPER

For several years I have been making a careful and prayerful study of our teachings with the motive of finding their underlying principles and whether or not these teachings are soundly based. . . . I have studied the life and teachings of D.S. Warner in our literature, past and present, in *The Cleansing of the Sanctuary* by D.S. Warner and H.M. Riggle; *The Birth of a Reformation* by A.L. Byers; and other works. I knew D.S. Warner personally; I read his articles and editorials in the *Gospel Trumpet* for three and one-half years just prior to his death. I have read all the books and tracts he wrote and had published. I knew nearly all of the ministers who were associated with him. In my early ministry I was intimately associated with many of them, such as B.E. Warren, A.J. Kilpatrick, J.N. and George Howard, S.L. Speck, Otto Bolds, Mother Sarah Smith, and others who had been very closely connected with Brother Warner for many years. For some years I was a worker at the Gospel Trumpet Office. I attended several of the general camp meetings, also state camp meetings and assembly meetings. I was, so to speak, in the center of our work, and had full opportunity to know all that was believed and taught in those days. I have followed our teaching closely in all the days since. I believe, therefore, that I am competent to speak of our teachings for the last fifty years . . . .

WARNER AS A MAN

I knew D.S. Warner and loved him with reverential affection. I shall never forget his kindness to me, and the wise advice and counsel he gave me. I shall speak of his personality only in an attempt to give a portrait of him as I knew him. He was a highly spiritual man, very devoted and earnest, sincere, with the utmost loyalty to what he conceived to be the truth. He hated error as much as he loved truth, and attacked it on every possible occasion. With the weak, the suffering, or the discouraged, he could be as tender as a woman. With his associates he was humble, brotherly, kind. He loved to exalt the grace of God. He was bold, fearless, and a man of boundless energy. When aroused he was like a lion and roared mightily against evil. He was a poet, a dreamer, an idealist, and a perfectionist. He was not a logical thinker. He got most of his ideas which he did not absorb from others through his intuition rather than by careful logical thinking. Having an idea, he would go to the Bible to find scriptural support for it. In hundreds of instances he misinterpreted and misapplied texts, as do all who use his method. We have been compelled to reject a very large portion of his exegesis because it has proved to be unsound. Nevertheless, he was a great and good man of God, worthy of our highest regard, and we should cherish his memory. His teaching on a pure and spiritual church, incarnating anew the Christ and speaking to the world as the voice of God, was a potent message which should remain central in all our teaching. . . .

ASSUMPTIONS BY BROTHER WARNER

. . . . 2. . . . c) The sects were not the church, so a church must be brought into being as a distinct body by calling Christians out of the sects and into the 'one body.' There was not and had not been since the apostasy, any true and apostolic manifestation of the true church.

d) The harvest of souls was past. There was now only a 'gleaning time' and only a 'remnant' to be saved.

e) God would no longer save souls in the sects. He had moved out of 'Babylon' and forsaken her. 'No candle should shine' there and 'no sound of grinding be heard.'

f) The preachers were to constitute a 'flying ministry.' This led to all being evangelists and to the neglect of the local churches.

g) Babylon was to be 'threshed.' This idea led to great extremes and bitter attacks on other movements and all who were members of them.

h) The idea of unity was limited to one group. All must come to that group. Just leaving a sect did not avail anything. People must come to *us*.

i) No 'Babylon stones' could be used, so whatever was done in the sects was wrong. Even the experience of Christians in the sects was contaminated by the sect relation, so all who came out were expected to 'come by way of the altar.'

j) Unity meant, not so much unanimity as uniformity. It meant all must see 'eye to eye' and 'speak the same thing.' This left no place for individual thought. A few leaders formulated the doctrines, and all perforce must agree with them or be adjudged 'crooked in doctrine.' Complete doctrinal agreement was held necessary for acceptance or unity.

k) The advent being imminent, all the prophecies as to what should occur before it, which had not already been fulfilled, must be fulfilled in the immediate future. *Now* was the 'day of his preparation.' The year 1880 was accounted a 'prophetic year' and must mark the beginning of the work of preparation for the advent. There could be no doubt of the time—it was *now*.

3. . . . c) Since the denominations constituted 'Babylon,' it was evident that they were not the church nor any part of it, so the church must be 'called out' and reestablished *at once* or she would not be ready for the advent.

d) Since only Brother Warner and the few associated with him 'saw the light,' upon them was laid the responsibility of proclaiming it and bringing about 'the reformation' of the church, which must needs come at once.

e) Since those who accepted the call 'Come out' formed the nucleus of this 'reformation movement,' it naturally resulted that they felt and taught, directly or by implication, that all other Christians should and must leave their sects and come to this 'one body' and become a part of this group exclusively.

f) It was assumed that all Christians would at once recognize and accept 'God's call' to leave their sects when they heard that call. Those failing to respond would go into darkness and be lost.

g) The success of this method was not questioned. The results were prophesied and could not fail.

NOTE: Brother Warner accepted the imminence of the advent as did the premillennialists, but rejected the millennium and associated the advent with the end of the world, thus making the latter imminent, and so making necessary the fulfillment of all prophesies not already fulfilled almost immediately. Most others believing the advent imminent did not associate it with the end of the world, but with the setting up of an earthly kingdom. These rejected Brother Warner's assumptions, and will continue to do so. Since Brother Warner's assumptions are directly opposed to the premillennial assumptions of what the advent signifies, their position constitutes a denial of most of his assumptions. The great increase of the premillennial teaching and emphasis makes acceptance of the 'reformation message' increasingly difficult and improbably to all premillenialists, therefore the realization of Brother Warner's expectations becomes less and less likely.

To the premillennialists the advent will automatically settle all church problems as all Christians will be caught up together to meet Christ, and in the kingdom set up each will take his proper place and be in his proper relation. To the premillennialist, only personal preparation for the advent is necessary.

h) The movement was carried forward by the enthusiasm of attack, the zeal of conflict, and the sense of having a mission.

EFFECTS OF BROTHER WARNER'S ASSUMPTIONS

By classifying all religious movements except his own, including the holiness movements, as 'Babylon' and all their adherents as 'Babylonians,' he alienated his former associates and finally all denominational adherents. He vigorously condemned and bitterly attacked all those who did not agree with him even in matters of little importance. When aroused, and his emotions stirred, he became aggressive in attack and denunciation almost to abusiveness, and his langauge [sic] was often quite intemperate. By the use of such methods he further alienated his many friends and former associates, even his own wife, and needlessly made many enemies for himself and his cause. The chasm that came to exist between him and the other holiness bodies resulted very largely from his own actions and attitudes. Had his methods been different, his doctrines might have been tolerated if not accepted.

Brother Warner was a product of the time in which he lived, when intolerance and emotion in controversy were the usual thing. Today the scientific method of thought in general vogue leads to greater tolerance and poise in both manners and methods. . . .

IS THE ADVENT IMMINENT?

. . . . Brother Warner, in a meeting I attended, made the statement that the Lord has promised him that he should live until Jesus returned. Another brother recently told me that he heard him make this same statement in Missouri on more than one occasion. However, Brother Warner died about six months after I heard him make the statement. . . .

DO OLD TESTAMENT PROPHECIES HAVE TWO FULFILLMENTS?

Brother Warner, and most of the rest of us, have based our use of Old Testament scriptures in relation to our movement upon the theory that the Old Testament prophecies had their first application to Israel, and a secondary application to the church. This left us free to apply any Old Testament scripture we chose without regard to its context to present-day occurrences and movements. We have, therefore taken, many Old Testament scriptures out of their setting and without regard for their setting applied them to anything which, to us, they seemed to fit. In *The Birth of a Reformation* a chapter is devoted to stating and developing this idea, but after a careful and extensive study of the subject I am convinced that this position is not tenable and is not likely to reveal truth . . . .

. . . . Brother Warner's position, based on the idea of a two-fold fulfillment of the Old Testament prophecies, was the same as the position held with respect to the same thing by the millennialists, the Mormons, the Adventists, the Russellites, and others. The theory is the basis of their errors. They feel free to take Old Testament scriptures out of their setting, disregarding the context, and to apply them to anything, at any time, as they see fit. This is an untenable method, and no sound exegesis of Scripture can be based upon it. The things that are based upon it are unsoundly based. . . .

DO OLD TESTAMENT PROPHECIES RELATE SPECIFICALLY TO OUR MOVEMENT?

Brother Warner, and to a lesser extent we who have followed him, have definitely applied quite a number of Old Testament texts to this 'reformation movement. Is this use sound? Many Old Testament scriptures relating to ancient Babylon have been used as though they specifically applied to the Babylon of Revelation. It is wrong to use them in this way. The most we can say of them is that they illustrate spiritual Babylon. Certainly none of them refers directly to it. . . .

DOES GOD STILL WORK IN THE DENOMINATIONS?

Brother Warner constantly asserted, and the rest of us reiterated, that God had forsaken the denominations, that he would no longer save souls in them. Of course, that result would naturally follow if God called his people all out of a denomination locally or generally, and himself totally deserted it. But how has this theory worked out in practice during the years? We all know that God did not cease to save souls n thie [sic] denominations. We know he is still saving every soul that turns to him, regardless of where that soul is. We know that hundreds of thousands of people are being converted in the denominations every year. This is a certainty. What does it signify? It signifies ttha [sic] the harvest of souls is not past, as we had supposed. It signifies that God has not ceased to work in denominations. It signifies that we were wrong in what we taught on the subject. There is no use glossing it over—we were wrong. I see no reason to believe that fewer people are saved today in the denominations than there were sixty years ago. Can we draw any other conclusion from this but that God has not changed his attitude toward them? Denominations were always wrong; they are still wrong, but most of God's people are in them and he works among his people wherever they are.

'Threshing Babylon' never was God's plan. It did a great deal of harm. It created a great deal of prejudice, most of which was unnecessary. It has greatly hindered our work. What we said about the denominations and their preachers was often slanderous. We might as well face this. I am glad that most of us have stopped that sort of preaching . . . .

WHAT IS BABYLON?

We have assumed that the term 'Babylon' in the Book of Revelation included the Roman Catholic Church and all Protestant churches. We have interpreted the first beast of Revelation 13 as referring to Roman Catholicism, while the second beast and his image represented Protestantism. We have included everyone who belonged to these denominations as being in Babylon; in fact, we have called every religious organization of every kind Babylon except our own movement. That is an easy way of disposing of all other movements, but is it a correct definition of Babylon?. . .

It is asserted that these churches are all governed by man rule and have not the divine rule. It is true they have various forms of church government, but the implication we make that God has nothing to do with their church government is begging the question. It amounts to asserting that their leaders do not seek or receive divine guidance. It definitely implies that the gifts of the Spirit are not possessed or in operation in their organizations. We know that among the officers of these various organizations are many men of great piety and devotion. It is also true as a historical fact that in setting up these organizations divine guidance was earnestly sought. Moreover, whatever form these organizations took, the persons setting them up were thoroughly convinced that they were following out the teachings of the Scriptures. . . .

Those denominations having the congregational, the presbyterian, and the episcopal forms of church government all believe they find their particular form set forth in the New Testament. Who shall say that God may not work through any of these forms? The important thing, of course, is that the government be on a spiritual basis and be divinely guided. This we may expect it to be wherever true Christians have the leadership. To contend that all Christians must have the particular form of church government we have is to contend for something that has no scriptural support. We may, and should, insist upon a spiritual quality of church government, but we have no right to insist that it be clothed in a certain form . . . .

UNITY

. . . . Brother Warner had an extreme view of unity. He advocated a type of unity that never existed, and never can exist, in this world. He was sincere and thoroughly believed what he taught, but we have seen the necessity of modifying his teachings to make them conform more nearly to the possibility. I give a few quotations from his writings. Speaking of entire sanctification, he says:

'We now come to the great condition, and all potent means of perfect unity, found in the prayer of Christ' (*The Cleansing of the Sanctuary*, p. 260, par. 2).

'Here we say is secured to us the essential and all-sufficient means (entire sanctification) of producing perfect unity in all the body of Christ' (par. 3).

'Entire sanctification heals all division' (Ibid.).

'The all-pervading love of God . . . brings all hearts into the same harmony that reigns in heaven, into perfect unity, as the Father and Son are one' (Ibid.).

Of sanctification, he again says: 'Perfect oneness is its sure fruit' (Ibid., p. 262, par. 1).

W.G. Schell said: 'The absence of unity proves the absence of sanctification' (*The Biblical Trace of the Church*, p. 154). . . .

Sanctification is not once anywhere in the New Testament linked with unity in relation of cause and effect. Sanctification provides a good background for unity, but it does not produce and maintain unity in and of itself. Unity is dependent also upon many other things.

Brother Warner also taught that entire sanctification will produce unity of doctrine as a natural and inevitable fruit. Of the sanctified, he said: 'They are all brought into one faith . . . they are not left in various and conflicting views and interpretations of one faith. Nay, but the unity of the faith implies one faith, a perfect uniformity in the understanding of the same . . . God has made full provision, in every respect, for the perfect harmony in faith, life, and teaching of all who honestly wish to know the truth and obey the same' (*The Cleansing of the Sanctuary*, p. 263).

I add another quotation on the general subject of sanctification and unity: 'Where the professed followers of Christ are divided into a plurality of sects, they have not yet become thoroughly sanctified to God' (*The Birth of a Reformation*, p. 219).

The trouble with such views is that they never have worked out in practice; neither we nor any other body of people has ever possessed or maintained such unity. Such views are a hindrance to unity rather than an aid in securing it. In all nature the law is unity in diversity. The church is not an exception. This law prevails in the church also. So there must be account taken of the wide variety in thought, feeling, outlook, and understanding of different people, and whatever unity is attained must be attained through accommodation to these differences.

PATTERN UNITY

. . . the unity that is preached is commonly a pattern unity. By pattern unity I mean a pattern of doctrine is preached, a theology that everyone is expected to accept; a pattern of behavior is set up and all are expected to behave according to this pattern. A pattern of organization and church government is set up which everyone is expected to accept and to which he is expected to conform. A pattern of worship is set up, and this pattern is made a standard; in other words, the unity sought is uniformity. Uniformity is unattainable.

When people go into a community and preach a pattern unity they set forth a blueprint of unity, along the lines mentioned, to which everybody is supposed to conform in order to enter into the unity. The fact is, most people are already patterned. They already have their beliefs, their standard of Christian behavior, their ideas of church organization and government and worship. These ideas may differ very widely from those of the pattern of unity being preached to them. Some people in a community will be able to fit into the pattern of unity that is preached; they will likely accept the preaching. The majority of the people will not be able to fit into the pattern being preached; they have already been molded into a pattern. They cannot change their pattern just because one preaches a different one, therefore they will not accept the pattern that is preached and consequently cannot come into the unity that is set up. Pattern unity, therefore, can never bring about the unity of all Christians. It is the wrong type of unity.

BASIS OF UNITY

Unity does not mean uniformity; it means unanimity. Unanimity depends on an attitude of soul and mind. This can never be attained by accepting a pattern of unity. It must come by experiencing unity within.

There are four things that are the basis of true Christian unity. The first is the recognition and acceptance of all Christians, simply because of their relation with Christ. The second is love of all Christians, just because they are Christians. The third, fellowship with all Christians, based on confidence toward all Christians. Fourth, a co-operative attitude toward all Christians. These four bases of Christian unity must be universal in their nature. They must include all Christians. A unity that is limited to a group is not Christian Unity—it is group unity. The unity of the church must be on a universal basis or it never will be attained, and it must have unanimity as its keynote.

FOUR ROADS TO UNITY

. . . The fourth road to unity is calling people out of other groups into one group. This may or may not produce unity. Merely bringing people together in an organic relationship cannot create unity. We know all too well from sad experience that many people have come to us as a group and have professed to be in unity who very soon proved they were not in unity, but were troublemakers or never were able to fit in. So calling people into one group does not guarantee the unity of that group, neither does it create unity with other groups of Christians. On the contrary, it is likely to set up within the group a narrow and exclusive type of unity which is often a hindrance to true universal Christian unity. . . .

RECONSTITUTING THE CHURCH

Brother Warner held, and our prophetic writers who followed him have held, that there was no visible manifestation of the church from the time of the Apostasy down to the beginning of our movement. There was 'no visible, corporate, concrete exhibition of God's true church' (*Revelation Explained*, Rev. ed., p. 268). The reformation is to call out Christians from the different sects and re-establish the church as a visible body. 'The true church is again concretely, institutionally restored' (Ibid., p. 269). This seems to be a misapprehension of the facts. The body of Christ as a spiritually organized body has always existed from the time he created it. To say that body had no manifestation that could be recognized during the ages seems to be to deny a thousand facts. Were there no local churches of God until we formed some? Did God deal with his people only as scattered individuals? Did he not work through them in any way collectively? If he did work through them collectively, then that collective group was a church of God without regard to anything else.

We are not the only body of people who claim that the church ceased to exist during the Apostasy and had to be reconstituted. Some of the Baptist bodies teach this same thing; likewise, the Mormons, the Seventh Day Adventists, the Church of Christ, the Russellites, a number of holiness sects and other bodies, all teach that to them was given the task of reconstituting the lost church. They have built up bodies which they claim are *the* church. Nothing outside their bodies is the church. Our claim is an a par with theirs. I think we shall do well to see what effects their making such claims has had upon them in making them feel superior to others, proud of their movement, intolerant. When their attention is called to others who make the same claim that they make, they say, 'Oh, but they are wrong; we are right. God has called us to re-establish his church, not them.' Let us be warned by their example . . . .

WHAT MAKES US A DISTINCT BODY?

We are not made a distinct body through salvation. Many persons and groups are saved the same as we are, yet are not a part of our group. We are not made a distinct body by any essential Christian thing, for we are not exclusive in our possession of any such thing. Neither are we made a distinct group by a special attitude of God toward us, as a group or personally, for his attitude is the same toward all his people. . . .

The universal church may be organized as local congregations in a formal way, but it cannot be organized formally as a general body in any practical way. Any attempt to so organize it results in a denomination, for that which unites some local churches into a visible, distinct organic group at the same time separates them from all other Christian groups. This separation is denominational and strongly tends to and usually does violate Christian unity.

WHAT LIES AHEAD?

. . . Brother Warner expected all Christians to be brought into this movement in a single generation—this I know from his own lips. He said so publicly in a meeting I attended, and from others I learn that he repeated the statement at other times and in other places. His expectations are not only far from being realized, but they have not even begun to be realized. No large number of Christians have heard and accepted our 'come out' message. Of those who have come to us from other movements, by far the greater number have come not because of hearing that message but because they wanted the salvation we preach or because they sought greater freedom among a more spiritual people.

Our 'come out' message has never proved effective except in a most limited way, and I see no reason to expect it to be more effective in the future. If we should count the number of those who were Christians in the denominations and who heard our prophetic message and because of it came to us, we would find the number surprisingly small, the percentage of our whole number very low.

There are more Christians in the denominations every year in spite of our message. There are probably a million persons converted in the world every year. The hope of ever bringing these Christians into our group is futile.

. . . One can be a member of a denomination and yet be wholly unsectarian. On the other hand, one can be undenominational or antidenominational and still be thoroughly sectarian. The task of reuniting Christians is a most difficult task, and it will take a long time; but it must be done by whatever means, and by all means, by which it can be accomplished.

I love our movement. I have given my life to it. I love its people. They are my dearest friends. I expect to end my days on earth in this movement and to contribute all I possibly can to its advancement. But I long to see it freed from the things that have impeded its progress and have caused it to be misunderstood. I am sure that better, richer, more glorious days lie ahead of us for we are making genuine progress and getting rid of many of the things that have stood in our way.

If we would stop preaching our theories of phophecy [sic] which few will ever believe, and with power preach salvation, righteous living, true unity, a spiritual church— and exemplify these things—we would prosper and be blessed as at no past time and our message would not be misunderstood as it has been so far. The way of victory is the way of simple, plain, gospel truth, loved, preached, and lived in the Bible way. If instead of being doctrine-centered or movement-centered we would become more and more Christ-centered, we would find many of our problems automatically solved and the glow of holy fervor would melt all hearts together. . . .

To sum up, if we should suddenly be taken out of the world as a movement, and there be no loss to Christianity or to society, then we have neither excuse nor reason to exist; but whatever losses of any and all sorts that would ensue from our going, the sum of those losses, for the present and future, is the sum of our reasons for our existence.

APPENDIX D

Shortly after Charles Naylor's booklet appeared, Andrew L. Byers, Warner's biographer, wrote a formal rebuttal against Naylor. In a letter to the editorial department of the *Gospel Trumpet*, Byers expressed his desire to be granted space in the periodical for a defense of Warner which would span several installments. The letter, dated 9 July 1950, was attached to the first of the proposed essays Byers intended to write. This installment was never published and there is no evidence that Byers did further work on the project. In 1976, the editor of *Vital Christianity* [successor to the *Gospel Trumpet*], Harold L. Phillips forwarded the Byers letter and essay to the Warner collection in the Church of God archives as an historical document. The underlining belongs to Byers.

IN VINDICATION OF D.S. WARNER AND HIS WORK

By Andrew L. Byers

Some months ago there was published a pamphlet entitled, 'The Teachings of D.S. Warner and His Associates,' the objective being, it seems, not simply a criticism of those teachings, but an attack intended to put them down and out, to undermine and destroy them completely. As I was an 'associate' of D.S. Warner and also the author of BIRTH OF A REFORMATION, LIFE AND LABORS OF D.S. WARNER, my teachings also fall a victim of this attack. As my life has been hanging in the balance because of a heart illness I promised God if he would spare me for the purpose I would say something about this apparent crisis. Well, God has spared me.

The author of the pamphlet has deceased since it was published and one dislikes to speak depreciatingly of such a one. But this sentiment must sometimes be laid aside. Brother Warner too has gone, and the message he gave his life for is being unworthily trampled under foot.

I knew our author intimately over a long period of years. He was my companion in song composition, and he had gifts on this line which helped to keep the quality of our hymnody on a high level. We have had none better than he. His whole effort was spent in the direction of the truth Brother Warner was advocating. And one appreciates this all the more and with the greater sympathy when it is remembered that for many years he was bedfast with pain and weakness. No doubt he was greatly comforted by many of his productions under those circumstances. His face would beam with joy if I happened along then, and he would want to read it to me at once.

But it must be said there were times when he could be quite harsh and outspoken in criticism. Yet if he could be shown where he was wrong he would accept the correction immediately.

But this time something went seriously wrong. Not so long ago he began to write perverse things about the church and to turn his back on the reformation truth he had always upheld. If individuals do not like the truth a man of God is teaching they have only to get together and start to discolor and misrepresent what he has SAID. This has always been a most effective weapon. This poor man lost his way and his flounderings have only brought error and confusion to his position.

He gives a peculiar twist to his argument. He draws our minds back to the times when he had the advantage of knowing Brother Warner personally and things which were being taught in those days, and he could 'follow our teachings closely in all the days since.' He speaks as if he had been at that time an opponent of Brother Warner and would have us believe that his knowing those things to point back to would help to show himself 'competent' NOW to speak judgingly of him. But the truth is he was NOT at that time an opponent of Brother Warner but was FOR him. Since then he has been composing such songs as <u>The Reformation Glory</u>, <u>The Church's Jubilee</u>, the 4th and 5th verses of <u>The Church Has One Foundation</u>, <u>Thy Children Are Gathering Home</u>, <u>I'll Never Go Back</u>, and other songs and writings of similar character. He wrote some splendid articles on the church during times when sectarian elements were showing themselves in some ministerial bodies and elsewhere in the movement. When he was writing those things he was not in a mood to judge Brother Warner because he was really for him. So his argument is spoiled and has no weight.

A PETTY ACCUSATION

One of the first and most prominent things in which he boasts of catching Brother Warner in the wrong is the latter's statement that the Lord showed him he would be alive when Jesus comes. Possibly he spoke this out of sheer enthusiasm without full regard to what he was saying. Anyway some of the early apostles almost said it. But note how Warner talked and wrote in his later and more sober reflections. In a hymn begun shortly before his death and called "The Last Hymn" (365 in the old SELECT HYMNS) he had composed one stanza and the first two lines of the chorus. Here they are:

'Shall my soul ascend with rapture
When the day of life is past?

> While my house of clay shall slumber,
> Shall I then with Jesus rest?'
> 'O my soul, press on to glory!
> Worlds of bliss invite thee on.'

A few of his poems show the same reflections.

Brother Warner was a chosen vessel of God if there ever was one. I first met him on a Saturday afternoon, April 7, 1888. By previous arrangement he and his evangelistic company had come to my home in Illinois to hold a series of meetings. I was eighteen then and had just arrived home on vacation from teaching in Iowa, and my father and I had gone that afternoon to engage a place for services. In Iowa I had made my decision for Christ by rising to my feet in a revival held by the 'River Brethren.' When Father and I returned from our trip that afternoon he introduced me to Brother Warner as having just been converted. The latter then said in all fervency of spirit and sincerity, 'Well, that's good news!' And as he continued talking to me there beamed from those soft blue eyes a something which pierced my soul with an illumination which has never left me. He made me feel for the first time in my life that salvation <u>is a thing of value and of joy to possess</u>.

I remained home for nearly three years and began preaching by helping to care for the little flock which had started there. Was ordained by A.B. Palmer in 1890. I attended the general camp meetings and of course continued to read the Gospel Trumpet which my parents had taken for many years. In February of 1891 I was called to join Brother Warner's singing company, who were then in Mississippi.

Some time after that, while visiting the Gospel Trumpet office at Grand Junction, Michigan, I felt certain inward movings that my work was to be with that institution. For thirty-one years that was my home, beginning at Grand Junction. As editor of the Trumpet, Brother Warner made it his home also when not engaged in meetings elsewhere, and I had opportunity many times over to know him thoroughly. He died there December 12, 1895.

BROTHER WARNER'S TEMPERAMENT

Brother Warner was one of the meekest and humblest of men and very easy to approach and converse with. Instances of his speaking rebukingly or with denunciation were when he would encounter evil and deceptive spirits in more or less open opposition to the truth, and sometimes in preaching, where it would be proper to do so. In his private life and deportment he was NEVER repulsive. In his counsel to other ministers I have heard him use such texts as Acts 14:1; 1 Cor.10:32 and 2 Cor.6:3. I shall not attempt to answer in detail all the wrong things taught in the pamphlet, but to set forth such general truth as will reveal the error.

HUMAN THINKING VERSUS DIVINE INTUITION

A new term is coming into the field of truth determination. It is the word 'think'. Such and such a brother is said to be a 'thinker'. It naturally suggests itself as a commendable thing, for we are given minds with which to think, so why not think? It seems to have no bearing on general education, but intrudes itself into the doctrinal field of human salvation, where it interferes with Christ's own prerogative and is expressly forbidden by him. Furthermore, by what standard would every one think? Would not every 'thinker' be thinking his own thoughts and with these find himself judging his own brother? It is the road to modernism.

If we go to Matthew 16, that chapter where the Christ-central scheme of salvation and the church is unfolded and called a 'rock', we shall find two classes of people brought into discussion through Jesus' question, 'Whom do men say that I the Son of man am?' (vs.13). St. Paul mentions the same two groups in 1 Cor.2:14, 15. The first group represents the thinkers, the New Testament counterpart of the modernists of today, who would deem it foolishness and quite impossible to conceive of Christ as really the Son of God; so they go the limit with their human thinking.

The other group, represented by Simon Peter and the disciples, replied to Jesus, 'Thou art the Christ, the Son of the living God.' Jesus then pronounced a blessing upon Peter because his answer was prompted by a REVELATION FROM THE FATHER and did not come by human agency ('FLESH AND BLOOD') or thinking. He said also that he was going to build his church (of course not your church or my church) on just such a rock principle of divine confession by heaven-born revelation and not by the agency of man. Was not this to be a divine intuition for all his followers? Note also what assurance this intuition affords—Peter was SURE of it! (See John 6:69 and Luke 1:77, 'to give KNOWLEDGE of salvation unto his people'. See also John 1:13, where all possible human element is sifted out from the series and only the divine retained.) What counts with God is not to be a 'thinker', but a RECEIVER, an open-hearted BELIEVER in the spiritual things of Christ.

Brother Warner was preaching a highly spiritual sermon on the line of perfect holiness through full consecration. It was in my home vicinity back in 1888. After he had finished my oldest brother came forward to greet Brother Warner and said, 'I guess I don't have brains enough to understand it.' He probably had been trying to <u>think</u> it out. Brother Warner then gently stroked my brother's cheeks and replied tenderly, 'God bless you, brother John, it doesn't take brains!' My brother ever after had the highest respect for and confidence in Brother Warner, though he did not continue a profession.

Peter and John, even as 'unlearned and ignorant men', were by this divine intuition equipped for leadership in the gospel such as none of the other early apostles were ever honored with. The Scribes and Pharisees marvelled at these men but remembered that 'they had been with Jesus'. They were thrown into prison for a night, then released and commanded under threat not to teach any more in the name of Jesus. Then came the aftermath. They went to their own company (of believers) and fell to such praying that the very place where they were gathered was shaken (Acts 4:31). Could that ever result from 'thinking?' They placed the responsibility upon the Lord and went ahead.

Now and then one hears, as if it were the announcement of a discovery, 'I tell you what this church needs is to become more Christ-centered! Good! How true! But listen—this Christ-centeredness' dwells right there in Matthew 16 where he makes known the divine secret of salvation and the church. Why not settle right there and stay instead of wandering again in the field of human 'thinking'?

One time when I was with Brother Warner in a southern state we spent the night together at a brother's house in a rural district. We had just experienced two molestations by a mob over in Mississippi. After dressing he suggested, 'Well, let's take a walk.' After strolling through the refreshing morning air amid sparsely-distributed woods we came to a place suitable for prayer. There he poured out his soul to God for spiritual anointing and strength for the work before him. Any one who has not heard Brother Warner in earnest prayer has missed a spiritual thrill. That was HIS method of keeping spiritually fed and fit.

APPENDIX E

A Selection of Hymns written by Daniel S. Warner

A = *Anthems from the Throne*, eds., Barney Warren and Daniel S. Warner
E = *Echoes from Glory*, eds., Barney Warren and Daniel S. Warner
S = *Songs of the Evening Light*, eds., Barney Warren and Andrew L. Byers
SE = *Salvation Echoes*, eds., Barney Warren, Andrew Byers, *et al.*
SV = *Songs of Victory*, ed., Joseph C. Fisher

A Hymn of Morning Praise A69
A Mansion in Glory E217
A Solemn Charge S64
Angels Gathering the Elect A90
Anthems from the Throne A1
Are you coming here tonight E155
Are you ready waiting E209
Awake O sinner A33

Beautiful Zion SE55
Behold the Dying Savior A12
Buried with Jesus A59

Captured by love SV45
Christ the friend we need E32
Church of God SE197
Come and be free A38
Come and be saved A38
Come to the Savior A6
Coming back to Salem SV18

Don't Resist the Holy Spirit SE102
Do you triumph E79

Endure Temptation E41
Escape the judgment day A64

Evening Praise E93
Everlasting Joy E20

Faith E23
Far Down, O'er the Ages E60
Farewell to sin E153
Fill me with thy spirit E172
Fire in the soul A26
Flee to the cross E124
Flee to the refuge A7
From Time to Eternity SE43

God of mercy E108
God is love A52
Gone to bloom above E213

Great peace SV50
Good news to all E118
Guide us with thine eye E174

Happy little saints S122
Have you thought of heaven A34
Hear the voice of our commander E34
Hear ye the moan E166
Here we meet E232

His yoke is easy E26
Holy fellowship A85
How often I've pondered E192
How sweet is my walk with Jesus E45

I am a child of the king E97
I am going home today A15
I know my name is there E221
I lost my life for Jesus E109
I ought to love my savior E144
I wake to sober thought E80
I will trust in thee E36
I will trust thee SV38
If thou wilt know the fountain S231
I'll say the great word S193
I'm beginning in this life A74
I'm sitting with Jesus S27
In the heart of my God SV20
In the holy hand A54
In the light of God E17
It is well with my soul E74
I've found a friend in Jesus E21
I've found it lord in thee E4
I've found my lord S248

Jesus all to me E3
Jesus will save A76
Joy in the service of the master E2
Joyful meeting in glory A16

Knock and it shall be opened A82

Land of bliss E220

Lift up your hands and sing A2
Listen sinner E168
Lo! heaven now opens E197
Lonely I ponder E147
Louder, louder S51
Love is freedoms law A49
Low at his feet E171

Morning hymn S219
Mother has gone home A73
My soul is satisfied E81

No peace to the wicked A11
Not saved by works A89
Now my pilgrim toils are over E203

O, careless sinner E116
O lord thou healest me A72
Obedience A84
O'er the door E162
Our God is love S130
Oh how can anyone refuse E194
Oh praise the lord E6
O worship God E110
Oh ye pilgrims E122
Only Christ I owe S54
Only thine E173

Perishing souls E125
Praise the lord E99
Praise the lord! SV68
Prayer E69
Precious Bible E62
Prophetic truth E190
Pure river of peace A67

Rays of hope E225
Redeemed, redeemed E33
Reigning in this life S124
Rejoicing E98
Rejoicing evermore A56
Repent A80
Resting in Jesus E28
River of Peace E83

Safe on the rock E12
Salvation E52
Salvation is flowing E67
Say it again E95

Sing an invitation SV35

Appendices

Sing of salvation A13
Sing the love of Jesus SV41
Singing joyful praise A4
Sitting at the feet of Jesus S225
Something for children to do S128
Sowing seeds of love E61
Sowing the seeds A78
Sweet haven of love A46

Table hymn S120
Take my yoke E131
Tell me pilgrim E195
That's enough for me E48
The angel choir S181
The angel of mercy A5
The awful question A81
The bond of perfectness E5
The children's meeting S144
The church triumphant E185
The crucifixion scene A14
The curse of rum E120
The evening is glorious A58
The evening light S1
The fight of faith A21
The golden morning E208
The gospel trumpet SV80
The great sacrifice E186
The hand of God on the wall A70
The holy of holies E11
The holy remnant E182
The home of the soul S10
The immortal soul A30
The kingdom of God E159
The kingdom of heaven E46
The last great day E215
The last hymn S56
The lord is coming S2
The lord is my shepherd E88
The lost alien E156
The love of Jesus E160
The music of his name E91
The new campground E104
The new Jerusalem E189

The redemption story S78
The resurrection morn E210
The royal servant E199
The sea of glass A17
The shield of faith E19
The spirit and the bride say come A8
The temple of God E49
The universe is God's domain E117
The valley of decision A77
The valley of judgment E178
The white horse calvary S48
The wonderful change A44
The world in awful sleep E158
There we'll sing a nobler song A25
There's a fountain of blood E16
There's an awful day E167
There's mercy poor sinner E165
There's music in my soul E100
This is why I love my savior E51
Thy precious soul E129
Tidings of a happy land E218
Time enough E132
Time onward plows E204
Two little hands E207
Trusting in Jesus E53

Unheeding winters cruel blast E90

Waiting for the lord A19
We must be holy E76
We stand upon the sea of glass E193
We tread upon the awful verge E121
We will work for Jesus S36
We're a happy pilgrim band E107
What manner of love A68
When lost in the darkness of sin E35
When we pass the golden summer E230
Where shall we look E59
While sleeping careless E163
Whiter than snow in the blood A31
Who are the happy people E24
Who shall dwell with Christ S201

Who will meet me there? A53
Who will suffer for Jesus? E169
Whosoever will may come A87
We know our home above A88
Why should a mortal complain? SV9
Will you go with us to heaven E73
Will you have a crown E217
Wisdom crieth in the streets E123
Won by dying love A71
Wonderful fountain E39

BIBLIOGRAPHY

Abzug, Robert H. *Cosmos Crumbling: American Reform and the Religious Imagination*. New York and Oxford: Oxford University Press, 1994.
Adams, Dickenson W., ed. *The Papers of Thomas Jefferson*, second series. Princeton: Princeton University Press, 1983.
Adams, Robert A. 'Hymnody of the Church of God (1885-1980) as a Reflection of that Church's Theological and Cultural Change'. unpublished thesis, Southwestern Baptist Theological Seminary, Fort Worth, Texas, 1980.
Adamson, Christopher. 'God's Continent Divided: Politics and Religion in Upper Canada and the Northern and Western United States, 1775 to 1841'. *Comparative Studies in Society and History* 36 (1994): 417-46.
Albanese, Catherine L. 'Savage, Sinner, and Saved: Davy Crockett, Camp Meetings, and the Wild Frontier'. *American Quarterly* 33 (No. 5, 1981): 482-501.
Asbury, Francis. *The Journal and Letters of Francis Asbury*. 3 volumes. eds., Elmer T. Clark, J. Manning Potts and Jacob S. Payton. London and Nashville: Epworth Press and Abingdon Press, 1958.
Asworth, John. *Slavery, Capitalism, and Politics in the Antebellum Republic*. Volume 1: *Commerce and Compromise, 1820-1850*. Cambridge: Cambridge University Press, 1995.
Balmer, Randall H. 'From Frontier Phenomenon to Victorian Institution: The Methodist Camp Meeting in Ocean Grove, New Jersey'. *Methodist History* 25 (No. 3, 1987): 194-200.
Banner, Lois W. 'Religious Benevolence as Social Control: A Critique of an Interpretation'. *The Journal of American History* 60 (No. 1, 1973): 23-41.
Barkun, Michael. *Crucible of the Millennium: The Burned-Over District of New York in the 1840s*. Syracuse: Syracuse University Press, 1986.
Barnes, Gilbert H. and Dwight L. Drumond, eds. *Letters of Theodore Dwight Weld, Angelina Grimké Weld and Sarah Grimké, 1822-1844*. 2 vols. New York and London: D. Appleton-Century Company, Inc., 1934.
Barlow, Philip. *Mormons and the Bible: The Place of the Latter-day Saints in American Religion*. New York and Oxford: Oxford University Press, 1991.
Bass, Dorothy C. 'Sex Roles, Sexual Symbolism, and Social Change: A Study in Religious Popular Culture of Nineteenth-Century American Women'. *Radical Religion* 4 (No. 1, 1978): 21-7.

Bassett, Paul M. 'A Study in the Theology of the Early Holiness Movement'. *Methodist History* 13 (April 1975): 61-84.

_____. 'Culture and Concupiscence: The Changing Definition of Sanctity in the Wesleyan Holiness Movement, 1867-1920'. *Wesleyan Theological Journal* 28 (Nos. 1-2, 1993): 59-127.

Berry, Robert L. *Golden Jubilee Book*. Anderson: Gospel Trumpet Company, 1931.

Billington, Ray Allen. *The Protestant Crusade 1800-1860: A Study of the Origins of American Nativism*. Chicago: Quadrangle, 1964.

Bloch, Ruth L. 'The Social and Political Base of Millennial Literature in Late Eighteenth-Century America'. *American Quarterly* 40 (No. 3, 1988): 378-96.

Bolitho, Axchie A. *To the Chief Singer: A Brief Story of the Work and Influence of Barney E. Warren*. Anderson: Gospel Trumpet Company, 1942.

Boyer, Paul. *When Time Shall Be No More: Prophecy and Belief in Modern American Culture*. Cambridge: The Belknap Press of Harvard University Press, 1992.

Brauer, Jerald C. 'Regionalism and Religion in America'. *Church History* 54 (No. 3, 1985): 366-78.

Brendlinger, Irv A. 'A Study of the Views of Major Eighteenth-Century Evangelicals on Slavery and Race, with special attention to John Wesley'. unpublished Ph.D. dissertation, University of Edinburgh, 1982.

Brooks, John P. *The Divine Church*. New York and London: Garland Publishing, Inc., 1984.

Brown, Charles E. *When the Trumpet Sounded: A History of the Church of God Reformation Movement*. Anderson: Warner Press, 1951.

_____. *When Souls Awaken: An Interpretation of Radical Christianity*. Anderson: Gospel Trumpet Company, 1954.

Brown, Ira V. 'Watchers for the Second Coming: The Millenarian Tradition in America'. *The Mississippi Valley Historical Review* 39 (No. 3, 1952): 441-58.

Brown, Kenneth O. *Holy Ground: A Study of the American Camp Meeting*. New York and London: Garland Publishing, Inc., 1992.

Bruce, Dickson D. Jr. *And They All Sang Hallelujah: Plain-Folk Camp Meeting Religion, 1800-1845*. Knoxville: The University of Tennessee Press, 1974.

Byrum, Enoch E. *Life Experiences*. Anderson: Gospel Trumpet Company, 1928.

Buell, Lawrence. 'The Unitarian Movement and the Art of Preaching in 19th Century America'. *American Quarterly* 24 (No. 2, 1972): 166-90.

Bundy, David. 'The Historiography of the Wesleyan/Holiness Tradition'. *Wesleyan Theological Journal* 30 (No. 1, 1995): 55-77.

Bushman, Richard L. 'The Book of Mormon and the American Revolution'. *Brigham Young University Studies* 17 (1976): 3-20.

Butler, Diana Hochstedt. 'The Church and American Destiny: Evangelical Episcopalians and Voluntary Societies in Antebellum America'. *Religion and American Culture* 4 (No. 2, 1994): 193-219.

Butler, Jon. 'Enthusiasm Described and Decried: The Great Awakening as Interpretive Fiction'. *The Journal of American History* 69 (No. 2, 1982): 305-25.

Byers, Andrew L. *Birth of a Reformation or the Life and Labors of Daniel S. Warner*. Anderson: Gospel Trumpet Company, 1921.

_____. 'Pioneers of the Present Reformation.' *Gospel Trumpet* (5 February 1920): 18-19.

_____. 'In Vindication of D.S. Warner and his Work', MS., 1950. The A.L. (Andrew L.) Byers Papers, Archives of the Church of God, Anderson University, Anderson, Indiana. Archives B620 1995.

Byrum, Enoch E. 'Customs and Traditions'. *Gospel Trumpet* (1 July 1915): 3, 11-12.

Callen, Barry L. *It's God's Church! The Life and Ministry of Daniel Warner*. Anderson: Warner Press, 1995.

_____. ed. *A Time to Remember: Beginnings* (Church of God Heritage Series, volume 1). Anderson: Warner Press, 1977.

_____. ed. *A Time to Remember: Testimonies* (Church of God Heritage series, volume 2). Anderson: Warner Press, 1978.

_____. ed. *A Time to Remember: Teachings* (Church of God Heritage Series, volume 3). Anderson: Warner Press, 1978.

_____. 'Church of God Reformation Movement (Anderson, Indiana): A Study in Ecumenical Idealism'. unpublished Masters thesis, Asbury Theological Seminary, 1969.

_____. 'Daniel Sydney [sic] Warner: Joining Holiness and all Truth'. *Wesleyan Theological Journal* 30 (No. 1, 1995): 92-110.

_____. *Contours of a Cause: The Theological Vision of the Church of God Movement (Anderson)*. Anderson: Anderson University School of Theology, 1995.

Cannon, William R. 'John Wesley's Doctrine of Sanctification and Perfection'. *Mennonite Quarterly Review* 35 (No. 2, 1961): 91-5.

Cartwright, Peter. *Autobiography of Peter Cartwright*. ed., Charles L. Wallis. Nashville: Abingdon Press, 1984.

Carwardine, Richard. *Trans-Atlantic Revivalism: Popular Evangelicalism in Britain and America, 1790-1865*. London and Westport: Greenwood Press, 1978.

_____. *Evangelicals and Politics in Antebellum America*. New Haven and London: Yale University Press, 1993.

_____. 'The Second Great Awakening in the Urban Centers: An Examination of Methodism and the New Measures' *Journal of American History* 59 (No. 2, 1972): 327-40.

Chrisman, Richard A. 'Peter Cartwright as a Presiding Elder'. *Methodist History* 27 (No. 3, 1989): 151-62.

Clark, Christopher. *The Roots of Rural Capitalism: Western Massachusetts, 1780-1860*. Ithaca and London: Cornell University Press, 1990.
Clarke, Clifford E. *Henry Ward Beecher: Spokesman for a Middle Class America*. Urbana: University of Illinois Press, 1978.
Clear, Valorous B. *Where the Saints Have Trod: A Social History of the Church of God Reformation Movement*. Chesterfield, IN: Midwest Publications, 1977.
Conkin, Paul K. *Cane Ridge: America's Pentecost*. Madison: University of Wisconsin Press, 1990.
Cooley, Steven D. 'Applying the Vagueness of Language: Poetic Strategies and Campmeeting Piety in the Mid-Nineteenth Century'. *Church History* 63 (No. 4, 1994): 570-86.
Coppedge, Allan. 'Entire Sanctification in Early American Methodism: 1812-1835'. *Wesleyan Theological Journal* 13 (Spring 1978): 34-50.
Corbin, J. Wesley. 'Christian Perfection and the Evangelical Association through 1875'. *Methodist History* 7 (No. 2, 1969): 28-44.
Coward, S.L.C. *Entire Santification from 1739 to 1900*. Louisville: Pentecostal Herald Press, 1900.
Cowing, Cedric B. 'Sex and Preaching in the Great Awakening'. *American Quarterly* 20 (No. 3, 1968): 624-44.
Cox, Leo George. *John Wesley's Concept of Perfection*. Kansas City, MO: Beacon Hill Press, 1964.
Cross, Barbara, ed. *The Autobiography of Lyman Beecher*. 2 vols. Cambridge: Belknap Press, 1961.
Cunningham, Raymond J. 'From Holiness to Healing: The Faith Cure in America 1872-1892'. *Church History* 43 (No. 4, 1974): 499-513.
Davis, David Brion. *The Problem of Slavery in the age of Revolution, 1770-1823*. Ithaca and London: Cornell University Press, 1975.
Davidson, Robert. *History of the Presbyterian Church in the State of Kentucky; with a preliminary Sketch of the churches in the valley of Virginia*. New York: Robert Carter, 1847.
Dayton, Donald W. 'Asa Mahan and the Development of American Holiness Theology'. *Wesleyan Theological Journal* 9 (Spring 1974): 60-9.
_____, ed. *Holiness Tracts defending the ministry of Women*. New York and London: Garland Publishing Inc., 1985.
Dieter, Melvin E. *The Holiness Revival of the Nineteenth Century*. Metuchen, NJ: The Scarecrow Press, Inc., 1980.
_____. 'Primitivism in the American Holiness Tradition'. *Wesleyan Theological Journal* 30 (No. 1, 1995): 78-91.
_____. 'The Development of Nineteenth Century Holiness Theology'. *Wesleyan Theological Journal* 20 (No. 1, 1985): 61-77.
Dillenberger, John. *The Visual Arts and Christianity in America*. New York: Crossroad Publishing Company, 1988.

Doan, Ruth Alden. *The Miller Heresy, Millennialism, and American Culture*. Philadelphia: Temple University Press, 1987.
Dolan, Jay P. *The Immigrant Church: New York's Irish and German Catholics, 1815-1865*. Baltimore: The Johns Hopkins Press, 1975.
Dorr, Donal J. 'Wesley's Teaching on the Nature of Holiness'. *The London Quarterly and Holborn Review* 190 (1965): 234-9.
Dow, Lorenzo. *The Dealings of God, Man, and the Devil; as exemplified in the Life, Experience, and Travels of Lorenzo Dow, in a period of over half a century: Together with his Polemic and Miscellaneous Writings, Complete. To which is added the Vicissitudes of Life by Peggy Dow*. 2 volumes. New York: Sheldon, Lamport & Blakeman, 1856.
Dunlop, Dale E. 'Tuesday Meetings, Camp Meetings, and Cabinet Meetings: A Perspective on the Holiness Movement in the Methodist Church in the United States in the Nineteenth Century'. *Methodist History* 13 (April 1975): 85-106.
Dvorak, Katherine L. 'Peter Cartwright and Charisma'. *Methodist History* 26 (No. 2, 1988): 113-26.
Eaton, S.J.M. *History of the Presbytery of Erie; Embracing in its Ancient Boundaries the whole of Northwestern Pennsylvania and Northwestern Ohio, with Biographical Sketches of all its Ministers, etc.* New York: Hurd and Houghton, 1868.
Elliott, Daryl M. 'Entire Sanctification and the Church of the United Brethren in Christ to 1860'. *Methodist History* 24 (No. 4, 1987): 203-21.
Endy, Melvin B. Jr. 'Just War, Holy War, and Millennialism in Revolutionary America'. *The William and Mary Quarterly*, third series 42 (No. 1, 1985): 3-25.
Eslinger, Ellen T. 'The Great Revival in Bourbon County, Kentucky'. unpublished Ph.D. dissertation, University of Chicago, 1988.
Farish, Hunter Dickinson. *The Circuit Rider Dismounts: A Social History of Southern Methodism 1865-1900*. New York: Da Carpo Press, 1969.
Faust, Clarence H. and Thomas H. Johnson, eds. *Jonathan Edwards: Representative Selections*. New York: Hill and Wang, 1962.
Fick, Edward W.H. 'John Wesley's Teaching on Perfection'. *Andrews University Seminary Studies* 4 (1966): 201-17.
Findlay, James. 'Agency, Denominations and the Western Colleges, 1830-1860: Some Connections Between Evangelicalism and American Higher Education'. *Church History* 50 (No. 1, 1981): 64-80.
Finke, Roger and Rodney Stark. 'Turning Pews into People: Estimating 19th Century Church Membership'. *Journal for the Scientific Study of Religion* 25 (No. 2, 1986): 180-92.
Finley, James B. *Autobiography of Rev. James B. Finley or, Pioneer Life in the West*. Cincinnati: Cranston and Curts; New York: Hunt and Eaton, 1853.

Finney, Charles G. *Sermons on Various Subjects*. New York: Taylor & Gould, 1835.
_____. *Lectures on Systematic Theology*. ed., J.H. Fairchild. South Gate, CA: Colporter Kemp, 1944.
_____. *Lectures on Revivals of Religion*. Oberlin: E.J. Goodrich, 1868.
_____. *Lectures to Professing Christians*. New York: Fleming H. Revell, 1878.
_____. *Sermons on Gospel Themes*. Oberlin: E.J. Goodrich, 1876.
_____. *Sermons on the Way of Salvation*. Oberlin: E.J. Goodrich, 1891.
Fisher, Joseph C., ed. *Songs of Victory*. fourth edition. Grand Junction, 1885.
_____. '"Vision and Interpretation" by the Lord'. *Gospel Trumpet* (1 September 1884).
Fogarty, Robert S. *All Things New: American Communes and Utopian Movements, 1869-1914*. Chicago and London: University of Chicago Press, 1990.
_____. 'Oneida: A Utopian Search for Religious Security'. *Labor History* 14 (No. 2, 1973): 202-27.
Foner, Philip S. *The Factory Girls*. Urbana, University of Illinois Press, 1977.
Forney, C [hristian]. H [enry]. *History of the Churches of God in the United States of North America*. Harrisburg, PA: Publishing House of the Churches of God, 1914.
Forrest, Aubrey L. 'A Study of the Development of the Basic Doctrines and Institutional Patterns in the Church of God (Anderson, Indiana).' unpublished Ph.D. dissertation, University of Southern California, 1948.
Foster, Lawrence. *Religion and Sexuality: Three American Communal Experiments of the Nineteenth Century*. New York and Oxford: Oxford University Press, 1981.
Fudge, Thomas A. and Laurie L. Moore, 'Daniel and Sarah Warner: Witnesses of the Evening Light'. unpublished paper, 1995.
Gaustad, Edwin. 'Regionalism in American Religion'. in *Religion in the South*. pp. 155-72. ed. Charles Reagan Wilson. Jackson: University of Mississippi Press, 1985.
_____. *Historical Atlas of Religion in America*. New York: Harper & Row, Publishers, 1976.
_____, ed. *The Rise of Adventism: Religion and Society in Mid-Nineteenth-Century America*. New York: Harper & Row, Publishers, 1974.
_____. *Sworn on the Altar of God: A Religious Biography of Thomas Jefferson*. Grand Rapids: William B. Eerdmans, 1996.
George, Carol V.R. *Segregated Sabbaths: Richard Allen and the Rise of the Independent Black Churches, 1760-1840*. New York: Oxford University Press, 1973.
German, James D. 'The Social Utility of Wicked Self-Love: Calvinism, Capitalism, and Public Policy in Revolutionary New England'. *The Journal of American History* 82 (No. 3, 1995): 965-98.

Gladden, Washington. *Burning Questions of the life that now is, and of which is to come*. New York: The Century Co., 1891.

Goodwin, Charles H. 'The Greatest Itinerant Francis Asbury 1745-1816'. *Proceedings of the Wesley Historical Society* 50 (May 1995): 47-53.

Gospel Trumpet [*Vital Christianity*], 1881-1996.

Gossard, J. Harvey. 'John Winebrenner: Founder, Reformer, and Businessman'. in *Pennsylvania Religious Leaders*, pp. 87-101. ed., John M. Coleman, John B. Frantz and Robert G. Crist. [Pennsylvania History Studies: No. 16]. University Park, PA: The Pennsylvania Historical Association, 1986.

Graham, Stephen R. *Cosmos in the Chaos: Philip Schaff's Interpretation of Nineteenth-Century American Religion*. Grand Rapids and Cambridge: William B. Eerdmans, 1995.

Gray, Albert F. 'Distinctive Features of the Present Movement'. *Gospel Trumpet* (23 February 1922): 5-6.

Green, Della J. 'In Memory of Bro. D.S. Warner'. *Gospel Trumpet* (19 December 1895).

Green, Roger Joseph. 'Charles Grandison Finney: The Social Implications of his Ministry'. *The Asbury Theological Journal* 48 (No. 2, 1993): 5-26.

Greene, Jack P. and J.R. Pole, eds. *Colonial British America: Essays in the New History of the Early Modern Era*. Baltimore: The Johns Hopkins University Press, 1984.

Griffin, Clifford S. 'Religious Benevolence as Social Control, 1815-1860'. *The Mississippi Valley Historical Review* 44 (No. 3, 1957): 423-44.

Hackett, David G. 'Gender and Religion in American Culture, 1870-1930'. *Religion and American Culture* 5 (No. 2, 1995): 127-57.

Hall, David D. *Worlds of Wonder, Days of Judgment: Popular Religious Belief in Early New England*. New York: Alfred A. Knopf, 1989.

_____. *Cultures of Print: Essays in the History of the Book*. Amherst: University of Massachusetts Press, 1996.

Hambrick-Stowe, Charles E. *Charles G. Finney and the Spirit of American Evangelicalism*. Grand Rapids and Cambridge: William B. Eerdmans, 1996.

Hamilton, James E. 'Nineteenth Century Philosophy and Holiness Theology: A Study in the Thought of Asa Mahan'. *Wesleyan Theological Journal* 13 (Spring 1978): 51-64.

Hammond, John L. 'Revivals, Consensus, and the American Political Culture'. *Journal of the American Academy of Religion* 46 (No. 3, 1978): 293-314.

Handlin, Oscar. *The Uprooted*. Boston: Little, Brown, 1951.

Handy, Robert T. 'American Methodism and its Historic Frontier: Interpreting Methodism on the Western Frontier: Between Romanticism and Realism'. *Methodist History* 23 (No. 1, 1984): 44-53.

Hardesty, Nancy. *Great Women of Faith: The Strength and Influence of Christian Women*. Grand Rapids: Baker Book House, 1980.

Hardesty, Nancy. *Women Called to Witness: Evangelical Feminism in the 19th Century*. Nashville: Abingdon Press, 1984.

Hardman, Keith J. *Charles Grandison Finney 1792-1875: Revivalist and Reformer*. Syracuse: Syracuse University Press, 1987.

Hatch, Nathan O. *The Democratization of American Christianity*. New Haven and London: Yale University Press, 1989.

_____. 'The Origins of Civil Millennialism in America: New England Clergymen, War with France and the Revolution'. *The William and Mary Quarterly*, third series 31 (No. 3, 1974): 407-30.

_____. 'The Christian Movement and the Demand for a Theology of the People'. *The Journal of American History* 67 (No. 3, 1980): 545-67.

_____. *The Sacred Cause of Liberty: Republican Thought and the Millennium in Revolutionary New England*. New Haven and London: Yale University Press, 1977.

_____. 'The Puzzle of American Methodism'. *Church History* 63 (No. 2, 1994): 175-89.

_____, and Mark A. Noll, eds. *The Bible in America: Essays in Cultural History*. New York and Oxford: Oxford University Press, 1982.

Hayden, Dolores. *Seven American Utopias: The Architecture of Communitarian Socialism, 1790-1915*. Cambridge, MA and London: The MIT Press, 1976.

Heisey, Terry. 'Singet Hallelujah! Music in the Evangelical Association, 1800-1894'. *Methodist History* 28 (No. 4, 1990): 237-51.

Herbert, T. Walter. *Moby-Dick and Calvinism: A World Dismantled*. New Brunswick, NJ: Rutgers University Press, 1977.

Hetrick, Gale. *Laughter Among the Trumpets: A History of the Church of God in Michigan*. Lansing: Church of God in Michigan, 1980.

Hewitt, Glenn A. *Regeneration and Morality: A Study of Charles Finney, Charles Hodge, John W. Nevin, and Horace Bushnell*. Brooklyn: Carlson Publishers, Inc., 1991.

Hill, E.J. 'A Visit to Grand Junction'. *Gospel Trumpet* (7 January 1892).

Hill, Marvin S. 'Cultural Crisis in the Mormon Kingdom: A Reconsideration of the Causes of the Kirtland Dissent'. *Church History* 49 (No. 3, 1980): 286-97.

Hills, Margaret T., ed. *The English Bible in America: A Bibliography of Editions of the Bible & the New Testament Published in America 1777-1957*. New York: American Bible Society and The New York Public Library, 1961.

Hovet, Theodore. 'Phoebe Palmer's "altar phraseology" and the Spiritual Dimension of Women's Sphere'. *The Journal of Religion* 63 (No. 3, 1983): 264-80.

Howard, Ivan. 'Wesley versus Phoebe Palmer: An Extended Controversy'. *Wesleyan Theological Journal* 6 (No. 1, 1971): 31-40.

Howard, John Alan. 'The Chronology of the Development of Daniel Sidney Warner's Belief in Holiness and Sanctification with Special Attention Given to his Library and Reading Concerning the Subjects of Holiness and Sanctification plus a section including Bibliographical Listings and General Observations regarding the D.S. Warner Private Library Collection'. Archives, Anderson University. unpublished paper, 1970.

Howe, David Walker. 'The Decline of Calvinism: An Approach to its Study' *Comparative Studies in Society and History* 14 (No. 3, 1972): 306-27.

Hudson, Winthrop S. *Religion in America*. fourth edition. New York: MacMillan Publishing Company, 1987.

Hughes, Richard. 'The Apocalyptic Origins of Churches of Christ and the Triumph of Modernism'. *Religion and American Culture* 2 (No. 2, 1992): 181-214.

Irwin, Joyce, ed. *Sacred Sound: Music in Religious Thought and Practice*. Chico, CA: Scholars Press, 1983.

Johnson, Benton. 'Do Holiness Sects Socialize in Dominant Values?' *Social Forces* 39 (No. 4, 1961): 309-16.

Johnson, Charles A. 'The Frontier Camp Meeting: Contemporary and Historical Appraisals, 1805-1840'. *The Mississippi Valley Historical Review* 37 (No. 1, 1950): 91-110.

_____. 'Camp Meeting Hymnody'. *American Quarterly* 4 (No. 2, 1952): 110-26.

_____. *The Frontier Camp Meeting: Religion's Harvest Time*. second edition. Dallas: Southern Methodist University Press, 1985.

Johnson, Curtis D. *Islands of Holiness: Rural Religion in Upstate New York, 1790-1860*. Ithaca and London: Cornell University Press, 1989.

Johnson, Frank E. '"Inspired by Grace": Methodist Itinerants in the Early Midwest'. *Methodist History* 35 (No. 2, 1997): 81-94.

Johnson, James E. 'Charles G. Finney and a Theology of Revivalism'. *Church History* 38 (No. 3, 1969): 338-58.

Johnson, Paul. *A Shopkeeper's Millennium: Society and Revivals in Rochester, New York, 1815-1837*. New York: Hill and Wang, 1978.

_____, and Sean Wilentz. *The Kingdom of Matthias*. New York and Oxford: Oxford University Press, 1994.

Jones, Charles E. *Perfectionist Persuasion: The Holiness Movement and American Methodism, 1867-1936*. Metuchen, NJ: The Scarecrow Press, Inc., 1974.

_____. *A Guide to the Study of the Holiness Movement*. Metuchen: The Scarecrow Press, Inc., 1974.

_____. 'The Inverted Shadow of Phoebe Palmer'. *Wesleyan Theological Journal* 31 (No. 2, 1996): 120-31.

Jones, Maldwyn Allen. *American Immigration*. second edition. Chicago and London: The University of Chicago Press, 1992.

Joyce, William L., David D. Hall, Richard D. Brown and John B. Hench, eds. *Printing and Society in Early America*. Worcester, MA: American Antiquarian Society, 1983.

Kern, Richard. *John Winebrenner: Nineteenth-Century Reformer*. Harrisburg, PA: Central Publishing House, 1974.

Kettner, James H. *The Development of American Citizenship, 1608-1870*. Chapel Hill: University of North Carolina Press, 1978.

Koeth, Robert E. 'A History of Anti-Catholicism in the Church of God Reformation Movement'. unpublished M.A. thesis, School of Theology, Anderson College, 1983.

Kostlevy, William. *Holiness Manuscripts: A Guide to Sources Documenting the Wesleyan Holiness Movement in the United States and Canada*. Metuchen and London: The American Theological Library Association and The Scarecrow Press, Inc., 1994.

Land, Gary, ed. *Adventism in America: A History*. Grand Rapids: William B. Eerdmans, 1986.

Licht, Walter. *Industrializing America: The Nineteenth Century*. Baltimore and London: The Johns Hopkins University Press, 1995.

Life Sketches of Mother Sarah Smith. Anderson: Gospel Trumpet Company, n.d.

Lippy, Charles H. 'The Camp Meeting in Transition: The Character and Legacy of the Late Nineteenth Century'. *Methodist History* 34 (No. 1, 1995): 3-17.

Loetscher, Lefferts A. 'The Problem of Christian Unity in Nineteenth-Century America'. *Church History* 32 (No. 1, 1963): 3-16.

Luchetti, Cathy. *Under God's Spell: Frontier Evangelists 1772-1915*. New York: Harcourt Brace Jovanovich, Publishers, 1989.

Lyman, R.W. 'Idolatry Exposed'. *Gospel Trumpet* (1 June 1884).

Madden, Edward H. and James E. Hamilton. *Freedom and Grace: The Life of Asa Mahan*. Metuchen and London: The Scarecrow Press, Inc., 1982.

Maddox, Randy L. *Responsible Grace: John Wesley's Practical Theology*. Nashville: Kingswood Books, Abingdon Press, 1994.

_____. ed. *Aldersgate Reconsidered*. Nashville: Kingswood Books, 1990.

Mahan, Asa. *The Baptism of the Holy Ghost*. New York: Palmer & Hughes, 1870.

_____. *Scripture Doctrine of Christian Perfection*. Boston: D.S. King, 1839.

Marks, Lynne. *Revivals and Roller Rinks: Religion, Leisure, and Identity in Late-Nineteenth-Century Small-Town Ontario*. Toronto: University of Toronto Press, 1996.

Marini, Stephen A. *Radical Sects of Revolutionary New England*. Cambridge, MA: Harvard University Press, 1982.

Marsden, George M. *Fundamentalism and American Culture: The Shaping of Twentieth-Century Evangelicalism 1870-1925*. New York and Oxford: Oxford University Press, 1980.

_____. *The Soul of the American University: From Protestant Establishment to Established Nonbelief*. Oxford /New York: Oxford University Press, 1994.

Marsden, George M. and Bradley J. Longfield, eds., *The Secularization of the Academy*. Oxford and New York: Oxford University Press, 1992.

Marty, Martin E. *Pilgrims in Their Own Land: 500 Years of Religion in America*. Boston and Toronto: Little, Brown and Company, 1984.

Matthews, Donald G. 'The Second Great Awakening as an Organizing Process, 1780-1830: An Hypothesis'. *American Quarterly* 21 (No. 1, 1969): 23-43.

McDonald, William and John E. Searles. *The Life of Rev. John S. Inskip, President of the National Association for the Promotion of Holiness*. Boston: McDonald & Gill, 1885.

McFadden, Margaret. 'The Ironies of Pentecost: Phoebe Palmer, World Evangelism, and Female Networks'. *Methodist History* 31 (No. 2, 1993): 63-75.

McLoughlin, William G. *Revivals, Awakenings, and Reform*. Chicago and London: The University of Chicago Press, 1978.

_____. *New England Dissent, 1630-1833: The Baptists and the Separation of Church and State*. 2 volumes. Cambridge: Harvard University Press, 1971.

_____. *Modern Revivalism: Charles Grandison Finney to Billy Graham*. New York: The Ronald Press Company, 1959.

_____. *The Meaning of Henry Ward Beecher: An Essay on the Shifting Values of Mid-Victorian America, 1840-1870*. New York: Knopf, 1970.

Moore, R. Lawrence. 'Religion, Secularization, and the Shaping of the Culture Industry in Antebellum America'. *American Quarterly* 41 (No. 2, 1989): 216-42.

_____. *Religious Outsiders and the Making of Americans*. New York and Oxford: Oxford University Press, 1986.

Moorhead, James H. 'Between Progress and Apocalypse: A Reassessment of Millennialism in American Religious Thought, 1800-1880'. *The Journal of American History* 71 (No. 3, 1984): 524-42.

Morgan, Douglas. 'Adventism, Apocalyptic, and the Cause of Liberty'. *Church History* 63 (No. 2, 1994): 235-49.

Morgan, Edmund S. *The Challenge of the American Revolution*. New York: W.W. Norton & Company, 1976.

Morrow, Ralph E. *Northern Methodism and Reconstruction*. East Lansing: Michigan State University Press, 1956.

Morse, James King. *Jedidiah Morse: A Champion of New England Orthodoxy*. New York: AMS Press, 1967.

Naylor, C.W. *The Teachings of D.S. Warner and his Associates*. Privately published, n.d. [1949]

_____. 'Heart Talks: Some Questions about the Church'. *Gospel Trumpet* (28 February 1929): 11-13.

_____. 'Some Thoughts for Consideration'. [unpublished paper on the church]. Archives, Anderson University, Anderson, Indiana.

Naylor, Charles W. 'What Shall the Church Do?' Article II 'The Church and Education'. unpublished paper. Archives, Anderson University, Anderson, Indiana.

Neidert, David L. 'Reformation's Song'. unpublished manuscript. Anderson University, 1985.

Nevin, John W. *Anti-christ; or the Spirit of Sect and Schism*. New York: John S. Taylor, 1848.

Nichols, James Hastings, ed. *The Mercersburg Theology*. New York: Oxford University Press, 1966.

Niebuhr, H. Richard. *The Social Sources of Denominationalism*. New York: Meridian Books, 1957.

Noll, Mark A. *A History of Christianity in the United States and Canada*. Grand Rapids: William B. Eerdmans, 1992.

_____. 'Common Sense Traditions and American Evangelical Thought'. *American Quarterly* 37 (No. 2, 1985): 216-38.

_____. *Princeton and the Republic 1768-1822*. Princeton: Princeton University Press, 1989.

_____. ed. *Religion and American Politics*. Oxford and New York: Oxford University Press, 1990.

_____, David W. Bebbington and George A. Rawlyk, eds. *Evangelicalism: Comparative Studies of Popular Protestantism in North America, the British Isles, and Beyond, 1700-1990*. New York and Oxford: Oxford University Press, 1994.

_____, Nathan O. Hatch and George M. Marsden, eds. *The Search for Christian America*. Westchester, Ill: Crossway Books, 1983.

Nord, David Paul. 'The Evangelical Origins of Mass Media in America, 1815-1835'. *Journalism Monographs* 88 (May 1984): 1-30.

Norwood, Frederick A. *The Story of American Methodism*. New York and Nashville: Abingdon Press, 1974.

Noyes, George Wallingford, ed. *Religious Experience of John Humphrey Noyes Founder of the Oneida Community*. New York: The MacMillan Company, 1923.

Noyes, Pierrepont. *My Father's House: An Oneida Boyhood*. Gloucester, MA: Peter Smith, 1966.

Numbers, Ronald L. and Jonathan M. Butler, eds. *The Disappointed: Millerism and Millenarianism in the Nineteenth Century*. Bloomington and Indianapolis: Indiana University Press, 1987.

Oblinger, Carl. *Religious Mimesis: Social Bases for the Holiness Schism in Late Nineteenth-Century Methodism. The Illinois Case, 1869-1885*. Evanston: The Institute for the Study of American Religion, 1973.

O'Dea, Thomas F. *The Mormons*. Chicago: University of Chicago Press, 1957.

Oden, Thomas C., ed. *Phoebe Palmer: Selected Writings*. New York and Mahwah: Paulist Press, 1988.

Olin, Spencer C. Jr. 'The Oneida Community and the Instability of Charismatic Authority'. *The Journal of American History* 67 (No. 2, 1980): 285-300.
Orr, Charles E. 'Self-Examination'. *Gospel Trumpet* (29 November 1906): 6-7.
Palmer, Phoebe. *Entire Devotion to God*. London: Salvationist Publishing and Supplies, Ltd., n.d.
_____. ed. *Pioneer Experiences*. New York, 1867.
_____. *The Way of Holiness*. New York: Palmer & Hughes, 1868.
Parker, Charles A. 'The Camp Meeting on the Frontier and the Methodist Religious Resort in the East—Before 1900'. *Methodist History* 18 (No. 3, 1980): 179-92.
Peacock, James L. and Ruel W. Tyson, Jr. *Pilgrims of Paradox: Calvinism and Experience Among the Primitive Baptists of the Blue Ridge*. Washington and London: Smithsonian Institution Press, 1989.
Peters, John Leland. *Christian Perfection and American Methodism*. New York and Nashville: Abingdon Press, 1956.
Phillips, Harold L. *Miracle of Survival*. Anderson: Warner Press, 1979.
_____. 'Warner and Charles G. Finney'. *Vital Christianity* (6 October 1974): 7-8.
_____. 'Editorial'. *Vital Christianity*. (9 June 1974): 7-8.
Pillis, Mario S. De. 'The Quest for Religious Authority and the Rise of Mormonism'. *Dialogue: A Journal of Mormon Thought* 1 (March 1966): 68-88.
Polley, J.B. 'A Description of Babylon'. *Gospel Trumpet* (8 December 1892).
Raboteau, Albert J. *Slave Religion: The 'Invisible Institution' in the Antebellum South*. New York: Oxford University Press, 1978
Rack, Henry. *Reasonable Enthusiast: John Wesley and the Rise of Methodism*. Philadelphia: Trinity Press International,1989.
Raser, Harold E. *Phoebe Palmer: Her Life and Thought*. Lewiston: The Edwin Mellen Press, 1987.
Reardon, Robert H. *The Early Morning Light*. Anderson: Warner Press, 1979.
_____. 'Charles Wesley Naylor'. in *Worship the Lord: Hymnal of the Church of God—Hymnal Companion*. pp. 29-38. eds. Lloyd A. Larson and Frank Poncé. Anderson: Warner Press, 1991
Reasoner, Victor D. 'The American Holiness Movement's Paradigm Shift Concerning Pentecost'. *Wesleyan Theological Journal* 31 (No. 2, 1996): 132-46.
Reynolds, David S. 'From Doctrine to Narrative: The Rise of Pulpit Storytelling in America'. *American Quarterly* 32 (No. 5, 1980): 479-98.
Richardson, Harry V. *Dark Salvation: The Story of Methodism as it Developed among Blacks in America*. Garden City, N.Y.: Doubleday, 1976.
Richey, Russell E. 'From Quarterly to Camp Meeting: A Reconsideration of Early American Methodism'. *Methodist History* 23 (No. 4, 1985): 199-213.
Riggle, Herbert M. *The Christian Church: It's Rise and Progress*. Anderson: Gospel Trumpet Company, 1912.

Riggle, Herbert M. *Pioneer Evangelism*. Anderson: Gospel Trumpet Company, 1924.
Roberts, B.T. *Why another Sect: Containing a review of articles by Bishop Simpson and others on the Free Methodist Church*. Rochester, N.Y.: 'The Earnest Christian' Publishing House, 1879.
Robins, Roger. 'Vernacular American Landscape: Methodists, Camp Meetings, and Social Respectability'. *Religion and American Culture* 4 (No. 2, 1994): 165-91.
Rose, Anne C. 'Social Sources of Denominationalism Reconsidered: Post-Revolutionary Boston as a Case Study'. *American Quarterly* 38 (No. 2, 1986): 243-64.
Rosell, Garth M. and Richard A.G. Dupuis, eds. *The Memoirs of Charles G. Finney*. Grand Rapids: Academie Books, 1989.
Rowe, Alexander T. 'What we Believe'. *Gospel Trumpet* (6 January 1898): 3.
Ruether, Rosemary Radford and Rosemary Skinner Keller, eds. *Women and Religion in America*, volume 1 (San Francisco: Harper & Row, 1981).
Runyon, Theodore, ed. *Sanctification & Liberation: Liberation Theologies in Light of the Wesleyan Tradition*. Nashville: Abingdon Press, 1981.
Schaff, Philip. *America: A Sketch of its Political, Social, and Religious Character*. ed. Perry Miller. Cambridge, MA: The Belknap Press of Harvard University Press, 1961.
Schell, William G. untitled memorial article. *Gospel Trumpet* (19 December 1895).
Schmidt, Leigh Eric. *Holy Fairs: Scottish Communions and American Revivals in the Early Modern Period*. Princeton: Princeton University Press, 1989.
Scott, Donald M. 'The Popular Lecture and the Creation of a Public in Mid-Nineteenth Century America'. *The Journal of American History* 66 (No. 4, 1980): 791-809.
Sellers, Charles. *The Market Revolution: Jacksonian America, 1815-1846*. New York and Oxford: Oxford University Press, 1991.
Sernett, Milton C. *Black Religion and American Evangelicalism: White Protestants, Plantation Missions and the Flowering of Negro Christianity, 1787-1865*. Metuchen, N.J.: The Scarecrow Press, Inc., 1975.
Shaw, S.B., ed. *Echoes of the General Holiness Assembly* [1901]. Chicago: S.B. Shaw, n.d.
Shipps, Jan. *Mormonism: The Story of a New Religious Tradition*. Chicago and Urbana: University of Illinois Press, 1985.
Shiels, Richard D. 'The Second Great Awakening in Connecticut: Critique of the Traditional Interpretation'. *Church History* 49 (No. 4, 1980): 401-15.
Simkins, Francis Butler and Robert Hilliard Woody, *South Carolina During Reconstruction*. Gloucester, MA: Peter Smith, 1966.
Sizer, Sandra. *Gospel Hymns and Social Religion: The Rhetoric of Nineteenth-Century Revivalism*. Philadelphia: Temple University Press, 1978.

Sizer, Sandra. 'Politics and Apolitical Religion: The Great Urban Revivals of the Late Nineteenth Century'. *Church History* 48 (No. 1, 1979): 81-98.

Slagle, John N. 'Stumbling Stonefruits'. *Gospel Trumpet* (15 September 1887).

Sloat, William A. II. 'The Role of the Methodists and the United Brethren in the Formation of John Winebrenner's Church of God'. *Evangelical Journal* 10 (No. 2, 1992): 55-64.

Smith, Elizabeth M. 'William Roberts: Circuit Rider of the Far West'. *Methodist History* 20 (No. 2, 1982): 60-74.

Smith, John W.V. *The Quest for Holiness and Unity: A Centennial History of the Church of God (Anderson, Indiana)*. Anderson: Warner Press, 1980.

_____. *Heralds of a Brighter Day: Biographical Sketches of Early Leaders in the Church of God Reformation Movement*. Anderson: Warner Press, 1955.

_____. 'Holiness and Unity'. *Wesleyan Theological Journal* 10 (Spring 1975): 24-37.

Smith, Joseph. *History of the Church of Jesus Christ of Latter-day Saints*. ed. Brigham H. Roberts. 8 volumes. Salt Lake City: Deseret News Press, 1932-51.

Smith, Timothy L. *Revivalism and Social Reform: American Protestantism on the Eve of the Civil War*. New York: Harper & Row, Publishers, 1965.

_____. 'Righteousness and Hope: Christian Holiness and the Millennial Vision in America, 1800-1900'. *American Quarterly* 31 (No. 1, 1979): 21-45.

_____. 'Congregation, State and Denomination: The Forming of the American Religious Structure'. *The William and Mary Quarterly*, third series 35 (No. 2, 1968): 155-76.

_____. *Called Unto Holiness: The Story of the Nazarenes: The Formative Years*. Kansas City, MO: Nazarene Publishing House, 1962.

_____. 'The Doctrine of the Sanctifying Spirit: Charles G. Finney's Synthesis of Wesleyan and Covenant Theology'. *Wesleyan Theological Journal* 13 (Spring 1978): 92-113.

Solberg, Winton U. 'The Conflict Between Religion and Secularism at the University of Illinois, 1867-1894'. *American Quarterly* 18 (No. 2, 1966): 183-99.

Stanley, John E. 'Unity amid Diversity: Interpreting the Book of Revelation in the Church of God (Anderson)'. *Wesleyan Theological Journal* 25 (No. 2, 1990): 74-98.

Stephanson, Anders. *Manifest Destiny: American Expansionism and the Empire of the Right*. New York: Hill and Wang, 1995.

Stout, Harry S. 'Religion, Communications, and the Ideological Origins of the American Revolution'. *The William and Mary Quarterly*, third series 34 (No. 4, 1977): 519-41.

Strege, Merle D. *Tell me the Tale: Historical Reflections on the Church of God*. Anderson: Warner Press, 1991.

Strege, Merle D. *Tell me Another Tale: Further Reflections on the Church of God*. Anderson: Warner Press, 1993.

_____. 'The Demise [?] of a Peace Church: The Church of God (Anderson), Pacifism and Civil Religion'. *Mennonite Quarterly Review* 65 (April 1991): 128-140.

Strong, Douglas M. 'The Crusade for Women's Rights and the Formative Antecedents of the Holiness Movement'. *Wesleyan Theological Journal* 27 (Nos. 1-2, 1992): 132-60.

Sutton, William R. 'Benevolent Calvinism and the Moral Government of God: The Influence of Nathaniel W. Taylor on Revivalism in the Second Great Awakening'. *Religion and American Culture* 2 (No. 1, 192): 23-47.

Sweet, William Warren, ed. *Religion on the American Frontier, 1783-1840: A Collection of Source Materials*. 4 volumes. New York: Cooper Square Publishers, Inc., 1964.

Synan, Vinson. *The Holiness-Pentecostal Movement in the United States*. Grand Rapids: William B. Eerdmans, 1971.

Szasz, Ferenc Morton. *The Protestant Clergy in the Great Plains and Mountain West, 1865-1915*. Albuquerque: University of New Mexico Press, 1988.

Tamke, Susan S. *Make a Joyful Noise unto the Lord: Hymns as a Reflection of Victorian Social Attitudes*. Athens, Ohio: Ohio University Press, 1978.

Telford, John, ed. *The Letters of the Rev. John Wesley, A.M.* 8 volumes. London: The Epworth Press, 1931.

Thomas, George M. *Revivalism and Cultural Change: Christianity, Nation Building, and the Market in the Nineteenth-Century United States*. Chicago and London: University of Chicago Press, 1989.

Thomas, Robert David. *The Man Who Would Be Perfect: John Humphrey Noyes and the Utopian Impulse*. Philadelphia: University of Pennsylvania Press, 1977.

Tocqueville, Alexis de. *Democracy in America*. trans., George Lawrence. ed., J.P. Mayer. Garden City, NY: Doubleday & Company, Inc., 1969.

Tragle, Henry I. *The Southampton Slave Revolt of 1834: A Compilation of Source Material*. New York: Random House, 1973.

Tripp, Bramwell, et al., eds. *Heritage of Holiness: A Compilation of Papers on the Historical Background of Holiness Teaching*. New York: Salvation Army, 1977.

Trollope, Francis. *Domestic Manners of the Americans*. ed. Donald Smalley. New York: Vintage Books, 1949.

Truesdale, Al. 'Reification of the Experience of Entire Sanctification in the American Holiness Movement'. *Wesleyan Theological Journal* 31 (No. 2, 1996): 95-119.

Underwood, Grant. 'Early Mormon Millenarianism: Another Look'. *Church History* 54 (No. 2, 1985): 215-29.

Van Dussen, D. Gregory. 'The Bergen Camp Meeting in the American Holiness Movement'. *Methodist History* 21 (January 1983): 69-89.

Vick, Edward W.H. 'John Wesley's Teaching Concerning Perfection'. *Andrews University Seminary Studies* 4 (1966): 201-17.

Wacker, Grant. 'The Holy Spirit and the Spirit of the Age in American Protestantism, 1880-1910'. *The Journal of American History* 72 (No. 1, 1985): 45-62.

Walker, Clarence E. *A Rock in a Weary Land: The African Methodist Episcopal Church During the Civil War and Reconstruction*. Baton Rouge and London: Louisiana State University Press, 1982.

Waller, Ethan Henry. 'The Doctrine of the Holy Spirit in the Preaching and Teaching of Daniel S. Warner'. unpublished B.D. Thesis. School of Religion, Butler University, 1954.

Walters, Orville S. 'John Wesley's Footnotes to Christian Perfection'. *Methodist History* 12 (No. 1, 1973): 19-36.

Warburton, T. Rennie. 'Holiness Religion: An Anomaly of Sectarian Typologies'. *Journal for the Scientific Study of Religion* 8 (No. 1, 1969): 130-9.

Ward, W.R. *The Protestant Evangelical Awakening*. Cambridge: Cambridge University Press, 1992.

Warner, D. Sidney. 'The Meeting at Sycamore Chapel'. typescript. Archives, Anderson University, Anderson, Indiana.

Warner, Daniel Sidney. D.S. Warner papers. Archives, Anderson University, Anderson, Indiana. Archives W656 1994A.

Journal. 6 volumes.

Book 07: Scratch Book.

Book 15: Accounts and Other Notes.

Letter to William Ryland, 21 May 1889.

———. *Poems of Grace and Truth*. Grand Junction, MI: Gospel Trumpet Publishing House, 1890.

———. *The Sabbath; or Which Day to Keep*. Moundsville, WV: Gospel Trumpet Publishing Company, 1899.

———. *Salvation: Present, Perfect, Now or Never*. Moundsville, WV: Gospel Trumpet Publishing Company, n.d.

———. *Innocence: A Poem Giving a Description of the Author's Experience from Innocence into Sin, and from Sin to Full Salvation*. Grand Junction, MI: Gospel Trumpet Publishing Company, 1896.

———. *Bible Proofs of the Second Work of Grace*. Goshen, IN: E.U. Mennonite Pub. Society, 1880.

———. *An Exclusive Christ*. Anderson: Gospel Trumpet Company, n.d.

———. *Questions and Answers on the Church*. Grand Junction, MI: Gospel Trumpet Publishing Company, n.d.

———. *No Sectism; or a Review of a Tract Bearing the Above Title written by A. Sims*. Moundsville, WV: Gospel Trumpet Company, n.d.

Warner, Daniel Sidney. *The Church of God; or What is the Church, and What is Not*. (Moundsville, WV: Gospel Trumpet Company, 1885.
_____. *Altar and Mercy Seat*. Grand Junction, MI: Gospel Trumpet Publishing Company, n.d.
_____. *What is the Soul?* Anderson: Gospel Trumpet Company, 1908.
_____. *Must We Sin*. Grand Junction, MI: The Gospel Trumpet Company, n.d.
_____. 'Church of God', in *Reformation Glory*, no. 33. Anderson: Gospel Trumpet Co., 1923.
_____. 'A Fallen Woman'. *Gospel Trumpet* (15 July 1884).
_____. 'Our Tour in Ohio'. *Gospel Trumpet* (22 September 1882).
_____. 'A Sad and Sudden end of this Life'. *Gospel Trumpet* (1 June 1893).
_____. 'News From the Field'. *Gospel Trumpet* (1 November 1886).
_____. 'A New-Spun Line of Lies'. *Gospel Trumpet* (1 November 1887).
_____. 'Sin in High Places'. *Gospel Trumpet* (15 September 1883).
_____. 'To our Contemporaries'. *Gospel Trumpet* (16 January 1882).
_____. 'Babylon Leaders and Dragon Authority'. *Gospel Trumpet* (15 October 1883).
_____. 'New Year's Greetings'. *Gospel Trumpet* (1 January 1882).
_____. 'Holiness Triumph over Dragon Zeal'. *Gospel Trumpet* (1 November 1883).
_____. 'Note'. *Gospel Trumpet* (15 September 1887).
_____. 'The Devil's Love'. *Gospel Trumpet* (15 October 1885).
_____. 'Harvester Twisting'. *Gospel Trumpet* (15 November 1885).
_____. 'Do Ministers of God See Eye to Eye?' *Gospel Trumpet* (14 December 1893).
_____. 'The Ministers of God See Eye to Eye'. *Gospel Trumpet* (21 December 1893).
_____. 'The Ministers of God Must See Eye to Eye'. *Gospel Trumpet* (28 December 1893).
_____. 'Erroneous Sayings'. *Gospel Trumpet* (18 February 1892).
_____. 'Woe to the Inhabitants of the Earth'. *Gospel Trumpet* (1 September 1884).
_____. 'The Jewish Exodus'. *Gospel Trumpet* (1 January 1885).
_____. 'Present Awful Truth - The End Drawing Nigh'. *Gospel Trumpet* (15 November 1881).
_____. 'The Glorious Return'. *Gospel Trumpet* (1 June 1885).
_____. 'Questions Answered'. *Gospel Trumpet* (15 August 1881).
_____. 'That Ye Break Every Yoke'. *Gospel Trumpet* (1 June 1881).
_____. 'Questions Answered'. *Gospel Trumpet* (15 September 1887).
_____. 'The Two Witnesses'. *Gospel Trumpet* (1 June 1884 and 1 July 1884).
_____. 'Square Come-Outism'. *Gospel Trumpet* (1 June 1881).
_____. 'The Shaft Giving Way'. *Gospel Trumpet* (1 November 1881).
_____. 'Propping Up the Walls'. *Gospel Trumpet* (1 December 1884).
_____. 'Our Tour Southwest'. *Gospel Trumpet* (1 March 1885).

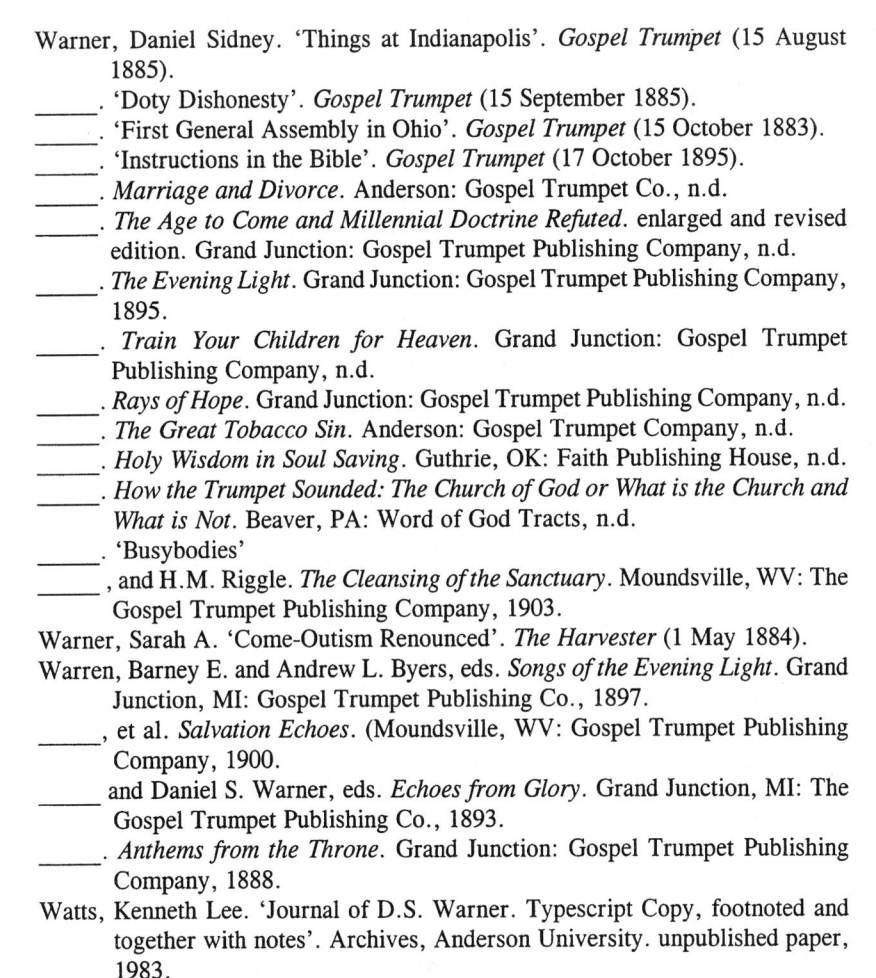

Warner, Daniel Sidney. 'Things at Indianapolis'. *Gospel Trumpet* (15 August 1885).
_____. 'Doty Dishonesty'. *Gospel Trumpet* (15 September 1885).
_____. 'First General Assembly in Ohio'. *Gospel Trumpet* (15 October 1883).
_____. 'Instructions in the Bible'. *Gospel Trumpet* (17 October 1895).
_____. *Marriage and Divorce*. Anderson: Gospel Trumpet Co., n.d.
_____. *The Age to Come and Millennial Doctrine Refuted*. enlarged and revised edition. Grand Junction: Gospel Trumpet Publishing Company, n.d.
_____. *The Evening Light*. Grand Junction: Gospel Trumpet Publishing Company, 1895.
_____. *Train Your Children for Heaven*. Grand Junction: Gospel Trumpet Publishing Company, n.d.
_____. *Rays of Hope*. Grand Junction: Gospel Trumpet Publishing Company, n.d.
_____. *The Great Tobacco Sin*. Anderson: Gospel Trumpet Company, n.d.
_____. *Holy Wisdom in Soul Saving*. Guthrie, OK: Faith Publishing House, n.d.
_____. *How the Trumpet Sounded: The Church of God or What is the Church and What is Not*. Beaver, PA: Word of God Tracts, n.d.
_____. 'Busybodies'
_____, and H.M. Riggle. *The Cleansing of the Sanctuary*. Moundsville, WV: The Gospel Trumpet Publishing Company, 1903.
Warner, Sarah A. 'Come-Outism Renounced'. *The Harvester* (1 May 1884).
Warren, Barney E. and Andrew L. Byers, eds. *Songs of the Evening Light*. Grand Junction, MI: Gospel Trumpet Publishing Co., 1897.
_____, et al. *Salvation Echoes*. (Moundsville, WV: Gospel Trumpet Publishing Company, 1900.
_____ and Daniel S. Warner, eds. *Echoes from Glory*. Grand Junction, MI: The Gospel Trumpet Publishing Co., 1893.
_____. *Anthems from the Throne*. Grand Junction: Gospel Trumpet Publishing Company, 1888.
Watts, Kenneth Lee. 'Journal of D.S. Warner. Typescript Copy, footnoted and together with notes'. Archives, Anderson University. unpublished paper, 1983.
Weber, Timothy P. *Living in the Shadow of the Second Coming: American Premillennialism, 1875-1982*. Chicago and London: University of Chicago Press, 1987.
Weinsberger, Bernard A. *They Gathered at the River: The Story of the Great Revivalists and their Impact upon Religion in America*. New York: Quadrangle, 1958.
Weiss, Ellen. *City in the Woods: The Life and Design of an American Camp Meeting on Martha's Vineyard*. New York and Oxford: Oxford University Press. 1987.
Wesley, John. *The Works of John Wesley*. 14 volumes. Grand Rapids: Baker, 1979.

Whalen, Robert. 'Calvinism and Chiliasm: The Sociology of Nineteenth Century American Millenarianism'. *American Presbyterians* 70 (Fall, 1992): 163-72.
White, Charles E. *The Beauty of Holiness: Phoebe Palmer as Theologian, Revivalist, Feminist, and Humanitarian*. Grand Rapids: Francis Asbury Press, 1986.
Wickersham, Henry C. *A History of the Church*. Moundsville, WV: Gospel Trumpet Publishing Co., 1900.
Wiebe, Robert H. *The Search for Order 1877-1920*. New York: Hill and Wang, 1967.
Wilhoit, Mel R. 'American Holiness Hymnody Some Questions: A Methodology'. *Wesleyan Theological Journal* 25 (No. 2, 1990): 39-63.
Williams, Donald E. 'How we View Holiness'. unpublished paper presented at Open Forum, Indianapolis, 1 March, 1989.
Wilmore, Gayrand S. *Black Religion and Black Radicalism*. Garden City, N.Y.: Doubleday, 1972.
Winebrenner, John. *History of all the Religious Denominations in the United States: containing authentic accounts of the rise and progress, faith and practice, localities and statistics, of the different persuasions: written expressly for the work, by fifty-three eminent authors, belonging to the respective denominations*. Harrisburg, PA: John Winebrenner, 1854.
_____. *A Brief View of the Formation, Government, and Discipline of the Church of God*. Harrisburg, PA: Montgomery and Dexter, 1829.
Wood, Gordon S. 'Evangelical America and Early Mormonism'. *New York History* 61 (October 1980): 359-86.
_____. *The Creation of the American Republic 1776-1787*. New York: Norton, 1972.
_____. ed. *The Rising Glory of America, 1760-1820*. New York: George Braziller, 1971.
Wood, Laurence W. 'Thoughts Upon the Wesleyan Doctrine of Entire Sanctification with Special reference to Some Similarities with the Roman Catholic Church Doctrine of Confirmation'. *Wesleyan Theological Journal* 15 (No. 1, 1980): 88-99.
Wood, William. *Culture and Personality: Aspects of the Pentecostal Holiness Religion*. The Hague and Paris: Mouton & Co, Publishers, 1965.
Yrigoyen, Jr. Charles. 'Methodists and Roman Catholics in 19th Century America'. *Methodist History* 28 (No. 3, 1990): 172-86.
_____, and George H. Bricker, eds. *Catholic and Reformed: Selected Theological Writings* of John Williamson Nevin. Pittsburgh: The Pickwick Press, 1978.

INDEX

Adventism 32, 49, 87, 91, 109, 236, 239, 276-7, 294, 318-19, 334-5, 339 *see* also Miller, William *and* Millerites
African Methodist Episcopal Church 43 *see* also Allen, Richard *and* Jones, Absalom
Alabama 37, 80, 235
Alcohol 11, 14, 46, 61, 66, 70, 73, 76, 78, 80, 81, 95-6, 99, 148, 150-1, 152-3, 154, 156, 171, 190
Allen, 'Camp Meeting' John 75
Allen, Richard 43, 292 *see* also African Methodist Episcopal Church
America, western expansion of 27, 35-6, 38, 84, 115
American Bible Society 86, 88
American Revolution 3, 5, 12, 13, 19, 20, 28, 34, 44, 48, 60, 85, 101, 104, 111, 288, 290
American Tract Society 86, 88
Amish 31, 239
Anabaptists 173, 181, 238, 316
Anderson University 220, 226
Anglicanism, *see* Episcopalians
Anthony, Susan B. 23
Antichrist 41, 48, 75, 106, 173, 212, 236, 246, 247, 253
Anticlericalism 38-9, 56, 61, 97-8, 142, 293, 296
Anti-intellectualism 61
Antinomianism 106, 118, 120, 137

Apocalypticism 48-9, 51, 60, 68, 85, 87, 195, 268, 269, 277, 294-5
Appomattox 48
Arminianism 117, 259
Asbury, Frances 31, 39-40, 42, 51, 60, 63-4, 76, 84, 125, 129, 143, 151, 159, 218, 237, 259, 292
   authority of 39-40, 42
Augsburg Confession 43
Augustine 17, 119, 121, 217
Authority, religious 4-5, 19, 35, 38-44, 45-6, 47, 84, 89-90, 94, 97, 100, 103, 111, 136-7, 162, 169, 171, 173, 174, 191, 193, 197, 247-8, 250-1, 267, 287-9, 302
   and order 34-5, 40, 47, 288-90
   autocratic 39, 41-3, 47, 103-4, 105, 169, 248, 270, 287, 292-3
   based on biblical exegesis 4, 39, 42-3, 169-70, 248, 302
Axley, James 63, 150-1

Babcock, William Smythe 98
Bangs, Nathan 126, 129, 132, 159
Baptists 32-3, 36, 56, 61, 70, 73, 88, 105-6, 108, 145, 149, 154, 237, 238, 240, 316, 339
Barth, Karl 94, 102, 217
Baur, Ferdinand Christian 101 *see* also Higher criticism

Beecher, Henry Ward 22, 58, 103
Beecher, Lyman 63, 109
Bellah, Ralph 22
Bennett, James Gordon 46
Bethune, Joanna Graham 23
Bible 4, 11, 39, 42-3, 46, 59, 78, 80, 85-6, 88, 90-1, 92-4, 95, 99, 101, 102, 119, 124, 127, 137, 141, 165, 173, 174, 186, 194-5, 236, 239, 243, 263, 292, 294, 297, 302, 306, 309, 310, 318, 322-3, 324, 332, 340, 348
    as symbol 4, 43, 85, 86, 91-2, 95
    authority of 43, 46, 59, 90, 91, 93-4, 119, 165, 170, 247, 263, 265, 297, 301
    exegesis controlled 4, 39, 42-3, 93-4, 236, 302
    uses of 39, 46, 78, 85-6, 89-90, 91-7, 104, 127, 165, 186, 234, 247, 256, 265, 268, 273, 293, 297, 332, 334-5
Bolitho, Axchie A. 198
Booth, William 239, 319-20, 322 *see also* Salvation Army
Boston 27, 53, 57, 63, 107, 110, 126
Bourbon County, Kentucky, *see* Cane Ridge
Bower, Jacob 56
Brendlinger, Irv A. 8, 114, 124
Brooks, John P. 161, 177-8, 180, 260
Brooks, Philip S. 58
Brown, Charles E. 3, 219, 220, 232, 261, 267, 284, 292
Bruegel, Peter 14, 16
    'The Fight Between Carnival and Lent' 14-16
Bucyrus, Ohio 184, 210, 230, 257, 264, 266, 309
'Burned Over District' 69, 98

Bushnell, Horace 25, 58
Byers, Andrew L. 3, 7, 220, 221, 260, 282-4, 299-300, 342-6
Byers, Jacob W. 217
Byrum, Enoch E. 280-2

California 12, 35, 36, 75, 161, 247, 260
Callen, Barry L. 3, 8
Calvin, John 16-17, 28, 62, 66, 106, 217, 238, 316
Calvinism 4, 5, 13, 16-22, 28, 38, 39, 45, 47, 62, 67, 68, 75, 85, 95, 103, 107, 115, 121, 126, 134, 137, 167, 238, 296 *see also* Predestination
    decline of 4, 5, 18-22, 28, 45, 296
    historical development of 16-18
    incompatibility in the New World 126
Camp meetings 5, 37, 54, 59, 63-81, 82, 99-100, 115, 128, 142, 143, 144-6, 150, 158-9, 164-5, 179, 199-200, 203, 217, 218, 259, 265, 280 *see also* Revivalism
    segregation at 70
Campbell, Alexander and Campbellites 41, 70, 81, 87, 92, 105, 106, 108, 217, 236, 295, 317
Canada 3, 199
Candler, Warren 151
Cane Ridge 10, 64-7, 77, 146, 184, 245, 265
Cartwright, Peter xiii, 43, 54, 63, 67, 81, 107, 108, 125, 141, 151, 158, 172, 237, 293 *see also* Circuit riding preachers *and* Methodism
Chapman, Milo L. 8, 220, 251, 282
China 82

Chicago 27, 139, 147, 275
Christian Harvester 211-12, 214, 228, 229, 234, 247, 259, 264, 273, 275, 278, 285, 305, 306, 308, 311 *see* also Doty, Thomas
Christian Science 32 *see* also Eddy, Mary Baker
Christianity as Babylon 194, 211-13, 230, 237, 239-40, 243, 245, 246-7, 257, 261, 268, 271, 275, 295, 297, 299, 301, 306, 311, 314, 332-4 *see* also Warner, Daniel S.
'Church of God' 92, 93, 105, 171-2, 173, 174-6, 178-9, 196-7, 207, 226, 234, 238, 242, 244, 253-4, 267-8, 279, 282-3 *see* also Winebrenner, John *and* Winebrennerians
Church Of God Reformation Movement xiv, 2, 6, 132, 179, 198, 201, 205, 206, 212, 216, 223, 232, 233, 243, 247, 251, 253-4, 255-7, 267, 276, 284, 292, 297, 301, 302 *see* also Warner, Daniel S.
Cincinnati 48, 64, 177, 210, 232
Circuit riding preachers 51-3, 54-5, 59, 82, 84, 87, 125, 129, 144, 158, 293, 294 *see* also Cartwright, Peter *and* Methodism
Civil War 19, 30, 32, 48-9, 71, 85-6, 96, 185
Clarke, Adam 295
Clear, Valorous B. 203, 243
Cleveland, Grover 93
Colleges and universities 29, 96, 101-2, 135
Come-out Movement 2, 5, 161-2, 163, 166-7, 176, 177, 178-80, 181-2, 183, 194-6, 199-200, 201, 205, 211, 212-13, 216, 223, 224, 229, 234, 240, 243-4, 245, 249, 250-1, 252-3, 255-7, 258, 260-4, 266, 268, 271, 275, 277-8, 284, 291, 294, 301 *see* also Warner, Daniel S. *and* Winebrenner, John
    as reaction 162, 234, 243, 291
    defined 252-6, 268
    denounced 156-7, 205, 212-13
Congregationalists 36, 74, 105, 106, 108, 145, 239, 318
Connecticut 23, 63
Cowdery, Oliver 40 *see* also Mormons
Crandall, Prudence 23
Crosby, Fanny J. 73

Dancing 31, 66, 148, 149, 151, 156, 267 *see* also Holiness standards *and* Worldliness
Darby, John Nelson 50 *see* also Dispensationalism
Darwin, Charles and Darwinism 101, 153
Delaware 218
Democracy, religious 4-5, 20, 22, 32, 33, 37, 38-9, 42-3, 44-5, 48, 65, 69, 74-5, 84, 90, 92, 99-100, 115, 157, 159, 163, 179, 180, 184, 188, 196, 205, 209, 212, 240, 241, 246, 250, 267, 279-80, 287, 288, 291, 294, 296, 300, 302, 303
Democracy, political 5, 16, 20, 21, 22, 40, 42-3, 47, 69, 70, 71, 85, 86, 163, 248, 288, 290, 298
Democrats 46
Denominationalism 5, 36, 60, 75, 77, 108-9, 111, 128, 132, 145, 156, 161, 162, 168, 179, 186, 187, 196, 207, 215, 220, 234,

236, 237-43, 244, 248, 253, 254, 257, 262, 292, 298, 313-30, 334, 339, 340 *see* also Christianity as Babylon *and* Warner, Daniel S.
  contentious 108, 161, 234
  exacerbated by revivalism 60
  perceived as erroneous 161, 162, 196, 234, 236-7, 238-9, 242, 243, 279, 313-30
Devil 11, 37, 48, 62, 72, 80, 98, 107, 108, 111, 118, 135, 140, 150, 156, 162, 187, 189, 196, 229, 230, 234, 238-9, 242-3, 263, 265, 269, 274, 275, 306, 307, 308, 309, 310, 311, 312
  and Sarah Warner 229, 274-5, 305-12
  corrupts true religion 187, 196, 238-9, 242-3, 272, 274-5, 314-15, 318, 324
  cosmic war 48, 140
  in popular religion 62, 71, 72, 80, 111, 162, 244, 265-6
  polemical device 106-7, 108, 135, 187, 244, 247, 269
Disciples of Christ 36, 70, 92, 169, 237 *see* also Campbell, Alexander *and* Stone, Barton
Discipline, spiritual 148, 149, 151-2, 153-5 *see* also Holiness standards
Dispensationalism 50 *see* also Darby, John Nelson
Dort, Synod of 16-17 *see* also Calvinism
Doty, Thomas K. 211, 212, 257, 259, 275 *see* also *Christian Harvester*

Dow, Lorenzo xiii, 18, 45, 53-4, 56, 58, 71, 291 *see* also Preaching
Dred Scott decision 31
Dunkers 148, 237, 316
Dutch Reformed 145

Ecumenism 111, 127, 129, 145, 163-4
Eddy, Mary Baker 23, 32, 105 *see* also Christian Science
Edwards, Jonathan 14, 20, 60, 63, 133
Election, doctrine of *see* Predestination
Emerson, Ralph Waldo 58 *see* also Transcendentalists
Episcopalians 21, 29, 36, 39, 205, 238, 316, 336
Erie Canal 27, 69, 98
Eucharist 46, 65, 74, 145, 149, 167, 171, 190
Evans, J.E. 139

Factories 24-5, 27, 30, 99 *see* also Industrialization
Faith healing 47, 101, 210, 269, 281, 282
Fanaticism 47, 59, 64-5, 66-7, 106, 153, 154, 156, 173, 179, 213, 216, 264-8, 277, 278
Fear tactics 19, 67-8, 142-3, 154, 295, 296
Federalism 19
Ferguson, Katherine 23
Fillmore, Charles and Myrtle 32
Finley, James B. 18, 66, 68, 76, 292
Finney, Charles G. 18, 26, 30, 41-2, 48, 55, 60, 63, 68, 69, 74, 91, 98-9, 103, 106, 129, 133-5, 136, 137, 140, 141, 142, 143, 148, 55, 159, 185 *see* also Holiness, Oberlin College, Preaching *and* Revivalism
  and slavery 74
  and Warner 185
  authority of 41-2, 91

heresy 135-6
strategies for revival 31, 55, 63, 68, 133-4
Fisher, Orceneth 61, 150
Fisk, William 109
'Flying Messengers' 198, 200, 332 see also Warner, Daniel S.
Footwashing, practice of 167, 171, 186, 190
Forney, Christian Henry 207
Fort Sumter 48
Franklin, Benjamin 301
Franklin, Samuel 146
Fugitive Slave Law 31
Fundamentalism 32, 88, 94, 100, 102-3, 159

Georgia 81, 84, 117, 125, 151
German Reformed Church 163-8, 170, 175-6, 191 see also Winebrenner, John
Gilruth, James 54-5
Gladden, Washington 32, 50 see also Social Gospel
Gospel Trumpet 6, 8, 197, 199, 200, 208-9, 210, 211-12, 213, 214, 219, 230, 231-2, 239-40, 246-7, 255, 259, 280-3, 284, 291, 301, 307, 313, 331, 342, 344 see also Church of God Reformation Movement, Come-Out Movement, Periodicals, religious *and* Warner, Daniel S.
as 'God's paper' 87-8, 246, 255, 291
dispute over 210, 309
Graham, Isabella Marshall 23
Grand Junction, Michigan 200, 201, 218, 219, 280, 281, 344 see also Warner, Daniel S.
Grant, Ulysses S. 46
Gray, Albert F. 242, 251, 283

Gray, James M. 147
Great Awakening, Second 19, 57, 60, 61, 68 see also Revivalism
Great Awakening, The 60, 66, 68
Greeley, Horace 58
Grimké, Angelina 23
Grimké, Sarah 23

Hardman, Keith 135
Hastings, Thomas 73
Hatch, Nathan O. 4, 21, 38-9, 87, 88-9
Haviland, Laura 23
Hayes, Rutherford B. 46
Helffenstein, Samuel 166 see also Winebrenner, John
Hell 17, 30, 37, 59, 63, 67, 71-2, 73, 76, 82, 106, 125, 140, 142, 143, 147, 148, 149, 150, 155, 156, 159, 162, 166, 239, 242, 245, 272, 274, 275, 291, 295, 296, 301 see also Fear tactics
as manipulation 37, 67, 71-2, 239, 245
result of worldliness 149-50, 167
Heresy 61, 92, 105, 107, 135, 157, 229, 230, 232, 237, 257, 279, 291
Higher criticism 101-3, 153
Himes, Joshua V. 110-11 see also Miller, William
Hodge, Charles 93
Holiness 5, 39, 113-60, 183, 185, 188, 189, 190, 199
Holiness Movements 5, 32, 44, 49, 73, 75, 107, 115, 121, 122, 125, 126-7, 128, 129, 130-1, 132, 133, 135, 137, 139-40, 143-5, 146, 148, 153, 155-6, 157-9, 161-2, 177-8, 179, 184, 191-2, 193-4, 196, 201, 205-6, 209, 212, 213, 218, 224, 247,

253, 257, 259, 273, 294
  as socially transformative 32, 115, 130, 140, 294-5
  divisions among 156-60, 161, 257-8
  eschatology in 49, 75
  hymnody of 73
  literature of 126-7, 129
  uniformity within 148-50
Holiness standards 63, 128, 148, 167, 177-8, 179, 264-5, 266-7
Holmes, Oliver Wendell 20, 58
Homiletics 56, 60, 96 *see also* Preaching
Hughes, George 259
Hutterites 31, 36
Hymnody 6, 9, 71-2, 73, 130-1, 196, 208, 248-9, 267, 282, 284

Illinois 42, 74, 77, 89, 105, 108, 146, 150, 161, 259-60
Immigration 5, 28-9, 33-4
Indiana 59, 80, 184, 194, 201, 217, 226, 244, 252, 262
Industrialization 5, 24-9, 74 *see also* Factories
Inskip, John S. 144, 259
Intolerance 85, 103-5, 109, 156, 287 *see also* Polemical language
Iowa 161

Jackson, Andrew *and* Jacksonianism 16, 22, 46, 47, 69
Jackson, Stonewall 141
Jefferson, Thomas 9, 22, 34, 39, 97, 111
Jehovah's Witnesses 49, 239, 335, 339 *see also* Russell, Charles Taze
Jerking 66-7, 265
Johnson, Lyman 239, 321-2, 328 *see also* Quakers
Jones, Abner 98
Jones, Absalom 43 *see* African Methodist Episcopal Church
Jones, Charles E. 153
'Jumping Jesus', *see* Matthews, Robert
Justification 114, 118, 121, 122, 123, 130, 131, 134, 143, 155

Kansas 161
Kent, L.B. 259
Kentucky 54, 64-5, 66, 108, 152, 154, 184
Kern, Richard 164, 165, 168, 170, 175, 191
Kerr, Tamzen 186, 206, 225, 232
Keswick 129, 259 *see also* Holiness
Kierkegaard, Søren 93
Kigar, Nannie 198
King, Starr 58
Kingdom of God 3, 5, 32, 42, 51, 65, 68, 74, 102, 106, 109, 115, 156, 195, 194, 197
Korea 82

Laity 38-42, 70, 127, 138, 155, 177
Lakin, Benjamin 55, 67, 105, 147
Lampoons, religious 78-80, 82, 110-11
Lankford, Sarah 23, 127, 259
Latourette, Kenneth Scott 241, 251
Lee, Ann 32 *see also* Shakers
Lee, Jason 35
Leland, John 292
Lincoln, Abraham 46, 150
'Lives of Jesus' 102
Loisy, Alfred 102
Lotta, James 150
Lowell, John 107
Lowell, Josephine Shaw 23
Lowell, Massachusetts 24, 27, 30, 99
Luther, Martin 91, 94, 106, 117, 123, 138, 140, 201, 217, 221, 270, 316
Lutherans 21, 36, 236, 238, 316
Lyon, Mary 23

MacDonald, William 259
Mahan, Asa 129, 135, 137, 141, 259 *see* also Oberlin College
Manifest Destiny 32, 47, 86
'Marital Purity', doctrine of 210, 214, 278 *see* also Stockwell, R.S. *and* Warner, Sarah
Marshall, Andrew 100
Marshall, Robert 97
Marty, Martin E. 1
Maryland 55, 125
Masons 61
Massachusetts 24, 27, 33, 98, 99 *see* also Puritans
Matthews, Robert 41, 54, 70, 98 (also known as 'Jumping Jesus')
McKinley, William 46
Melanchthon, Philip 221
Mennonites 238, 241, 316
Merritt, Timothy 126-7, 143
    Guide to Christian Perfection 126-7, 143
Methodism 36, 39-40, 43, 45-6, 47, 50, 51, 55, 61, 62, 63, 64, 73, 77, 81, 87, 88, 95, 96, 105, 106, 107, 114, 118-19, 124-6, 127, 129, 130, 131-2, 133, 139, 142, 143, 144, 145, 149, 150, 152, 153, 155, 157, 158, 159, 161, 164, 166, 184, 190, 237, 238, 240, 245, 252, 293, 316
    aggressive action of 61, 96, 137, 184
    growth of 49, 62, 87, 96, 137, 184
    holiness emphases 124-5, 149-50, 153, 252
    literature of 87, 126-7, 129
    political involvement of 45-6, 96, 129
Michigan 106, 179, 194-5, 198, 200, 201, 218, 252, 259

Millennialism 49, 68, 69, 85, 86
Miller, Frances 'Frankie' 198, 200, 232, 260 *see* also Warner, Daniel S.
Miller, William 32, 45, 49, 69, 87, 91, 110, 111, 239, 290, 292, 295, 318, 319 *see* also Adventists *and* Millerites
Millerites 49, 69, 73, 82, 87, 111, 137, 172, 319 *see* also Adventists *and* Miller, William
Missionary activity 36, 86-7, 163, 186, 188, 191
Mississippi 125, 198
Missouri 35, 77, 107, 154, 161, 198, 222, 265
Moby Dick 13-14, 39
Moody Bible Institute 147
Moody, Dwight 12, 58, 68, 71, 129
Moravians 116, 237 *see* also Zinzendorf, Nikolaus
Mormon, Book of 40, 70, 89-90
Mormonism 32, 35, 40, 42, 49, 69, 73, 89-90, 98, 104-5, 106, 173, 335, 339 *see* also Cowdery, Oliver, Smith, Joseph *and* Young, Brigham
Mormons, extermination order against 107
Morse, Jedidiah 107
Moundsville, West Virginia 199
Mourners's benches 68

National Camp Meeting Association for the Promotion of Holiness 144, 259
Native Americans 36-7, 116
Naylor, Charles W. 7, 242, 245, 246-7, 251, 253, 270, 282-4, 294, 299, 331-41, 342-4
    attacked 283-4, 299, 342-4
    definition of 'Church of God'

242, 251
de-mythologizer of Warner 282-4, 331-41
hymn writer 7, 282, 322, 343
Nebraska 161, 186, 187-8, 189
Nevin, John W. 41-2, 92, 165-6, 172-3, 174-5
New England 12, 24, 35, 40, 63, 66, 69, 84, 85, 87, 92, 109
New Hampshire 98
New Mexico 35
New York 23, 30, 41, 46, 69, 70, 87, 89, 98, 135, 144, 152, 154, 158, 184
New York City 23, 54, 57, 74, 98, 127, 177
Newspapers 87-8, 90, 95
Niebuhr, Reinhold 22, 94
Noll, Mark 85, 86, 254
Nolley, Richard 125
North Carolina 153
Noyes, John Humphrey 32, 41, 69, 77-8, 87, 88, 104-5, 135-7, 144, 219 *see* also Oneida community

Oberlin College 128, 129, 133, 135, 137, 185, 187, 189, 252, 259, 292 *see* also Finney, Charles G. *and* Mahan, Asa
Ohio 40, 64, 69, 81, 176, 184, 185, 186, 188, 190, 191, 206, 209, 210, 213, 216, 237, 257, 262, 264-5, 266, 278
Oliver, W.H. 190-1
Oneida community 32, 41, 49, 75, 88, 136, 138 *see* Noyes, John Humphrey
Oregon 35, 61, 75, 84, 125

Pacifism 172
Paine, Thomas 21, 62, 68, 301
Palmer, Alfred B. 217, 344

Palmer, Phoebe 23, 126, 127, 128, 130, 132, 134, 136, 140-1, 143, 146, 149-50, 151, 155, 159, 259, 260-1
  holiness proponent 127, 128, 132, 140-1, 259, 261
  leadership rôle of 23, 127, 129, 141, 259
  theology of 130-1, 132, 134, 136, 140-1, 146, 149
  'Tuesday Meeting' 127
Palmer, Walter C. 143, 259
Peck, George 132
Pelagianism 117, 134
Pennsylvania 139, 145, 165, 167, 170, 203, 222, 238
Pentecostalism 73, 130, 132-3, 159
Perfection 44, 113, 116-24 *see* Holiness *and* Sanctification
Periodicals, religious 87-91, 143, 208, 255, 259-60
Phillips, Harold L. 9, 232, 251, 283, 342
Polemical language 106-8, 235-6, 240-1, 250, 257, 272-3
Polk, James K. 46
Popular religion 5, 59-81
Popular songs 61-2, 71-3, 99
Preaching xiii, 5, 37-58, 61, 63-4, 65, 66, 67, 70, 71, 74, 77, 78, 81, 82, 86-7, 89, 90, 91, 96, 98, 99, 100, 107, 164-5, 166-7, 171, 186-7, 200, 203, 217-19, 235, 241, 293-4, 296, 298, 301
Predestination 17, 19, 22, 68, 117, 121, 167 *see* also Calvinism
Presbyterians 11, 26, 29, 36, 37, 40, 55, 63, 65, 77, 80-1, 95, 105-6, 108, 145, 152, 154, 239, 240
Print 5, 82-96, 143-4, 208, 256, 273-4, 294 *see* also Periodicals, religious

Puritans 18, 27-8, 29, 33, 49, 66, 85
Putney, Vermont, community at 41, 88, 137

Quakers 23, 32, 36, 145, 148, 230, 237, 238, 239, 316, 320, 322, 328

Raub, Henry 230
Rauschenbusch, Walter 32 *see* also Social Gospel
Reardon, Robert H. 9, 249-50, 282-3
Reid, Isaiah 259
Religion, social influence of 11-12, 22-3, 28-9, 30-1, 44-5, 46-8, 57, 69-70, 73-4, 84-5, 90-1, 97-100, 178
  blending of ideas 28-9
  control 31, 47, 85, 97-100
  especially in America 12
  relation to politics 44-6, 73-4
  social reform 22-3, 47, 74-5, 98-100
  transformative 12, 47
Religious freedom 33-5, 109
Republicanism 21-2
Revivalism 5, 26, 32, 36, 38, 48, 49, 61, 62, 63, 63, 66, 68-9, 70-5, 85, 95, 96, 98, 107, 115, 127, 128, 129, 140, 156, 157, 158, 159, 162, 163-5, 166, 177, 204, 218, 237, 265, 266, 293, 294, 295, 296 *see* Asbury, Francis, 'Burned Over District', Camp meetings, Cane Ridge, Circuit riding preachers, Finney, Charles G., Great Awakening, Methodism *and* Popular religion
Rhode Island 27, 37
Rich, Caleb 98
Ricoeur, Paul 96
Riggle, Herbert M. 221, 331

Roberts, Benjamin 153
Roberts, William 125
Rochester, New York 70
Roman Catholicism 21, 36, 55, 93, 105, 108, 109, 173, 235, 240, 268, 315, 333 *see* also Intolerance
Rowe, Alexander T. 241-2, 251
Rupp, I. Daniel 172
Russell, Charles Taze 239, 323-5 *see* also Jehovah's Witnesses

Sale, John 64
Salvation 4, 19, 20, 21, 26, 38, 42, 68, 70, 72, 73, 98, 103, 116, 131-5, 219, 243, 245, 246, 248, 262, 267
Salvation Army 31, 133, 239, 319-20 *see* also Booth, William
Sanctification 115, 118-24, 126, 127, 129, 130, 131, 132, 133-4, 137, 138-40, 141, 143, 146, 149, 151, 157, 159, 187, 189-90, 195, 196, 207, 210, 215-16, 234, 240, 244, 256, 259-61, 262, 263, 266, 279, 336-7 *see* also Finney, Charles G., Holiness, Methodism, Oberlin College, Perfection, Palmer, Phoebe, Wesley, John *and* Warner, Daniel Sidney
  and perfection 120, 136-8, 153, 260
  divine act 118
  human participation 134, 266-7
  salvific nature of 124, 131, 134-5, 141, 150-1, 182-3, 240, 260, 261-2
Sankey, Ira D. 73
Schaff, Philip 12, 33, 86, 90, 105, 109, 152, 162, 172, 173-4, 180, 195-6
Schell, William G. 270, 337

Schweitzer, Albert 102
Second work of grace, *see* Sanctification
Sectarianism 37, 97, 106, 109, 162, 169, 172-3, 174, 177, 190, 193-4, 195, 196, 208, 234, 244, 246, 257, 290, 291
Secularism 1, 21, 29, 60, 96, 98, 129
Sex 32 *see* 'Marital Purity' doctrine of *and* Oneida community
Sexual misconduct 77-8, 80-1, 99, 136, 149, 229-30, 274, 295-6 *see* also Discipline, spiritual
Shakers 32, 49, 61, 70, 95, 238, 316 *see* also Lee, Ann
Shaw, Solomon B. 161, 179, 260 *see* also Come-out Movement
Simul iustus et peccator 123, 140 *see* also Luther, Martin
'Slain in the Spirit' 59, 67, 76, 77, 175-6 *see* also Fanaticism *and* Jerking
Slavery 23, 31, 32, 46, 57, 69, 74, 75, 88, 100, 172
Smith, Amanda Berry 23
Smith, Elias 39, 72, 87, 98
Smith, Frederick G. 198, 242, 251
Smith, John W.V. 3, 211, 231, 247, 250, 277
Smith, Joseph 32, 40, 42, 45, 69, 89-90, 98, 105, 107, 290, 292 *see* also Mormonism
Smith, Lucy Mack 98
Smith, Samuel Stanhope 22
Smith, Sarah 183, 198, 246, 331
Smith, Steele 282
Smith, Uriah 295
Social Gospel 32, 50 *see* also Gladden, Washington *and* Rauschenbusch, Walter
Sola fide 118, 133, 155
Sola scriptura 95, 174 *see* also Bible
South Carolina 109, 138, 152

Stanton, Elizabeth Cady 23
Steele, Daniel 241, 259
Stocking, Frances 185, 206
Stockwell, R.S. 209-10, 214, 231, 266, 272, 273, 300, 309-10 *see* also 'Marital Purity' doctrine of, Warner, Daniel S. *and* Warner, Sarah
Stone, Barton 70, 97, 245, 292 *see* also Campbell, Alexander *and* Disciples of Christ
Stow, Harriet Beecher 23
Strauss, David Friedrich 101-2
Strege, Merle D. 7-8, 184, 201, 233, 279, 282
Sunday, Billy 54

Tappan, Lewis 135
Thirty-Nine Articles, The 43
Thompson, John 97
Tobacco 63, 76, 82, 147-8, 156, 167 *see* also Holiness standards *and* Worldliness
Tocqueville, Alexis de 10, 34-5, 40-1
Transcendentalists 32 *see* also Emerson, Ralph Waldo
Troeltsch, Ernst 254
Trollope, Frances 59
Truth, Sojourner 23
Tübingen School 101, 102
Tubman, Harriet 23
Turner, Nat 46-7, 57 *see* also Religion, social influence of *and* Slavery

Unitarianism 27-8, 32, 36, 58, 106, 107, 318 *see* also Boston
United Brethren, Church of the 126, 164, 169, 235, 239, 240, 318
Universalism 98, 106, 323
Universalists 32, 61, 87, 105, 237, 239, 318
Urbanization 21, 24-5, 29-30, 74 *see*

Index 381

Utah 42, also Industrialization

Vermont 41
Virginia 55, 109, 125
Volunteerism 21, 163

Wallace, Hardin 161, 260
Warner, D. Sidney 182, 211, 217, 231, 260, 278
Warner, Daniel S. xiv, 1-9, 54, 87, 91, 105, 109, 147, 161, 163, 176, 177, 178, 179, 181-202, 203-12, 213-23, 224-7, 229-86, 293, 296, 297, 298-303
- and Sarah Keller (Warner) 6, 7, 188-90, 205, 206-7, 209-11, 212-15, 257-8, 264, 271-6, 277, 285-6, 305-12, 334
- at Oberlin College 185, 187, 189, 292
- attitude toward other Christians 105, 147, 179, 186-7, 234-41, 248-50, 257-8, 300, 313-30, 332-3
- authority of 102, 197-8, 207-8, 221, 239-40, 245-7, 250-1, 254-6, 257, 262-3, 277-8, 281, 291-2, 293, 298, 301-2
- biblicism of 91, 109, 302, 332, 334-5
- Come-Out leader 161, 163, 176, 178, 179, 181, 183, 194, 200, 242-4, 250-1, 252-3, 254-5, 260, 279, 302-3
- connection to the Winebrennerians 5, 163, 176, 179, 185-7, 188, 190-4, 206, 252
- death of 201, 270, 280
- early life 183-7, 206-7
- editor of *Gospel Trumpet* 87, 197, 200, 208, 210, 211-12, 247, 255, 281, 291, 301
- 'evening light' motif 3, 204, 208, 222, 223, 239, 247, 249, 268, 276, 277, 279, 285-6, 297, 300
- expulsion from the Winebrennerian Church of God 192-3, 207, 256
- hymn-writer 6, 176-7, 204, 208, 248-9, 261, 284, 347-50
- interest in eschatology 268, 277, 279, 295, 333
- myth of 2-3, 181, 201-2, 216-23, 229
- opposes sanctification 185, 187, 258
- preacher 54, 185-6, 187, 217-18
- promotes holiness 181-2, 190-1, 196, 207-8, 260-1
- reputation as a religious leader 183, 189, 216-17
- sources for his life 183-4

Warner Pacific College 6, 7, 8, 9, 203, 283
Warner, Sarah 6-7, 9, 187-8, 189, 190, 205, 206-8, 209-17, 218, 223-33, 234, 241, 251, 252, 255, 256, 258, 260, 264, 268, 270-9, 285-6, 305-12
- and 'Marital Purity' doctrine of 210, 214, 278
- attacked Warner 6, 205, 211, 215-16, 234, 241, 256, 264, 271, 273-4

'Come-outism Renounced' 211, 212-16, 223, 224, 243, 256, 257, 272-3, 274-5, 277, 305
death of 232
divorced Warner 6, 198, 205, 211, 231
leadership rôle 209, 224
marital woes 206-7, 210, 214, 227-8
marriage to Warner 188, 205, 206, 223-4, 285
poetry of 226-8
professes sanctification 189, 258, 260
reputation of 224-6, 229-31, 271-5
sources for her life 6-7, 224-9, 275
Warren, Barney E. 197, 201-2, 235, 267, 273, 331
Washington 31
Washington, George 46
Watson, George D. 259
Watts, Isaac 73
Webb, Thomas 131
Weld, Theodore Dwight 48, 63
Wells, H.G. 138
Wells, Ida B. 23
Wesley, Charles 122, 131, 259
Wesley, John 8, 39-40, 53, 91, 113-14, 115-24, 131, 132, 133, 136, 139, 148, 153, 155-6, 217, 237, 238, 259, 316 see also Holiness and Sanctification
Aldersgate experience 116
and the Bible 91, 119, 123
cautions against 'perfection' 122, 123, 155
definition of sin 119-20, 121-2, 136
doctrine of sanctification 114, 115, 116-24, 132-3
father of Methodism 114, 122-3, 126, 148, 259
in America 116-17
on ecclesiastical titles 39-40
Plain Account of Christian Perfection 119-21, 136, 148
relation to Calvinism 117-18
Whatcoat, Richard 54, 155
Wheat, T.J. 161
Whigs 46
White, Alma 23
White, Ellen G. 23 see also Adventism *and* Millerites
Whitefield, George 60, 122, 237, 259
Whitman, Marcus and Narcissa 35
Wilberforce, Samuel 37
Williams, Roger 37
Wilson, Woodrow 22
Winchester, Elhanan 98
Winebrenner, John 5-6, 92, 161-80, 186, 190, 191, 238, 254 see also 'Church of God'
Winebrennerians 73, 185-6, 187, 188, 190, 191-3, 206, 207, 237-8, 252, 256, 258
anti-holiness of 186, 190-1, 207
hymnody 73
Winthrop, John 14
Wisconsin 108
Witchcraft trials 230
Witherspoon, John 22
Women 23, 24, 25, 69, 70, 127-8
Wood, J.A. 259
Wood, John A. 144
Worldliness 31, 63, 130, 138-9, 147-56, 159, 187, 264-5, 267 see also Holiness standards *and* Revivalism
Wyoming 31

Young, Brigham 32, 42 *see* also Mormonism

Zinzendorf, Nikolaus 237 *see* also Moravians

STUDIES IN AMERICAN RELIGION

1. Suzanne Geissler, **Jonathan Edwards to Aaron Burr, Jr.: From the Great Awakening to Democratic Politics**
2. Erwin Smith, **The Ethics of Martin Luther King, Jr.**
3. Nancy Manspeaker, **Jonathan Edwards: Bibliographical Synopses**
4. Erling Jorstad, **Evangelicals in the White House: The Cultural Maturation of Born-Again Christianity 1960-1981**
5. Anson Shupe and William A. Stacey, **Born Again Politics and the Moral Majority: What Social Surveys Really Show**
6. Edward Tabor Linenthal, **Changing Images of the Warrior Hero in America: A History of Popular Symbolism**
7. Philip D. Jordan, **The Evangelical Alliance for the United States of America, 1847-1900: Ecumenism, Identity, and the Religion of the Republic**
8. Jon Alexander, **American Personal Religious Accounts, 1600-1980: Toward an Inner History of America's Faiths**
9. Richard Libowitz, **Mordecai M. Kaplan and the Development of Reconstructionism**
10. David A. Rausch, **Arno C. Gaebelein, 1861-1945: Irenic Fundamentalist and Scholar**
11. Ralph Luker, **A Southern Tradition in Theology and Social Criticism 1830-1930: The Religious Liberalism and Social Conservatism of James Warley Miles, William Porcher Dubose, and Edgar Gardner Murphy**
12. Barry Jay Seltser, **The Principles and Practice of Political Compromise: A Case Study of the United States Senate**
13. Kathleen Margaret Dugan, **The Vision Quest of the Plains Indians: Its Spiritual Significance**
14. Peter C. Erb (ed.), **Johann Conrad Beissel and the Ephrata Community: Mystical and Historical Texts**
15. William L. Portier, **Isaac Hecker and the First Vatican Council**
16. Paula M. Cooey, **Jonathan Edwards on Nature and Destiny: A Systematic Analysis**
17. Helen Westra, **The Minister's Task and Calling in the Sermons of Jonathan Edwards**
18. D. G. Paz, **The Priesthoods and Apostasies of Pierce Connelly: A Study of Victorian Conversion and Anticatholicism**
19. Thomas E. Graham (ed.), **The Agricultural Social Gospel in America:** *The Gospel of the Farm* **by Jenkin Lloyd Jones**
20. Jane Rasmussen, **Musical Taste as a Religious Question in Nineteenth-Century America**

21. E. H. McKinley, **Somebody's Brother: A History of the Salvation Army Men's Social Service Department 1891-1985**
22. Stafford Poole and Douglas J. Slawson, **Church And Slave in Perry County, Missouri, 1818-1865**
23. Rebecca Moore, **The Jonestown Letters: Correspondence of the Moore Family 1970-1985**
24. Lawrence H. Williams, **Black Higher Education in Kentucky 1879-1930: The History of Simmons University**
25. Erling Jorstad, **The New Christian Right, 1981- 1988: Prospects for the Post-Reagan Decade**
26. Joseph H. Hall, **Presbyterian Conflict and Resolution on the Missouri Frontier**
27. Jonathan Wells, **Charles Hodges' Critique of Darwinism: An Historical-Critical Analysis of Concepts Basic to the 19th Century Debate**
28. Donald R. Tuck, **Buddhist Churches of America: Jodo Shinshu**
29. Suzanne Geissler, **Lutheranism and Anglicanism in Colonial New Jersey: An Early Ecumenical Experiment in New Sweden**
30. David Hein, **A Student's View of The College of St. James on the Eve of the Civil War: The Letters of W. Wilkins Davis (1842-1866)**
31. Char Miller, **Selected Writings of Hiram Bingham (1814-1869), Missionary To The Hawaiian Islands: To Raise the Lord's Banner**
32. Rebecca Moore, **In Defense of Peoples Temple-And Other Essays**
33. Donald L. Huber, **Educating Lutheran Pastors in Ohio, 1830-1980: A History of Trinity Lutheran Seminary and its Predecessors**
34. Hugh Spurgin, **Roger Williams and Puritan Radicalism in the English Separatist Tradition**
35. Michael Meiers, **Was Jonestown A CIA Medical Experiment?: A Review of the Evidence**
36. L. Raymond Camp, **Roger Williams, God's Apostle of Advocacy: Biography and Rhetoric**
37. Rebecca Moore & Fielding M. McGehee III (eds.), **New Religious Movements, Mass Suicide, and Peoples Temple: Scholarly Perspectives on a Tragedy**
38. Annabelle S. Wenzke, **Timothy Dwight (1752-1817)**
39. Joseph R. Washington, Jr., **Race and Religion in Early Nineteenth Century America 1800-1850: Constitution, Conscience, and Calvinist Compromise** (2 vols.)
40. Joseph R. Washington, Jr., **Race and Religion in Mid-Nineteenth Century America 1850-1877: Protestant Parochial Philanthropists** (2 vols.)
41. Rebecca Moore & Fielding M. McGehee III (eds.), **The Need for a Second Look at Jonestown**

42. Joel Fetzer, **Selective Prosecution of Religiously Motivated Offenders in America: Scrutinizing the Myth of Neutrality**
43. Charles H. Lippy, **The Christadelphians in North America**
44. N. Gordon Thomas, **The Millennial Impulse in Michigan, 1830-1860: The Second Coming in the Third New England**
45. John S. Erwin, **The Millennialism of Cotton Mather: An Historical and Theological Analysis**
46. William E. Ellis, **Patrick Henry Callahan (1866-1940): Progressive Catholic Layman in the American South**
47. Virginia Peacock, **Problems in the Interpretation of Jonathan Edwards' *The Nature of True Virtue***
48. Francis W. Sacks, **The Philadelphia Baptist Tradition of Church and Church Authority 1707-1814: An Ecumenical Analysis and Theological Interpretation**
49. Joseph R. Washington, Jr., **Rulers of Reality and the Ruled Races: The Struggle of Black Ministers to Bring Afro-Americans to Full Citizenship in America**
50. Joseph Forcinelli, **The Democratization of Religion in America: A Commonwealth of Religious Freedom by Design**
51. Joseph R. Washington, Jr., **The First Fugitive Foreign and Domestic Doctor of Divinity: Rational Race Rules of Religion and Realism Revered and Reversed or Revised by The Reverend Doctor James William Charles Pennington**
52. Richard A. S. Hall, **The Neglected Northampton Texts of Jonathan Edwards: Edwards on Society and Politics**
53. Hugh Barbour, **William Penn on Religion and Ethics: The Emergence of Liberal Quakerism**
54. Joseph Forcinelli, **The Global Democratization of Religion and Theology: An Evolution of Spiritual Freedom**
55. Francis J. Beckwith and Stephen E. Parrish, **The Mormon Concept of God: A Philosophical Analysis**
56. William Harder Squires, **The Edwardean: A Quarterly Devoted to the History of Thought in America**
57. Steven R. Pointer, **Joseph Cook, Boston Lecturer and Evangelical Apologist: A Bridge Between Popular Culture and Academia in Late Nineteenth Century America**
58. Gary Holloway, **O.B. Perkins and the Southern Oratorical Preaching Tradition**
59. Bruce M. Stephens, **The Holy Spirit in American Protestant Thought, 1750-1850**
60. M. Darrol Bryant, **Jonathan Edwards' Grammar of Time, Self, and Society: A Critique of the Heimert Thesis**

61. Robert K. Gustafson, **James Woodrow (1828-1907) - Scientist, Theologian, Intellectual Leader**
62. Claude E. Cox (editor), **The Campbell-Stone Movement in Ontario: Christian Church (Disciples of Christ), Churches of Christ, Independent Christian Churches/Churches of Christ**
63. Francis Ellingwood Abbot, **The Collected Essays of Francis Ellingwood Abbot (1836-1903), American Philosopher and Free Religionist**, edited by W. Creighton Peden and Everett J. Tarbox, Jr. (4 volumes)
64. Robert K. Hudnut, **The Aesthetics of Ralph Waldo Emerson: The Materials and Methods of His Poetry**
65. Peter Hicks, **The Philosophy of Charles Hodge: A 19th Century Evangelical Approach to Reason, Knowledge and Truth**
66a. W. Creighton Peden and Jerome A. Stone (editors), **The Chicago School of Theology–Pioneers in Religious Inquiry, Volume I, The Early Chicago School, 1906-1959**
66b. W. Creighton Peden and Jerome A. Stone (editors), **The Chicago School of Theology–Pioneers in Religious Inquiry, Volume II, The Later Chicago School, 1919-1988**
67. Michael W. Casey, **The Battle Over Hermeneutics in The Stone-Campbell Movement, 1800-1870**
68. Thomas A. Fudge, **Daniel Warner and the Paradox of Religious Democracy in Nineteenth-Century America**